T0180958

History of Computing

The History of Computing series publishes high-quality books which address the history of computing, with an emphasis on the 'externalist' view of this history, more accessible to a wider audience. The series examines content and history from four main quadrants: the history of relevant technologies, the history of the core science, the history of relevant business and economic developments, and the history of computing as it pertains to social history and societal developments.

Titles can span a variety of product types, including but not exclusively, themed volumes, biographies, 'profile' books (with brief biographies of a number of key people), expansions of workshop proceedings, general readers, scholarly expositions, titles used as ancillary textbooks, revivals and new editions of previous worthy titles.

These books will appeal, varyingly, to academics and students in computer science, history, mathematics, business and technology studies. Some titles will also directly appeal to professionals and practitioners of different backgrounds.

For further volumes:
http://www.springer.com/series/8442

Gerard Alberts • Ruth Oldenziel
Editors

Hacking Europe

From Computer Cultures to Demoscenes

Editors
Gerard Alberts
Korteweg-de Vries Institute
for Mathematics
University of Amsterdam
Amsterdam, The Netherlands

Ruth Oldenziel
School of Innovation Sciences,
History Department
Eindhoven University of Technology
Eindhoven, The Netherlands

ISSN 2190-6831 ISSN 2190-684X (electronic)
ISBN 978-1-4471-7069-3 ISBN 978-1-4471-5493-8 (eBook)
DOI 10.1007/978-1-4471-5493-8
Springer London Heidelberg New York Dordrecht

Softcover reprint of the hardcover 1st edition 2014

Printed on acid-free paper

Springer is part of Springer Science+Business Media (www.springer.com)

Preface

This book had its genesis at the Lorentz Center research week on the History of Software held in Leiden, the Netherlands, in September 2010. The enthusiasm of the early career scholars at the workshop inspired us to shepherd the book to publication.

Hacking Europe has been the outcome of a collaboration of two research projects: the *Software for Europe* and the *European Ways of Life in the American Century*. Both projects were part of the ESF-funded Eurocores program *Inventing Europe: Technology and the Making of Europe, 1850–Present*, which brought together a transatlantic community of scholars. We would like to thank Ron Kline, Nathan Ensmenger, and Valérie Schafer for their careful reading of the manuscript and Johan Schot for his leadership of the *Inventing Europe* program.

We thank Dutch Science Foundation (NWO), European Science Foundation (ESF), the Lorentz Center, Foundation for the History of Technology in Eindhoven (SHT), and the Informatics Institute at the University of Amsterdam for their financial support, and Martijn van der Eerden for some last-minute assistance with the bibliography.

Amsterdam, The Netherlands — Gerard Alberts
Eindhoven, The Netherlands — Ruth Oldenziel

Contents

1 **Introduction: How European Players Captured the Computer and Created the Scenes** 1
Gerard Alberts and Ruth Oldenziel

Part I Appropriating America: Making One's Own

2 **Transnational (Dis)Connection in Localizing Personal Computing in the Netherlands, 1975–1990** 25
Frank C.A. Veraart

3 **"Inside a Day You Will Be Talking to It Like an Old Friend": The Making and Remaking of Sinclair Personal Computing in 1980s Britain** 49
Thomas Lean

4 **Legal Pirates Ltd: Home Computing Cultures in Early 1980s Greece** 73
Theodoros Lekkas

Part II Bastard Sons of the Cold War: Creating Computer Scences

5 **Galaxy and the New Wave: Yugoslav Computer Culture in the 1980s** 107
Bruno Jakić

6 **Playing and Copying: Social Practices of Home Computer Users in Poland during the 1980s** 129
Patryk Wasiak

7 **Multiple Users, Diverse Users: Appropriation of Personal Computers by Demoscene Hackers** 151
Antti Silvast and Markku Reunanen

Part III Going Public: How to Change the World

8 **Heroes Yet Criminals of the German Computer Revolution** 167
Kai Denker

9 **How Amsterdam Invented the Internet: European Networks of Significance, 1980–1995** 189
Caroline Nevejan and Alexander Badenoch

10 **Users in the Dark: The Development of a User-Controlled Technology in the Czech Wireless Network Community** 219
Johan Söderberg

Bibliography 241

About the Authors 257

Index 261

Chapter 1
Introduction: How European Players Captured the Computer and Created the Scenes

Gerard Alberts and Ruth Oldenziel

Playfulness was at the heart of how European players appropriated microcomputers in the last quarter of the twentieth century. Although gaming has been important for computer development, that is not the subject of *Hacking Europe*. Our book's main focus is the playfulness of hacker culture. The essays argue that no matter how detailed or unfinished the design projecting the use of computers, users playfully assigned their own meanings to the machines in unexpected ways. Chopping games in Warsaw, hacking software in Athens, creating chaos in Hamburg, producing demos in Turku, or partying with computing in Zagreb and Amsterdam—wherever computers came with specific meanings that designers had attached to them—local communities throughout Europe found them technically fascinating, culturally inspiring, and politically motivating machines. They began tinkering with the new technology with boundless enthusiasm and helped revolutionize the use and meaning of computers by incorporating them into people's daily lives. As tinkerers, hackers appropriated the machine and created a new culture around it. Perhaps best known and most visible were the hacker cultures that toyed with the meaning of ownership in the domain of information technology. In several parts of Europe, hackers created a counterculture akin to the squatter movement that challenged individual ownership, demanded equal access, and celebrated shared use of the new technological potential. The German Chaos Computer Club best embodied the European version of the political fusion of the counterculture movement and the love of technology. Linguistically, in Dutch, the

G. Alberts (✉)
The Korteweg-de Vries Institute for Mathematics, University of Amsterdam, Amsterdam, The Netherlands
e-mail: G.Alberts@uva.nl

R. Oldenziel
School of Innovation Sciences, History Department, Eindhoven University of Technology, Eindhoven, The Netherlands
e-mail: ruth@oldenziel.com

G. Alberts and R. Oldenziel (eds.), *Hacking Europe. From Computer Cultures to Demoscenes*, History of Computing, DOI 10.1007/978-1-4471-5493-8_1,

slang word "*kraken*," the term used for both hacking and squatting, pointedly expressed such creative fusion that is the subject of this book.[1]

1.1 The Hacker Phenomenon

In his *Computer Power and Human Reason*, Joseph Weizenbaum first portrayed hackers as compulsive programmers, "their arms tensed and waiting to fire their fingers, already poised to strike."[2] Investigative reporter Tracy Kidder in contrast took a more ethnographic and sympathetic attitude in order to understand the "midnight programmer."[3] In 1984, Sherry Turkle offered a "thick description" of the phenomenon. She was arguably the first to conceptualize the phenomenon as "hacker culture."[4] The "hack," the Holy Grail of that culture, signified more than a neat programming trick. It was, she wrote, a "magician's gesture: a truly surprising result produced with ridiculously simple means." Through a great trick, these computer users showed mastery of their trade, revealing an expertise "acquired unofficially and at the expense of a big system. The hacker is a person outside the system who is never excluded by its rules."[5] Turkle noted that in the eyes of the hacker, who deliberately chose an outsider role, complexities are there to be mastered, locks exist to be cracked, and exclusion is to be countered with intrusion. A crucial aspect of the hacker's ethos was to leave a fingerprint of the intrusion, but to do no harm. Just as hackers were "loving the machine for itself," breaking in was done for the "hack" of it.[6] The self-representation of hackers-as-outsiders "knowing things better" than the experts-on-the-inside resembles the attitude of members of a counterculture. She portrays hackers-as-outsiders engaging with computers to show mastery, enjoying science fiction, and practicing rites of passage to form communities. The element of game, abound in her description of the hacker culture, remains implicit. Since, the emerging field of games studies, in rediscovering the historian Johan Huizinga's work, has drawn attention to what has come to be called the ludological element: play as an essential element of culture.[7] In our book, we combine these elements to focus

---

[1] See the contribution by Caroline Nevejan, and Alexander Badenoch. 2014. How Amsterdam invented the Internet: European networks of significance, 1980–1995. In *Hacking Europe. From computer cultures to demoscenes*, ed. Gerard Alberts and Ruth Oldenziel, 189–217. New York: Springer; Ine Poppe, and Sandra Rottenberg. 2000. *De KRAAKgeneratie*. Amsterdam: De Balie.

[2] Joseph Weizenbaum. 1976. *Computer power and human reason: From judgment to calculation*, 116. San Francisco: W. H. Freeman.

[3] Tracy Kidder. 1981. *The soul of a new machine*. Boston: Little Brown.

[4] Turkle explicitly refers to the method of thick description made famous by anthropologist Clifford Geertz in her ethnography of hacker culture. Sherry Turkle. 1984. *The second self: Computers and the human spirit*. New York: Simon & Schuster.

[5] Ibid., 227.

[6] Ibid., Chapter 6.

[7] Espen Aarseth. 1997. *Cybertext: Perspectives on ergodic literature*. Baltimore: Johns Hopkins University Press; Gonzalo Frasca. 2007. *Play the message: Play, game and videogame rhetoric*. PhD thesis, University of Copenhagen; Gonzalo Frasca. 2003. Simulation vs. narrative:

on the playfulness of hacker culture to understand it in its larger cultural context. Greek users went about "interfering" (*Επεμβάσεις*) with any given software. Under socialism, Yugoslav teenagers and students "riffed" computers as part of a subculture of party and music. Polish hackers demonstrated pride in their intrusion by appropriating the opening page of a copied game. Finnish demoscenes formed closed communities where newcomers could become members by rite of passage if they could show off with an intricate piece of software, the so-called demo. As if playing a game, German hacker Wau Holland openly and proudly intruded the Hamburg bank's computer system to expose security flaws; and when officials accused him of criminal activities, he sought protection from the Chaos Computer Club. Finally, the powerful spatial metaphor of the city in the online world allowed Amsterdam activists to "play city" as citizens and mayors in a bid to influence local politics. In short, play was a quintessential element of the culture of personal computing.

The creation of an alternative or space outside the system generated a host of issues. When in November 1984 two German hackers found their way into the files of the Hamburger *Sparkasse*, they were outsiders hacking their way into the system. Finnish demosceners created their own outsider-insider oppositional playground. The question is, what kind of inside-outside opposition these hackers in numerous countries created? Were they opposing "the computer," IBM, the bank, the banking system, the network, the web, the economic system, or "the system" as such? To what extent did these users position themselves outside that system and to what extent did they also refuse to be excluded?

The history of hacker culture suffers from being read as an American story that, by extension, claims universality.[8] Many first-person narratives reinforce the idea of universal appeal as they celebrate the sense of control users felt when using personal computers.[9] Yet, two aspects complicate the claim of universality. In a technical

---

Introduction to ludology. In *The video game theory reader*, ed. J.P. Mark Wolf and Bernard Perron, 221–236. London: Routledge; Johan Huizinga. 1949 [1938]. *Homo Ludens: A study of the play-element in culture*. London: Routledge & Kegan Paul.

[8] Fred Turner. 2006. *From counterculture to cyberculture: Stewart brand, the Whole Earth Network, and the rise of digital utopianism*. Chicago: University of Chicago. Other classics are Steven Levy. 1984. *Hackers: Heroes of the computer revolution*. Garden City, NY: Anchor Press/Doubleday. For a general survey offering context to this story cf. Martin Campbell-Kelly, William Aspray, Nathan Ensmenger, and Jeffrey R. Yost. 2014 [1996]. *Computer: A history of the information machine*, The Sloan technology series, 233. Boulder, CO: Westview Press; Steven Lubar. 1993. *Infoculture. The Smithsonian book of information age inventions*. Boston/ New York: Houghton Mifflin Company.

[9] The fascination with the technique is ubiquitous in the traditional literature of personal accounts and journalism. John Chirillo. 2001. *Hack attacks encyclopedia: A complete history of hacks, cracks, phreaks, and spies over time*. New York: Wiley; Constantin Gillies. 2003. *Wie wir waren: die wilden Jahre der Web-Generation*. Weinheim: Wiley-VCH; Katie Hafner, and John Markoff. 1991. *Cyberpunk: Outlaws and hackers on the computer frontier.* London: Touchstone; Steven L. Kent. 2001. *The ultimate history of video games. From Pong to Pokémon and beyond: The story behind the craze that touched our lives and changed the world.* New York: Three Rivers Press; Brad King, and John Borland. 2003. *Dungeons and dreamers. The rise of computer game culture from geek to chic*. New York: McGraw-Hill; David Kushner. 2003. *Masters of Doom. How two guys created an empire and transformed pop culture*. New York: Random House; Fred Moody. 1999. *The visionary position. The inside story of the digital dreamers who are making virtual reality a reality*. New York: Times Business.

sense, hacking defies clear demarcation; a more helpful definition of hacking is to look at the motives of computer users who "hacked." Hacking is defined by users' unconventional, playful mastery and unique, outsider expertise. That very definition undermines the claim of technological universality. In geographical terms, the global influence of computers beyond the US borders has been wide and deep; in Europe, the rapid appropriation of personal computers on both sides of the Iron Curtain was impressive indeed.[10] Yet, by examining how such a technological culture became embedded in other cultural and political contexts, we can appreciate the severe limits to the computers' claim of universality. The appeal of personal computers was neither inherent in the technology nor a foregone conclusion.

In this book, the authors examine the local appropriation of hacker cultures in several European countries at the end of the Cold War. Given the American dominance in computing, we need to consider the prominent position of the United States as a geopolitical power in its ability to set global standards and position itself as a seductive symbol of market capitalism in postwar Europe. Whether it was kitchens, nuclear reactors, or computers, historical research shows that in the context of the US postwar global power, the ability of American social actors to shape industry standards better explains why computers were adopted relatively quickly than their intrinsic appeal.[11] US-based products and technologies often came with elaborate global public-relations campaigns; moreover, many consumer goods ranging from blue jeans to computers came to be associated with America's youth culture, acquiring a status of superiority and sensuality. In other words, US-based artifacts like computers travelled across the Atlantic with an elaborate story of power in their luggage. When it came to computing, Europeans struggled with the sense of their outsider position in relation to the U.S. global power. That ambivalence resulted in the double appeal of intense hacking practices and the eager adoption of computers. Were the hacking Europeans outsiders to an American corporate culture, who nevertheless mastered the artifacts and knowledge of the system? Or were they outsiders to their local community, who showed their mastery by flaunting their ability to access exquisite, global products and who participated in a global, transnational community defying national boundaries?

These questions point to a crucial juncture at which European histories of hacker culture diverge from the US narratives. Hacker communities played an active role in appropriating the technology. The very meanings they gave to computers helped embed these complicated and unfinished products in their local context. On the one hand, users were trying to make sense of microcomputers and networks in their own way. On the other hand, European users explored how much room they had to create

---

[10]Victoria de Grazia. 2005. *Irresistible empire. America's advance through twentieth-century Europe*. Cambridge, MA: Belknap Press.

[11]John Krige. 2006. *American hegemony and the postwar reconstruction of science in Europe*. Cambridge, MA: MIT Press; John Krige. 2008. The peaceful atom as political weapon: Euratom and American foreign policy in the late 1950s. *Historical Studies in the Natural Sciences* 38(1): 5–44; Ruth Oldenziel, and Karin Zachmann (eds.). 2009. *Cold War kitchen. Americanization, technology, and European users*. Cambridge, MA: MIT Press. On nuclear reactors see, for example, Irene Cieraad. 2009. The radiant American kitchen: Domesticating Dutch nuclear energy. In *Cold War kitchen. Americanization, technology, and European users*, ed. Ruth Oldenziel and Karin Zachmann, 113–136. Cambridge, MA: MIT Press.

their own codes within the context of US cultural, political, and technological dominance. It turns out, quite a bit, as the activities of Greek pirates, Yugoslav partygoers, and Polish copiers confirm. In the UK, it was still possible to design alternative products to the US standards. Experiments in Amsterdam to create a public domain on the web offer a peek into an even more fundamental alternative to the American model of commercialization of the Internet.

1.2 Appropriating Computers and Making Technology

The act of appropriation is a general aspect of how technologies become domesticated. Appropriation processes are not particular to hacking as such, but in the case of computing, they were more intense. In *Hacking Europe*, we focus on the gap between the universal expectations of computers and the way users playfully created a practice that often contradicted the designers' intentions. The case of computers justifies the scholarship arguing that users matter a great deal in shaping technologies.[12] Not only do designers configure projected users in their design, but the reverse is also true. Designers' choices are shaped by technology users and their organizations. In the now classic case of the bicycle, sociologist of technology and science Wiebe Bijker has argued that by the end of the nineteenth century, elderly men and women pushed the development of the perilous high-wheeled vehicle in new directions that helped pave the way for the safety bike. The example of the bicycle illustrates how a young man's culture celebrating the dangerous and pleasurable aspects of cycling shifted to a broader culture of cycling demanding safety and usefulness. The new meaning became imprinted in a newfound technological development that led to the safety bike.[13] Furthermore, French anthropologist Madeleine Akrich and sociologist Bruno Latour introduced the notion of "script" or scenario to suggest that designers attribute and delegate competencies, actions, and responsibilities in their designs to both users and technological artifacts.[14] Feminist scholars have extended that notion to include one of

[12] Nelly Oudshoorn, and Trevor J. Pinch (eds.). 2003. *How users matter. The co-construction of users and technology*. Cambridge, MA: MIT Press.

[13] Wiebe E. Bijker, Thomas P. Hughes, and Trevor J. Pinch (eds.). 1987. *The social construction of technological systems. New directions in the sociology and history of technology*. Cambridge, MA: MIT Press.

[14] Bruno Latour. 1992. Where are the hidden masses. Sociology of a few mundane artifacts. In *Shaping technology/building society: Studies in sociotechnical change*, ed. Wiebe E. Bijker and John Law, 225–258. Cambridge, MA: MIT Press; Madeleine Akrich. 1992. The de-scription of technical objects. In *Shaping technology/building society: Studies in sociotechnical change*, ed. Wiebe E. Bijker and John Law, 205–224. Cambridge, MA: MIT Press; Madeleine Akrich, and Bruno Latour. 1992. A summary of convenient vocabulary for the semiotics of human and nonhuman assemblies. In *Shaping technology/building society: Studies in sociotechnical change*, ed. Wiebe E. Bijker and John Law, 259–264. Cambridge, MA: MIT Press. Steve Woolgar. 1991. Configuring the user: The case of usability trials. In *A sociology of monsters: Essays on power, technology and domination*, ed. John Law, 57–100. London: Routledge; Christina Lindsay. 2003. From the shadows: Users as designers, producers, marketers, distributors, and technical support. In *How users matter. The co-construction of users and technology*, ed. Nelly Oudshoorn and Trevor J. Pinch, 29–50. Cambridge, MA: MIT Press.

gender in the equation.[15] A focus on "gender scripts" seeks to understand how representations of femininity and masculinity are inscribed in technological artifacts in ways that define and reinforce power relations of who is included or excluded in their use. The notion of scripts can also be seen as a complex cultural web of representations or "cultural scripts" that frame and constrain the choices designers and users make. Thus, in referring to cultural script, we stretch the concept from the original idea of a specific scenario imprinted in the machine to include a cultural practice. Class distinctions are perceptible in some of the contributions in this book as well. Lean shows how the microcomputer could evolve into a middle-class machine; Wasiak describes how different social segments of society had access to different technologies; Nevejan and Badenoch's actors were specific of a certain tier of the Amsterdam society. Yet, class scripts are not the binding theme of this book. Such a history of social stratifications of computer cultures of use must for the moment remain a desideratum. Gender specificity is omnipresent in hacker culture. Even blindfolded one could not overlook the gendered encoding of the demoscenes with their cocky pride in the power of ridiculously simple code and their technophile rites of passage.[16] Again, with examples abound in this book of the gendering of computing, and a study on the theme for Europe urgently wanted—such a gender script is not the binding thread of the present volume either, but cultural script is. The contributions show a differentiated palette of cultural practices by which European users appropriated computer. But how did such appropriations occur?

Users and producers never meet in person, of course.[17] Their interaction is always mediated. To enable a deeper understanding of the relationship between designer communities and user communities, historians have developed the concept of the consumption or mediation junction to focus more sharply on the role numerous organizations and institutions play in the interaction. Such organizations often assume the status of spokespersons for users or of gatekeepers, claiming user expertise that no one else possesses.[18] Mediators are often the carriers of the local script.

---

[15] Nelly Oudshoorn. 1996. Genderscripts in technologie: Noodlot of uitdaging? *Tijdschrift voor Vrouwenstudies* 17(4): 350–368.

[16] For an analysis of De Digitale Stad through this lens, see Els Rommes. 2002. *Gender scripts and the Internet: The design and use of Amsterdam's digital city*. PhD thesis, University Twente. For the ubiquity of the gendered scripts: Thomas J. Misa (ed.). 2010. *Gender codes: Why women are leaving computing*. Hoboken: Wiley.

[17] With the notable exception of the IBM user groups as revealed by Atusushi Akera. 2001. Voluntarism and the fruits of collaboration: The IBM user group, SHARE. *Technology and Culture* 42(4): 710–736.

[18] Ruth Schwartz Cowan. 1987. The consumption junction: A proposal for research strategies in the sociology of technology, in *The social construction of technological systems*, ed. Wiebe E. Bijker, Thomas P. Hughes, and Trevor J. Pinch, 261–280; Ruth Oldenziel. 2001. Woman the consumer: The consumption junction revisited. In *Feminism in twentieth-century science, technology and medicine*, ed. Angela N.H. Creager, Elizabeth Lunbeck, and Londa Schiebinger, 128–148. Chicago: Chicago University Press; Ruth Oldenziel, and Adri A. de la Bruhèze. 2009. Theorizing the mediation junction for technology and consumption. In *Manufacturing technology, manufacturing consumers. The making of Dutch consumer society*, ed. Adri A. de la Bruhèze and Ruth Oldenziel, 9–40. Amsterdam: Aksant.

They translate a practice from a very general idea such as working with computers to an actual practice. Although users often do not form official organizations, they do come together in communities that shape the direction of innovations.

In 1980, the way computers were supposed to be used was not standardized either in the USA or in Europe. By the time personal computers entered the market, user regimes had been evolving in specialized areas over several decades. A variety and separate forms of user practices had developed but were not standardized, ranging from large mainframe computing in data-processing to military control equipment and mini-computing in laboratories. In the late 1960s, the cultural rebellion opposing the quest for control and centralization in bureaucracies as well as large computer systems broke open a pathway that was about to close at the time.[19] As a result, with each innovation that followed, computer technology acquired different and diverse meanings, despite the claim of universality computers had thus far projected. After 1971, when Intel introduced the microcomputer with the marketing slogan "a computer on a chip," new user groups joined the computer world, adding new meanings.[20] The introduction of microcomputers and the changing views on the use of mainframe computers offered alternative avenues for how users could appropriate the new technology. Indeed, by 1978 the small computer had become "personal" rather than "professional." The early computer users tinkered and domesticated them in the novel setting of their homes. They became responsible for how the "personal" became a major part of the "script" of the computer, of how the innovation should be read, interpreted, designed, and sold. In turn, these novel and alternative modes of configuration then found their way back into the well-established culture of mainframe computers, challenging engineers to consider design questions like why not "phreaking" and tinkering with mainframes as well or why not personalize the university computer and print ASCII-art. As a result, "personal" computer script as a form of personal expression found its way to mainframe computers. Because mainframes were more widely used in Europe, a personal computer industry was less dominant than in the USA. Personal computer practices were also based on different European traditions.

For one, European governments sought to introduce computers as educational machines. In the late 1970s, several countries started computer literacy programs, using the argument that computers would bring economic prosperity. In the UK, a 1978 BBC documentary *Now the Chips are down* presented the coming microcomputer revolution and predicted massive unemployment, while a report to the government argued that the looming crisis could only be averted if the British became computer literate. Then BBC produced a TV series explaining how computers worked, attracting 7.7 million viewers, and developed an ACORN BBC computer for the purpose. Complete with educational software and manual, the ACORN's script was explicitly educational and cultural. Unlike the cheaper and low-end Sinclair computer, the

---

[19] Steven Lubar. 1992. 'Do not fold, spindle or mutilate': A cultural history of the punched card. *Journal of American Culture* 15(4): 43–55. Turner, *From counterculture to cyberculture*.

[20] William Aspray. 1997. The intel 4004 microprocessor: What constituted invention. *IEEE Annals of the History of Computing* 19(3): 4–15.

ACORN catered to the middle-class sector and became the standard for British schools before finding its way to the USA and West Germany in the early 1980s. Almost simultaneously, the Dutch government commissioned former industry director of research, G.W. Rathenau (1911–1989) to report on the social impact of the "micro." The 1978 report became the basis for Dutch educational policy to bring computers into the classroom. Various models appeared in schools like the Philips computer based on its Austrian division's R&D and the Dutch Compudata, later renamed Tulip.[21] By embracing the notion of "informatization" to pinpoint social impact, the 1978 Nora and Minc report commissioned by the French government on *L'informatisation de la société* impressed its readers even more. An English translation gave it further resonance.[22] The same year, Sweden's social democratic government sponsored the Compis computer, distributed by Esselte to grammar school level and exported to Norway and Finland as well.[23] Socialist governments in Eastern Europe subsidized computer clubs to introduce their citizens to the new technology in the hope that computer education would bring socialist progress.[24] In the late 1980s, Poland started its computer literacy programs.[25] A broad coalition sought to popularize computing. It included members of the Polish Association of Informatics and the Association of Polish Socialist Youth and journalists from *The Young Technician* (*Młody Technik*). They lobbied decision makers and encouraged children and teenagers to use computers, but were also worried that computer games would do little to enhance the national economy.[26] West European social democrats and East European socialist educators alike not only complained that teenagers used computers inappropriately, but were concerned that gaming would subvert nationalistic goals.

Most government programs were short lived. They were often linked to attempts to solve the 1980s economic crisis by subsidizing the nation's manufacturers. In particular, the subsidy programs often failed to allocate sufficient funds for maintenance, support, and rapidly changing standards. Furthermore, software

[21] Thomas Lean, 'Inside a day you'll be talking to it like an old friend': The making and remaking of Sinclair personal computing in 1980s Britain, in Alberts and Oldenziel, *Hacking Europe*, 49–71. Frank Veraart, Transnational (dis)connection in localizing personal computing in the Netherlands, 1975–1990, in Alberts and Oldenziel, *Hacking Europe*, 25–48.

[22] Simon Nora, and Alain Minc. 1978. *L'informatisation de la société: rapport à M. le Président de la République*. Paris: La Documentation française.

[23] Thomas Kaiserfeld. 1996. Computerizing the Swedish welfare state: The middle way of technological success and failure. *Technology and Culture* 37(2): 249–279.

[24] Bruno Jakić. 2014. Galaxy and the new wave: Yugoslav computer culture in 1980s, in Alberts and Oldenziel, *Hacking Europe*, 107–128.

[25] Maciej M. Sysło, and Anna B. Kwiatkowska. 2008. The challenging face of informatics education in Poland. In *Informatics education – Supporting computational thinking*, ed. Roland T. Mittermeir and Maciej M. Sysło, 1–18. Berlin/Heidelberg: Springer, as cited in Patryk Wasiak, Playing and copying: Social practices of home computer users in Poland during the 1980s, in Alberts and Oldenziel, *Hacking Europe*, 129–150, fn. 33.

[26] Ibid.

designed for the classroom was either unavailable or of poor quality. And when gaming became popular, raising teenagers' expectations and demands for faster processors and graphics, it pushed computer software in a different direction. State funding could not—and in principle would not—respond to such expectations of young computer users. Dutch Tulip, Swedish Compis, Yugoslav Lola, and Polish Meritum all rather unsuccessfully competed with IBM as national alternative to the US model.[27] National governments intervened in the struggle over the meaning of computers by assigning their "proper" place in society. Except for the successful BBC micros, which experienced a relatively long life in British schools, government policies to support national industry largely failed in the long run; programs fostering citizens' computer literacy were equally short lived. An alternative user culture of computers undermined these efforts both locally and nationally. Home-grown groups provided the new microcomputers with local contexts, while connecting them transnationally to a burgeoning youth culture.

Hacking first developed as a practice among computer mainframe users: typically students and researchers playing out their fascination at the terminal of a mainframe computer at a university, "phreaking" connected computer systems or harassing fellow workers and students.[28] When the micro arrived, the new machine fundamentally altered the computer landscape. Firstly, the micro helped pry open the limited range of what the technology could mean and how it could be used. Secondly, the microcomputer user generally became the owner of a small-scale system. The sense of autonomy for the user, often a consumer who bought an assembled product rather than a hobbyist who built it with components, developed as a more important aspect of how to "use" the computer. From then on, for computer owners, appropriating the machine was intimately connected to personal autonomy in using the system. With the development of microcomputers, the fascination of personal autonomy and control took on new forms. Users were able to closely identify with the technology as a personal device in the intimacy of their homes rather than in the factory or office-like environment of mainframe computers.[29]

Hacking went beyond using a private machine for personal use; it also involved using computers in a network. Networking as such was not a novel phenomenon; after all, in the 1970s and 1980s, large bureaucratic organizations from the military to academic computing centers and large corporations had already connected mainframe computers through telephone lines or the incidental dedicated cable. By the 1990s, when users of personal computers joined in vast numbers the already connected world of the Internet, their entry was the defining moment when hacking became hacking.

Or was their joining of the interconnected world the moment when hacking stopped? While the playfulness of computers remained an important element in

---

[27] Lean, Inside a day you'll be talking to it like an old friend; Veraart, Transnational (dis)connection; Jakić, Galaxy and the new wave; Kaiserfeld, Computerizing the Swedish welfare state.

[28] Weizenbaum, Kidder, and Turkle all focus on users of a big university computer or in the research department of a major enterprise.

[29] Turkle, *The second self*.

creating communities, what changed was the character of counterculture. Tim Jordan and Paul Taylor suggest a major shift from hacking to hacktivism. "Initially hacking was predicated upon the imaginative re-appropriation of technology's potential within the countercultural and oppositional communities." By the mid-1990s, these authors believe that "hacking's technological expertise had become, on the one hand, increasingly co-opted by the commercial mentality of the pre-dot.com-bust Internet 'industries' and, on the other hand, was equated largely with illicit, illegal or unwanted computer intrusion."[30]

Against the stream of a disappearing hacker culture that Jordan and Taylor describe, however, communities in Europe emerged that took a more overt political stance. The "hacktivist" movement did not seek to change politics in general, but developed a well-defined political activism that looked to shape computer use and the Internet. Hacktivism targeted the very scripts of the technology. The politicization of the computer was expressed in terms of autonomy, trust, openness, access, ownership, privacy, and security. Hacktivists sought to prevent the threatening commodification and state control of information. We therefore suggest a different path for European personal computing.[31]

1.3 Appropriating America and Making Europe

Europeans participated enthusiastically in the hacktivist movement, but the European story diverged from the US narrative. In Europe, the commercialization of the Internet was less prominent or overpowering than in the USA. Moreover, while Americans routinely celebrated technology, in Europe, there was a strong cultural tradition critiquing the overreliance on technological developments and warning about the effects of alienation. The political attitude of challenging the form and shape of the technological developments was less exceptional. In this respect, the 1994 Amsterdam initiative of a digital city (DDS) was one of the first attempts to create a public space on the Internet with the explicit goal of enabling access for all. The fate of the German hackers, who were first welcomed as heroes before being criminalized as villains, also illustrates a transatlantic difference between Europe and the USA in understanding the goals of the Internet and hacking. Finally, when computers became micros, thus smaller and more accessible to consumers outside the large-scale computing centers, the technology moved across the well-defined boundary between work and leisure. In this space between work and leisure, new habits and an alternative ethos emerged, embracing pleasure rather than utility as

---

[30]Tim Jordan, and Paul A. Taylor. 2004. *Hacktivism and cyberwars. Rebels with a cause?*, 5. London: Routledge.

[31]Ibid., 18.

the guiding principle of hackers.[32] In this particular area, the European appropriation of computing followed a different course.

The unfinished business of ready-made user scripts was even more incomplete in Europe than in the USA. In Europe, the emerging *lingua franca* of computers, the English language, was not a foregone conclusion. In the postwar era, English-language education was still competing with other preferred international languages like French (e.g., in France, the Netherlands, and Greece), German (e.g., in the Netherlands and Eastern Europe), and Russian (e.g., in Finland, Poland, and Yugoslavia). Using English was not just a matter of translation, but also of adopting a mindset and a culture. From the start, US standards and terminology sought to dominate computer development. Ksenia Tatarchenko studied how, in the 1960s, English became the *lingua franca* in the International Federation of Information Processing, IFIP.[33] Even though the French government campaigned to develop its own terminology, none of that remains, except for the term *Informatics* as a label for computer science, which was readily adopted throughout Europe. Perhaps even more noticeable was the fact that personal computers came with a keyboard modeled after American standards. The US keyboard with only 26 characters of the alphabet was introduced both in West and East European nations using Latin-based alphabets. Former IFIP president Heinz Zemanek laments, "[o]ne simple example is sufficient to prove the dependence [of Europe on the USA]: the computer character set, the two times 26 letters which ignore the needs of the larger and smaller countries in Europe. This restriction damages the European language culture."[34] Indeed, the problem Greek users faced in trying to use their alphabet, for example, similarly questioned the routine assumption that computers were universal machines that could be plugged into any culture at any time without any modification.[35] When the technology was still new and largely undetermined, the early computer users were positioned simultaneously as producers and consumers. At times they were acting as hackers, at others as software tinkerers, yet they were always zealously typing away, plugging connections, and even soldering parts. What was available to these social actors was neither the ready-made product nor the well-sketched projection of a personal computing practice.

---

[32] As Rachel Maines writes: "Any technology that privileges the pleasures of production over the value and/or significance of the product, can be a hedonizing technology." Maines discusses technologies once professional that have become popular hobbies like photography, sewing, cooking, car dragsters, and ham radio amateurs, but could also have included hackers. Rachel P. Maines. 2009. *Hedonizing technologies. Paths to pleasure in hobbies and leisure*. Baltimore: The Johns Hopkins University Press.

[33] Ksenia Tatarchenko. 2010. Not lost in translation: How did English become the common language of information processing (1960–1974)? Paper presented at the Software for Europe workshop. Lorentz Center, Leiden, The Netherlands, September 2010.

[34] Heinz Zemanek. 2002. Computers in small countries. In *Computing technology past & future*, ed. J. Folta, 157–170. Prague: National Technical Museum in Prague.

[35] Aristotle Tympas, Fotini Tsaglioti, and Theodore Lekkas. 2008. *Universal machines vs. national languages: Computerization as production of new localities*. Paper presented at the international conference 'Technologies of Globalization', Darmstadt.

This volume's contributions show how the culture of hacking came into being. The authors focus on the different choices local users faced when US-based innovations and related practices travelled across the Atlantic. The act of appropriation gave local meaning to the fascination with computers through a playful culture of youthful rebellion and collective use. In appropriating computers in the local context, users joined the connected world and turned the personal use of computing into hacking. The authors show how the rebellion of young users toying with personal computers without a prescribed purpose, the sense of personal control, and the celebration of "connectedness" came together in specific European ways and how engineers, teenagers, media artists, and social activists participated in the process of appropriation, helping to bridge the gap between the globally produced products and their—at times—exaggerated technological expectations. They offer stories about the fine tuning between design and use in the process of appropriation. In appropriating the machine into their daily routines and local contexts, users spent a great deal of time and resources tinkering and tweaking the technology to forge a link between what was promised and what was required in practice; they also accepted the computer as an essentially instable consumer product. Indeed, few technologies have come with scripts as unfinished as those of personal computers.[36] Thus computer users rather than designers occupied center stage in shaping this particular piece of technology. And they had plenty of room to play.

After developing hobby computers and building kits for personal computers, by the 1980s a few major American brands like IBM, Apple, and Commodore dominated the PC industry. Game computers also entered the scene. In 1981, IBM claimed that the generic term "personal computer" created a new standard, shaping a process that led to a multiplication of the overall market size by a factor of 10. Breaking with its conventional, established corporate strategy, IBM created a PC from component parts not strictly developed in-house. The IBM PC was an open standard that others could follow. The "IBM-compatible" soon acquired a magical meaning for manufacturers seeking to conquer a share of the PC market. Although European firms sold IBM clones that were cheaper, brandless, and sometimes earlier than the American original, the clones were assembled from computer components manufactured in Taiwan, based on US standards. Domestic production in European countries turned into a cottage industry for the assembly of Taiwanese parts. Multinationals like Dutch electronics firm Philips, Italian Olivetti, and German Siemens managed to take a market share only by producing IBM-compatible machines. With the exception of Sinclair and Osborne in the UK, start-up computer firms who designed their own parts and architecture were short lived.

IBM-compatible operating systems were also made according to US standards, something like Microsoft: the MS-DOS system before it was surpassed by Windows in 1985. When the World Wide Web was introduced in 1994, it became clear how much the Windows standard had become the one to follow, turning into a global lock-in. Before the globalizing force of the Web, there was only compliance to a

[36] Thierry Bardini, and A.T. Horvath. 1995. The social construction of the personal computer user. *Journal of Communication* 45(3): 40–66; Thierry Bardini. 2000. *Bootstrapping: Douglas Engelbart, coevolution, and the origins of personal computing*. Stanford: Stanford University Press.

standard among those users who formed a community and were looking for ways to exchange software among like-minded. Apple consumers and music lovers using Commodore often preferred to maintain their own operating systems; game computers operated under another and more restrictive regime; and user communities sharing programs exchanged software such as games, word-processing software, and bookkeeping programs within a dedicated operating system. Committing to an Apple or the Commodore Amiga, computer served as a mark of distinction and was often the first step in participating in a computer habitat with its own routines and codes.

Despite the technical confines of these US-dominated standards, many scenarios remained open ended for computer users. Specifications and user habits still had to be decided for a computer to work properly, for computing practices to evolve in a user-friendly fashion, and for local communities to emerge around them. For example, if you bought an Amiga on the Polish market and brought the machine home to Krakow, you could not simply plug it in with US manuals and scripts, as if it were a universal machine with a fixed meaning and stable functionality. What it meant to own a computer in Poland within the Cold War context, the implications of having one, and what it would be used for—all such aspects of a cultural script—were yet to be inscribed into the machine. Neither the itinerary nor the form of ownership was firmly set; nor could the route or mediation process which shaped the use be assumed. In most cases, hackers adopted US-standardized parts, rejected some, tinkered with others, and created new assemblies and new meanings to fit local uses. In the process, these users helped co-construct the new products.

Recent Cold War scholarship has shown that the mythical Iron Curtain was often gauze, through which frequent exchanges between East and West occurred and through which technical knowledge flowed back and forth.[37] Many routes were open to prospective Polish users to purchase a personal computer.[38] Young Yugoslavs, interested in assembling computers, found ways of circumventing official restrictions and acquiring imported parts. Thus, transnational and international circulation of ideas and expertise took place broadly, but the political meanings of computer hacker culture on both sides of the Cold War divide played out in different ways. While German computer clubs like Chaos Computer Club and Dutch hobby clubs at times presented themselves as anti-establishment and countercultural movements, such oppositional political associations remained rather weak or even absent in Yugoslavia or Poland.[39]

---

[37] Simon Donig. 2010. Appropriating American technology in the 1960s: Cold War politics and the GDR computer industry. *IEEE Annals in the History of Computing* 32(2): 32–45; Petri Paju, and Helena Durnová. 2009. Computing close to the iron curtain: Inter/national computing practices in Czechoslovakia and Finland. *Comparative Technology Transfer and Society* 7(3): 303–322.

[38] Patryk Wasiak. 2010. Computing behind the iron curtain: Social impact of home computers in Polish People's Republic. In *Tensions of Europe and Inventing Europe Working Paper series*, working paper No. 2010/ 08. Accessible online at http://tensionsofeurope.eu/www/en/publications/working-papers.

[39] Kai Denker. 2014. Heroes yet criminals of the German computer revolution, in Alberts and Oldenziel, *Hacking Europe*, 167–188; Wasiak, Playing and copying; Veraart, Transnational (dis) connection; Jakić, Galaxy and the new wave.

Even so, despite the polarizing politics of the Cold War, what is so remarkable is not so much the differences but the similarities between the ways East and West European users appropriated microcomputer technology into their daily lives. On both sides of the political divide, microcomputers were domesticated into a culture where they became marks of cultural exclusivity, social distinction, and close-knit communities or "scenes." Given the strong rituals, sense of exclusivity, and feeling of community, it is little wonder that hackers have generated their mythologies and national heroes; but such national focus is only one part of the story.[40]

What the chapters in *Hacking Europe* bring to the fore is how, despite the Cold War, there were numerous ways computers defied and crossed national borders.[41] Indeed a more explicitly transnational lens helps us to focus on the circulation of technological artifacts and the practices of technology-in-use. Contrary to stories of national pride and production, motherboards manufactured in Taiwan travelled to local start-up firms in Europe that assembled the machines according to US "IBM-compatible" standards.[42] A transnational perspective, moreover, allows us to see how national governments and international bodies wielded their influence over the flow of computer expertise and hardware. Government-sponsored programs in Sweden and the Netherlands promoted personal computers on a national scale. At the same time, the European Community encouraged them through ESPRIT, while in Warsaw Pact countries, state policies deferred their adoption.

1.4 European Diversity and Common Ground

Hacking Europe brings together for the first time essays on European computing events. Collectively the essays offer us new insights. First of all, the contributions show that tinkering with computers was not all about hacking: fun and fascination

[40] Chirillo, *Hack attacks*; Hafner and Markoff, *Cyberpunk*; Kent, *The ultimate history of video games*; King and Borland, *Dungeons and dreamers*; Kushner, *Masters of doom*. The French Micral computer, a 1973 product based on the Intel 4004 processor, advances the French claim of having invented the microcomputer. It is a favorite website story but lacks proper historiographical groundings. For historically based cases on domestication of the PC in Finland, the Netherlands, the UK, and Germany, see, respectively, the works of Petri Saarikoski, Frank Veraart, Thomas Lean, and Kai Denker. Petri Saarikoski, and Jaakko Suominen. 2009. Computer hobbyists and the gaming industry in Finland. *IEEE Annals of the History of Computing* 31(3): 20–33; Petri Saarikoski. 2005. Club activity in the early phases of microcomputing in Finland. In *History of Nordic computing*, ed. Janis Bubenko, John Impagliazzo, and Arne Sølvberg, 277–288. Berlin: Springer; Frank Veraart. 2008c. *Vormgevers van Persoonlijk Computergebruik: De ontwikkeling van computers voor kleingebruikers in Nederland 1970–1990*. PhD thesis, TU Eindhoven. Frank Veraart. 2008b. De domesticatie van de computer in Nederland 1975–1990. *Studium* 2(1): 145–164; Thomas Lean. 2008. *'The making of the micro': Producers, mediators, users and the development of popular microcomputing in Britain (1980–1989)*. PhD thesis, University of Manchester, Manchester.

[41] Helena Durnová. 2010. Sovietization of Czechoslovakian computing: The rise and fall of the SAPO Project. *IEEE Annals of the History of Computing* 32(2): 21–31.

[42] On this topic of microcomputers in Taiwan, see Honghong Tinn. 2011. From DIY computers to illegal copies: The controversy over tinkering in Taiwan, 1980–1984. *IEEE Annals of the History of Computing* 33(2): 75–88.

were equally inspiring. In addition, the authors describe specific European forms of community like the digital public domains best symbolized by the Amsterdam "Digital City" project and by the Polish and Finnish creative "demoscenes" communities. Indeed, European hacking was embedded in play rather than work. Serendipity, mischievousness, and humor played a large role. In appropriating and tinkering with the new technology, the "ludological" element was part of the effort to make the computers one's own. Perhaps that is not unique to European ways of appropriating the new technology because similar processes occurred on the other side of the Atlantic. But European users did face specific challenges.

In the 1980s, users from Greece to Finland and from Zagreb to Amsterdam were confronted with computers' incompatibilities, universal language claims, projected uses, and technical standards that had little to do with local circumstances. Hacker communities' elaborate appropriation procedures through piracy as well as illegal copying and tinkering were the key to personal computers' success outside the American orbit. Thus far, hacker culture had been known primarily as a phenomenon of how users appropriated a technology embedded in the military-academic communities for their own uses. The current collection provides insights into the unique ways European subcultures domesticated computers (Part I); appropriated computers in political ways, forming tight communities or "scenes" (Part II); and created public space in computing (Part III).

We present this collection with a strict theme (hackers) and in chronological (1980s–1990s) order, while contributions from Yugoslavia, Poland, Greece, and the Czech Republic lend a wide geographical balance. Part I "Appropriating America" covers three case studies (the Netherlands, the UK, and Greece) where the transatlantic circulation of English-language computer technologies and knowledge was appropriated through mediating channels like magazines, computer stores, computer clubs, and educational institutions. Part II "Bastards Sons of the Cold War" looks at three portals countries between the Cold War in East and West (Yugoslavia, Poland, and Finland): computer subcultures helped create unique niches that were neither private nor public and in which neither the state nor the market was pushing the envelope of digital cultures and innovations. "Creating the Scenes" is the common denominator for these hybrid communities. Finally, Part III "Going Public" shows how subcultures of hacking became part of a political movement to make computer technologies and the Internet accessible for all, by placing it squarely in the public domain in Hamburg, Amsterdam, and Prague. The Internet acquired an aspect of public space.

Each contribution explores the mediating actors instrumental in appropriating and spreading the cultures of computing around Europe. The most noticeable aspect of all these cultures is their strong internal coherence and the small size of their communities. Consequently, the narrow entry point through which the US-based innovation of PCs and operating systems passed gave the gatekeepers a great deal of influence over the diffusion of computing practices. In Eastern Europe, these communities formed subcultural spaces rather than overt political countercultural communities like the American homebrew computer clubs. Depending on the national context, these communities acted as subcultures which inscribed local meanings and habits into the machines. In the UK, the educational script and utility led to specific computer choices and designs. In Yugoslavia, the urge to be independent of industrial standards governed the logic of individual computer use. Yugoslavian users purposefully tinkered with the American standards to suit their local needs.

Thus, the first section looks at how American standards did or did not shape local choices. In his case study, Frank Veraart presents the diffusion of personal computers in the final decades of the twentieth century as an archetypical example of Americanization. Although North-American personal computers sold like wildfire in the Netherlands, a closer look at how they were appropriated in Dutch households, schools, and small printing industries demonstrates the various ways computer technologies and uses were localized. The introduction and appropriation of personal computers was not an inevitable and smooth process of international technology and knowledge transfer to a local context. Depending on local needs, habits, and cultural settings, many actors developed different strategies to deal with North-American suppliers. In his analysis of how British Sinclair personal computing was created in the 1980s, Thomas Lean argues that compared to the USA, prices and preferences determined the UK users' choice of computer. Potential computer users preferred low cost over high performance and educational benefits (or "computer literacy") over general purpose utility. The British culture of thrift and social uplift explains why the Cambridge manufactured and cheaper Sinclair (ZX 81 and ZX Spectrum) was more popular than the gadget-oriented Apple and Commodore computers. The chapter is a classic example of how user preferences coproduced the outcome of British home computing in the 1980s.[43] Theodore Lekkas shows how a home-computing culture of software use was built around the publication of a computer magazine called *Pixel*. It integrated newcomers into a community of users who collectively reconfigured critical software components to make the computer usable in Greece. The journal also functioned as a channel of transnational mediation between Greek and foreign computer users.[44]

The next three chapters look at copying and cracking cultures. Bruno Jakić's chapter on Yugoslavian computer culture maps how the nonaligned socialist state of Yugoslavia, sandwiched between the superpowers during the Cold War, developed a long-standing culture of technological and military expertise independent of both the USA and the Soviet Union. The introduction of computing practices in the 1980s profited from the thriving local manufacturing industries. While computer hardware and software were imported through various routes from Italy and Germany and computer expertise travelled from the UK, Yugoslavia also established its own PC manufacturing. The development of independent Yugoslav software through the exchange of cassette tapes, radio broadcasts, and transcriptions was similar to that in

[43] For a striking parallel, see Joy Parr. 1997. What makes washday less blue? Gender, nation, and technology choice in postwar Canada. *Technology and Culture* 38(1): 153–186.

[44] Theodore Lekkas, Legal Pirates Ltd: Home computing cultures in early 1980s Greece, in Alberts and Oldenziel, *Hacking Europe*, 73–103.

the Netherlands.[45] But in Yugoslavia, the autonomy was hard wired. The architecture of the locally produced kits and computers was such that the software protection, either hacked from the US standards or locally produced, had to be removed before it could be installed. The thriving hacker scene in Yugoslavia was elitist, participated in a culture of alternative music and art, but was not driven by political motives. Patryk Wasiak focuses on the playing and copying practices of home computing in Poland. Part of a wider hacker culture of "cracking" and the "demoscene," Polish hobby computing was shaped by similar practices in Western Europe. Despite Cold War restrictions, Polish users had access to specialized literature, computer magazines, and grassroots publications while maintaining contact with Western computer clubs and periodicals. Antti Silvast and Markku Reunanen detail the Finnish demoscene, a subculture of programmers, graphics artists, and musicians who created real-time audiovisual presentations with personal computers. Calling themselves "demosceners" or "sceners," they presented real-time demonstrations ("demos"). An exclusive European phenomenon, the demoscene is viewed as an artistic activity: "art of the real-time" or digital art form and a way of life. A characterization of the culture of the demoscene may be distilled from the combined reading to the Chaps. 6 and 7 by Wasiak and Silvast and Reunanen.[46]

The last three chapters describe how the hacker movement sought to go public and create shared spaces. Kai Denker describes the West German Chaos Computer Club as a politically driven organization. Here the communities facilitating the introduction of computing to a larger audience resembled more closely the US countercultural movement. Even so, the counterculture movement in Germany meant something else than the Californian Whole Earth Network, which Fred Turner argues was the origin of the cyber culture.[47] Caroline Nevejan and Alec Badenoch detail how Amsterdam invented the Internet as a public space and how the city served as a portal for Europe's computer networks. The influential Amsterdam Digital City (De Digitale Stad or DDS) embraced elements of the countercultural movement from California and the German Chaos Computer Club, and successfully empowered ordinary Dutch citizens by turning them into digital ones. Applying early Internet applications, the project built virtual communities supported by the local social democratic government and political grassroot movements. Besides, Amsterdam served as a crucial node in Europe's emerging Internet infrastructure, while the digital city also made transnational connections between Amsterdam and Belgrade on the eve of the political disintegration of Yugoslavia. Johan Söderberg studies the Czech Wireless Community's "Ronja" hardware used for sending data by means of visible light. The technology was developed by users in the Czech wireless network community. The philosophy behind the project was that you did not need any previous knowledge of electronics to build the device yourself. To realize

---

[45] See Frank C.A. Veraart. 2011. Losing meanings: Computer games in Dutch domestic use, 1975–2000. *IEEE Annals of the History of Computing* 33(1): 52–65.

[46] Antti Silvast, and Markku Reunanen, Multiple users, diverse users: Appropriation of personal computers by demoscene hackers, in Alberts and Oldenziel, *Hacking Europe*, 151–163.

[47] See: note 1; Turner, *From counterculture to cyberculture*; Gillies, *Wie wir waren.*

this vision, the mechanics and electronics were designed with generally available, off-the-shelf components, while the assembly instructions were published on the Internet under a free license. Guided by the principles of "user-controlled technology," the case study also uncovers the split in the Czech wireless community over the commercialization of Ronja.[48]

We hope these essays will collectively contribute to the current scholarship in several ways: they will help to focus on the understudied European cultures of appropriation that have been an early subfield of the history of technology.[49] The case studies also point out the ways in which an American product became embedded through elaborate cultural scripts in local contexts in Eastern and Western Europe during the 1980s and 1990s; they thus enrich the European American Studies scholarship dealing with the process of Americanization: how American products and culture are appropriated outside the geographical boundaries of the USA and domesticated in a local context.[50] Finally, the contributions show the many ways computer user communities activated various means of communication ranging from hobby computer clubs, specialized magazines to classified ads, computer stores, and radio programs. Exploring these—predominantly male—hacker scenes lets us see how practices were reproduced on an individual level. This compilation of essays paints a rich picture of how personal computers found their way into local European contexts, thus helping us understand whether computers could rightly or not claim a US-based sense of universality.

Bibliography

Aarseth, Espen. 1997. *Cybertext: Perspectives on ergodic literature*. Baltimore: Johns Hopkins University Press.

Akera, Atusushi. 2001. Voluntarism and the fruits of collaboration: The IBM user group, SHARE. *Technology and Culture* 42(4): 710–736.

Akrich, Madeleine. 1992. The de-scription of technical objects. In *Shaping technology/building society: Studies in sociotechnical change*, ed. Wiebe E. Bijker and John Law, 205–224. Cambridge, MA: MIT Press.

---

48 Johan Söderberg, Users in the dark: The development of a user-controlled technology in the Czech Wireless Network Community, in Alberts and Oldenziel, *Hacking Europe*, 219–239.

49 The burgeoning of the European history of technology can be followed in the research agenda of *Tensions of Europe* established in 1999. See www.tensionsofeurope.eu

50 Richard Pells. 1997. *Not like us: How Europeans have loved, hated, and transformed American culture since World War II*. New York: Basic Books. Mel Van Elteren. 2006. *Americanism and Americanization. A critical history of domestic and global influence*. Jefferson/London: McFarland; Pells, *Not like us*; Jonathan Zeitlin, and Gary Herrigel (eds.). 2000. *Americanization and its limits. Reworking US technology and management in post-war Europe and Japan*. Oxford: Oxford University Press; Mattias Kipping, and Ove Bjarnar (eds.). 1998. *The Americanisation of European business. The Marshall plan and the transfer of US management models*. London: Routledge. Richard F. Kuisel. 1993. *Seducing the French: The dilemma of Americanization*. Berkeley: University of California Press. Oldenziel and Zachmann, eds., *Cold War kitchen*.

Akrich, Madeleine, and Bruno Latour. 1992. A summary of convenient vocabulary for the semiotics of human and nonhuman assemblies. In *Shaping technology/building society: Studies in sociotechnical change*, ed. Wiebe E. Bijker and John Law, 259–264. Cambridge, MA: MIT Press.

Aspray, William. 1997. The Intel 4004 microprocessor: What constituted invention. *IEEE Annals of the History of Computing* 19(3): 4–15.

Bardini, Thierry. 2000. *Bootstrapping: Douglas Engelbart, coevolution, and the origins of personal computing*. Stanford: Stanford University Press.

Bardini, Thierry, and A.T. Horvath. 1995. The social construction of the personal computer user. *Journal of Communication* 45(3): 40–66.

Bijker, Wiebe E., Thomas P. Hughes, and Trevor J. Pinch (eds.). 1987. *The social construction of technological systems. New directions in the sociology and history of technology*. Cambridge, MA: MIT Press.

Campbell-Kelly, Martin, William Aspray, Nathan Ensmenger, and Jeffrey R. Yost. 2014 [1996]. *Computer: A history of the information machine*, The Sloan technology series. Boulder: Westview Press.

Chirillo, John. 2001. *Hack attacks encyclopedia: A complete history of hacks, cracks, phreaks, and spies over time*. New York: Wiley.

Cieraad, Irene. 2009. The radiant American kitchen: Domesticating Dutch nuclear energy. In *Cold War kitchen. Americanization, technology, and European users*, ed. Ruth Oldenziel and Karin Zachmann, 113–136. Cambridge, MA: MIT Press.

Cowan, Ruth Schwartz. 1987. The consumption junction: A proposal for research strategies in the sociology of technology. In *The social construction of technological systems. New directions in the sociology and history of technology*, ed. Wiebe E. Bijker, Thomas P. Hughes, and Trevor J. Pinch, 261–280. Cambridge, MA: MIT Press.

de Grazia, Victoria. 2005. *Irresistible empire. America's advance through twentieth-century Europe*. Cambridge, MA: Belknap.

Denker, Kai. 2014. Heroes yet criminals of the German computer revolution. In *Hacking Europe. From computer cultures to demoscenes*, ed. Gerard Alberts and Ruth Oldenziel, 167–188. New York: Springer.

Donig, Simon. 2010. Appropriating American technology in the 1960s: Cold War politics and the GDR computer industry. *IEEE Annals of the History of Computing* 32(2): 32–45.

Durnová, Helena. 2010. Sovietization of Czechoslovakian computing: The rise and fall of the SAPO project. *IEEE Annals of the History of Computing* 32(2): 21–31.

Frasca, Gonzalo. 2003. Simulation vs. narrative: Introduction to ludology. In *The video game theory reader*, ed. J.P. Mark Wolf and Bernard Perron, 221–236. London: Routledge.

Frasca, Gonzalo. 2007. *Play the message: Play, game and videogame rhetoric*. PhD thesis, University of Copenhagen.

Gillies, Constantin. 2003. *Wie wir waren: die wilden Jahre der Web-Generation*. Weinheim: Wiley-VCH.

Hafner, Katie, and John Markoff. 1991. *Cyberpunk: Outlaws and hackers on the computer frontier*. London: Touchstone.

Huizinga, Johan. 1949 [1938]. *Homo Ludens: A study of the play-element in culture*. London: Routledge & Kegan Paul.

Jakić, Bruno. 2014. Galaxy and the new wave: Yugoslav computer culture in 1980s. In *Hacking Europe. From computer cultures to demoscenes*, ed. Gerard Alberts and Ruth Oldenziel, 107–128. New York: Springer.

Jordan, Tim, and Paul A. Taylor. 2004. *Hacktivism and cyberwars. Rebels with a cause?* London: Routledge.

Kaiserfeld, Thomas. 1996. Computerizing the Swedish welfare state: The middle way of technological success and failure. *Technology and Culture* 37(2): 249–279.

Kent, Steven L. 2001. *The ultimate history of video games. From Pong to Pokémon and beyond: The story behind the craze that touched our lives and changed the world*. New York: Three Rivers Press.

Kidder, Tracy. 1981. *The soul of a new machine*. Boston: Little Brown.

King, Brad, and John Borland. 2003. *Dungeons and dreamers. The rise of computer game culture from geek to chic*. New York: McGraw-Hill.

Kipping, Mattias, and Ove Bjarnar (eds.). 1998. *The Americanisation of European business. The Marshall plan and the transfer of US management models*. London: Routledge.

Krige, John. 2006. *American hegemony and the postwar reconstruction of science in Europe*. Cambridge, MA: MIT Press.

Krige, John. 2008. The peaceful atom as political weapon: Euratom and American foreign policy in the late 1950s. *Historical Studies in the Natural Sciences* 38(1): 5–44.

Kuisel, Richard F. 1993. *Seducing the French: The dilemma of Americanization*. Berkeley: University of California Press.

Kushner, David. 2003. *Masters of Doom. How two guys created an empire and transformed pop culture*. New York: Random House.

Latour, Bruno. 1992. Where are the hidden masses. Sociology of a few mundane artifacts. In *Shaping technology/building society: Studies in sociotechnical change*, ed. Wiebe E. Bijker and John Law, 225–258. Cambridge, MA: MIT Press.

Lean, Thomas. 2008. *'The making of the micro': Producers, mediators, users and the development of popular microcomputing in Britain (1980–1989)*. PhD thesis, University of Manchester, Manchester.

Lean, Thomas. 2014. 'Inside a day you'll be talking to it like an old friend': The making and remaking of Sinclair personal computing in 1980s Britain. In *Hacking Europe. From computer cultures to demoscenes*, ed. Gerard Alberts and Ruth Oldenziel, 49–71. New York: Springer.

Lekkas, Theodore. 2014. Legal Pirates Ltd: Home computing cultures in early 1980s Greece. In *Hacking Europe. From computer cultures to demoscenes*, ed. Gerard Alberts and Ruth Oldenziel, 73–103. New York: Springer.

Levy, Steven. 1984. *Hackers: Heroes of the computer revolution*. Garden City, NY: Anchor Press/Doubleday.

Lindsay, Christina. 2003. From the shadows: Users as designers, producers, marketers, distributors, and technical support. In *How users matter. The co-construction of users and technology*, ed. Nelly Oudshoorn and Trevor J. Pinch, 29–50. Cambridge, MA: MIT Press.

Lubar, Steven. 1992. 'Do not fold, spindle or mutilate': A cultural history of the punched card. *Journal of American Culture* 15(4): 43–55.

Lubar, Steven. 1993. *Infoculture. The Smithsonian book of information age inventions*. Boston/New York: Houghton Mifflin Company.

Maines, Rachel P. 2009. *Hedonizing technologies. Paths to pleasure in hobbies and leisure*. Baltimore: The Johns Hopkins University Press.

Misa, Thomas J. (ed.). 2010. *Gender codes: Why women are leaving computing*. Hoboken: Wiley.

Moody, Fred. 1999. *The visionary position. The inside story of the digital dreamers who are making virtual reality a reality*. New York: Times Business.

Nevejan, Caroline, and Alexander Badenoch. 2014. How Amsterdam invented the Internet: European networks of significance, 1980–1995. In *Hacking Europe. From computer cultures to demoscenes*, ed. Gerard Alberts and Ruth Oldenziel, 189–217. New York: Springer.

Nora, Simon, and Alain Minc. 1978. *L'informatisation de la société: rapport à M. le Président de la République*. Paris: La Documentation française.

Oldenziel, Ruth. 2001. Woman the consumer: The consumption junction revisited. In *Feminism in twentieth-century science, technology and medicine*, ed. Angela N.H. Creager, Elizabeth Lunbeck, and Londa Schiebinger, 128–148. Chicago: Chicago University Press.

Oldenziel, Ruth, and Adri A. de la Bruhèze. 2009. Theorizing the mediation junction for technology and consumption. In *Manufacturing technology, manufacturing consumers. The making of Dutch consumer society*, ed. Adri A. de la Bruhèze and Ruth Oldenziel, 9–40. Amsterdam: Aksant.

Oldenziel, Ruth, and Karin Zachmann (eds.). 2009. *Cold War kitchen. Americanization, technology, and European users*. Cambridge, MA: MIT Press.

Oudshoorn, Nelly. 1996. Genderscripts in technologie: Noodlot of uitdaging? *Tijdschrift voor Vrouwenstudies* 17(4): 350–368.

Oudshoorn, Nelly, and Trevor J. Pinch (eds.). 2003. *How users matter. The co-construction of users and technology*. Cambridge, MA: MIT Press.

Paju, Petri, and Helena Durnová. 2009. Computing close to the iron curtain: Inter/national computing practices in Czechoslovakia and Finland. *Comparative Technology Transfer and Society* 7(3): 303–322.

Parr, Joy. 1997. What makes washday less blue? Gender, nation, and technology choice in postwar Canada. *Technology and Culture* 38(1): 153–186.

Pells, Richard. 1997. *Not like us: How Europeans have loved, hated, and transformed American culture since World War II*. New York: Basic Books.

Poppe, Ine, and Sandra Rottenberg. 2000. *De KRAAKgeneratie*. Amsterdam: De Balie.

Rommes, Els. 2002. *Gender scripts and the Internet: The design and use of Amsterdam's digital city*. PhD thesis, University Twente.

Saarikoski, Petri. 2005. Club activity in the early phases of microcomputing in Finland. In *History of Nordic computing*, ed. Janis Bubenko, John Impagliazzo, and Arne Sølvberg, 277–288. Berlin: Springer.

Saarikoski, Petri, and Jaakko Suominen. 2009. Computer hobbyists and the gaming industry in Finland. *IEEE Annals of the History of Computing* 31(3): 20–33.

Silvast, Antti, and Markku Reunanen. 2014. Multiple users, diverse users: Appropriation of personal computers by demoscene hackers. In *Hacking Europe. From computer cultures to demoscenes*, ed. Gerard Alberts and Ruth Oldenziel, 151–163. New York: Springer.

Söderberg, Johan. 2014. Users in the dark: The development of a user-controlled technology in the Czech Wireless Network Community. In *Hacking Europe. From computer cultures to demoscenes*, ed. Gerard Alberts and Ruth Oldenziel, 219–239. New York: Springer.

Sysło, Maciej M., and Anna B. Kwiatkowska. 2008. The challenging face of informatics education in Poland. In *Informatics education – Supporting computational thinking*, ed. Roland T. Mittermeir and Maciej M. Sysło, 1–18. Berlin/Heidelberg: Springer.

Tatarchenko, Ksenia. 2010. Not lost in translation: How did English become the common language of information processing (1960–1974)? Paper presented at the Software for Europe workshop. Lorentz Center, Leiden, The Netherlands, September 2010.

Tinn, Honghong. 2011. From DIY computers to illegal copies: The controversy over tinkering in Taiwan, 1980–1984. *IEEE Annals of the History of Computing* 33(2): 75–88.

Turkle, Sherry. 1984. *The second self: Computers and the human spirit*. New York: Simon & Schuster.

Turner, Fred. 2006. *From counterculture to cyberculture: Stewart Brand, the Whole Earth Network, and the rise of digital utopianism*. Chicago: University of Chicago Press.

Tympas, Aristotle, Fotini Tsaglioti, and Theodore Lekkas. 2008. *Universal machines vs. national languages: Computerization as production of new localities*. Paper presented at the international conference 'Technologies of Globalization', Darmstadt.

Van Elteren, Mel. 2006. *Americanism and Americanization. A critical history of domestic and global influence*. Jefferson/London: McFarland.

Veraart, Frank. 2008b. De domesticatie van de computer in Nederland 1975–1990. *Studium* 2(1): 145–164.

Veraart, Frank. 2008c. *Vormgevers van Persoonlijk Computergebruik: De ontwikkeling van computers voor kleingebruikers in Nederland 1970–1990*. PhD thesis, TU Eindhoven.

Veraart, Frank. 2011. Losing meanings: Computer games in Dutch domestic use, 1975–2000. *IEEE Annals of the History of Computing* 33(1):52–65

Veraart, Frank. 2014. Transnational (dis)connection in localizing personal computing in the Netherlands, 1975–1990. In *Hacking Europe. From computer cultures to demoscenes*, ed. Gerard Alberts and Ruth Oldenziel, 25–48. New York: Springer.

Wasiak, Patryk. 2010. Computing behind the iron curtain: Social impact of home computers in Polish People's Republic. In *Tensions of Europe and Inventing Europe Working Paper series*, working paper no. 2010/08. Accessible online at http://tensionsofeurope.eu/www/en/publications/working-papers

Wasiak, Patryk. 2014. Playing and copying: Social practices of home computer users in Poland during the 1980s. In *Hacking Europe. From computer cultures to demoscenes*, ed. Gerard Alberts and Ruth Oldenziel, 129–150. New York: Springer.
Weizenbaum, Joseph. 1976. *Computer power and human reason: From judgment to calculation*. San Francisco: W. H. Freeman.
Woolgar, Steve. 1991. Configuring the user: The case of usability trials. In *A sociology of monsters: Essays on power, technology and domination*, ed. John Law, 57–100. London: Routledge.
Zeitlin, Jonathan, and Gary Herrigel (eds.). 2000. *Americanization and its limits. Reworking US technology and management in post-war Europe and Japan*. Oxford: Oxford University Press.
Zemanek, Heinz. 2002. Computers in small countries. In *Computing technology past & future*, ed. J. Folta, 157–170. Prague: National Technical Museum in Prague.

Part I
Appropriating America: Making One's Own

Chapter 2
Transnational (Dis)Connection in Localizing Personal Computing in the Netherlands, 1975–1990

Frank C.A. Veraart

2.1 Introduction[1]

In September 1989, Microsoft's CEO Bill Gates traveled to the Netherlands to sign a contract with the Dutch Ministry of Education to provide all the elementary and high schools in the country with Microsoft Windows. After more than a decade of experimenting with computers, the Dutch education system switched to the infamous American software producer. The Netherlands was the world's first country to do so, and this was just one of Microsoft's many successes during its domination of personal computers starting in the 1980s. Microsoft's conquest is a typical example of Americanization resulting from the United States dominating computer developments in the 1970s and 1980s. The story charting the rise of personal computers in these decades mirrors the classic example of American business success when personal computers conquered the world. Business histories showed evidence of the growing revenue from computer hardware and software industries in those years.[2] Combined with the entrepreneurial accounts of garage shops transforming into million dollar businesses, these histories turned into modern-day versions of "the American dream" of self-made man, the twentieth century pioneer of the

[1]The chapter is based on my PhD research on the development of personal computing in the Netherlands. Frank Veraart. 2008c. *Vormgevers van Persoonlijk Computergebruik*. PhD thesis, TU Eindhoven. An earlier version was presented at the European Science Foundation's Appropriating America workshop in 2009 in Amsterdam. I wish to thank Per Lundin, Gerard Alberts, and Ruth Oldenziel for their stimulating comments on this and earlier versions.

[2]Alfred D. Chandler Jr. 2007. *Inventing the electronic century: The epic story of the consumer electronics and computer industries*. New York: The Free Press; Martin Campbell-Kelly. 2003. *From airline reservations to sonic the hedgehog, a history of the software industry*. Cambridge MA/London: MIT Press.

F.C.A. Veraart (✉)
Foundation of the History of Technology (SHT), Eindhoven University of Technology, Eindhoven, The Netherlands
e-mail: f.c.a.veraart@tue.nl

G. Alberts and R. Oldenziel (eds.), *Hacking Europe. From Computer Cultures to Demoscenes*, History of Computing, DOI 10.1007/978-1-4471-5493-8_2,

digital world.[3] Such a producer-centered view of personal computer developments represents a grand narrative of Americanization – a world dominated by American technology.[4]

Simply interpreting the adoption and appropriation of personal computers as Americanization, however, does not do justice to the more interactive dynamics of these processes. On both sides of the Atlantic, actors were working hard to introduce computer technologies into society. From a user's viewpoint, a different story emerges. Users and intermediary social actors shaped and co-constructed the adoption and appropriation of computer technologies.[5] Through transnational links, technology and knowledge were transferred and translated, both figuratively and at times literally, from producers to end users via many intermediary actors.[6] For example, small-scale users such as households and schools were of interest to producers as mass consumers. Unlike business applications, these communities lacked a direct economic interest in computing technology but were rather seeking suitable applications for their own specific needs. Their search led to flexible processes of appropriation involving users, producers, and intermediaries on both sides of the Atlantic.

Processes of appropriation, like the one under discussion here, may evoke many different reactions and innovating activities. Using Americanization as an analytical concept, instead of an actor's category, Dutch sociologist Mel van Elteren talks of "dialectic contra-flows of modernity, [...] informal patterns of resistance characteristic of institutions to various strategies of control by managerial elites."[7] Elaborating on such notions, this chapter explains the various responses to the appropriation of

---

[3] William H. Gates III. 1995. *The road ahead.* New York: Penguin; Jeffrey S. Young, and William L. Simon. 2005. *iCon Steve Jobs, the greatest second act in the history of business.* Hoboken: Wiley; Steve Wozniak. 2006. *iWoz, computer geek to computer icon.* New York: W.W. Norton and Company.

[4] Leading histories of computing underline this view with a very strong focus on the American influence in computer development: Martin Campbell-Kelly, William Aspray, Nathan Ensmenger, and Jeffrey R. Yost. 2014 [1996]. *Computer: A history of the information machine.* Boulder, CO: Westview Press. Paul E. Ceruzzi. 2003 [1988]. *A history of modern computing.* Cambridge, MA/London: MIT Press; James W. Cortada. 2004. *The digital hand: How computers changed the work of American manufacturing, transportation, and retail industries.* Oxford: Oxford University Press.

[5] Nelly Oudshoorn, and Trevor J. Pinch (eds.). 2003. *How users matter. The co-construction of users and technologies.* Cambridge, MA: MIT Press; Adri Albert de la Bruhèze, and Ruth Oldenziel (eds.). 2009. *Manufacturing technology, manufacturing consumers. The making of Dutch consumer society.* Amsterdam: Aksant.

[6] An overview of transnational studies in technological development in Erik van der Vleuten. 2008. Toward a transnational history of technology: Meanings, promises, pitfalls. *Technology and Culture* 49(4): 974–994. The methodological approach builds on notions of technology and knowledge circulation in the context of business innovation. These studies show how innovation is supported by the development of (inter)national networks that allow information and technology flows. More on this in Arjan van Rooij, Eric Berkers, Mila Davids, and Frank Veraart. 2008. National innovation system and international knowledge flows: An exploratory investigation with cases from the Netherlands. *Technology Transfer and Strategic Management* 20(2): 149–168.

[7] Mel van Elteren. 1994. *Imagining America, Dutch youth and its sense of place.* Tilburg: Tilburg University Press.

US-based personal computer technologies. We see the transnational dynamics involved throughout the development of computer technologies at home and at schools in the Netherlands.

2.2 Personal Computing Pioneers: Bridging the Atlantic

In the early 1970s, hardly anyone envisaged that personal computers would be for the masses. Computers were capital-intensive, million dollar machines for large industries, government agencies, research institutes, the military, and universities. The rise of computer industries and informatics was indeed fostered by the military's complex and administrative demands. Computers were the mainly invisible heart of modern society, and the possibilities with these programmable machines seemed endless. In visions of the future, computers played an iconic role as an unlimited knowledge resource, a robotized and efficient management system. By 1970, actors in the established computer regime developed plans for education, entertainment, and other public services based on centralized mainframe computers and databases that could be accessed by home-owned terminals.

As part of the emerging counterculture movement, critical groups both in the United States and Europe, however, viewed these ideas as yet another attempt by the establishment to increase centralization and control. In an effort to shift the balance, these groups adopted amateurs' methods of self-building and programming computers to empower a general audience of people with computer knowledge. In their view, self-education could liberate people from the technology and knowledge monopolies held by authorities and businesses. The movement popularized computers as a hobby and established the production and trade of the first personal computers based on microprocessors. In California, similar initiatives resulted in the Homebrew Computer Club that blossomed into a fertile breeding ground for grass roots businesses. Club meetings, magazines, and fairs became arenas for exchanging new knowledge, technologies, and applications.[8]

The first computer to gain some commercial success from these activities was called the Altair. Ed Roberts had been commissioned to develop the machine in 1977 by the magazine *Popular Electronics*. The computer côuld be purchased as a kit for US$395. Its price and potential to build add-ons made the Altair an icon of the personal computer development in a technophile subculture of computer amateurs. In the Netherlands, a handful of computer amateurs had introduced such personal computers as early as 1975, along with information developed by the American and British user groups. Some established small shops that imported complete and semifinished computers from the United States. They aimed mainly at the niche markets of electronic and amateur radio enthusiasts. These customers

[8] More on the development of American computer amateurs and clubs in relation to social critics, in Steven Levy. 1984. *Hackers: Heroes of the computer revolution*. Garden City, NY: Anchor Press/Doubleday; Campbell-Kelly e.a., *Computer* and Ceruzzi, *A history of modern computing*.

were tinkering with their electronics in attics and hobby rooms. The roots of personal computer technology in the Netherlands were established in an atmosphere of experimentation, similar to their American and British counterparts.[9]

The Dutch followed the British lead. The January 1976 issue of the Dutch magazine *Elektuur*, catering to electronics hobbyists, reviewed the possibilities of microprocessors. "The avalanche of applications of the μP (microprocessor, F.V.) will take off within 2 years and we will gratefully enjoy it as an addition to our technological capacities. For now, we are awaiting the man that can present it: a micro-professor."[10] The first Dutch edition of the Australian-based electronics magazine *Electronics TOP International* (ETI), issued in October 1976, took the bull by the horns.[11] This Dutch edition of the magazine was issued by *Radio Rotor*, a wholesale trader in electronics. The magazine featured the so-called study computers which could be hooked up to television sets, enabling people to study the new electronics. These computers were featured in a series of articles, offering many electronics hobbyists the first opportunity to build their own computer. The Dutch wholesaler produced several kit computers as a licensee for the Dutch, Belgian, and British markets. Importers of electronics such as Radio Rotor opened up the microprocessor markets in the United States and the United Kingdom, preparing the ground for the first Dutch computer clubs.

In March 1977, Dik Barnhoorn, a math student at Leiden University, established the Dutch computer club along the same lines as the British Amateur Computer Club (ACC) founded in 1973. Barnhoorn had joined the British club during his studies and was looking for local peers. Proposing the idea of a Dutch computer club, he sent out calls to professional computer journals, amateur radio, and electronic hobbyist magazines.[12] These resulted in a first meeting on April 27, 1977, at which Barnhoorn and two fellow students from Leiden, Gerrit Slot and Rob van Spaandonk, along with Jaap van Duffelen of the Technical University Delft founded the Hobby Computer Club (HCC).

Van Duffelen ran a small electronics shop that had been importing computer kits by American producers Southwest Technical Systems Co. since 1975. He was interested in new ways of selling his goods and offered to compile the Hobby Computer Club's newsletter. The first issues ran articles from the British ACC's newsletters with the permission of the editors. Thus, the newsletter translated and distributed the international information to its Dutch audience.[13]

---

[9] Veraart, *Vormgevers*, 71–83.

[10] "Microprofessor," *Elektuur* (March 1976): 322.

[11] *Electronics TOP International* was the Dutch edition of *Electronics Today International*, Veraart, *Vormgevers*, 79.

[12] These magazines were *Computable, De Automatiseringgids, Radio Electronica*, and *Radio Bulletin.*

[13] Ed van Eeden. 2002. *Allemaal enen en nullen*, 52–68. Utrecht: AW Bruna; Veraart, *Vormgevers*, 67–91.

Dutch computer clubs adopted the model of sharing learning and knowledge after the example of the American hacker culture.[14] Unlike their transatlantic peers, the Dutch referred to themselves as "hobbyist" users, whereas their counterparts called themselves amateurs so they could be distinguished from computer professionals. Hobbyists signaled how much they enjoyed the relaxing nature of their activities. Clubs supported the computer hobbyist activities of exchanging know-how and technology through journals, meetings, and fairs. In the early 1980s, hobbyists in the Netherlands shifted their main interest from computer electronics to programming. A larger group of hobbyists interested in programming and applying computers in various domains and building interfaces overtook the homebrew computer builders. They used computer hardware, drawing on a wide variety of predominantly American and British microcomputers that they traded at fairs and small shops.

Clubs, journals, and hobbyist shops bridged the divide between the users and producers of technology. They were responsible for removing national boundaries by translating knowledge and technology literally and figuratively to local contexts and by providing the necessary contact between producers and users. Nevertheless, the gap between users and foreign producers was still vast. How would Dutch hobbyist users react?

2.3 Resolving Design Differences: Basicode as Computer Esperanto

The world of the computer hobbyist in the early 1980s consisted of many different types and brands of computers configured around microprocessors produced by US firms Zilog, Motorola, and Intel. Such microcomputers all shared BASIC as a common programming language that also served as the computers' operating system. The use was a legacy of the compiler used for the 1977 Altair computer, developed by Harvard students Paul Allen and William (Bill) Gates III. The initial revenue for their company Microsoft came mainly from developing different compilers for the various microcomputers.[15]

---

[14]The Hacker culture was widely studied by sociologists in the 1970s, 1980s, and 1990s. These studies show the diversity of hacker cultures but also the common values of peer learning, knowledge sharing, and competition. Sherry Turkle. 1984. *The second self: Computers and the human spirit.* New York: Simon & Schuster; Tove Håpnes. 1996. Not in their machines. How hackers transform computers into subcultural artifacts. In *Making technology our own? Domesticating technology into everyday life*, ed. Merete Lie and Knut Sørensen, 121–150. Oslo/Stockholm/Copenhagen/Oxford/Boston: Scandinavian University Press; Pekka Himanen. 2001. *The hacker ethic: A radical approach to the philosophy of business.* New York: Random House. Levy, *Hackers*.

[15]Ceruzzi, *A history of modern computing*, 232–236; Campbell-Kelly e.a., *Computer*, 240–244.

In the late 1970s and early 1980s, many different types of microcomputers were developed, not all using one common BASIC. Rather the computer language was adapted to the specificities of the computer and its manufacturer. The differences were down to technological developments with the microprocessor and a wide range of design decisions by producers. These allowed specialized functions such as various graphics modes, color, and instructions for additional equipment such as reading and storing on cassette players, disk drives, and output signals for printers. The ambivalent purposes and audiences for microcomputers resulted in many different configurations and therefore variants of BASIC. Producers created and used such variations in BASIC to shield their technology from competitors. Computer models became popular by virtue of the amount of available software rather than their capacities.

These brand-specific variations in BASIC prevented users from easily sharing and exchanging programs between computers. The lack of standardization annoyed hobbyist users, who were keen to exchange computer programs based on their shared interests. Hobbyist teachers were among the first to come up with a solution. The British Association of Microcomputer Users in Secondary Education (MUSE) developed a protocol that prescribed the use of common BASIC commands: a limited set of commands that could be run irrespective of the type of computer. The protocol also included a standardized layout of a computer program in recognizable blocks to clarify the program structure. Their protocol facilitated type-specific alterations that the hobbyist teachers could add to the programs. Applying programs for their own activities therefore still required some programming skills on the part of the hobbyist users, but at least the protocol helped in tackling the incompatibility problem. The Dutch hobbyist teacher groups adopted the British protocol to exchange their homemade programs. Thanks to teachers, the protocol paved the way for a system of software exchange by radio transmission called Basicode.

Basicode was an initiative of the Dutch radio show *Hobbyscoop*. The weekly program on national radio discussed the latest developments in consumer electronics. From the mid-1970s, the show was involved in several experiments such as the first radio broadcast in stereo, broadcasts of telex, facsimile, and videotext pages. In the spirit of these experiments, the show tested the broadcasting of computer programs in 1978, adding new features to the Kansas City code developed 3 years earlier by American computer amateurs. Binary codes were captured in audio signals of 1,200 and 2,400 Hz that listeners could then tape, store on cassettes, and copy with regular recorders, and also radio broadcasting.

Hobbyscoop's experimental radio broadcasting of software gained momentum in 1979 when the Television Academy (TELEAC) produced a programming course "Microprocessors 2" on Dutch national television. The course was a follow-up to the first course that had started the year before. The Dutch course was probably the first of its kind in Europe and 4 years earlier than comparable series by the BBC in the United Kingdom, the leading European country in microcomputing.[16] The first

[16] Thomas Lean. 2014. 'Inside a day you'll be talking to it like an old friend': The making and remaking of Sinclair personal computing in 1980s Britain. In *Hacking Europe. From computer cultures to demoscenes*, ed. Gerard Alberts and Ruth Oldenziel, 49–71. New York: Springer.

Fig. 2.1 Basicode–Dutch computer hobbyists build a computer Esperanto called Basicode. Hobbyists designed this feature to overcome incompatibility issues because of the variations of computer language BASIC that manufacturers installed on their computers. Basicode software was transferred either via cassette tape or via radio transmission before it was presented on national television in 1981. In this images, radio broadcasted software is captured on tape by a simple radio receiver (*top right*). The tape is fed to four different types of microcomputers operated by hobbyist developers (*in front*). Source: Reprint from Hans G. Janssen. 1983. *Basicode.* Hilversum: NOS

course on microprocessors started in October 1978, giving a general overview of the implications of microprocessor technologies. It had an informative character, whereas the second course, taken by nearly 10,000 people, assumed hands-on experience. Participants needed an Apple II clone computer to practice their programming skills while *Hobbyscoop*'s radio broadcasts distributed the supporting software for the course. After the television course, *Hobbyscoop* decided to continue radio broadcasting software for the four most popular types of microcomputers in the Netherlands at the time: Tandy TRS-80, Apple II, Commodore PET, and Exidy Sorcerer. The weekly scheduling of *Hobbyscoop* restricted the broadcasters to transmitting software only once a month for each type. The show's producers tried to solve this issue. The answer came from a befriended radio amateur Klaas Robers, a research engineer at the Dutch electronics company Philips that at that point had entered the laser disc market. He suggested producing specific translation programs for each type of computer. These would translate programs from strictly defined common BASIC into a computer-specific version of the programming language. A set of commonly used BASIC commands, conventions on programming similar to the MUSE protocols, and computer-specific translating programs defined a system they called "Basicode." Dutch computer hobbyists went on to develop translation programs for a wide variety of computers. The whole system elaborated on American and British developments, but added a new dimension of spreading software by radio transmission.

In 1981, the system was launched with a demonstration on one of the two Dutch national television channels (see Fig. 2.1) and was used throughout the 1980s. In its heyday during the late 1980s, there were three broadcasts a week. A second improved version launched in 1984 caught the attention of international radio broadcasters. In Britain, BBC radio took up Basicode in association with the Radio 4 computer-enthusiast show *Chip Shop*. The BBC Basicode transmissions took place in the early hours of Sunday mornings, in order not to disturb the general listeners. Furthermore, the German WDR3 and broadcasters in Belgium, Denmark, and Australia and, in the late 1980s, even Eastern Germany adopted the Basicode format to send software into the air.[17]

The development of Basicode allowed Dutch computer hobbyists to align the differences in design that foreign computer manufacturers had created.

Basicode enabled users to exchange and develop software in domains with many different types of computers. However, the way Basicode was set up limited the full use of a computer's capabilities and was always applied as an addition rather than a replacement of computer-specific software. Through radio broadcasts, Basicode provided free software to all types of computers, thus enabling cheap and simple computers to be functional. By applying Basicode, hobbyists bridged variations between computers. However, the programs in Basicode were limited because they needed to comply with the computer with the least capabilities. For the computer owners these limits highlighted the real differences of the various computer types.

The development of Basicode was the first liberating step by Dutch hobbyists from terms set by (American) producers and allowed a local exchange of programs without (foreign) limitations. Although the hobbyists' designers acknowledged they were indebted to the international efforts that formed the building blocks for Basicode, they hailed the establishment of the "microcomputer Esperanto" as their own Dutch accomplishment. The local programming effort nurtured national self-esteem. Later some hobbyists distanced themselves further in order to rebel more directly/openly against their foreign counterparts.

2.4 Alienation from Producers: Hobbyist Cracking Software

Software became an important issue in the 1980s hobbyist scene. In the pioneering days, hobbyists could gain prestige with homemade software. Lists of programs were published in the hobbyist newsletters or specific magazines. Alternatively, software was exchanged on cassette tapes using the aforementioned Kansas City Code, while Trade Fairs and meetings served as market places for the barter trade (see Fig. 2.2). Hobbyists were coproducers of software and viewed other software producers, whether firms or individuals, as equals. Many American producers indeed originated from a similar technophile user context. A few entrepreneurs turned their hobbyist activities into a commercial microcomputer

[17] Hans G. Janssen (ed.). 1984. *Basicode-2*, 9–17. Hilversum: Nederlandse Omroep Stichting; "Hobbyscoop boekt succes in binnen en buitenland", in *Viditelgids*, (August 1984): 80–81 (documentation and library of Dutch National Broadcasting Co-operations); "A look back at Basicode," *Beebug*, 3 (1984): 8–9. For more on Basicode development, see Frank Veraart. 2008a. Basicode: Co-producing a microcomputer Esperanto. *History and Technology* 28: 129–147.

Fig. 2.2 Opening page of German cracking group 5211. The illustration shows various cracking groups, companies and services, across Western Europe in June 1987. Cracking groups would 'greet' each other by showing their activities to peers. Cracked software was distributed through barter trade and other informal channels of users. Source: Courtesy: *The C-64 scene database.* http://csdb.dk/. Accessed 12 Nov 2013 (Public domain)

and software manufacturing business, among many others Apple and Microsoft. They made ready-to-use computers and software for small businesses, education, and home application.

The accessibility of these computers increased further with the spread of more computer shops and the expansion of the range in general stores. The microcomputer craze that hit the Netherlands in the early 1980s was similar to other West European countries.[18] Dutch department stores *Vroom en Dreesmann* (V&D) reacted to the growing interest and began selling Sinclair Spectrum and Commodore computers in 1984. As a part of their marketing strategy, V&D founded the *Microcomputer Club Netherlands* (MCN). Free membership was included with a computer purchased in store, and they also offered educational software to entice parents to buy a computer. The marketing campaign was a huge success. In 1985,

[18] More on developments in other European countries: for UK, see Leslie G. Haddon. 1988a. The home computer, the making of a consumer electronic. *Science as Culture* 2: 7–51; Leslie G. Haddon. 1988b. *The roots and early history of the British home computer market: Origins of the masculine micro.* PhD thesis, University of London; and Lean, Inside a day you'll be talking to it like an old friend; for Finland, see: Petri Saarikoski. 2005. The role of club activity in the early phases of microcomputing in Finland. In *History of Nordic computing*, IFIP international federation for information processing, ed. Janis A. Bubenko Jr., John Impagliazzo, and Arne Sølvberg, 277–287. Berlin: Springer; for Greece, see: Theodore Lekkas, Legal Pirates Ltd: Greek home computing cultures in early 1980s Greece, in Alberts and Oldenziel, *Hacking Europe*, 73–103.

Table 2.1 Hobby Computer Club activities 1977–1992

Year	Members	Visitors to annual fairs
1977	100	200
1978	770	2,000
1979		
1980		
1981	5,000	14,000
1982	7,000	20,000
1983	10,800	27,000
1984	15,000	34,000
1985	20,500	45,000
1986	20,600	55,000
1987	35,000	
1988	46,000	51,000
1989	67,000	51,000
1990	50,000	53,500
1991		
1992	58,000	

Source: Veraart, *Vormgevers*, 146–152

the MCN had 30,000 members, only to double the following year. By the mid-1980s, computers were sold alongside television sets, video recorders, washing machines, hairdryers, and other electrical consumer goods.

In the same year, the Dutch consumers association *Consumentenbond* offered a review of domestic computer applications. Its assessment was rather skeptical: "Some common sense for the interested user seems appropriate...No matter how immense the opportunities might seem, the home computer is less suited for household use. It mainly serves as a toy. A toy costing more than 6,000 guilders [ca. $2500, F.V.]." Despite the skepticism, the association felt it should start a debate on the use of computers in the home. The sale of computers in department stores and the public debate about their application marked a turning point, and hereafter computers were seen as regular consumer goods. By the mid-1980s, computer clubs were flourishing (see Table 2.1) and microcomputers became a craze, with public fairs, debates, and computers featuring in many arenas.

Modern, more user-friendly computers of the early 1980s attracted new hobbyists who went on to change computer practices and attitudes to software. These newfound hobbyists transformed the machines from programming devices to software players.[19] For the newer groups, the consumption rather than production of software represented a mark of prestige. Club meetings and fairs turned into locations of software exchange. In overwhelming numbers, users copied software to tapes and diskettes. Hobbyist users had easy access to the means and places of exchange. In this way they were able to build up software libraries, which gained

[19] The concept of software players was introduced by Haddon, *The roots and early history of the British home computer market*.

them the esteem of their peers. The availability of software became an important consideration for new users when deciding which computer to purchase, thus boosting the popularity of some types of computers over others.

The increasing importance of software generated a huge informal market of copied software. Among friends, colleagues, and students, software was swapped for free and sold cheaply compared to retail prices. Whether the software was homebrew, cracked, or illegally copied mattered little to these users who yearned for new computer programs. Copying was an easy and cheap way to acquire vast amounts of software and cast aside compassion and fair compensation for producers. The Dutch users' rich copying practice highlighted how they distanced themselves from the anonymous, predominantly American producers. This was a phenomenon seen in many places where the division between users and producers was becoming more and more noticeable. As early as 1976, Bill Gates, for example, had sent an open letter to the American hobbyists and questioned the practice directly, saying: "The amount of royalties we have received from sales to hobbyists makes the time spent on Altair basic worth less than $2 an hour. Why is this? As the majority of hobbyists must be aware, most of you steal your software. Hardware must be paid for, but software is something to share. Who cares if the people who worked on it get paid?"[20] Gates and others denounced the practice as illegal copying or piracy, claiming the practice infringed the copyrights and economic interests of (foreign) producers. From a user perspective, there were virtually no restraints, except moral ethics, as the HCC's reactions to the illegal copying showed. In the early 1980s, the HCC's newsletter began discussing the topic in order to ethically inform and educate the members. The columnists questioned the user's conscience: "Besides gains such as cheaply acquiring collections of amusing and useful programs, the rash copying of software also has unfavorable long-term effects. With insufficient turnover, it will be difficult to keep professional programmers interested in the hobby market."[21] The Dutch followed Gates' economic argument to convey its principal warning. Continued piracy practices, discoveries of copyrighted programs in the HCC software library, and a report by the American journal *Byte* on European illegal copying practices forced a stronger response from the HCC board. But instead of issuing a clear statement, the board began discussing whether the HCC should change to a "Hobby Copy Club" an "Honest Computer Club" or a "Happy Computer Club." The board also put forward three scenarios: the first scenario required hiring a good lawyer to proceed with the software producers' lawsuits. The second scenario suggested a ban on copying and predicted a decline in hardware sales, while the third involved a high turnover of software at such low prices that hardly anyone would be tempted to copy. The last suggestion was the board's attempt to achieve the joint responsibility of both producers and users. Producers should lower prices; users

---

[20] Bill Gates. 1976. Open letter to hobbyists. *Homebrew Computer Club Newsletter* (Letter dated February 3, 1976). http://en.wikipedia.org/wiki/Open_Letter_to_Hobbyists. Accessed 31 Dec 2011.

[21] Henk Wevers. 1980. Softtalk. *HCC Newsletter* 18, June/July, 23.

Table 2.2 Profile of the HCC members in 1986

Job in computers businesses	16 %		
Job in relation to computers	62 %		
Software use		*Job/position*	
Administrative purposes	74 %	Higher employees	31 %
Documentation (database)	66 %	Medium employees	45 %
Program development	61 %		
Scientific purposes	40 %	*Job*	83 %
Games	75 %	Studying	10 %
Wish to extend gaming	21 %	No job position	6 %
Education		*Age*	
University of Technology	11 %	24 years and younger	14 %
University (general)	18 %	25–34 years	34 %
Polytechnic	16 %	35–49 years	40 %
Higher Vocational (others)	13 %	50 years and older	11 %
High school	10 %		
Technical education	38 %		

Source: De Automatiseringsgids*
* "HCC geen club meer voor computerfreaks" (HCC a club no longer for computer freaks) in *De Automatisering Gids* (Automation Directory), 27 augustus 1986, p. 4; R.P.N. Bronckers. 1986. Microcomputer buiten werktijd. *De Automatisering Gids*, November 5, 30–32

should refrain from illegal copying.[22] By debating the issue of copying practices, the club was clearly analyzing the problem in terms of two opposing actors: software producers and hobbyist users. In the process, hobbyist and producers evidently alienated each other and were no longer peers in the HCC's view.

In the mid-1980s, the HCC tried to professionalize its activities and worked on changing its reputation among computer professionals. This became present in their gradual dismissal of gaming as a computing activity. Gaming was by far the most popular application of computer hobbyists. Initially games were manifestation of programming skills. But with the transition to software players games became the favorite software collectable of mainly young computer users. In an attempt to distinguish themselves from the "computer freaks" and "gamers," the HCC published the results of an inquiry among members in the journal for computer professionals *Automatisering Gids* (see Table 2.2). The results showed the profile of the HCC members of 1986. The inquiry presented a number of interesting categories. It depicted the computer club as a set of ordinary people with a various characteristics in education, age, job positions, and education. It explicitly emphasized that only a minority (38 %) had a technical education. Another interesting category showed the breakdown of software use. It proved that games were the most used application by HCC members. The inquiry to the "wish to extend gaming," however, illustrated the hidden agenda the HCC had with this survey. The result stressed only a minority (21 %) of the members had intentions to stick

[22] "Kopiëren van Software," (Copying software) *HCC Newsletter* no. 29 (June 1981): 4–7.

Fig. 2.3 Opening page of German cracking group 5211. The illustration shows various cracking groups, companies and services, across Western Europe in June 1987. Cracking groups would 'greet' each other by showing their activities to peers. Cracked software was distributed through barter trade and other informal channels of users. Source: Courtesy: *The C-64 scene database*. http://csdb.dk/. Accessed 12 Nov 2013 (Public domain)

to game play. In other words, in the long run most of the members were in other, what they called "serious," applications of personal computers. The dismissal of gaming could also liberate the club from its difficult position between the software producers and its illegal copying members.[23]

Increasingly, the club requested members to behave more responsibly. The editors formally condemned illegal copying and officially forbade the exchange of illegal software at their meetings and in libraries. Nevertheless, in practice their call hardly had any effect.

Copying and cracking were international phenomena. A distinct cracking culture in games and demos distanced itself from other computer hobbyists focused on domestic use. Cracking communities grew throughout Europe (see Fig. 2.3), exchanging new cracked material and sending each other greetings in credit pages added to the programs. Through established channels of communication, fairs, and meetings, the software also reached more mundane hobbyists and new users. Presumably copying practices fostered the Dutch adoption of personal computing.

---

[23] On the shift in status, see Frank Veraart. 2011. Losing meanings: Computer games in Dutch domestic use, 1975–2000. *IEEE Annals for the History of Computing* 33(1): 52–65.

Table 2.3 Possession of home and personal computers in all Dutch households 1985–1995

	1985	1986	1987	1988	1989	1990	1991	1992	1993	1994	1995
Home and/or PC	7	10	13	17	18	21	25	29	31	34	39
Home computer		9[a]			10	11	10	10	8		
Personal computer					9	13	17	21	26		
Game computer									9	12	13

Source: Central Bureau of Statistics (CBS)*
*Socioeconomic panel research
1985–1988 October measurement, 1989–1995 April measurement
CBS *Jaarboek inkomen en consumptie* [Year book Wages and Consumption] 1990–1995, and CBS www.StatLine.nl (accessed June 25, 2006). No explanation is given for the "and/or" category not being the sum of the other two.
[a]April measurement

The great variety of computer models faded in the second half of the 1980s. In 1981 IBM introduced its personal computer to compete with other microcomputers popular in the managerial and office markets. IBM's reputation as a renowned computer builder for businesses pushed their personal computer in the office markets. This model and its copycats became known as IBM-compatible Personal Computers or PCs by the mid-1980s. Other new computer types such as MSX computers (1983) by Japanese and European producers introduced advanced uses of color and also an interoperable operation system. The Apple Macintosh (1984), Atari ST (1986), and Commodore Amiga (1986) introduced graphical interfaces and mouse control. Clones of the IBM personal computer spread like wildfire in the offices. Computers were reframed as "home" and "office" computers or microcomputers and PCs; however, the technical differences gradually diminished due to processor and software developments.

The transition from home computers to IBM-compatible PCs in Dutch households occurred in the late 1980s (see Table 2.3). The switch was encouraged by a so-called "PC-private" initiative that started in 1985. This was a financial measure allowing businesses and agencies to resell new computers to their employees without tax.[24] This lowered the prices of PCs for these consumers. In this way, companies and many governmental agencies could determine the computer standards at home for employees involved in the PC-private-use programs. Most institutions decided to adapt their office equipment, which mostly consisted of IBM-compatible PCs. These decisions secured the interoperability of computers at home and in the office, enabling overtime work to be done at home. Furthermore, providing their employees with PCs at home was cost-effective for employers, saving them expensive and elaborate on-the-job training, since most employers' PC-private initiatives included small home training programs.

The influx of PCs transformed the Dutch computer landscape at home. In the early 1990s, home computers gradually gave way to IBM-compatible PCs.

[24]PC-private programs became massive in the 1990s. At festive events, businesses would give out thousands of PCs to their employees. By 2000, 35 % of Dutch employers had PC-private programs. The system was abolished in August 2004. More on these programs see: Veraart, *Vormgevers*, 230–233.

Table 2.4 Possession vs. acquisition of Dutch users' ten most popular computer programs in 1991

Name	Application	% possession	% bought
WordPerfect	Text editing	92	36
Lotus 123	Spreadsheet	61	62
Pc tools	Utilities/service	46	34
dBase III	Database	42	61
Harvard graphics	Draw/slide shows	33	9
Norton utility	Utilities/service	32	16
dBase IV	Database	16	37
DrawPerfect	Draw	11	24
Dr Halo	Draw	10	67
Copy II PC	Utilities/service	9	12

Source: Jacobs (1993)*

Note: Games are not visible in this investigation because of their great variety and the subordinate status of this application

* For results of an inquiry among 2000 Dutch computer users in 1991, see: Marc A. Jacobs. 1993. *Software kopen of kopiëren? Een sociaal-wetenschappelijk onderzoek onder pc-gebruikers.* Den Haag: [s.n.]

However, this shift did not radically change computing habits. Like home computers, PCs were mainly used as software players, executing commercial software packages. Domestic PC users adopted home computer user practices like illegal copying and gaming.

In fact, social networks like the computer clubs facilitated users' illegal copying habits in the late 1980s. An important aspect of copying was that the intelligibility of the software further facilitated the practice. This explains why text editors and drawing programs were copied profusely (see Table 2.4). Users also copied computer games in overwhelming numbers. These, however, do not show up in the investigation because of their great variety and the subordinate status they had for the inquirers.[25]

As their confidence and self-esteem grew, Dutch hobbyists now felt more independent from their transatlantic counterparts. The HCC had become a key player in the shaping of Dutch personal computing. By 1992, it boasted almost 60,000 members, thereby becoming Europe's largest consumer organization for computing. The growth of these intermediary organizations caused a divide between users and producers. The latter (American) producers of computer technologies were no longer seen as peers, rather as anonymous and foreign outsiders by individual hobbyist users. Dutch home users viewed the dominant US corporations as "others," who, in their opinion, did not suffer from hobbyists' copying habits. This dramatic change from a peer to peer relationship to one between anonymous outsiders was an unintentional development. The shift contrasted with the Dutch government initiatives for computers at elementary and high schools that deliberately aimed to develop home-grown manufacturing and markets.

[25] On the shift in status, see Veraart, Losing meanings.

2.5 Protected Educational Market: From Niche to Microsoft Monopoly

The arrival of American microcomputers evoked a more calculated reaction from policy makers. They saw computers as strategically important technologies and supported the development of national computer industries. Just as in many European countries, Dutch policy makers were addressing the consequences of computer technology for society and the economy.[26] The Netherlands' first technology assessment report on "Microelectronics" by G.W. Rathenau increased the focus on these electronics and microcomputers. The report assessed the consequences and opportunities for a transition of the Netherlands into an "Information Society." The report embraced the notion of a technological lag between the Netherlands and the United States, especially when it came to computer technology. It concluded that quick and firm actions were needed to avoid a backslide in technological development. Presented during the economic crises of the late 1970s, the report concluded that the long-term benefits of computer technology and automation outweighed the short-term consequences of possible unemployment. The report echoed the science and technology-driven developing neoliberal views that developed in different places in Europe.[27] Despite the unfavorable timing of such a message, the advice in the report was widely accepted by politicians in power and the industry alike. The report presented in November 1979 gave the impulse for future developments in personal computing. In her speech opening the Dutch parliamentary year in 1980, Queen Beatrix declared: "Although the future is uncertain, we see a number of developments emerging that will rapidly become significant for the 1980s. These include the importance of information in terms of its availability and its uses. The impact on society will be huge."[28] The actors already involved in computing, whether they had centralized or decentralized computer systems in mind, tailored their activities to the new agenda of the information society. Many new experiments and schemes emerged, using microcomputers in various domains of society.

At the time, there were many proposals for centralized computer systems, such as mainframe computers for a general audience in the form of experiments with so-called view-data services. These services gave access to centralized

---

[26] Many European countries were exploring policies for the information society. For Sweden, see: Thomas Kaiserfeld. 1996. Computerizing the Swedish welfare state: The middle way of technological success and failure. *Technology and Culture* 37(2): 249–279.

[27] Another example of such views is British case is given by Lean, Inside a day you'll be talking to it like an old friend.

[28] Translation of the Queen's following words: "Hoeveel onzekerheid toekomststudies ook in zich bergen, een aantal ontwikkelingen tekent zich voor de jaren tachtig duidelijk af. Daartoe behoort dat het kunnen beschikken over en omgaan met informatie in snel toenemende mate aan betekenis wint. Dat zal in de samenleving grote gevolgen krijgen." Carla van Baalen, Anne Bos, Jan Willem Brouwers, Peter van Griendsven, Ron de Jong, and Jan Ramakers. 2005. *Koningin Beatrix aan het woord, 25 jaar troonredes, officiële redevoeringen en kersttoespraken.* Den Haag: Sdu.

computer databases at home. The Dutch telephone company PTT together with electronics multinational Philips developed Viditel that used telephone lines and a TV set to display the information. The Dutch broadcasting corporation NOS and Philips developed Teletext, a database accessible via the TV remote and transmitted along with television signals. Both experiments received government support to stimulate the economy. Such experiments and their financial backing followed similar European view-data experiments like the French Minitel and the British Prestel and Ceefax.[29]

Like in the United Kingdom, a larger proportion of the Dutch government support was dedicated to preparing future generations for the "information society" through educational programs. A wide educational support scheme not only assisted the establishment of informatics in further education, but also sought to introduce computer courses in all schools, starting with high school education. In 1982, the Dutch Ministry of Education adopted an experiment to develop computer literacy courses which concentrated on explaining computer technology and its impact on society. Computers were subsidized by the Ministry of Education in conjunction with the Ministry of Economic Affairs. Thus national economic interests favored Dutch industries to deliver the required equipment. Philips and a small company called Music-print Computer Products (MCP) acquired these exclusive rights. MCP supplied Aster CT-80 computers, presented as "the computer that has it all."[30] The computer was assembled in the Netherlands based on the American Zilog Z-80 processor. It was compatible with various operating systems and had interfaces for various computer languages including BASIC and Basicode. As the second supplier for the Ministry of Education's program, Philips brought in its P2000 microcomputers. The machine had its roots in Philips' Austrian cassette recorder branch in Vienna and was not originally Dutch. At the heart of the computer was also a Zilog Z-80 processor with a specially designed operating system and computer language developed in Austria. Programs were stored on micro-tapes and special abilities could be added to the computers by using cartridges (see Fig. 2.4).

A 100 schools could take part in the experiment to develop courses in computer literacy. The Ministry organized inaugural festivities to celebrate the first delivery of computers for the experiment on August 30, 1983. However, the Ministry of Education was overwhelmed by the number of schools wanting to participate. Although it had only budgeted for 100, over 750 schools applied.

The response to the experimental project was huge both from within and beyond the field of education. Schools used computers to lure new students as parents judged schools with computer classes as modern. The Dutch Ministry of Economic Affairs' nationalistic policy became only partially effective. Philips and Aster profited from government support thanks to direct sales to the experiment and the huge media attention. Both companies received additional orders from schools outside

---

[29] Christopher McDonald. 2010. Technology in the political landscape. *IEEE Annals of the History of Computing* 32(2): 87–88; Kenneth Lipartito. 2003. Picturephone and the information age: The social meaning of failure. *Technology and Culture* 44(1): 50–81.

[30] Advertisement in *HCC Newsletter* no. 23 (March 1983) advertorial supplement.

Fig. 2.4 Spreading 'digital literacy.' In 1983, the Dutch ministry of education started a program to prepare future generation for the information society. The initiative included new courses at primary and high schools. These teachers receive training on Philips 2000 computers at the primary school Teacher Education College (PABO) in Eindhoven in 1984. Source: Courtesy Chris de Boer (private collection)

the government-sponsored experiment. MCP was literally overwhelmed with orders and forced to file for bankruptcy in 1984 because of managerial problems caused by the massive attention and its inability to fulfill expectations. Many schools that could not participate in the government-sponsored project established their own initiatives. Sponsoring from local banks, computer businesses, and private investments provided 75 % of all high schools with computers. Some schools kept to the standard choices in the experiment, whereas many others chose less expensive microcomputers. The ministerial coordination and societal microcomputer craze of the early 1980s resulted in a patchwork of different computer types in schools. By the mid-1980s, it was nevertheless North-American Commodore instead of Dutch companies that had become the main supplier of computers in high schools (see Table 2.5).

When the Ministry of Education reviewed the computer literacy programs in high schools in 1985, it concluded that many schools had computers, but were finding it difficult to integrate computer literacy courses in their teaching program. Reviewers of the computer experiments blamed the lack of software developed to introduce computer classes in schools. The massive influx of very different computers had resulted in a lack of compatibility, according to the reviewers. In

Table 2.5 Microcomputers in Dutch high schools, 1985

Brand (Country)	Price in Euros 1985 (*1982)	Number of schools 1983–1984	Number of computers 1983–1984	Computers/school 1983–1984	Number of computers 1985	Growth 1984–1985
Commodore (CAN/US)		39	208	5.3	4,450	21×
VIC-20	113					
C-64	363					
Philips P2000 (NL/A)	542	28	140	5.0	2,136	15×
Tandy (US)		23	98	4.2	695	7×
Apple (US)		18	85	4.7	597	7×
Apple II	1,359*					
Apple IIe	1,872					
Aster CT-80 (NL)	1,795	5	32	6.4	718	22×
Sinclair (GB)		10	35	3.5	244	7×
Exidy Sorcerer (US/NL)	1,497*	6	26	4.3	179	7×
Acorn (GB)		–	21		591	28×
Sharp (Jap)		2	9	4.5	n.a.	–

Source: Carleer and Valkenburg (1985), Muylwijk and Moonen (1985) and prices Veraart (2008c)**
*points at prices of 1982 instead of 1985
**Table 2.1 data based on Gerrit J. Carleer, and H.D. Valkenburg. 1985. *Burgerinformatica, meer dan computers alleen, resultaat van het Landelijk Onderzoek Burgerinformatica en Evaluatie-onderzoek 100-scholenproject*, 28. Den Haag: Ministerie van Onderwijs en Wetenschappen and Bert Van Muylwijk, and Jef Moonen. 1985. Computerapparatuur op school. *Computers op School* 6: 15–19; Veraart, *Vormgevers*, 134

talks with educational publishers, the reviewers nevertheless expected this would be solved in the future: operational compatibility would provide a platform for software developments.[31] Elaborating on these ideas, Dutch manufacturers of computers Philips and Compudata (later renamed Tulip) along with American IBM proposed to jointly sponsor computers for all high schools in the Netherlands in 1985. The Ministry of Education responded favorably and announced the new cosponsored program later that year. The three companies jointly invested EUR21 million, while the Ministry of Economic Affairs matched with another EUR15 million. As a result of these investments, every Dutch high school received eight IBM-compatible personal computers, made by Philips, Tulip, or IBM. These computers, all with the same Microsoft disk operating system (MS-DOS), were mainly used for teaching computer technology through hands-on experience.

[31] Gerrit J. Carleer, and H.D. Valkenburg. 1985. *Burgerinformatica, meer dan computers alleen, resultaat van het Landelijk Onderzoek Burgerinformatica en Evaluatie-onderzoek 100-scholenproject.* Den Haag: Ministerie van Onderwijs en Wetenschappen; Projectgroep Burgerinformatica. 1985. *Burgerinformatica of informatiekunde*, 9–10. Report of a national conference on informatics for citizens held in May 1985 in Apeldoorn. Enschede: Stichting voor de Leerplanontwikkeling. More detailed information in Veraart, *Vormgevers*, 245–266.

In elementary schools, computers served a different purpose. There they were used as educational tools, as training devices for general subjects such as mathematics, Dutch language, and geography. Software was either supplied by educational publishers or homemade by hobbyist teachers and user groups. By the mid-1980s, the hardware was a kaleidoscope of computer types very similar to the computers used in secondary education. In order to encourage developments in educational software, in 1988 the Ministry of Education urged for a computer standard in elementary schools. These schools' advisory boards argued in favor of computers with user-friendly graphical interfaces. For that reason, especially the Apple Macintosh and Atari ST were advised as the best machines. The de facto standard for secondary education, however, served as a lock-in for the Ministry. This lured policy makers into favoring IBM compatibles, with a similar standard at both elementary and high schools as persuasive argument. IBM proponents additionally pointed to the announced release of a third version of Microsoft Windows as an alternative for graphical interfaces. A fierce debate followed between IBM and Apple proponents. The latter favored the proven technologies of the Macintosh over the potential teething troubles with the Windows system. The debate resulted in the establishment of an additional feature to the new standard: the use of a graphical interface.

Parallel to the discussion among educational advisors, civil servants at the Ministry of Education and Microsoft officials negotiated an agreement to provide all Dutch elementary schools with MS Windows 3.0. In 1989, the Dutch Minister of Education announced the new standard: an IBM-compatible computer with MS Windows. Bill Gates in person came to the Netherlands to present the worldwide premiere of a nationwide use of Microsoft Windows in elementary schools.

In the debates, national exclusivity had been lost as an argument in the selection of software. Although two of the three companies that supplied computer hardware to high schools had a Dutch base, American companies IBM and Microsoft had set the technical standards of hard and software developments in the Dutch educational system. Eventually Dutch firms Philips and Tulip gained a considerable share of the education market. By the mid-1980s, the automation of offices and industries had accelerated through price cuts, mainly caused by Asiatic clone production of the IBM PC. In 1989, an overview of PC use in various markets in the Netherlands showed that education was the only market not dominated by IBM (see Table 2.6).

The policy makers' aversion to American dominance had vanished by the late 1980s. Ministry of Education officials welcomed the Philips, Tulip, and IBM cooperation and negotiated the Windows deal for elementary schools with Microsoft. The impact of the Ministry of Economic Affairs' policies favoring Dutch computer industries remained rather fuzzy other than offering a head start to Philips and Tulip in the education market.

Table 2.6 Seven most popular PC brands by sector in 1989

Brand (Country)	Trading firm	Production firm	Independent profession	Government	Services	Education	Non-profit	Other
IBM (USA)	28	57	30	46	38	39	24	48
Tulip (NL)	8	8	3	20	17	50	18	22
Philips (NL)	13	14	8	14	5	28	18	10
Olivetti (Italy)	4	5	8	14	11	28	6	12
Apple (USA)	7	–	8	6	8	22	9	12
Compaq (USA)	8	19	–	1	8	6	6	10
Wang z (Japan)	8	3	3	8	8	–	9	8

Source: Magazine *Kantoor en Efficiency**

* Survey among 669 subscribers of the magazine Kantoor en Efficiency. K&E Trendspeiling 1989. *Kantoor en Efficiency*, September 1989, 29–30

Government investment in the education system had enabled Tulip, Philips, and IBM to secure a strong market hold. In the meantime, however, the Dutch firms had modified their products in line with the originally American Personal Computer standards. By the mid-1980s, these had become the worldwide de facto standards for PCs.[32] One might even argue that incorporating the new standard PCs in secondary education enabled the Dutch firms to transfer production from independent microcomputers towards IBM-compatible PCs. In the earlier stages of computer development, both Tulip and Philips had supplied alternative non-IBM-compatible types of computers. The Ministry of Foreign Affairs' policies kept Dutch firms in competition and allowed them to shift standards.

Protective policy measures created some market space for Dutch firms such as Philips and Tulip. The outer shells of their computers looked Dutch, but they were based on American PC standards. Facing fierce competition in the PC market, both companies, Philips (1992) and Tulip (1998), finally stopped producing personal computers, nullifying the lasting effects of these protective policies. The discontinuation should, however, be seen in the context of the consciously changing improvements in computer technologies and applications. The activities carried out by these firms were beneficial. They served as the building blocks in supporting the tide of ICT expansion that changed the course of personal computing developments in the Netherlands. Compatibility demands in schools resulted in a monopoly on the use of Microsoft Windows. Microsoft software is now widely used throughout the Dutch education system and on PCs at home. In first decade of the twenty-first

[32] James Sumner. 2008. Standards and compatibility: The rise of the PC platform. *History and Technology* 28: 101–127.

Table 2.7 Operating systems used on computers in various European countries and the United States 2008 and 2011

	2008			2011		
	Microsoft[a]	MacOSX	Other	Microsoft[a]	MacOSX	Other
Netherlands	93,1	4,7	2,2	86,4	9,0	4,6
Germany	95,2	2,9	1,9	91,8	6,3	1,9
France	93,3	5,2	1,5	87,9	10,0	2,1
United Kingdom	92,7	5,3	2,0	85,5	10,5	4,0
Italy	92,3	5,4	2,3	90,9	7,5	1,7
Sweden	92,2	6,1	1,7	85,5	12,0	2,5
Greece	96,6	1,8	1,5	96,3	2,7	1,1
Europe	95,0	3,3	1,7	91,3	6,6	2,1
USA	91,3	6,2	2,5	84,0	14,1	1,9

Source: gs.statcounter.com

[a]This includes Microsoft operating systems Windows 2003, Windows XP, Vista, and Windows 7

century, the Microsoft Windows operating system still dominated Dutch computers, with market shares of 90 % and over, typical for many European countries (see Table 2.7).[33] The government's actions were effective, not in distancing from American suppliers but paradoxically in limiting variations and creating some American-dominated monopolies.

2.6 Multiple American Appropriations

The snapshots presented of the appropriation of personal computing at home and in schools in the Netherlands illustrate the wide variety of interactions actors had both with the United States and other nations. American appropriation therefore cannot be perceived as a singular process or as a one-way flow of knowledge and technology. Rather the appropriation of personal computing should be seen as a very transnational process with flows of information back and forth and a multitude of connections to many different countries.

The influx of American technologies evoked many different implicit and explicit reactions that changed over time. Actors with direct links to America considered themselves as coproducers of the American technology. Hobbyists developed Basicode that filled the gaps created by American hardware producers. Growing self-esteem among these actors alienated them from their American peers. Crackers and home users even felt they were at a safe distance to distribute and use illegally copied software, thus violating international copyrights, but beyond the reach of

[33]Recently, the rate has dropped slightly to 75 % in September 2013. Statcounter at http://gs.statcounter.com/. Accessed Sept 2013.

American stakeholders. Appropriation in this case involved a process of expropriation from the original American interests.

The actions and reactions of hobbyists were rather unreserved and implicit. An explicit challenge to Americanization came from the Dutch Ministry of Economic Affairs in its support of national computer producers in the education experiments. Their views were based on the technological theories put forward by the Rathenau Report. The final result, however, was an all-American setup in elementary and high schools of personal computers with IBM architecture operated by Microsoft Windows.

Bibliography

Albert de la Bruhèze, Adri, and Ruth Oldenziel (eds.). 2009. *Manufacturing technology, manufacturing consumers. The making of Dutch consumer society*. Amsterdam: Aksant.

Bronckers, R.P.N. 1986. Microcomputer buiten werktijd. *De Automatisering Gids*, November 5, 30–32.

Campbell-Kelly, Martin. 2003. *From airline reservations to sonic the hedgehog, a history of the software industry*. Cambridge MA/London: MIT Press.

Campbell-Kelly, Martin, William Aspray, Nathan Ensmenger, and Jeffrey R. Yost. 2014 [1996]. *Computer: A history of the information machine*. Boulder, CO: Westview Press.

Carleer, Gerrit J., and H.D. Valkenburg. 1985. *Burgerinformatica, meer dan computers alleen, resultaat van het Landelijk Onderzoek Burgerinformatica en Evaluatie-onderzoek 100-scholenproject*. Den Haag: Ministerie van Onderwijs en Wetenschappen.

Ceruzzi, Paul E. 2003 [1988]. *A history of modern computing*. Cambridge, MA/London: MIT Press.

Chandler Jr., Alfred D. 2007. *Inventing the electronic century: The epic story of the consumer electronics and computer industries*. New York: The Free Press.

Cortada, James W. 2004. *The digital hand: How computers changed the work of American manufacturing, transportation, and retail industries*. Oxford: Oxford University Press.

Gates, Bill. 1976. Open letter to hobbyists. *Homebrew Computer Club Newsletter* (Letter dated February 3, 1976). http://en.wikipedia.org/wiki/Open_Letter_to_Hobbyists. Accessed 31 Dec 2011.

Gates III, William H. 1995. *The road ahead*. New York: Penguin.

Haddon, Leslie G. 1988a. The home computer, the making of a consumer electronic. *Science as Culture* 2: 7–51.

Haddon, Leslie G. 1988b. *The roots and early history of the British home computer market: Origins of the masculine micro*. PhD thesis, University of London.

Håpnes, Tove. 1996. Not in their machines. How hackers transform computers into subcultural artifacts. In *Making technology our own? Domesticating technology into everyday life*, ed. Merete Lie and Knut Sørensen, 121–150. Oslo/Stockholm/Copenhagen/Oxford/Boston: Scandinavian University Press.

Himanen, Pekka. 2001. *The hacker ethic: A radical approach to the philosophy of business*. New York: Random House.

Jacobs, Marc A. 1993. *Software kopen of kopiëren? Een sociaal-wetenschappelijk onderzoek onder pc-gebruikers*. Den Haag: [s.n.].

Janssen, Hans G. (ed.). 1984. *Basicode-2*, 9–17. Hilversum: Nederlandse Omroep Stichting.

Kaiserfeld, Thomas. 1996. Computerizing the Swedish welfare state: The middle way of technological success and failure. *Technology and Culture* 37(2): 249–279.

Lean, Thomas. 2014. 'Inside a day you'll be talking to it like an old friend': The making and remaking of Sinclair personal computing in 1980s Britain. In *Hacking Europe. From computer cultures to demoscenes*, ed. Gerard Alberts and Ruth Oldenziel, 49–71. New York: Springer.

Lekkas, Theodore. 2014. Legal Pirates Ltd: Greek home computing cultures in early 1980s Greece. In *Hacking Europe. From computer cultures to demoscenes*, ed. Gerard Alberts and Ruth Oldenziel, 73–103. New York: Springer.

Levy, Steven. 1984. *Hackers: Heroes of the computer revolution*. Garden City, NY: Anchor Press/ Doubleday.

Lipartito, Kenneth. 2003. Picturephone and the information age: The social meaning of failure. *Technology and Culture* 44(1): 50–81.

McDonald, Christopher. 2010. Technology in the political landscape. *IEEE Annals of the History of Computing* 32(2): 87–88.

Oudshoorn, Nelly, and Trevor J. Pinch (eds.). 2003. *How users matter. The co-construction of users and technologies*. Cambridge, MA: MIT Press.

Projectgroep Burgerinformatica. 1985. *Burgerinformatica of informatiekunde*. Enschede: Stichting voor de Leerplanontwikkeling.

Saarikoski, Petri. 2005. The role of club activity in the early phases of microcomputing in Finland. In *History of Nordic computing*, IFIP international federation for information processing, ed. Janis A. Bubenko Jr., John Impagliazzo, and Arne Sølvberg, 277–287. Berlin: Springer.

Sumner, James. 2008. Standards and compatibility: The rise of the PC platform. *History and Technology* 28: 101–127.

The C-64 scene database. http://csdb.dk/. Accessed 12 Nov 2013.

Turkle, Sherry. 1984. *The second self: Computers and the human spirit*. New York: Simon & Schuster.

van Baalen, Carla, Anne Bos, Jan Willem Brouwers, Peter van Griendsven, Ron de Jong, and Jan Ramakers. 2005. *Koningin Beatrix aan het woord, 25 jaar troonredes, officiële redevoeringen en kersttoespraken*. Den Haag: Sdu.

van der Vleuten, Erik. 2008. Toward a transnational history of technology: Meanings, promises, pitfalls. *Technology and Culture* 49(4): 974–994.

van Eeden, Ed. 2002. *Allemaal enen en nullen*, 52–68. Utrecht: AW Bruna.

van Elteren, Mel. 1994. *Imagining America, Dutch youth and its sense of place*. Tilburg: Tilburg University Press.

van Muylwijk, Bert, and Jef Moonen. 1985. Computerapparatuur op school. Computers op School 6: 15–19.

van Rooij, Arjan, Eric Berkers, Mila Davids, and Frank Veraart. 2008. National innovation system and international knowledge flows: An exploratory investigation with cases from the Netherlands. *Technology Transfer and Strategic Management* 20(2): 149–168.

Veraart, Frank. 2008a. Basicode: Co-producing a microcomputer Esperanto. *History and Technology* 28: 129–147.

Veraart, Frank. 2008c. *Vormgevers van Persoonlijk Computergebruik*. PhD thesis, TU Eindhoven. Published: Eindhoven: Stichting Historie der Techniek.

Veraart, Frank. 2011. Losing meanings: Computer games in Dutch domestic use, 1975–2000. *IEEE Annals for the History of Computing* 33(1): 52–65.

Wevers, Henk. 1980. Softtalk. *HCC Newsletter* 18, June/July, 23.

Wozniak, Steve. 2006. *iWoz, computer geek to computer icon*. New York: W.W. Norton and Company.

Young, Jeffrey S., and William L. Simon. 2005. *iCon Steve Jobs, the greatest second act in the history of business*. Hoboken: Wiley.

Chapter 3
"Inside a Day You Will Be Talking to It Like an Old Friend": The Making and Remaking of Sinclair Personal Computing in 1980s Britain

Thomas Lean

In early 1980 advertisements began appearing in British national newspapers for the latest domestic technology, the Sinclair ZX80 personal computer, available ready built for the bargain price of just £99.95. Personal computing had first emerged in the mid-1970s as an outgrowth of the activities of electronics hobbyists, but its costs and complexities had restricted it to a technically able niche market.[1] The ZX80 was quite different, combining low-cost, nontechnical marketing and neat design to create a more consumer-friendly computer, configured as an affordable introduction to computing. Britain took to the low-cost introductory personal computer enthusiastically in the early 1980s. By 1983 the country boasted the highest level of computer ownership in the world and a booming personal computer industry.[2] This computer marketplace was diverse and the differences between machines gave rise to friendly rivalries between their users. However, the context was common, and the trends that defined early British home computing at their strongest in Sinclair, making it an excellent case study.

Two 1980s popular books, the semiofficial *The Sinclair Story* by Rodney Dale and the more critical *Sinclair and the Sunrise Technology* by Ian Adamson and Richard Kennedy, already provide a view into the company's computer business.[3]

[1] For standard accounts of personal computing's hobbyist roots, see Martin Campbell-Kelly, William Aspray, Nathan Ensmenger, and Jeffrey R. Yost. 2014 [1996]. *Computer: A history of the information machine*. Boulder, CO: Westview Press, ch. 10; Paul E. Ceruzzi. 2003 [1998]. *A history of modern computing*. Cambridge, MA/London: MIT Press, ch. 7.

[2] An oft repeated though apparently unverified claim. For one prominent instance, see the *Conservative General Election Manifesto* (1983). For discussion of the figures behind the claim, see Thomas Lean. 2012. Mediating the microcomputer: The educational character of the 1980s British popular computing boom. *Public Understanding of Science*, first published online on 30 October, 2012 as doi:10.1177/0963662512457904.

[3] Ian Adamson, and Richard Kennedy. 1986. *Sinclair and the sunrise technology: The deconstruction of a myth*. Harmondsworth: Penguin; Rodney Dale. 1985. *The Sinclair story*. London: Duckworth.

T. Lean (✉)
National Life Stories, The British Library, London, UK
e-mail: thomas.lean@bl.uk

G. Alberts and R. Oldenziel (eds.), *Hacking Europe. From Computer Cultures to Demoscenes*, History of Computing, DOI 10.1007/978-1-4471-5493-8_3,

Originally founded by Clive Sinclair in 1961 as Sinclair Radionics, the company's embrace of innovation and economically minimalistic style led to successes, such as the earliest affordable pocket calculators, and failures, such as digital watch kits whose electronics could reputedly be scrambled by the static of a synthetic material shirt.[4] However, this experience of hobbyist and consumer electronics put them in an excellent position to enter the personal computer market as it began the transition from enthusiasts' kit computers to domestic appliances for the general population. For the first few years of the 1980s Sinclair's machines, the ZX80, ZX81, and ZX Spectrum, would be the most popular computers in Britain, and the company struggled to meet demand for its products. As Adamson and Kennedy discuss, the low-cost machines had limitations and problems, but I argue that these should not overshadow their place in computer history. They have become iconic of Britain's early years of home computing. In 2010 the BBC even considered their development worthy of retelling in a nostalgia heavy television comedy drama, *Micromen,* which focused on the rivalry between Sinclair and Acorn Computers. In this essay, I use Sinclair's early computers, the ZX80, ZX81, and ZX Spectrum, as a case study in the early development of personal computing in 1980s Britain and as an example of how user activity can help to shape the representation and form of technology.

Accounts of the early development of personal computing have tended to concentrate on 1970s America, where skilled electronics hobbyists and hackers created the first personal computers for their own interest. As Stephen Levy captures in *Hackers,* there was a countercultural edge to this, an excitement with technology and hope to bring computers to the people, rather than having them restricted to corporate or academic elites.[5] Home computing in early 1980s Britain was more officially sanctioned than it was countercultural. David Skinner has amply demonstrated that the widespread uptake of home computing in 1980s Britain was fuelled, in large part, by a view of information technology as a transforming force.[6] The personal "microcomputer" was seen as an introduction to the information technologies which were anticipated to have sweeping social and economic effects in the next few years. Leslie Haddon has characterized much early home computing in Britain as "self-referential," using the computer to understand it.[7] In a context of "computer literacy," which was prominently supported by the government and media, computers became seen as almost inherently educational.[8] In this environment, activities commonly associated

[4]To save a lengthy diversion into a complex company history, already well covered by Adamson and Kennedy, in this essay I refer to the producer of Sinclair computers simply as Sinclair. In fact Clive Sinclair left the troubled Sinclair Radionics in 1979, to join Science of Cambridge, previously set up as a "lifeboat company" for him. Science of Cambridge became Sinclair Computers in 1980 and then Sinclair Research in 1981. It was bought by Amstrad in 1986.

[5]Steven Levy. 1984. *Hackers: Heroes of the computer revolution.* Garden City, NY: Anchor Press/Doubleday.

[6]David Ian Skinner. 1992. *Technology, consumption and the future: The experience of home computing*. PhD thesis, Brunel University.

[7]Leslie G. Haddon. 1988b. *The roots and early history of the British home computer market: Origins of the masculine micro*. PhD thesis, University of London.

[8]Neil Selwyn. 2002. Learning to love the micro: The discursive construction of educational computing in the UK, 1979–89. *British Journal of Sociology of Education* 23: 427–443.

with the hacker, such as modifying hardware, programming, and developing an intimate knowledge of the computer, were less countercultural than they were officially sanctioned as part of learning about computers. However, as Skinner and Haddon make clear in their studies of personal computing in Britain, within a few years these original educational hopes were dashed, as video gaming dominated the British home computer scene.[9] On no other home computer was this change quite as dramatic as those of Sinclair, where games became synonymous with the machines, in spite of their original educational characteristics.

The transformation of the Sinclair computer from educational "passport to the future" to games system presents a prime example of how users can shape a technology. In her essay on the development of the TRS80 personal computer, Christina Lindsay outlines how "the user" appears in different stages and guises over the machine's life.[10] Lindsay suggests how these different users helped to shape a computer's development over time, as the electronics enthusiast imagined by designers was replaced by real users with different impressions of the machine. In doing so, she usefully bridges the gap between production and use by suggesting how user activity could contribute to the ongoing development of the technology, a cycle of co-construction over the lifetime of a product. My approach here follows a similar basic model to Lindsay, but expands on it by embedding the Sinclair computer in the wider society around it. I begin by exploring the initial construction of the Sinclair computer and its configuration for educational use. I then explore the actual use of these computers by a variety of different parties. Finally, I demonstrate how as one of these uses, games, came to dominate, the Sinclair computer was reconfigured in response to this user activity.

3.1 The Challenge of the Chip

Rising unemployment, high levels of inflation, a decline in traditional industry, and troubles with the trade unions had made the 1970s an unhappy decade for Britain. Matters reached their nadir with the widespread strikes of the 1978–1979 "Winter of Discontent." With the country apparently in crisis, Margaret Thatcher's Conservative Party entered government in 1979, promising dramatic changes to create a more enterprising Britain. Meanwhile, another potential source of change was coming to prominence. In 1978, the BBC broadcast *Now the Chips are Down*, an influential documentary examining the expected impact of the microprocessor and

---

[9] Haddon, *The roots and early history of the British home computer market*, ch. 7; Skinner, *Technology, consumption and the future*.

[10] Christina Lindsay. 2003. From the shadows: Users as designers, producers, marketers, distributors, and technical support. In *How users matter: The co-construction of users and technologies*, ed. Nelly Oudshoorn and Trevor J. Pinch, 29–50. Cambridge, MA: MIT Press.

the cheap computer power it offered, an event often seen as the moment when "microchips" came to greater public attention in Britain.[11]

From its opening awe at what microchips could do, to unsettling conclusion that Britain is ill prepared for their social and economic consequences, *Now the Chips are Down* presents the "chip" in a manner typical of the considerable media attention they received elsewhere in late 1970s Britain.[12] On one hand, benefits, easier lifestyles, greater productivity, and economic prosperity. On the other, the threats of massive unemployment, a technology whose benefits were restricted to a wealthy elite, or a Britain overwhelmed by computerized foreign competition. Yet beyond the inevitability of change, *Now the Chips are Down* offers no firm conclusions about the impact of the chip, a technological uncertainty common to late 1970s discussion of the chip's impact and succinctly summed up by David Skinner as "deliverance or damnation."[13,14]

To realize the opportunities of the microchip and guard against the threats, Britain needed to prepare a position at the vanguard of this new industrial revolution. Reports to the government highlighted the importance of a population educated about these technologies to the future well-being of the nation.[15] The alternative was obsolescence, as *The Mighty Micro*, the best known of a thriving genre of popular books on the implications of the "microchip revolution," warned in the stark language common to these discussions: "For those who are informed [about the new technologies] employment opportunities will be prodigal, while those who remain ignorant, resistant or unwilling to learn will find the world an alarmingly alien place."[16]

As in the USA, personal computing in Britain first took hold with electronics hobbyists, people fascinated by the technology, and its possibilities. With American computer magazines, such as *Byte* available in Britain and the British computer press regularly reporting on computing on the other side of the Atlantic, developments in the USA were influential. To give one example, Bruce Everiss, an accountancy computing manager, was inspired by developments in the United States to open one of Britain's earliest computer shops, Microdigital, in Liverpool:

> I… started reading *Computing* and *Computer Weekly*, the two trade magazines for the computer industry in the UK. And in those there were lots of articles about what was happening with microprocessors and microcomputers in California and America in general, and how

[11] Paul Kriwaczek. 1997. *Documentary for the small screen*, 237. Oxford: Focal Press.

[12] Thomas Lean. 2008a. From mechanical brains to microcomputers: Representations of the computer in Britain 1948–1984. In *Science and its publics*, ed. A. Bell, S. Davies, and F. Mellor, 179–200. Newcastle: Cambridge Scholars Publishing, 190–192

[13] See, for examples, Bryan Rimmer. 1978. Tomorrow's world. In the eye of a needle. *Daily Mirror*, September 21; Kenneth Owen. 1978. Microelectronics: This could be man's greatest leap forward. *The Times*, October 10.

[14] Skinner, *Technology, consumption and the future*, 68.

[15] Advisory Council for Applied Research and Development. 1978. *The applications of semiconductor technology.* London: HMSO.

[16] Christopher Evans. 1979. *The mighty micro: The impact of the computer revolution*, 96. London: Victor Gollancz.

> this was, you know, the up and coming thing and everything…I read about these strange things called computer stores that were starting up. And I thought, 'this is interesting, they're in America now, they'll come to the UK. I should start one.'[17]

In such ways personal computing ideas made the transatlantic crossing, but hardware was harder to import. Although British hobbyists could mail-order equipment from American suppliers, American products were distinctly expensive in a Britain undergoing economic crisis, especially when some manufacturers charged a premium for exported computers. By the late 1970s British computer kits were starting to appear, such as the £200 NASCOM 1 and Sinclair's first computer, the Science of Cambridge MK14. Developed as a cheaper alternative to American imports, the £39.95 MK14 was typical of hobbyist computers.[18] Sold by mail order through electronics hobby magazines, the MK14 arrived as a kit of components for the enthusiast to solder together into a chip encrusted circuit board, complete with calculator style keypad and LED display for input and output. A way for the user to tinker with a microprocessor of their own using complicated hexadecimal instructions, it was computing for computing's sake, a niche technical hobby requiring skills, and interest beyond those of the general populace.

3.2 The Making of an Educational Home Computer

While the MK14 was providing British enthusiasts with an affordable way to explore microprocessors, the first "appliance computers," the Commodore PET2001 and Apple II, were being released in the USA. Unlike hobby machines these shipped as factory-built appliances. Hardware complexities were wrapped in sleek casing, they were equipped with the beginners' programming language BASIC, and were advertised to appeal to wider audiences than just enthusiasts. The overall effect was of a more consumer-oriented product, more user friendly, and with wider appeal, but more expensive. While the Apple II in particular has become iconic of computing's domestication in the USA, with prices starting at around £800 in 1978 it was simply too costly to have the same mass appeal in Britain, whatever its merits as a user-friendly appliance. As Clive Sinclair recalled it there were "some very good machines [already on the market] but pretty expensive, so my idea was, that if we could get the price way, way down, five times down, to £100, we could aim straight at the general public."[19]

What the British mass market needed to develop beyond the hobbyists and the well-healed was a product offering the accessible appliance-like nature of the Apple II, at a price accessible to a wider audience. In 1980 Sinclair released the ZX80, costing £79.95 as a kit or £99.95 ready built, the first complete computer under the

[17] Bruce Everiss, interview (2007).

[18] Adamson and Kennedy, *Sinclair and the sunrise technology*, 69.

[19] Clive Sinclair, interview (2008).

symbolic £100 mark. More appliance like than the MK14, the ZX80's complexities were hidden by plastic casing, like the more expensive Apple or PET. The ZX80 sold perhaps 50,000 units, before being replaced by an improved version, the ZX81, where changes in industrial design and internal logic created a sleeker, even more consumer-oriented product. Thanks to greater integration of components, the price of the machine dropped to £69.95 assembled or £49.95 as a kit. This adaptation of the computer to the British home did not just make it affordable and appropriate for novice users, but configured it to support educational use.

Christina Lindsay highlights the importance of the "projected user" during the computer design process, the user whom the machine's creators had in mind. In Lindsay's case of the TRS80, the projected user was the electronics enthusiast, and the machine consequently configured to support such users.[20] In Sinclair's case, the computers were intended for "the man in the street" who knew little about computers, but wanted to learn. As Clive Sinclair remarked: "The idea I had was that people could educate themselves and amuse themselves by understanding what programming meant and doing some programming at home."[21] While other uses were considered, the early Sinclair home computers were configured with education strongly in mind and directed toward a wide and unskilled audience.

Adamson and Kennedy have rather dismissively noted that the ZX80 was little more than a hobbyist computer wrapped up in a plastic case.[22] However, as Paul Atkinson has noted in respect to other forms of computer, a machine's industrial design embodies its wider culture and the intentions of those behind it.[23] That Sinclair's computers had their components and complexities hidden away was fundamental in creating the impression of a complete appliance. This was furthered on the ZX81, whose industrial designer, Rick Dickinson, made it clear about how he was aiming at a more consumer, rather than hobbyist-orientated design, with the domestic environment in mind:

> The product I think Clive [Sinclair] was pushing me towards was much more of a consumer product [than the ZX80] and… I found that very difficult because there were no home computers in the shops… what is a home computer? You know, how would people relate to it? How do you identify it? What should it look like? Should it have a feel of Dictaphone or tape recorder or a feel of television about it? Where will it sit in the home?… It had to reflect some level of hi-tech, it had to be elegant, well considered in its design and its detail… It certainly wasn't hi-fi but it certainly would live in the bedroom or in the lounge, certainly not in the kitchen or the bathroom or the garage.[24]

The ZX machines simply plugged into a television set for display and a tape recorder for data storage, reducing costs, and associating the computer with common household technologies. The existing market of hobbyists was still targeted

---

[20] Lindsay, From the shadows, 32–37.

[21] Clive Sinclair, interview (2008).

[22] Adamson and Kennedy, *Sinclair and the sunrise technology*, 87.

[23] Paul Atkinson. 2005. Man in a briefcase: The social construction of the laptop computer and the emergence of a type form. *Journal of Design History* 18: 191–205.

[24] Rick Dickinson, interview (2008).

Fig. 3.1 Tinkering Users: the Sinclair ZX81. The small, flat "membrane" keyboard of the ZX81 is readily apparent, as is the minimalistic aesthetic of the machine—a simple black box ready to be plugged into a television display. The BASIC commands visible on the keys indicate the use of a keyword BASIC that allowed commands to be entered at the touch of a key. Creative users tired of the small, unresponsive keypad frequently refitted the machine with a typewriter-style unit or rehoused it in a case with a better keyboard

with technical advertisements in electronics magazines, but at around the same time advertising in national newspapers introduced the computers to a new audience of nonspecialists. Using reassuring slogans, such as "inside a day you'll be talking to it like an old friend," Sinclair's marketing soothed potential unease over letting a computer into the home.[25] Phrases such as "take it out of it's box, plug into your TV and mains and start," and "designed with special consideration for the beginner" spelt out the nature of the ZX computer as an accessible introduction to computing in easy to understand language (Fig. 3.1).

Promises to deliver "genuine computer understanding" for both you and your children and to make "learning easy exciting and enjoyable" highlight the educational pitching of the Sinclair machines. Learning to program and understand computing is a running theme throughout the advertisements, such as the emphasizing of the manual as a BASIC programming course. The machine's features were also configured toward introducing programming. Rather than an expensive typewriter-style keyboard with moving keys, the ZX80 and ZX81 had a membrane keyboard: a flat plastic sheet with small "keys" printed on, overlaying electrical contacts. With just four moving parts, it typifies the minimalistic approach of Sinclair, a way of saving money with neat, innovative design, even if the resulting products were

[25] These examples of slogans are drawn from various Sinclair ZX80 and ZX81 adverts over the 1980–1982 period, found in the popular press.

criticized for their suboptimal nature. While the keyboard's lack of tactile feedback and small size made conventional typing difficult, this was not its raison d'être. As Rick Dickinson remarked of the ZX81, "there was no need to touch type, because data entry wasn't at that level for that particular market. People couldn't touch type, they weren't secretaries."[26] Coupled to a built-in version of BASIC that allowed keyword entry of commands by pressing a single key or key combination rather than typing them out in full, the membrane keyboard, and the computer itself for that matter, was oriented to make programming accessible, a key element of the wider computer literacy culture the machines existed in.

As I have discussed elsewhere, there was a strongly educational context to British home computing in the early 1980s.[27] Having identified the challenge of the chip in *Now the Chips are Down*, the BBC launched the Computer Literacy Project, a comprehensive and high-profile effort to introduce the nation to computing. Supported by a programming course and a best-selling book, the first television series, 1982s *The Computer Programme,* was watched by seven million people.[28] The BBC even developed their own home computer with Sinclair rivals Acorn, the BBC Microcomputer.[29] Like Sinclair's machines, the BBC Micro was designed with education in mind, but without the same degree of extreme economy and minimalistic esthetic.[30] While the ZX machines defined the lower end of the British home computer market, the solid middle-class respectability by association and £400 price tag of the BBC Micro marked its upper reaches. Between the two, a variety of manufacturers offered computers built along similar lines, almost invariably stressing educational benefits at low cost.

Alongside other measures to promote the use of information technologies by business and industry, the British Government launched a number of measures aimed at increasing public awareness of computing. 1982, for instance, was designated Information Technology Year, IT82, with events and exhibitions around the country.[31] There was an element of political spin to these policies. Maureen McNeil has highlighted the ideological role IT played in the Thatcher "reforms." The forward-looking nature of information technology broke from old-fashioned and ugly industrial connotations and its association with efficiency and new

---

[26] Rick Dickinson, interview (2008).

[27] Lean, Mediating the microcomputer.

[28] John Radcliffe, and Robert Salkeld. 1983. *Towards computer literacy: The BBC computer literacy project.* London: BBC Education.

[29] Acorn co-founder Chris Curry was an important figure in Sinclair's original move into computing in the late 1970s, before leaving to found Acorn. The rivalry between the two Cambridge-based companies, including a 1984 pub fight between Chris Curry and Clive Sinclair over Acorn attacking Sinclair computers' reliability in advertisements, has already been explored in the BBC's *Micromen.* A serious academic comparison of the two firms is long overdue.

[30] For an idea of the BBC's thinking behind the BBC Micro, see: Radcliffe and Salkeld, *Towards computer literacy*, 13.

[31] Clive Cookson. 1982. The times guide to information technology. *The Times*, January 14.

entrepreneurial "sunrise industries" helped to lay the ground for acceptance of Thatcher's new economic policies.[32] Against the background of decline over the 1970s, the success of Sinclair and other British computer manufacturers, selling not only to domestic markets but oversees too, was trumpeted as a success for British enterprise.

As Adamson and Kennedy describe in detail, Clive Sinclair himself became a high-profile face of technological entrepreneurship in Thatcher's Britain,[33] enjoying something of a reputation as a technological visionary at time. He spoke to the US Congressional Clearinghouse about the potential for information technology in 1984, and his next product announcements were eagerly awaited as a sign of where the future may lie. Curiously, Clive Sinclair was apparently more personally interested in other aspects of the company's work, miniature televisions, and electric vehicles, than he was on computers, but this made little difference to the company's image.[34] "Uncle Clive," as the computer press dubbed him, was a publicly appealing mix of successful entrepreneur and inventor, who harked back to the familiar figure of the lone, sometimes eccentric, British boffin. As such he was the perfect figure for introducing computing to 1980s Britain. He was knighted in 1983, and in 1982 Prime Minister Margaret Thatcher presented her Japanese counterpart with a Sinclair computer, her words making its value as a symbol of British ingenuity clear:

> I was pleased during my recent trip to Japan to be able to present to the Japanese Prime Minister, in the very temple of high technology, a Sinclair Home Computer conceived, designed and produced in this country. Out into the market ahead of its Japanese rival.[35]

Of longer lasting significance than political rhetoric was a drive for computer education in schools to prepare British children for the future. The Microcomputer Education Program helped to train teachers and develop and disseminate the necessary material "to help schools to prepare children for life in a society in which devices and systems based on microelectronics are commonplace and pervasive."[36] The Micros in Schools program gave schools financial support to purchase Department of Industry recommended computers, albeit not including those of Sinclair at first. Although the company's educational discount and later inclusion in the scheme made up for this somewhat, the approved Acorn BBC Microcomputer became the dominant British school computer by 1984,[37] while Sinclair concentrated on the home market.

[32] Maureen McNeil. 1991. The old and new world of information technology in Britain. In *Enterprise and heritage: Crosscurrents of national culture*, ed. John Corner and Sylvia Harvey, 120–124. London: Routledge.

[33] Adamson and Kennedy, *Sinclair and the sunrise technology*, 9–14.

[34] Ibid., 85–86.

[35] Margaret Thatcher. 1982. *Speech opening conference on information technology*, London.

[36] Department of Education and Science. 1981. *Microelectronics education program: The strategy*. London, Department of Education and Science.

[37] Lucy Hodges. 1985. Average school has nine micros. *The Times*, January 25.

At grassroots levels as well, interest in learning about computers was growing. The number of local and national computer clubs in Britain grew from around 43 in 1978 to at least 235 by 1983.[38] Commonly meeting in community buildings, such as libraries and pubs, these offered many people a hands-on friendly introduction to computing. Many of those joining the clubs were not the hacker enthusiasts who have attracted so much attention as personal computer pioneers, but everyday people who just wanted to learn about computers in a supportive environment. As Jean Farrington, a member of a local club in the Lancashire market town of Chorley, recalled:

> It was the only place you could get any information at all about any of it and we joined as a family… There was a general fear around at one time, in the 80s, that people were frightened of them [computers], fearful of the technology and I was, still am a bit! But they realized that unless they could get on board, they were frightened also of being left behind.[39]

Positioned in this wider social context of curiosity and concern, Sinclair's computers became best sellers as affordable introductions to computing. For good reason did Sinclair advertising imply the importance of computers for the future, such as linking the impact of the ZX computers with the prosperity associated with the Model T Ford, and suggest computers importance in tomorrow's workplace.

The low-cost design and marketing of the ZX machines made the computer accessible in a way that appealed to the pocket, concerns, and level of computer awareness of early 1980s Britain. The machines had something of a reputation for poor reliability, yet this did little to dampen enthusiasm for Sinclair' computers; indeed, overwhelming demand sometimes caused problems fulfilling orders in a timely fashion. The appeal of the computers to a general market was furthered by national bookshop chain W.H. Smith, who started selling the ZX81 off the shelf in their stores for Christmas 1981. Prior to this computers had mainly been sold via mail order or through the small number of specialist computer retailers, which could be intimidating places for the novice. Smith's profitable experiment took the computer onto the high street and reduced it to a box that could be bought without the complications associated with computers, even if Smith's had to give their own staff a basic computer education to be able to sell them.[40] They were soon followed by other major retailers, whose efforts and advertising further the impression of microcomputers as consumer products.

Sinclair's earliest home computers, the ZX80 and especially ZX81, were innovative in redefining computing in a new form suitable for the 1980s British home, with a strong focus on education and programming. Moving further from hobbyist computing, Sinclair's next offering, the ZX Spectrum of 1982, refined this concept, removed the option for kit construction, and added a host of improvements in light of experiences with the earlier machines. The Sinclair computer was

---

[38] Thomas Lean. 2008b. *'The making of the micro': Producers, mediators, users and the development of popular microcomputing in Britain (1980–1989).* PhD thesis, University of Manchester.

[39] Jean Farrington, interview (2007).

[40] Adamson and Kennedy, *Sinclair and the sunrise technology,* 109–110.

initially configured with educational use in mind, but as Christina Lindsay reminds us, projected and actual use can differ, with consequences for the future development of a technology.[41]

3.3 GOTO Education

In line with the expectations of computer designers, many of the people who first bought computers in the early 1980s did so for educational reasons. For example, a 1981 survey of around 150 users in consumer advice magazine *Which?* revealed that the two most important uses that people bought computers for, were "writing programs" and "helping to learn about computers."[42] Many parents purchased computers for their children in expectation of educational benefits,[43] and Neil Selwyn has made a persuasive case that the activities of IT firms, the media, and Government from the 1980s have enshrined the computer as being inherently educational.[44] A question remains of how much of this educational intent and ethos was actually carried through into use of the home computer, particularly in the case of Sinclair, where gaming eventually became paramount.

Leslie Haddon's idea of "self-referential" computer use, using the computer to understand it, is valuable here. This exploratory use of the computer is clear in the selection of software available for the early Sinclair machines, which often seem of tenuous practical application. We see many programs for such purposes as generating interesting patterns, plotting histograms, displaying "biorhythms," or using the computer as an alarm clock. While of some utility, such software seems more valuable as a demonstration of what the computer *could do* and as a simple way interacting with it and exploring its capabilities. It helped familiarize the computer through association with everyday activities and introduced some potential real-life applications on a small scale, such as telephone directory programs as an introduction to databases.

The importance of programming to the computer hobbyist generally has been established.[45] The Sinclair machines were popular with hobbyists, as availability of kit ZX80 and ZX81s and the use of the machines in electronics hobbies, such as amateur radio, demonstrate. However, the ZX computers had much wider appeal, and in the computer literacy culture of 1980s Britain, programming was an important element of mainstream home computing. In some ways learning programming seems as an act of empowerment, a way of mastering the machine rather than becoming its slave. Programming and learning about computers were closely

---

[41] Lindsay, From the shadows, 37–40.

[42] Anon. 1981a. Home computers. *Which?*, July, 376.

[43] Gowling Marketing Services. 1984. *The attitudes of parents and children to home computers and software.* Liverpool: Gowling Marketing Services.

[44] Selwyn, Learning to love the micro.

[45] Levy, *Hackers*, chs. 10 and 11.

associated, with programming an element of computer education books, television, and computer club activity. In general, as David Skinner points out it was a common aspect of people's initial computer use.[46]

Sinclair was no exception to this, well demonstrated by articles in *Sinclair User* magazine, notably "User of the Month," which profiled a variety of Sinclair computer users around 1982–1984. Programming features in most of them, among users as varied as pensioners looking for an interesting hobby, to sportsmen optimizing their performance, and to parents anxious about their children's education. Sinclair computing was embedded in a context that encouraged and facilitated programming. It featured heavily in Sinclair magazines, commonly in the form of teaching articles and type-in program listings. Further program listings and more detailed knowledge were available from a multitude of cheap and easily accessible books.

As David Skinner has revealed, there are different ways of programming and people engaged with it to a different extent.[47] It could be just about typing out listings from magazines and books into the computer to get a program to run. The process could be time consuming and laborious, particularly on the small keyboards of Sinclair machines. Type-in listings were often error ridden or might be mistyped, leading to bugs in the program which the user would have to hunt down. For some it just added to the difficulties in getting the computer to do something useful, but for others bug hunting could be a "challenge and a useful learning exercise."[48] Programming was not just the means to an end, but could be an end in itself. It can be seen as a mental pursuit akin to a crossword or other puzzle, as another user remarked, "it is the sheer logic of it which appeals to me."[49] As Skinner points out, programming did not necessarily have to lead to some finished end product. It did not have to have practical value beyond the practice of programming, as another Sinclair user recalled:

> I think the biggest challenge for me was attempting to write a rudimentary word processor. God knows why, I didn't have a printer. Never managed to succeed but it was an interesting side project.[50]

Advanced users could go even further than BASIC and start experimenting with more complicated lower-level languages, programming in assembler, and machine code; though such was the wide appeal of programming, that guides on machine code were even produced for children. Whatever the depth of an individual's programming activity, it was a commonplace practice, unrestricted to any particular subculture of home computer users. With little ready written software available at

---

[46] Skinner, *Technology, consumption and the future*, 254.

[47] Ibid., 255–257.

[48] J. Johnson. 1983. Letters: Illustrations waste space. *Sinclair User*, June, 17.

[49] Claudia Cooke. 1983a. User of the month: Retiring to the sea, the ship and his Sinclairs. *Sinclair User*, April, 48.

[50] Mark Patterson, correspondence (2005).

first, it was also something of a necessity. Initially a commercial home computer software industry did not exist on any meaningful scale, and users themselves became software producers. Most of the program listings printed in magazines were sent in by readers, and a cottage industry emerged of home produced software cassettes sold via the small ads pages of computer magazines.[51] This activity quickly became more organized as skilled home programmers began to set up small businesses themselves, employing others from similar backgrounds or publishing the submissions of others.[52] Many of these programmers were teenagers, some of whom rose to national attention, as newspapers began reporting their allegedly massive salaries as a demonstration of how knowing about computers was bringing prosperity.[53] The wide availability of ready written software would eventually become a game changer. It meant that users did not *have* to learn to program for themselves to use the computer. In time, this would challenge the original conception of an educational computer. However, education was not the only thing the Sinclair computers were capable of.

3.4 "Serious" Use

The drawbacks of Sinclair computers, such as reliability problems and design compromises, which cut costs at the expense of usability or capability, have frequently been highlighted by commentators. In all fairness, such problems were far from unique to Sinclair, but the machines were undoubtedly built to be cheap. To keep costs down, the ZX machines had basic features, even compared to many contemporaries. The ZX81 had just 1 kilobyte of random access memory (RAM), enough to hold about half an A4 page worth of text, limiting program size. The keyboard was a common target of criticism, described by consumer guide *Which*? as "small and tiring to use."[54] The display was low-resolution monochrome, it had a single nonstandard interface port, and it lacked such basic refinements as an on/off button. The machine had no sound, though enterprising users learned to play music, after a fashion, by connecting the cassette recorder output to a speaker. While the Spectrum had a color display, improved membrane keyboard with moveable rubber keys, a beeper for sound, and larger 16 or 48 kilobyte memory, it too lacked the refinement of more expensive machines. For example, while the BBC Micro was inferior in some respects to the Spectrum, such as smaller 32 kilobyte memory, the "Beeb's" better graphics and sound, full typewriter-style keyboard, and impressive expansion

---

[51] For a good example of the mechanics of this activity, see Chris Bourne. 1985. Fool's gold from the funny farm? *Sinclair User*, January, 138.

[52] For an atmospheric insight into the early British home computer software industry, connected with Sinclair's rival Acorn but typical of the time, see Francis Spufford. 2004. *Backroom boys*. London: Faber and Faber, ch. 3.

[53] Lean, From mechanical brains to microcomputers, 195–196.

[54] Anon. 1981b. Home computers. *Which?*, August, 439.

capabilities added up to a package that seemed of higher quality, particularly given Sinclairs' poor reputation for reliability.[55] The ZX machines' limitations have led to them being written off as "serious" computers, only useful for games or introductory use. For example, Leslie Haddon remarks that "Sinclair's earliest home computers were distinguished by the degree to which they had virtually no practical uses or benefits apart from being a vehicle for learning to program."[56]

Technological determinism would suggest that the machine's limitations should have limited their utility. However, these perspectives ignore the potential for Sinclair users to reinterpret and reshape their computers as they saw fit, and there are several indicators that the machines were used for more than just learning about computers. A 1984 survey of 2000 small businesses with computers revealed Sinclair machines were used by 9 %, the same share as Apple, and only 3 % behind market leader Acorn.[57] Applications software was available in some quantities for the machines, not just simple calculators, but feature rich programs, such as the popular *Tasword* word processor and *Masterfile* database. *Sinclair User's* "User of the Month" feature provides useful case studies of people putting these cheap and apparently limited computers to surprisingly sophisticated applications.

The 1970s programmable calculator had been used as a precursor to fully fledged personal computers.[58] In the early 1980s we see the situation reversed, as people made use of microcomputers as sophisticated calculators. From small businesses, there are stories of how ZX81s and Spectrums were used to calculate payrolls,[59] check taxes,[60] or work out engineering stressing calculations.[61] Outside the office, micros were used in hobbies, such as amateur archeology[62] to help calculate measurements of dig sites, or by canoeists to determine the optimum course across streams.[63] There still seems an element of exploratory use in many of these cases, as people found out what a computer could be useful for. However, in other examples the programs seem of more genuine utility, such as a ZX81-based antiques dealer's business system, combining databases for stock control and financial records with the ability to analyze the data to produce financial reports.[64]

---

[55] Ralph Bancroft. 1984. What the retailers said when they looked at the spectrum. *The Times*, December 4.

[56] Haddon, *The roots and early history of the British home computer market*, 125.

[57] Bill Johnstone. 1984. More small firms buy computers. *The Times*, June 14.

[58] Paul Ceruzzi. 1999. Inventing personal computing. In *The social shaping of technology*, 2nd ed, ed. Donald MacKenzie and Judy Wajcman, 66–68. Buckingham: Open University Press.

[59] Claudia Cooke. 1983b. User of the month: Taking the strain out of calculating wages. *Sinclair User*, August, 78–79.

[60] Claudia Cooke. 1983c. User of the month: Leading athletes quest for gold is boosted by ZX-81. *Sinclair User*, September, 84–85.

[61] John Heritage. 1984. Sinclair business user: A systematic start. *Sinclair User*, July, 120.

[62] Chris Bourne. 1984. Digging up the past. *Sinclair User*, August, 110–111.

[63] Nicola Serge. 1984. User of the month: Paddle your own canoe with the ZX81. *Sinclair User*, February, 58–59.

[64] Alan Proctor. 1984. Sinclair business user: ZX-81 in the antique shop. *Sinclair User*, November, 163–164.

Key to the use of simple computers for complex tasks was the availability of add-ons, peripherals, and upgrades, which allowed users to expand the capabilities of basic machines. While Sinclair produced around half a dozen key peripherals, many more were produced by a cottage industry of small manufacturers. At least 500 different peripherals were available for the ZX Spectrum: interfaces to adapt the machines' simple user port to standard interfaces, disc drives, enhancements for graphics and sound, and all manner of specialized gadgets.[65] While a few needed soldering or had other technicalities to grasp, many simply plugged into the computer's user port, a simple way of improving the machine. Sinclair membrane keyboards were often replaced by typewriter-style units,[66] and memory upgrade "RAM packs," from a variety of suppliers, became virtually standard kit on the ZX81. Illustrating the occasionally quirky nature of the machines in use, "RAM pack wobble" wiping the contents of a loosely fitted ZX81 memory upgrade could cost hours of programming effort. The range of solutions suggested in computer magazines, readers' letters advocating Blu-Tack or Velcro, adverts for specially made computer holders, and improved wobble-free RAM packs are insightful into the homespun ingenuity of users and to how peripheral suppliers helped to negate the ZX machines' drawbacks.

In keeping with the wider encouragement to learn to program, many of the users profiled in "User of the Month" relied on application software written themselves, frequently far beyond simple programs. Using a ZX81 or Spectrum for serious computing could be a complex task, requiring multiple add-ons and the additional complication of getting software to work with them all. While it certainly was not countercultural in the context of computer literacy, such efforts could share the fascination with technology typically associated with hacking. One user, for instance, boasted with pride of never having bought a commercial program, preferring to write software himself.[67] Another remarked on the "application that boarders on obsession" required for serious programming.[68] Most of those profiled reckoned that after the initial outlay in time and learning the computer made a positive difference. For example, a Methodist minister, who used his Spectrum to match circuit preachers with churches, reckoned that his timetabling program, after taking month to write, did a morning's scheduling work in 15 minutes.[69] While Sinclair's machines did not make ideal serious computers straight out of the box, with user innovation they could become useful small systems and were far from restricted to "self-referential" computing in the hands of determined users.

---

[65] Paul Jenkinson. 2007. Spectrum hardware page. http://www.worldofspectrum.org/hardware/. Accessed 15 Oct 2007.

[66] Franco Frey. 1984. Dk'tronics revisited. *Crash*, October, 52–53.

[67] Cooke, User of the month: Leading athletes quest for gold is boosted by ZX-81.

[68] Proctor, Sinclair business user: ZX-81 in the antique shop.

[69] Flo Barker. 1984. Programs lighten the load of a methodist minister. *Sinclair User*, January, 102–103.

Fig. 3.2 Responding to Users: Sinclair ZX Spectrum. The larger size of the "Speccy" improved the computer's usability compared to the ZX81 model, notably through the raised "dead flesh" rubber keys that gave computer users better tactile feedback. The machine, now with a simple sound generation and color display, was better optimized for entertainment uses than its predecessors, but BASIC programming remained a prominent part of the design

3.5 Just a Toy Computer?

Today the Sinclair computer is not primarily known as an introductory computer, or valuable electronic office aid, but as a computer game system. Sinclair had anticipated that games would be among the uses of their home computers, but seem to have been surprised to the extent to which this occurred.[70] The low price and small size of Sinclair's computer put them dangerously close to expensive toys, and many were purchased for children. In his discussion of how the home computer turned into a games system, Leslie Haddon draws attention to how the software industry and magazines turned computer games into a desirable commodity for computer users, particularly children and teenagers.[71] The extent to which this happened actually varied considerably across the market. Acorn's educational user base, for example, insulated them from such changes, but the transformation of Sinclair into a games system was dramatic (Fig. 3.2).

Games playing quickly emerged as a prominent use of the ZX81. Games were a good demonstration of what the computer could do and many of the listings printed in magazines were for game programs. Indeed, home programmers learned how to make effective use of the machine's tiny memory to an extent where there was even a one kilobyte version of chess. From the computer press and a flow of programs and suggestions sent in directly from users, Sinclair was aware of the growing

[70] Clive Sinclair, interview (2008).

[71] Haddon, *The roots and early history of the British home computer market*, ch. 7.

importance of gaming. The design of the ZX Spectrum was thus configured with games more in mind.[72] As Clive Sinclair and Rick Dickson, respectively, remarked:

> Because of the games development the Spectrum was a logical next step: we improved the keyboard and we put in color.[73]
>
> Color was a pretty logical progression… I suppose it was a question of just think what you can do with color if it was a games product; it gives you so many new dimensions… I think by then Clive had probably accepted that it was a games product predominantly.[74]

As in Lindsay's case of the TRS80, the conception of the configured user had begun to change in response to actual users.[75] The Spectrum still possessed all the educational qualities inherent in its predecessors, and its greater capability was just as easily turned to other uses too. However, low-cost, high-profile, and color graphics also made it a particularity attractive games machine to younger users and an increasingly organized software industry. Unlike other forms of software, there is a disposable quality to games. After completion a game could simply be replaced by another one, a potentially lucrative cycle of software consumption. Analysis of the most comprehensive listing available of Sinclair software, from the website *World of Spectrum*, shows that in 1982 a little over 200 games were commercially released for the Spectrum and around 60 utilities. In 1983 there were around 170 new utilities compared to nearly 800 games, a discrepancy that grew.[76] Accompanying this came glossy advertising of games and the promotion of star programmers, which started to overshadow other forms of software.

Like other types of 1980s home computing, gaming actually had technical aspects too. The BASIC commands PEEK and POKE allowed memory locations to be examined and altered. PEEKing and POK(E)ing was a common facet of Sinclair gaming, as users explored programs in the hope of finding ways of modifying the game or cheating. Other users enjoyed the challenge of hacking into commercial releases to circumvent copy protection, wrote their own games from scratch or keyed in games from listings, making their own modifications as they went along, and altering commercial releases. As user Mark Patterson recalled of his childhood Spectrum use:

> In those days, you could play a game and think 'wouldn't it be great if you had a gun in *Manic Miner* [a popular game]' then go to work trying to build a level from scratch where you can go ahead and shoot the bad guys instead of jumping over them.[77]

Although programming was enjoyable for some, for others, it was a means that delayed the ends of playing the game. The ready written products of the games industry offered instant gratification, or at least in the time it took to load a cassette. There was little educational value in such activity, and the culture that went with it was more about consumption than education. Leslie Haddon has revealed elements

---

[72] Haddon, *The roots and early history of the British home computer market.*

[73] Clive Sinclair, interview (2008).

[74] Rick Dickinson, interview (2008).

[75] Lindsay, From the shadows.

[76] Thomas Lean. 2004. *'What would I do with a computer?' The shaping of the Sinclair computer 1980–1986*, 99. MA thesis, University of Kent.

[77] Mark Patterson, email (2005).

of masculine competitiveness in the culture of computer gaming among younger micro users.[78] At school, computer clubs and at home, young users, largely boys, traded hints and tips, gossiped about their game experiences, swapped pirated software, discussed the latest releases, and compared high scores – we even see them being compared in the letters pages of magazines. There was rivalry between the owners of different platforms and competition to own the largest games collections, new releases, or complete series of titles.

Consumption of entertainment software was fueled further by computer magazines. While the Sinclair magazine market had originally catered for a range of uses, with programming, gaming, and general interest publications, it became increasingly dominated by games coverage. *Sinclair User*, for instance, began as a general interest publication, with a pronounced programming and exploration element. By the later 1980s it was a gamer's magazine, altered by the change in the market, advertising revenue from software houses, and competition from game-focused rivals, such as *Your Sinclair* and *Crash*. The supportive context of the Sinclair computer thus shifted from supporting education to gaming. The computer code listings previously contained in magazines were replaced by cover-mounted cassettes of ready to run programs and reviews of commercial software.

In the context of computer literacy, the use of computers for such frivolous purposes as games was a misuse of their potential for some. In the computing press we see hints of frustration that people were not taking their home computers more seriously and that the concentration on games had left the serious user unsupported, as a reader lamented in *Sinclair User*:

> The Spectrum is a sophisticated, powerful machine having the capabilities of the minicomputers of a decade ago [which were] properly used as tools for serious applications. So why is the £130 home computer not similarly used in the same roles? Unfortunately they have become saddled with the image of toys. It is clear that the potential serious user of a Spectrum…is dissuaded from buying the computer.[79]

As the computer market matured, so too did the buying public. By 1984, prospective customers were likely to have some experience of microcomputing, and there was a gradual shift toward more sophisticated "real computers" rather than introductory machines.[80] Consumer electronics manufacturer Amstrad demonstrated this shift when they joined the home computer market in 1984. Dismissing Sinclair's products as "pregnant calculators" Amstrad head Alan Sugar demanded a professionally styled "real computer," modeled on those customers might encounter at airport check-in desks.[81] Even if the resulting Amstrad CPC464 was not that much more powerful than a Spectrum in many respects, it certainly looked more like a serious computer. Despite considerable user interest, Sinclair's own attempt at a business machine, the sophisticated £400 Quantum

---

[78] Haddon, *The roots and early history of the British home computer market*, ch. 8.

[79] G.A. Rooker. 1983. Letters: Technical uses need promoting. *Sinclair User*, October, 19.

[80] Bancroft, What the retailers said when they looked at the spectrum. Peter Large. 1984. Indian summer of cheaper micro. *The Guardian*, December 20.

[81] David Thomas. 1991. *The Amstrad story*, 123–124. London: Pan Books.

Leap (QL), was a failure, brought down by a mix of technical and production problems and confusion over whether it was a home or professional computer.[82] This failure, along with that of Sinclair's ill-fated C5 personal electronic vehicle, contributed to Sinclair's sale to Amstrad in 1985, who continued to produce the Spectrum and to further develop it.

One of the surprising things about the popularity of the Spectrum for gaming was that it was not especially well suited to such use from a technical standpoint. In original 1982 form, it lacked an interface that could directly connect to most joysticks, its sound was limited to a simple beeper, and its display suffered from an inherent technical issue known as "color clash" which caused screen colors to get mixed up in animations.[83] These drawbacks in an entertainment product were mitigated by add-on joystick interfaces from the cottage industry and programmers learning to lay out graphics to avoid color clash. However, as Spectrum gaming expanded, Sinclair, and later Amstrad, reconfigured the machine to enhance its suitability for gaming.

By the Amstrad developed Spectrum+2 of 1986, the addition of joystick ports, a proper sound synthesizer, and a built-in cassette recorder had created a "software player" orientated towards entertainment.[84] Concurrently the prominence of BASIC was depreciated. The programming oriented membrane keyboard was replaced by a typewriter-style unit without BASIC keywords on the keys, and BASIC was hidden behind a software loader screen rather than being the first thing the user saw on boot up. Marketing paid scant attention to education or programming, but instead emphasized that there were "more games available than you can wiggle a joystick at," to quote one Spectrum+2 advert from around 1986. Even while more powerful computers appeared on the home market, pushing the Spectrum into obsolescence, software houses continued to support the large Spectrum user base. Indeed, experienced programmers who knew the machine intimately could create games of a quality reckoned to exceed early efforts on newer computers, such as the Atari ST.[85] As the cumulative weight of gaming built up over the years, and the machines' design and representation changed to reflect this, the educational origins of the Sinclair computers slipped into memory. The Sinclair computer had changed from introduction to the future to mere gaming appliance.

Even as the emphasis on everybody learning to be a programmer declined, in the face of consumption of ready written commercial games, another form of self-referential use emerged for aging home computers like the Spectrum, albeit on a far smaller scale.

---

[82] Adamson and Kennedy, *Sinclair and the sunrise technology,* 153–182.

[83] The Spectrum's color display was essentially a monochrome bitmap image beneath an overlay which divided the screen into blocks of different colors. This saved on memory as it was unnecessary to store information on what color each pixel was, but it could cause color clash where the underlying bitmap image moved from a block of one color to one of a different color, appearing to change color itself in the process.

[84] Between the original ZX Spectrum and Spectrum+2, Sinclair had developed the Spectrum into the Spectrum+, little more than re-cased Spectrum with a new keyboard, and Spectrum 128, with extra memory, improved audio capabilities and other improvements.

[85] James Sumner. 2005. Retrieving micro histories: The strange case of the domestic microcomputer. Paper presented to University College London seminar series, London.

Demos, like earlier home computer software, were a demonstration of what the computer could do, but for artistic rather than instructional ends, for example:

> I modified a screen flipper to create a full screen dancing Dizzy character. Mashed two programs together, one was the screen flipper, and another did the flipping based on sound input through the MIC socket. The character would kind of dance to the music.[86]

Typically combining animations and sound effects to create an audio-visual experience for the user, demo programmers frequently pushed the Spectrum to the limits of its capability, to where one "wouldn't have believed the machine could do this."[87] Sometimes included on magazine cover tapes, demos were also swapped through less visible channels, such as mail-order public domain libraries or personal contacts. This non-mainstream movement had an international following, with prominent groups in Eastern Europe where Spectrum clones would continue to be produced after the machine's official end of production in 1992. Use, as David Edgerton reminds us, continues long after a technology is new.[88]

In the early twenty-first century, Sinclair's computers still have use, both as popular culture nostalgia, well demonstrated by *Micromen*, and within the niches of demo and "retrocomputing" communities, which continue to keep the machine alive, archiving and even producing new software. Indeed, considering the machines' cult status, the popularity of extensive sites, such as *World of Spectrum,* and premium prices commanded for Sinclair products on E-bay, 30 years from its birth the Sinclair computer is, in its afterlife, still thriving.[89]

3.6 Game Over

The history of Sinclair computing reveals much of the conditions that shaped the early British popular computing experience, particularly its original educational emphasis. In the context of computer literacy, developing an intimate knowledge of computing and programming was not just the niche interest of a subculture, but a part of a wider societal move toward computer mastery and common part of home computer use. The demise of this model of computing and the remaking of the Sinclair computer as a video games player demonstrates the importance of users, software houses, and magazines in the ongoing construction of computer technology. In particular, the redesign of the Spectrum to reflect the uses that gamers were finding for it closes the loop between production and use of technology, by demonstrating how producers and users could coproduce a computer over time. That the educational computer died out does not designate its failure, but rather its success in helping a computer-illiterate British society get used to

---

[86] David Womble, correspondence (2008).

[87] Paul Collins, personal communication (2008).

[88] David Edgerton. 2006. *The shock of the old: Technology and global history since 1900*. London: Profile.

[89] Martijn van der Heide, et al. 2010. *World of spectrum*. www.worldofspectrum.org. Accessed 10 Jan 2010.

the idea of computers. It was simply a concept with a finite lifespan that contained the seeds of its own obsolescence.

Sinclair computing provides an excellent case study of the British home computing experience, but it is only one example, albeit an important one. The British computer market was diverse,[90] and comparative work between different manufacturers and the users of their products is needed to reveal a more nuanced picture of popular computing cultures. Sinclair's computers also had stories outside Britain. The simple, economic model of personal computing inherent in the designs meant that they were widely copied, particularly in the Eastern bloc. Indeed Russian Spectrum clones, such as the Scorpion and Pentagon, expanded on Sinclair's basic design considerably.[91] In more affluent markets, the story was somewhat different. Sinclair's own efforts to market versions of the ZX81 and Spectrum in America through a deal with Timex were of fleeting, but not insignificant, success. According to Adamson and Kennedy, over half a million Timex Sinclair TS1000's, an Americanized ZX81, were sold in the USA in their first 5 months of sales in 1982, on top of 150,000 previous mail-order sales of ZX81s into the States by Sinclair.[92] Faced with a large marketplace of more affluent consumers better able to afford more powerful machines, this flow of British home computers into America seems to have been relatively short lived. However, according to Brian Bagnall's recent popular history of American home computer giant Commodore, the Sinclair concept of accessibly low-cost computing had more traction. Citing Commodore designer Chuck Peddle, Bagnall claims that Commodore's own move from the PET series to a cheaper personal computer, the VIC20, was directly influenced by the ZX80.[93] Such transfers of popular computing ideas *into* the USA, not just from it, demand that we consider the early development of personal computing as more of a global movement than has hitherto been the case.

Bibliography

Adamson, Ian, and Richard Kennedy. 1986. *Sinclair and the sunrise technology: The deconstruction of a myth*. Harmondsworth: Penguin.

Advisory Council for Applied Research and Development. 1978. *The applications of semiconductor technology*. London: HMSO.

Atkinson, Paul. 2005. Man in a briefcase: The social construction of the laptop computer and the emergence of a type form. *Journal of Design History* 18: 191–205.

---

[90] For discussion of the extent and reasons for this diversity of computer design, see Lean, *The making of the micro*, 217–232.

[91] Chris Owen. 2010. *Planet Sinclair: Clones and variants*. http://www.nvg.ntnu.no/sinclair/computers/clones/clones.htm. Accessed 10 Jan 2010.

[92] Adamson and Kennedy, *Sinclair and the sunrise technology*, 133–136.

[93] Brian Bagnall. 2006. *On the edge: The spectacular rise and fall of Commodore*. Winnipeg: Variant Press.

Bagnall, Brian. 2006. *On the edge: The spectacular rise and fall of Commodore*. Winnipeg: Variant Press.

Bancroft, Ralph. 1984. What the retailers said when they looked at the spectrum. *The Times*, December 4.

Barker, Flo. 1984. Programs lighten the load of a methodist minister. *Sinclair User*, January, 102–103.

Bourne, Chris. 1984. Digging up the past. *Sinclair User*, August, 110–111.

Bourne, Chris. 1985. Fool's gold from the funny farm? *Sinclair User*, January, 138.

Campbell-Kelly, Martin, William Aspray, Nathan Ensmenger, and Jeffrey R. Yost. 2014 [1996]. *Computer: A history of the information machine*. Boulder, CO: Westview Press.

Ceruzzi, Paul. 1999. Inventing personal computing. In *The social shaping of technology*, 2nd ed, ed. Donald MacKenzie and Judy Wajcman, 66–68. Buckingham: Open University Press.

Ceruzzi, Paul E. 2003 [1998]. *A history of modern computing*. Cambridge, MA/London: MIT Press, ch. 7.

Cooke, Claudia. 1983a. User of the month: Retiring to the sea, the ship and his Sinclairs. *Sinclair User*, April, 48.

Cooke, Claudia. 1983b. User of the month: Taking the strain out of calculating wages. *Sinclair User*, August, 78–79

Cooke, Claudia. 1983c. User of the month: Leading athletes quest for gold is boosted by ZX-81. *Sinclair User*, September, 84–85.

Cookson, Clive. 1982. The times guide to information technology. *The Times*, January 14.

Dale, Rodney. 1985. *The Sinclair story*. London: Duckworth.

Department of Education and Science. 1981. *Microelectronics education program: The strategy*. London, Department of Education and Science.

Edgerton, David. 2006. *The shock of the old: Technology and global history since 1900*. London: Profile.

Evans, Christopher. 1979. *The mighty micro: The impact of the computer revolution*, 96. London: Victor Gollancz.

Frey, Franco. 1984. Dk'tronics revisited. *Crash*, October, 52–53.

Gowling Marketing Services. 1984. *The attitudes of parents and children to home computers and software*. Liverpool: Gowling Marketing Services.

Haddon, Leslie G. 1988b. *The roots and early history of the British home computer market: Origins of the masculine micro*. PhD thesis, University of London.

Heritage, John. 1984. Sinclair business user: A systematic start. *Sinclair User*, July, 120.

Hodges, Lucy. 1985. Average school has nine micros. *The Times*, January 25.

Jenkinson, Paul. 2007. Spectrum hardware page. http://www.worldofspectrum.org/hardware/. Accessed 15 Oct 2007.

Johnson, J. 1983. Letters: Illustrations waste space. *Sinclair User*, June, 17.

Johnstone, Bill. 1984. More small firms buy computers. *The Times*, June 14.

Kriwaczek, Paul. 1997. *Documentary for the small screen*, 237. Oxford: Focal Press.

Large, Peter. 1984. Indian summer of cheaper micro. *The Guardian*, December 20.

Lean, Thomas. 2004. *'What would I do with a computer?' The shaping of the Sinclair computer 1980–1986*, 99. MA thesis, University of Kent.

Lean, Thomas. 2008a. From mechanical brains to microcomputers: Representations of the computer in Britain 1948–1984. In *Science and its publics*, ed. A. Bell, S. Davies, and F. Mellor, 179–200. Newcastle: Cambridge Scholars Publishing.

Lean, Thomas. 2008b. *'The making of the micro': Producers, mediators, users and the development of popular microcomputing in Britain (1980–1989)*. PhD thesis, University of Manchester, Manchester.

Lean, Thomas. 2012. Mediating the microcomputer: The educational character of the 1980s British popular computing boom. *Public Understanding of Science*, first published online on 30 October 2012 as doi:10.1177/0963662512457904.

Levy, Steven. 1984. *Hackers: Heroes of the computer revolution*. Garden City, NY: Anchor Press/Doubleday.

Lindsay, Christina. 2003. From the shadows: Users as designers, producers, marketers, distributors, and technical support. In *How users matter: The co-construction of users and technologies*, ed. Nelly Oudshoorn and Trevor J. Pinch, 29–50. Cambridge, MA: MIT Press.

McNeil, Maureen. 1991. The old and new world of information technology in Britain. In *Enterprise and heritage: Crosscurrents of national culture*, ed. John Corner and Sylvia Harvey, 120–124. London: Routledge.

Owen, Kenneth. 1978. Microelectronics: This could be man's greatest leap forward. *The Times*, October 10.

Owen, Chris. 2010. *Planet Sinclair: Clones and variants*. http://www.nvg.ntnu.no/sinclair/computers/clones/clones.htm. Accessed 10 Jan 2010.

Proctor, Alan. 1984. Sinclair business user: ZX-81 in the antique shop. *Sinclair User*, November, 163–164.

Radcliffe, John, and Robert Salkeld. 1983. *Towards computer literacy: The BBC computer literacy project*. London: BBC Education.

Rimmer, Bryan. 1978. Tomorrow's world. In the eye of a needle. *Daily Mirror*, September 21.

Rooker, G.A. 1983. Letters: Technical uses need promoting. *Sinclair User*, October, 19.

Selwyn, Neil. 2002. Learning to love the micro: The discursive construction of educational computing in the UK, 1979–89. *British Journal of Sociology of Education* 23: 427–443.

Serge, Nicola. 1984. User of the month: Paddle your own canoe with the ZX81. *Sinclair User*, February, 58–59.

Skinner, David Ian. 1992. *Technology, consumption and the future: The experience of home computing*. PhD thesis, Brunel University.

Spufford, Francis. 2004. *Backroom boys*. London: Faber and Faber, ch. 3.

Sumner, James. 2005. Retrieving micro histories: The strange case of the domestic microcomputer. Paper presented to University College London seminar series, London.

Thatcher, Margaret. 1982. *Speech opening conference on information technology*, London.

Thomas, David. 1991. *The Amstrad story*, 123–124. London: Pan Books.

van der Heide, Martijn, et al. 2010. *World of spectrum*. www.worldofspectrum.org. Accessed 10 Jan 2010.

Chapter 4
Legal Pirates Ltd: Home Computing Cultures in Early 1980s Greece

Theodoros Lekkas

4.1 Introduction

In 1987, about 15,000 men, women, and children gathered at the football stadium on Alexandras Avenue in Athens for the successful annual live lottery draw; while attending a concert featuring some of the most popular Greek singers of the time, the audience rushing to fill the stands were responding to a computer magazine's invitation to take part in an informatics competition, with home personal computers, software, and peripherals as prizes. Our interest in the case intensifies when we learn that said magazine does not even feature personal computers but only specifically home computers, which by the late 1980s were already a thing of the past in most countries (a recreational pastime for a few amateurs at best). The live draw was one of the largest of its kind ever held in Greece and invites us to explore the meaning of computing technology in 1980s Greece. (Fig. 4.1)

In April 1994, the editor of Greek computer magazine *RAM*, Theodore Spinoulas, reminisced about the early days of Greek personal computing: "In 1981, IBM presented its first personal computer. At that time (and until recently), IBM divided the countries where they supplied their computers into three categories. The first consisted of the USA, Germany, France, and the UK; the second was the Netherlands, Belgium etc., and the third was Greece along with countries such as Uganda, Zimbabwe, and Namibia. The first category had everything: local language support, books, people, and everything needed to enhance IBM sales. The second category only received part of these services. In countries like Greece though, as the reader might have guessed, IBM did not provide anything. Computers were sold, but the user could be long dead and gone before Greek characters would ever appear on his screen or on paper – not to mention that a manual in Greek was a faraway dream."

T. Lekkas (✉)
Philosophy and History of Science Department,
National and Kapodistrian University of Athens, Athens, Greece
e-mail: tlekkas@phs.uoa.gr

G. Alberts and R. Oldenziel (eds.), *Hacking Europe. From Computer Cultures to Demoscenes*, History of Computing, DOI 10.1007/978-1-4471-5493-8_4,

Fig. 4.1 Winning Computers in a Greek Stadium. For many Greeks, home microcomputers were their only link to computer technology. A distinct discourse developed surrounding computers as the vehicle to a "better society." *Pixel* magazine was the key actor in articulating the discourse, while also acting as the crucial mediator between the users and microcomputer technology. Its role was so prominent that when *Pixel* organized a public lottery in an Athenian soccer stadium, it attracted 15,000 people, mostly families, to the event. Source: *Pixel* 35(1987): 67

These two episodes evoke an image of a country which, although located within technologically advanced Western Europe, is characterized by unique features, not least its unique alphabet. The country remained excluded from the official support of major English-language multinational computer companies like IBM that treated Greece as a small underdeveloped market, forcing Greeks to tackle the various problems of adoption and adaptation of the available computer technology. Home computers in particular played an important role in the country's orientation towards technological adjustment. The literature usually treats home computers as devoid of historical significance or as mere gaming consoles at best. This chapter attempts to understand the historical context, while focusing the narrative on the concept of the hacker. From the Greek socio-technical perspective, the term hacker takes on a different meaning from what we see in popular computer articles that usually focus on North America.[1]

During the late 1970s, computer technology had achieved a relatively low penetration in those sectors of Greek society with minimal involvement in the world of electronics (TV, video, and fax). In Greece, as in many other countries, the term computer usually referred to the sizeable mainframe computers used by large enterprises like banks and telecommunication companies, the military, universities, or public sector agencies. Large computers managed vast and complex databases or were used for specific tasks requiring significant computing power – such as banking – but remained virtually invisible to the public at large.[2] Even though mainframes already affected daily life, most citizens, except the few technical and administrative staff in these organizations, remained unaware of computer developments. When developments in the USA changed the way people used computer technology and impacted people's lives, amateur enthusiasts began utilizing microchip technology.[3] They assembled cheap personal computers from readily available parts (RAM chips, microprocessors).[4] Some turned the activity into a full-time

[1]Recent literature presents the strategic challenge posed by American domination of computer technology as the shaping force behind any national identity concerning the production, distribution and marketing of technological products. Thomas J. Misa, and Johan Schot. 2005. Inventing Europe: Technology and the hidden integration of Europe. *History and Technology* 21: 1–19.

[2]The only study on the application of mainframe computers in Greece is Αλέξανδρος-Ανδρέας Κύρτσης, Εθνική Τράπεζα της Ελλάδος: Τεχνολογική και Οργανωτική Πρωτοπορία, 1950–2000, (Εθνική Τράπεζα της Ελλάδος: Πρόγραμμα Ερευνών Ιστορικού Αρχείου, 2008). On the use and history of mainframes, see Jeffrey R. Yost. 2005. *The computer industry, Emerging industries in the United States*. Westport: Greenwood Press; Emerson W. Pugh. 1995. *Building IBM: Shaping an industry and its technologies*. Cambridge, MA: MIT Press; Steve Usselman. 1993. IBM and its imitators: Organizational capabilities and the emergence of the international computer industry. *Business History Review* 22(1): 1–35; Arthur L. Norberg. 2005. *Computers and commerce: A study of technology and management at Eckert-Mauchly Computer Company, Engineering Research Associates, and Remington Rand, 1946–1957*. Cambridge, MA: MIT Press; Jamie Parke Pearson. 1992. *Digital at work: Snapshots from the first thirty-five years*. Burlington: Digital Press.

[3]Ross Knox Bassett. 2002. *To the digital age: Research labs, start-up companies, and the rise of MOS technology*. Baltimore: Johns Hopkins University Press; Christophe Lécuyer. 2005. *Making Silicon Valley: Innovation and the growth of high tech, 1930–1970*. Cambridge, MA: MIT Press; Joel N. Shurkin. 2006. *Broken genius: The rise and fall of William Shockley, creator of the electronic age*. London/New York: Palgrave Macmillan; Richard S. Tedlow. 2006. *Andy Grove: The life and times of an American business icon*. New York: Portfolio.

[4]A typical example of this personal computer was MITS Altair 8800, designed in 1975. Ceruzzi writes: "This ranks with IBM's announcement of the System/360 a decade earlier as one of the most significant in the history of computing." Paul E. Ceruzzi. 2003 [1998]. *A history of modern computing*, 226. Cambridge, MA/London: MIT Press. Despite all this, the early history of personal computers is rather neglected by the historians of technology and this gap is covered, in some extend, by columnists. See Paul Freiberger, and Michael Swaine. 1984. *Fire in the valley: The making of the personal computer*. Berkeley: Osborne/McGraw-Hill; and Robert X. Cringely. 1992. *Accidental empires: How the boys of Silicon Valley make their millions, battle foreign competition, and still can't get a date*. Reading: Addison-Wesley.

profession, selling personal computers already assembled that were ready to use.[5] By the late 1970s, a subcategory of personal computers,[6] the home microcomputers (or home micros) appeared on the market, featuring limited memory and computing power.[7] They were extremely cheap and simple to build without additional operating equipment and soon became extremely popular in America and Western Europe.[8] Despite their popularity, only recently have historians of technology shown any interest in them.[9] I argue that studying these home micros reveals a broader picture of computer technology use in countries like Greece.

---

[5] Steven Levy. 1984. *Hackers: The heroes of the computer revolution*. Garden City, NY: Anchor Press/Doubleday and John W. Markoff. 2005. *What the dormouse said: How the 60s counterculture shaped the personal computer industry*. New York: Viking.

[6] On the invention of the personal computer in the mid-1970s, see Paul E. Ceruzzi. 1996. From scientific instrument to everyday appliance: The emergence of personal computers, 1970–77. *History and Technology* 13(1): 1–31; James Chposky, and Ted Leonsis. 1988. *Blue magic: The people, power, and politics behind the IBM personal computer*. New York: Facts on File. On the emergence of PC as a standard in the early to mid-1980s, see J. Sumner. 2008. Standards and compatibility: The rise of the PC platform. *History and Technology* 28: 101–127. Sumner suggested that computing platforms are not simply rigid standards, but emerge thanks to negotiations between producers and users, J. Sumner. 2007. What makes a PC? Thoughts on computing platforms, standards, and compatibility. *IEEE Annals of History of Computing* 29(2): 87–88.

[7] The ZX Spectrum, an 8-bit home computer supplied in the UK in 1982 by Sinclair Research Ltd, was based on a Zilog Z80A CPU which ran at 3.5 MHz and featured a 16 KB RAM memory (in the basic version). A monitor or TV screen had to be added to display graphics along with a cassette player to run applications. ZX Spectrum Servicing Manual, 1984, ftp://ftp.worldofspectrum.org/pub/sinclair/technical-docs/ZXSpectrum48K_ServiceManual.pdf. The ZX Spectrum succeeded the earlier Sinclair computers, the ZX80 and ZX81, which came as homebuilt kits and were mainly for enthusiasts not beginners. See also Thomas Lean. 2014. 'Inside a day you'll be talking to it like an old friend': The making and remaking of Sinclair personal computing in 1980s Britain. In *Hacking Europe. From computer cultures to demoscenes*, ed. Gerard Alberts and Ruth Oldenziel, 49–71. New York: Springer.

[8] By 1982, an estimated 621,000 home computers were in use in the USA. Gregory S. Blundell. 1983. Personal computers in the eighties. *BYTE*, January, 166–182. This situation is often described as "micro moved from a restricted hobbyist audience to become a mainstream consumer electronic:" Leslie Haddon. 1990. Researching gender and home computers. In *Technology and everyday life: Trajectories and transformations*, ed. Knut Sørensen and Anne-Jorn Berg, 89–108. Trondheim: University of Trondheim. See also: Scott Cohen. 1984. *Zap! The rise and fall of Atari*. New York: McGraw Hill; Lewis Kornfeld. 1997. *To catch a mouse make a noise like a cheese*. Irving: The Summit Publishing Group; and Brian Bagnall. 2005. *On the edge: The spectacular rise and fall of Commodore*. Winnipeg: Variant Press.

[9] Thomas Lean. 2008. '*The making of the micro': Producers, mediators, users and the development of popular micro-computing in Britain (1980–1989)*. PhD thesis, University of Manchester; Frank Veraart. 2008a. Basicode: Co-producing a microcomputer esperanto. *History and Technology* 28: 129–147. There are also corporate, amateur, or journalistic histories of individual computer production companies: Ian Adamson, and Richard Kennedy. 1986. *Sinclair and the sunrise technology: The deconstruction of a myth*. Harmondsworth: Penguin; Bagnall, *On the edge*; Rodney Dale. 1985. *The Sinclair story*. London: Duckworth; David Thomas. 1991. *Alan Sugar: The Amstrad story*. London: Pan Books; Michael S. Tomczyk. 1984. *The home computer wars: An insider's account of Commodore and Jack Tramiel*. Greensboro: Compute! Publications; Michael Moritz. 1984. *The little kingdom: The private story of Apple computer*. New York: W. Morrow.

In Greece, as in other European countries, home computers soon gained a broader audience. They were tailored to the country's specific social, economic, and cultural characteristics, not just fulfilling the role of "entry level" machine before users could advance to "normal" personal computers (IBM PC compatibles) but becoming a distinctive general-purpose machine in their own right. Although associating personal computers with IBM PC compatibles and the perception of home computers mainly as game machines, such notions are rather restrictive and fail to recognize local aspects.[10] In Greece, their use found more general commercial applications. They were seen as an affordable alternative to IBM PC compatibles. Home computers found a place between the costly and complex mainframes of large companies and personal computers with a more professional orientation like the IBM PC. Users and the media saw home computers as the machines for ordinary, everyday users that, according to the 1960s slogan, "brought power to the people." Computer games were part and parcel of the broader cultural and social context that deserves historical research.[11] This chapter argues that home computers had a major impact on the adoption of computer technology in many aspects of Greek social life in small- and medium-sized firms like shops and households, which constituted in Greece (as they still do) the backbone of the economy.[12] As scholarship shows, we cannot understand technology separate from its users.[13] Seen in this light, studying amateur users becomes extremely relevant and important.[14]

Communities of amateur computer hobbyists developed during the 1970s along with rapid computer networking during the 1980s and 1990s, having emerged from

[10] As Aristotle Tympas has shown, one main premise of this historiography is the notion that the computer of the past decades is a global machine, invented in the USA, and transferred to the rest of the world, where it can be used by different people in the same way: Aristotle Tympas. 2006. Electronic era technologies, the European experience: Historiographical omissions and ambitions. In *Tensions of Europe network second plenary conference proceedings*, ed. Johan Schot, et al., Lappeenranta, Finland (CD-ROM).

[11] F. Mäyrä. 2002. Introduction: All your [base are] belong to us. In *Computer games and digital cultures conference proceedings studies in information sciences*, 5–8. Tampere: Tampere University Press. For their dynamic in Scandinavia, Petri Saarikoski. 2004. *Koneen lumo. Mikrotietokoneharrastus Suomessa 1970-luvulta 1990-luvun puoliväliin* [The Lure of the machine. The personal computer interest in Finland from the 1970s to the mid-1990s]. Nykykulttuurin tutkimuskeskuksen julkaisuja 83. Jyväskylä: Jyväskylän yliopisto.

[12] Even in 2010, out of a total of 4.4 million workers, 1.3 million are employed in companies with fewer than 20 employees: Ηλίας Γεωργάκης. 2010. Μείωση εισφορών έως 25%. *TA NEA*, December 21. http://www.tanea.gr/default.asp?pid=2&ct=3&artid=4609892. Accessed 2010.

[13] David Edgerton. 2006. *The shock of the old: Technology and global history since 1900*. London: Profile Books; Nelly Oudshoorn, and Trevor J. Pinch (eds.). 2003. *How users matter: The co-construction of users and technology*. Cambridge, MA/London: MIT Press; Steve Woolgar. 1991. Configuring the user: The case of usability trials. In *A sociology of monsters: Essays on power, technology and domination*, ed. John Law, 58–100. London/New York: Routledge.

[14] Sherry Turkle. 1984. *The second self: Computers and the human spirit*. New York: Simon & Schuster; Jörgen Nissen. 1993. *Pojkarna vid datorn: Unga entusiaster i datateknikens värld* [Boys in front of computers. Young enthusiasts in the world of computer technology]. PhD thesis, Lynköping Universitet.

the 1960s counterculture movement.[15] The social movement opposed the way computers were used by military and large corporations, which sought to centralize and concentrate power. In opposition, countercultural movements like the pacifist movements, anti-war activism, and lifestyle experimentation with drugs such as LSD sought to shift the use of computers to radically different purposes. For one, these movements focused on redistributing political power through ordinary citizens' use of computers to develop better living conditions. Countercultural movements fostered alternative cultural beliefs about computers and their use, which profoundly shaped the aspirations of the first enthusiasts and creators of the personal computer. Although highlighting the cultural dimensions of forming a technological framework, the current scholarship fails to describe how countries like Greece adopted home computer technology, where cultural conditions differed considerably and applications depended on local circumstances.[16]

I argue that we can substitute the concept of countercultures with an "open culture" which, in the case of Greece, was created by the use of home computers and bolstered by the technical structure of the home computer, but mostly by magazines and computer shops. The open culture described how the home computer "ought" to be used so the user could gain maximum benefit within a socioeconomic environment as well as educational opportunities, with minimum investments in computer technology. Proponents also considered the novel machines as means of achieving a better and modern society. Such a society could be achieved more readily by integrating Greece in the socio-technical framework of the early 1980s than by any ideology of democratization.

In this context, a software sharing culture emerged. In the early 1980s, users in Greece were perceived to be entitled to make their own copies of software and to distribute them at will. A user who acted in this way was considered to be utilizing the computer to its best potential – proudly carrying the title of hacker. In existing literature, the term hacker is usually applied to unconventional users of computer technology who operate beyond formal academic and professional environments. According to some studies, significant developments in computer technology, especially in software during the 1970s and 1980s, were attributed to the activity of hackers.[17] Some see hackers as social outcasts and unprofessional developers, while others consider them people of courage, visionaries, whose activities largely

[15] Fred Turner. 2006. *From counterculture to cyberculture: Stewart Brand, the Whole Earth Network, and the rise of digital utopianism*. Chicago: University of Chicago Press; Markoff, *What the dormouse said*.

[16] Robbie Guerreiro-Wilson, Lars Heide, Matthias Kipping, Cecilia Pahlberg, Adrienne van den Bogaard, and Aristotle Tympas. 2004. Information systems and technology in organizations and society (ISTOS): Review essay. In *Tensions of Europe. Network first plenary conference proceedings*, ed. Johan Schot, et al., Budapest, Hungary (CD-ROM). [Also accessible as: *Tensions of Europe Working Paper* http://www.tensionsofeurope.eu/www/en/files/get/Review_IT_Guerreiro.pdf. Accessed 30 Jan 2014]; Aristotle Tympas, Foteini Tsaglioti, and Theodore Lekkas. 2008. Universal machines vs. national languages: Computerization as production of new localities. Paper presented at the international conference 'Technologies of Globalization', Darmstadt.

[17] Levy, *Hackers*.

determined the way billions of people came to use personal computers.[18] In the latter interpretation, the hackers' culture represents the desire to release information from the confines of power structures like big companies and the army.[19]

Taking Greece as my example, I question whether the hacker only represents the "advanced" user who is seeking to acquire a thorough working knowledge of his/her computer and take advantage of its full potential – a user who copies software by cracking protection methods and alters codes to adapt the software to his needs for entertainment or work. Users involved in altering codes mostly applied this to cracking games, a process still valued in extending the lifetime of an application or acting as an informal research and development tool.[20] The Greek situation resembles the widespread "demoscene culture." Even though we cannot confirm contact with corresponding communities in Europe, we can see similarities in terms of cracking programs, while different in terms of their setup and objectives.[21] The major difference was perhaps that the computer scene was not a subculture, but the dominant culture of 1980s Greece. In a historiographical essay, historian of technology Aristotle Tympas has gone so far as to suggest that "for many actors of the early Greek PC computing scene (during the late 1980s), piracy was a functional prerequisite for developing computing in the country."[22]

This last point brings us to the question of software piracy, which today is considered an illegal act. Perpetrators face severe punishment.[23] Historians of computing have not sufficiently addressed piracy. This issue is monopolized by the social, legal, and economic sciences, leaning towards a stereotypical image of software piracy as primarily an economic phenomenon related to the purchase cost of software or issues concerning intellectual property rights and their effective protection.[24]

---

[18] McKenzie Wark. 2004. *A hacker manifesto*. Cambridge, MA: Harvard University Press.

[19] Douglas Thomas. 2002. *Hacker culture*. Minneapolis: University of Minnesota Press.

[20] O. Sotamaa. 2005. Creative user-centred design practices: Lessons from game cultures. In *Everyday innovators: Researching the role of users in shaping ICTs*, ed. Leslie Haddon, et al., 104–116. Dordrecht: Springer.

[21] Tamás Polgár. 2005. *Freax. The brief history of the demoscene*, vol. 1. Winnenden: CSW Verlag; Markku Reunanen, and Antti Silvast. 2009. Demoscene platforms: A case study on the adoption of home computers. In *History of Nordic computing 2*, IFIP advances in information and communication technology, ed. John Impagliazzo, Timo Järvi, and Petri Paju, 289–301. Berlin: Springer; L. Tasajärvi, B. Stamnes, and M. Schustin (eds.). 2004. *Demoscene: The art of real-time*. Even Lake Studios & katastro.fi; H. Lönnblad. 1997. Kahden tietokonedemon vertaileva analyysi [A comparative study of two computer demos]. *Musiikin Suunta* 19(2): 28–34. http://www.kameli.net/demoresearch2/

[22] Tympas, Electronic era technologies.

[23] For example, see how Australian law criminalises end-user piracy through the Australia-United States Free Trade Agreement: http://www.dfat.gov.au/fta/ausfta/final-text/chapter_17.html

[24] Many articles examine the advantages of organized bodies in protecting software authors and owners, the policy and economic implications of software piracy, the legal importance of instruments for IP rights protection, copyright acts and provisions for their enforcement, copyright laws, loss of revenues in the software industry, the effect of this loss on the software market, and the ethical dimensions. Even criminological theories have been proposed, Robert Willison, and Mikko Siponen. 2008. *Software piracy: Original insights from a criminological perspective*. Paper presented at the proceedings of the annual Hawaii international conference on system sciences, Maui.

My research shows that the meaning of piracy goes beyond the financial sphere and needs to be understood in its social and historical context.[25] The Social Construction of Technology (SCOT) model emphasizes the role users and consumers play in shaping the technology of social groups and actors.[26] While producers of technology and users mutually shape each other, in the case of Greece, the designer of the artifact is absent, as the sociology of technology demands.[27] By applying theoretical and methodological approaches to the historical context of this socio-technical framework, we will show the concepts of hacker, software pirate, and home computer in a new and original approach context, just as various social groups may view the same technological product from diverse aspects.

4.2 When IBM Provided Nothing

When in 1994 RAM's editor, Theodore Spinoulas, wrote, "in countries such as Greece, as the reader might guess, IBM provided nothing," he was expressing the prevailing view in the Greek computer market. The personal computer might have been imported in several countries as a "global machine" that could meet people's general needs, but as the utilization of computers proved, the social, cultural, and, especially in Greece's case, national framework largely shaped the terms of their use.[28] Since the mid-1980s, the problem of displaying and printing Greek characters on personal computers was a key issue. Solutions were sought both through software and hardware modifications. Since the user support by major computer companies was virtually nonexistent, users took it on themselves to adapt personal computers to their needs.

The most pressing need in localizing the computer, therefore, was adapting the personal computer's operation to the Greek language so that it could respond to the specific socioeconomic and cultural environment. The most famous attempt to resolve the issue of appropriate software took place in a Greek software house,

---

[25] Donald A. MacKenzie, and Judy Wajcman (eds.). 1985. *The social shaping of technology: How the refrigerator got its hum*. Milton Keynes: Open University Press; Merritt Roe Smith, and Leo Marx (eds.). 1994. *Does technology drive history? The dilemma of technological determinism*. Boston: MIT Press; Hughie Mackay, and Gareth Gillespie. 1992. Extending the social shaping of technology approach: Ideology and appropriation. *Social Studies of Science* 22(4): 685–716.

[26] Trevor J. Pinch, and Wiebe E. Bijker. 1984. The social construction of facts and artefacts: Or how the sociology of science and the sociology of technology might benefit each other. *Social Studies of Science* 14(August): 399–441; Wiebe E. Bijker, Thomas P. Hughes, and Trevor J. Pinch (eds.). 1987. *The social construction of technological systems. New directions in the sociology and history of technology*. Cambridge, MA: MIT Press; Langdon Winner. 1993. Upon opening the black box and finding it empty: Social constructivism and the philosophy of technology. *Science Technology & Human Values* 18(3): 362–378.

[27] Paul Glennie. 1995. Consumption within historical studies. In *Acknowledging consumption: A review of new studies*, ed. Daniel Miller, 164–203. London/New York: Routledge.

[28] D. Ortiz-Arroyo, F. Rodriguez-Henriquez, and C.A. Coello. 2010. The turing-850 project: Developing a personal computer in the early 1980s in Mexico. *IEEE Annals of the History of Computing* 32(4): 60–71.

Memotek, which developed its own standard of Greek characters, known as 437. IBM later tried to establish its own standard, the 851. Because computer manufacturers treated Greece as a regional market and one of limited commercial value, the response to problem solving was severely delayed. The delayed reaction by multinational corporations to the needs of the user created a "chaotic" situation, as contemporaries called it.[29]

The gap in personal computer support, particularly regarding the proper display and printing of Greek characters, was more than a transient phenomenon. It proved the computer was not really a "global" machine with universal applications as popular rhetoric would have it. Studying its use in the Greek setting brings to light the many difficulties, conflicts, and changes that took place before the personal computer could be configured to eventually become an object used by locals. The first Greek software houses' efforts to adapt computer technology, even their very formation, owed their existence to "negotiating" the terms of usage.

Already a few years before the first software houses appeared in Greece, individual users had taken up the task of adapting the computer and its software to Greek specifications. Before they could even use their personal computer, the first users had to understand and then interfere with its operating system because the accompanying software was not adapted to the specifics of the Greek language. The first users were naturally part of a very small community that included electronics amateurs and the first computer technology enthusiasts. As the technology was limited almost exclusively to large enterprises, universities, and public bodies, the first users – like their counterparts elsewhere – saw their computers as instruments to launch society into a modern era, with better living conditions and prospects for personal development. The most enthusiastic, already having a fleeting experience with radio technology, succeeded during the late 1970s in obtaining microprocessor units by mail from mainly American companies.[30] These units featured minimum technical capabilities, but if users fitted them correctly, they could build a very basic personal computer.[31]

During the late 1970s, a few amateurs developed limited interaction with the USA and mostly the UK, through the community of Greek informatics students.

[29] "A positive step by the multinational giants 6 years later to establish a certain standard brought even greater confusion, since retailers would now have to provide their clients with two different sets of characters, the IBM standard and 437, the de facto set by then," Κ. Καράλης. 1990. Στα άδυτα της ελληνικότητας. *RAM*, April, 69.

[30] One trade magazine in Greece was *Popular Electronics*, featuring in January 1975 instructions on how to build the first "mini-computer for home use," ALTAIR 8800, http://www.swtpc.com/mholley/PopularElectronics/Jan1975/PE_Jan1975.htm. Another popular source for the hobbyist of the 1980s was the Greek magazine Τεχνική Εκλογή (est. in 1965), which featured articles on building microcomputers. In the 1970s, the same editors produced the magazine Μικρός Επιστήμονας, an edition for young readers aged 12–18. By following instructions, teenagers could fit things like a small radio receiver: http://www.phorum.gr/viewtopic.php?f=39&t=79764&start=0

[31] Computers sold as kits that could be fitted by the hobbyist were, e.g., the Altair 8800, Sinclair ZX80, Sinclair ZX81, and Acorn Atom.

Unfortunately, the Greek community could not expand nor interact with peer communities abroad, because the necessary equipment was hard to obtain due to high customs fees and the lack of alternative technological expertise and materials. When the first home computers arrived in 1980s Greece, they helped to unleash the community's potential. An extensive nucleus of users was created in fields where computer technology had not yet penetrated, like private households and small businesses. The domestication of computer technology in homes and its adoption process have been the focus of considerable international research. This culture could be established not only thanks to its material role but in the way it would form the individual characteristics of a technological object used in everyday life.

The inexpensive and simple-to-operate home computers which appeared in Greek stores during the early 1980s became a powerful tool in the hands of experienced computer amateurs.[32] As the technical characteristics were essentially restricted and the available imported expansion peripherals limited, both amateurs and the first user enthusiasts turned to the software to customize computers to their needs, thereby solving the many problems of adjustment. Characteristically, the imported British Sinclair ZX-81, one of the most popular home computers in Greece, did not supply a sound chip, obliging the user who wanted to "extract" sound from the computer to run a small software program. He would have to either write in machine code himself, purchase one from a friend or shop, or find one in the popular trade magazines (in the form of a program listing). Moreover, the ZX-81 could only display graphics in very low resolution, which could only be resolved through a small program written in machine code.

Learning how to enter a command or change lines of code in software programs did not indicate unconventional behavior or a different approach to using the computer, but rather a necessity for the user. Likewise, the Greek user of the home computer Spectravideo could not type Greek characters. The solution came in the form of a short program written in machine code, which the user had to run in order to store Greek characters. The program had to either be written by the user himself or purchased from a specialized computer store (which was unlikely). He could also buy the third issue of *Pixel* magazine, where on page 112 he could find the appropriate program listing to be typed and thus solve the problem.[33] Many typical problems of home computers could be solved in the same way, such as mapping the so-called special keys known as F-Keys. In personal computers, the solution was appropriate BIOS settings, which were relatively easy for the typical user, but home computer users had to resort once again to a small program typed in machine code. Such a program was written and submitted for publication by a Pixel reader, labeled by the

[32] In the "Home Micros Buyers Guide," *Pixel* 3(1984): 51–69, the home computers selected for presentation and comparison of their technical capabilities were Laser 200, BIT-90, TI 99/4A, TRS-80, ZX Spectrum, SORD M-5, ORIC ATMOS, DRAGON 32, ATARI 600 XL, SPECTRAVIDEO SV-318, NEWBRAIN, COMMODORE 64, LYNX, and BBC MODEL B., "Αφιέρωμα: Οδηγός αγοράς για Home Micros" [Market Guide for Home Micros].

[33] "Software," *Pixel* 3(1984): 112.

editors as "one of the few crazy pioneers that would see their name written into the first page of the home micro-computing history in Greece."[34]

One way or another, the main feature that gave home computers the competitive edge in affordability also required the user's active participation if he wanted to perform any task beyond playing games. Within the framework of adopting home computer technology, a culture of use emerged highlighting the need for experimentation to obtain the "ghost in the machine" (i.e., the software), according to a popular expression in *Pixel*.[35] The attitude of Greek users towards home computer software developed in this way right from the start and under very different conditions than in other countries. As the accompanying software was minimal or even nonexistent, the user had to develop a more active attitude towards his new computer in order to perform even the simplest of tasks, such as printing a character. A user could only manage this by experimenting with the software. As most programs were first written in machine code, users had to acquire a rudimentary knowledge of this. They also had to know some basic commands to perform key functions, such as getting a backup for a program. Increasingly commercial programs were being written in BASIC programming language, which you had to understand if you wanted to adapt these programs to your requirements. Users who managed to develop their skills in these areas acquired the coveted title of hacker, as someone able to shape the software as he sees fit. Their identity was closely associated with the act of cracking ("σπάσιμο") programs (mainly games) by changing parts of their code and copying them.

This active involvement was a result of the lack of adequate technical support, along with the technical features of the imported personal computers themselves that allowed a more unmediated relationship. The ZX-Spectrum, a very popular home computer at that time, demanded that the software was uploaded from audio tapes that many Greek households used.[36] Before floppy disks and hard drives entered the market, tapes were the primary method of data storage for home computers.[37] The audiotape was already very popular in Greece as the cheapest and most efficient way to copy and play music. It is typical that such duplication was organized and well established not only among listeners and friends, but by the music stores selling music albums and original tapes. Thus, Greeks were already intimately familiar with audio tapes as a means of copying data. Computer users considered copying tapes containing data (instead of sound) a legitimate practice.[38]

[34] "Προγράμματα από εμάς για σάς," [Programs from us to you] *Pixel* 4(1984): 86.

[35] N. Μανούσος. 1983. Γράμμα από τον Εκδότη [Letter from the Editor]. *Pixel* 1: 3.

[36] Almost 10,000 were sold until 1985, according to the most well-known computer shop of that period, PLOT, M. Νικολάου. 1985. Νίκος Λουκίδης: Ο Έλληνας 'Mr. Chips' [Nikos Loukidis: The Greek "Mr. Chips"!]. *Pixel* 15: 158.

[37] For the development of home recording and the cultural and economic significance of this technology, see David L. Morton. 2000. *Off the record: The technology and culture of sound recording in America*. New Brunswick: Rutgers University Press.

[38] Copying software tapes seems to be very common practice among Greek users of home computers at this time. Issue 17 of Pixel informs users about an adaptor that could be connected to the cassette port of Commodore and Spectrum and enable a "one to one" cassette copy. This adaptor was

Gradually, copying tapes became more systematic. According to a famous software pirate of the era, an industry of tape piracy existed in 1985, the main actors being pirates/hackers and computer shops, which either received from the hackers copied programs to sell to their customers or even hired the pirates/hackers themselves.[39] The magnitude of this phenomenon is illustrated by the characteristic statement of a Pixel editor, who wrote that pirated tapes could be found everywhere, "even in the drawers of readers' homes."[40]

At the same time, home computers were becoming more popular thanks to their users, ranging from enthusiastic amateurs to those who saw the new computer technology as a cheap and accessible way to enter the world of informatics. Already in the second issue of *Pixel*, the editor explained the dynamic: "Since the first microcomputer appeared, our world is not the same. While the use and processing of information were in the hands of the powerful, nowadays, the key to the real changes in our society can be found, at last, in the hands of everyone. For us, microcomputers are more than just a game or simple entertainment; they are the road to a better and freer world."[41] Evidently, the home computers in the case of Greece were a substitute for personal computers in a socio-technical framework eager to adopt the technological advances of Western Europe and North America but deprived of the necessary technological infrastructure to achieve them.

So far we have seen that the idea that software could (and should) be configured to enable computers to serve user need was proven during the late 1970s by amateurs' early efforts. Then, in the early 1980s, the emergence of the home computer as a consumer product released the potential of the personal computer as the most appropriate entry to the world of informatics. Yet, the software was still scarce, the support even scarcer, and problems of adjustment to the Greek language were more pressing than ever. How would these issues be settled? Only through proper shaping of the hacker culture developed through the culture of the personal computer user.

4.3 "You Can Make Your Own Version of Software"

In the first article of *Pixel*, the editor welcomed new readers, pointing out that "we all know that software is the 'ghost in the machine' of every microcomputer and the hardware alone is as useful as a car without fuel."[42] *Pixel*, the highest-circulated

---

profoundly named "Doubler" and aimed, according to the magazine, at "potential pirates," Παυλής Δημ, "Αφιέρωμα: Χριστουγεννιάτικα δώρα για Home Micros" [Christmas gifts for Home Micros] *Pixel* 17(1985): 136. The machine was sold in a popular computer shop at the time in the heart of Athens.

[39] Χ. Κυριακός. 1986a. Οι Hackers αποκαλύπτουν [Hackers reveal]. *Pixel* 27: 76–81.

[40] Χ. Κυριακός. 1986b. Οι πειρατές του software [Software pirates]. *Pixel* 21: 55.

[41] Γ. Καραιωσηφόγλου. 1984. Τα νέα του *Pixel* [Pixel's news]. *Pixel* 2: 5. Similarly, Skinner supports that the widespread acceptance of home microcomputing should be understood in a wider context of an information revolution: David Ian Skinner. 1992. *Technology, consumption and the future: The experience of home computing*. PhD thesis, Brunel University.

[42] Μανούσος, Γράμμα από τον Εκδότη.

computer magazine in Greece during the 1980s, published articles emphasizing the use and study of computer software rather than hardware, which the editors considered non-modifiable, promoting a perception of the computer as a black box. Readers, personal computer amateurs for the most part, but also enthusiasts from universities and the private sector, soon became familiar with the idea that software is what makes the computer what it is. Therefore users must be personally involved in the search or design of the best possible software.

Because the available software was expensive and imported in small quantities, users quickly turned to copying commercial programs. *Pixel* had provided the technical knowledge on how to copy software tapes since its first issue. Specifically, in the third issue in August 1984, a new column appeared entitled "Interferences" ("Επεμβάσεις") providing users with instructions for cracking games like Manic Miner for the ZX-Spectrum[43] (Fig. 4.2). The 1984 article first taught the user step by step what keys to press and in what order to "unlock" the game and gain access to all levels, before instructing users to "create their own version of Manic Miner."[44]

The expression "your own version" meant users could copy the software from an original tape to a blank cartridge, while also creating a new version, modified so that the user could achieve "infinite lives" or access any level of play. It was relatively easy to do, but required a basic understanding of programming. *Pixel* provided technical knowledge not available elsewhere: special training (private or public) did not exist for personal computers until the mid-1980s when the first computer schools appeared, as advertisements in the magazine show. Computer magazines and shops thus took on the role of technically educating users and creating the user culture. Readers learned how to crack and copy a program by first typing a program listing, as shown in Fig. 4.2.

"Listings" refer to the way software was distributed in printed form, such as in magazines or books, allowing readers to enter the printed sets of orders into the computer manually and then run these commands or save them to a magnetic medium (e.g., tape) for later use. Program listings were a very effective way of sharing home computer software during the first half of the 1980s. Greek users considered storing data in printed form reliable, and as the programs were relatively short, program listings were very popular. For example, the ZX-Spectrum user had to type the listing printed in Pixel, check it for errors, and then run it. After that, the user loaded the original game from the tape until a message appeared ("NEW TAPE"). Next, the user placed the empty cartridge in the cassette recorder to record "his own game," as contemporaries called it. Copying a program from a cassette tape was thus very similar to modifying the software (hacking): copying prompted the user to run the appropriate program before "tricking" the computer. The procedure was called "cracking" ("σπάσιμο"); the user who applied the technique was a "pirate" or "hacker."

In the Greek socio-technical context of the early 1980s, the act of copying programs and adapting them to user needs contributed to the continued and successful use of computers. The software protection methods could be bypassed through the

---

[43] N. Τσουάνας. 1984. Σπάστε το Manic Miner [Break Manic Miner]. *Pixel* 3: 16.

[44] Ibid.

ΕΠΕΜΒΑΣΕΙΣ

Τοποθετήστε τώρα στο κασσετόφωνο μια καινούργια κασέτα για να γράψετε σε αυτή τη δική σας version Manic Miner.

Πιέστε τα πλήκτρα της εγγραφής στο κασετόφωνο και μετά ένα τυχαίο πλήκτρο του υπολογιστή. Το πρόγραμμα τώρα γράφεται στην κασέτα.

Μετά από λίγα δευτερόλεπτα, θα πρέπει να ξαναπιέσετε ένα τυχαίο πλήκτρο του υπολογιστή για να μπορέσει να γραφτεί και το δεύτερο κομμάτι του προγράμματος. Όταν εμφανισθεί το μήνυμα "O.K." σταματήστε το κασετόφωνο.

Η κασέτα που τώρα γράψατε, περιέχει τη δική σας πρωτότυπη εγγραφή. Στη συνέχεια, δεν έχετε παρά να καθαρίσετε τη μνήμη του υπολογιστή σας, διακόπτοντας την τροφοδοσία του, και να φορτώσετε όλο το πρόγραμμα της κασέτας, δίνοντας την εντολή:

LOAD "MANICMINER" ή LOAD""

Όταν τελειώσει το φόρτωμα, θα σας ζητηθεί από τον υπολογιστή να πιέσετε το "y" ή το "n" για την επιλογή "άπειρες ζωές". Αν πιέσετε το πλήκτρο "y", θα ξεκινήσει το παιχνίδι κανονικά και θα διαπιστώσετε ότι δεν ελαττώνονται καθόλου τα ανθρωπάκια, κάθε φορά που αποτυγχάνετε σε κάποια προσπάθεια.

Αν πιέσετε το πλήκτρο "n", τότε θα πρέπει στη συνέχεια να απαντήσετε στην ερώτηση "πόσες ζωές", με έναν αριθμό από το 1 έως το 16, και φυσικά μετά το ENTER.

Την πρώτη φορά συνιστάται να δώσετε σαν αριθμό το 16, οπότε θα παρατηρήσετε να εμφανίζεται στο κάτω μέρος της οθόνης μια ολόκληρη διμοιρία από ανθρωπάκια.

LISTING 1

```
  1 REM ⁂ NIKOS TSOYANAS ⁂
  2 REM ⁂ **** 1984 **** ⁂
 10 CLEAR 30000
 15 CLS : PRINT AT 10,5;"LOAD M
ANIC MINER"
 20 LOAD "MM2"CODE
120 CLS : PRINT AT 10,10;"NEW T
APE"
130 SAVE "MANICMINER" LINE 200
140 SAVE "N.T."CODE 32768,32768
150 CLS : PRINT AT 10,12; FLASH
 1; BRIGHT 1;"O.K.": PAUSE 1000:
 BEEP 2,25
160 STOP
200 CLEAR 30000
205 PRINT AT 10,12; BRIGHT 1;"M
ANICMINER";AT 14,11; BRIGHT 1; F
LASH 1;"PLEASE WAIT": LOAD ""COD
E
210 CLS : PRINT AT 4,2;" APEIRE
S ZOES ? "; FLASH 1; BRIGHT 1;"
Y/N "
220 IF INKEY$="Y" OR INKEY$="y"
 THEN GO TO 290
230 IF INKEY$="N" OR INKEY$="n"
 THEN GO TO 250
240 BEEP .1,20: GO TO 220
250 CLS : INPUT "POSES ZOES ?
1-16 ";n
260 IF n<1 OR n>16 THEN BEEP 2,
-15: GO TO 250
270 POKE 34269,n-1
280 GO TO 300
290 POKE 35136,0
300 PRINT USR 33792
```

ΔΕΥΤΕΡΗ VERSION

Αν η version του Manic Miner που μόλις φτιάξατε, δεν σας ικανοποιεί αρκετά, σας δίνουμε μιαν άλλη παραλλαγή της στο πρόγραμμα του Listing-2.

Για το πρόγραμμα αυτό, θα πρέπει να ακολουθήσετε την ίδια διαδικασία με το πρόγραμμα του Listing-1. Η διαφορά σε αυτή τη version είναι ότι το πρόγραμμα εδώ δίνει μόνιμα άπειρες ζωές, αλλά και τη δυνατότητα να ξεκινήσετε από την πίστα που θα θελήσετε εσείς.

Στο πρόγραμμα αυτό, θα πρέπει να ξεκινήσετε το παιχνίδι, πριν έλθει στην κατάσταση για το demonstration. Στην παραλλαγή αυτή, θα πρέπει να αποφύγετε να κάνετε BREAK στο πρόγραμμα.

ΕΠΕΜΒΑΣΗ ΣΤΟ ΙΔΙΟ ΤΟ ΠΑΙΧΝΙΔΙ

Αν και πάλι δεν είσαστε ικανοποιημένοι, γιατί δεν αλλάζετε την ίδια τη δομή του παιχνιδιού; Μπορείτε να κάνετε τις πίστες ευκολότερες ή δυσκολότερες. Για τον λόγο αυτό, θα πρέπει να διαθέτετε ένα πρόγραμμα Disassembler (γι'αυτούς που δεν έχουν, υπάρχει κάποιο σχετικό πρόγραμμα σε αυτό το τεύχος του PIXEL).

Το Manic Miner έχει την εξής δομή. Τα σχέδια της πρώτης πίστας ξεκινούν από τη διεύθυνση 8000 (δεκαεξαδική). Η κάθε πίστα καταλαμβάνει 1K, περίπου, μνήμης.

Σαν παράδειγμα για τις αλλαγές, σας δίνουμε μια μικρή τροποποίηση της πρώτης πίστας. Φορτώστε κανονικά το πρόγραμμα που δημιουργήσατε, την πρώτη version, με την βοήθεια του Listing-1. Στην ερώτηση "Άπειρες ζωές;", κάνετε BREAK. Δώστε τότε σαν εντολή άμεσης εκτέλεσης την:

POKE 45207,0:POKE 45211,0:POKE 45219,68:POKE 45333,0:POKE 45452,0 και φυσικά ENTER

Κατόπιν δίνετε την εντολή GOTO 210 και θα δείτε τις μικρές ➤

17

Fig. 4.2 Users and Programming. The publication of program listings was a main function of home microcomputer magazines during the 1980s in Greece as elsewhere. A program listing was a printout that listed in the correct sequence the instructions, routines, and other contents of a program for a home microcomputer. In an era of expensive, inaccessible, imported software, program listings included in magazines or books were a very popular method of distribution for software applications. At the same time, the typing of the commands listed was considered the first step toward programming, as a BASIC program listing was easy to read and understand. Users preferred the program listings designed to "crack" and copy games. Such a program listing for the Manic-Miner game is pictured here. Source: *Pixel* 3(1984): 17

program listings in *Pixel*, as well as by a more manual procedure which the magazine also published. The manual process involved the "headerless" loading of a computer program from tape. In order for a home computer to load a program, the computer should be told the starting address and the length of the load along with its type. This information was contained in the so-called header, which preceded the program and was replaced by a short machine code which put information into the appropriate computer registers and then called the routine in the ROM that performed the loading. Through the process of copying, the user was motivated substantially towards a personal involvement with his home computer, writing commands, manipulating existing code segments, and correcting code segments reproduced incorrectly.

Considered in that context, the process had no relevance to the current debate on piracy and user involvement as users were not in a position to download onto their computer already copied software or a specific program to unlock it (e.g., a key generator). If users opted against buying a copied program available only in the few places that supplied it, they had to experiment on their computers, exploring possibilities, gaining valuable experience, and ultimately forming a specific culture for its overall use. In a way, after purchase, software belonged to the home computer owner rather than to the creator, or so the current debate on piracy claims. At the time, software was still relatively rare and expensive. Home computers users believed that using, copying, and sharing inexpensive and free software was within their rights because the investment in the computer alone was already significant. A key element of this user culture developing in the early 1980s was the perception that users could interfere with the program code in order to achieve some of their culture's terms.

Amateurs' personal involvement with rudimentary programming led, in addition, to the effort of learning dialects of the BASIC programming language, some knowledge of which was essential for using home computers at the time. Many users spent hours typing in program listings they found in *Pixel* or attempted to build their own software. They addressed the adaptation problems or responded to the magazine's various "challenges."[45] One very popular pastime was writing program listings designed to circumvent mechanisms that locked the software. Forms containing program listings were sent in by readers to *Pixel* each month, in particular to the regular column "Interventions." Typically, every program published stated clearly both the contributor's name and home address, since the publication of their work was regarded as a great achievement by the user community and should be demonstrated accordingly.[46]

---

[45] By the 2nd issue, readers were encouraged to submit their programs for 1,000 drachmas. "Προγράμματα από εμάς για εσάς" [Programs from us to you], *Pixel* 4(1984): 86. The magazine also announced a competition for the best program listings, the three winners receiving 5,000 drachmas each, a respectable sum for that time. "HINTS & TIPS", *Pixel* 25(1986), 44–45.

[46] Indicatively, in the 15th issue of Pixel, the program written by Mr. Giorgos Zotos of Ag. Paraskeyi was published with compliments for his effort, N. Τσουάνας. 1985. Επεμβάσεις: Ξεκλειδώστε το Pole Position [Interferences: Unlock pole position]. *Pixel* 15: 134.

Because copying was not considered illegal in the standard context of the term, many amateurs began to advertise their business in journals. In a characteristic advertisement in *Pixel* in 1985, one reader announced he possessed and could make available across Greece a software package ("CRASHER") consisting of three separate utilities with which the ordinary user could crack the Amstrad computer and make copies of any program.[47] Significantly, the advertiser provided personal information, such as his home phone number. From 1985 to 1987, *Pixel* published hundreds of advertisements by amateurs, mostly students, who offered thousands of copied programs that could be purchased by personal appointment scheduled through the phone. Many hackers went as far as printing business cards, directly stating their occupation, believing it was a perfectly decent profession.[48] Lists of games and programs were also circulated by hand, allowing the prospective buyer to consider his choices. A scheduled appointment between hacker and client followed, usually within the euphemistically named Greek "Silicon Valley" Stournari Street and the surrounding area in downtown Athens, where most computer shops were located. The advertising declined when readers pointed out that this practice was prosecuted abroad and that Greek authorities would probably take similar measures to address the problem.

Pixel's editors referred to all amateur users who either wrote their own programs for cracking software or simply typed the program listings published in the magazine as "hackers." In June 1986, the magazine published a new feature under the heading "Hackers Column." Two pages of instructions guided the user through the process of overriding the software protection mechanisms and then creating an exact copy of the original program (minus initial protection). This aimed to instruct users in specific techniques that would "transform them into real hackers."[49] This particular culture emerged as a result of users' demand for a more active participation in computer technology than simply typing program listings, as the first step for any aspiring hacker was the "knowledge of how a commercial program can be copied."[50] Characteristically, the 14th issue presented the "Crasher" software, which removed such protections, informing readers they could obtain it for 1,900 drachmas through specific computer stores, an application considered essential in any hacker's arsenal.[51]

The identity of the "hacker" appeared to be almost identical to the pirate, as the cracking of software implied its replication. For this reason, the press did not always distinguish between both terms. The study of publications, however, indicates that the term hacker had a wider use and sounded more positive. It corresponded to the image of the user who had stepped beyond the amateur level and possessed advanced technical knowledge, obtained mainly through personal involvement with the home computer. The hacker, therefore, was neither a renegade developer nor an idealist,

[47] *Pixel* 13(1985): 96.

[48] Κυριακός, Οι Hackers αποκαλύπτουν.

[49] Φ. Γεωργιάδης. 1986a. Εισαγωγή στο Hacking [Introduction to hacking]. *Pixel* 23: 103.

[50] Ibid.

[51] ΕλληνικήΑγορά [Greek market]. *Pixel* 14: 24.

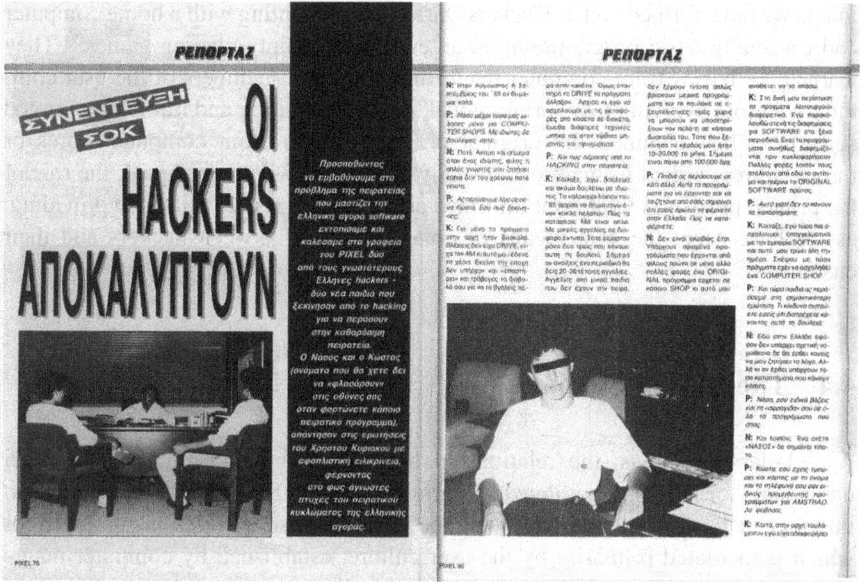
ΡΕΠΟΡΤΑΖ

ΣΥΝΕΝΤΕΥΞΗ ΣΟΚ

ΟΙ HACKERS ΑΠΟΚΑΛΥΠΤΟΥΝ

Προσπαθώντας να εμβαθύνουμε στο πρόβλημα της πειρατείας που μαστίζει την ελληνική αγορά software εντοπίσαμε και καλέσαμε στα γραφεία του PIXEL δύο από τους γνωστότερους Έλληνες hackers - δύο νέα παιδιά που ξεκίνησαν από το hacking για να περάσουν στην καθαρόαιμη πειρατεία. Ο Νάσος και ο Κώστας (ονόματα που θα 'χετε δει να «φλασάρουν» στις οθόνες σας όταν φορτώνετε κάποιο πειρατικό πρόγραμμα), απάντησαν στις ερωτήσεις του Χρήστου Κυριακού με αφοπλιστική ειλικρίνεια, φέρνοντας στο φως άγνωστες πτυχές του πειρατικού κυκλώματος της ελληνικής αγοράς.

ΡΕΠΟΡΤΑΖ

PIXEL 76 PIXEL 80

Fig. 4.3 Celebrating Cracking. The practices of "hacking" and "cracking" were very popular among home microcomputer users in Greece during the 1980s. At the time, the copying and modification of software were accepted practices. In Greece, "hackers" were celebrated as "advanced users" who knew how to take full advantage of computers' technical capabilities. Until 1987, hackers' identity was considered in a positive light and their practices perfectly legal. The publication of an interview with two known hackers of that time in *Pixel* did not surprise anyone. Source: *Pixel* 27 (1986): 76, 80

images generally portrayed by international histories of computing. In Greece, he was more like an advanced user who could crack the protection of a program and examine its programming properties, change elements of its code, and copy it before selling on to a third party for a certain price or use it himself according to his needs. Ultimately he was the one who could solve issues such as the adaptation of home computer software to the needs of the Greek user community, like "getting Greek characters in an English text editor or installing Greek on CP/M."[52]

The Greek socio-technical environment created this identity of the hacker and of course legitimized it, resulting in the magazine hosting an interview with two hackers. In this case too, it is clear that the term hacker and pirate are interchangeable, as in this interview entitled "The Hackers Reveal," the guests were two famous software pirates, Costas and Nassos, aged 17[53] (Fig. 4.3). After attending school, they had become professional software pirates, copying software either on behalf of popular computer stores or as freelancers. Both these hackers/pirates confirm the

[52] Γεωργιάδης, Εισαγωγή στο Hacking.

[53] Κυριακός, Οι Hackers αποκαλύπτουν.

image we have formed so far. Hackers started experimenting with a home computer and especially basic programming at an early age, mainly playing games.[54] They learned the basics from computer magazines and other members of the user community before evolving to a "professional" level by creating and trafficking pirated software. They obtained the original programs either from computer stores or through direct orders from abroad, usually the United Kingdom. Again, the role of the printed press was vital, as it informed about new releases, while also providing, as we have seen, the best means of communication between hackers and their customers.[55]

4.4 The Role of Mediators

As scholarship shows, the relationship between user and technology is never unmediated or pure but facilitated by various factors.[56] Between the manufacturer/importer of household computers and the consumer/user, a relationship develops which is mediated primarily by the user culture, established by computer magazines and computer stores. As our research demonstrates, magazines such as Pixel and computer stores were important social actors that significantly affected the way the technology of personal computers was adopted and eventually used by people.

In the early 1980s, the main Greek computer magazines not only in terms of circulation and readership but also influence were *Computers for All* (Computer για όλους), *RAM,* and *Pixel*.[57] All three magazines appeared at a time when the Greek community of users had reached such a critical size that it sought information on current developments and guidelines for the proper and effective use of computers. The first magazine, *Computers for All,* was published in January 1983 and it is still in circulation, despite having lost its initial momentum. The editors wrote in the first issue that the aim was "to make computers more accessible to all. One of its key themes was none other than answering: What is, in fact, a computer?"[58]

A few months later, in October 1983, a supplement appeared in *Computers for All* for home computer users. Until then, the amateur user could find the more popular

---

[54] For the significance of the relationship between young males, the main users of home micros, and the game's consumers, see Haddon, Researching gender and home computers.

[55] Κυριακός, Οι Hackers αποκαλύπτουν.

[56] According to the Actor-Network Theory, social "things" need to be constantly built or remodeled through complex correlations with mediators. That is, there is no specific and consolidated framework for the relationship between the technical and the social. Bruno Latour. 2005. *Reassembling the social: An introduction to actor-network-theory*. Oxford: Oxford University Press.

[57] For an example of using computer magazines as historical source, see Frank Veraart. 2008c. *Vormgevers van Persoonlijk Computergebruik: De ontwikkeling van computers voor kleingebruikers in Nederland 1970–1990*. PhD thesis, TU Eindhoven.

[58] http://www.cgomag.gr/firstissue.asp

trade magazines such as Byte and a few other English magazines in computer stores or specialist press kiosks in downtown Athens, but the Greek technical press was not in close or constant touch with international developments. The first critical step was founding the Compupress Company in 1982, whose objective was to publish information on new technologies. Between its two major titles, *Computers for All* was mainly aimed at users of IBM PC compatibles and *Pixel* (initially an insert) at home computer users. Soon the little sibling would surpass its bigger brother in circulation.

Pixel initially addressed the limited community of home computer users, publishing almost exclusively program listings and game applications. As the community gradually grew, *Pixel* became an autonomous monthly magazine for the typical home user in 1984, establishing a readership of over 30,000 in the 1980s. As the editor pointed out in its first issue, the magazine reflects the need of a growing number of amateurs involved with home computers to gain access to new programs. A survey published in the fifth issue confirmed the need. The focal point was the demand for free and, at the same time, open software.[59] The term "open" meant software whose code users could change and was not subject to copyright limitations. The most striking examples of open programs at the time were program listings. The software shared in this way was generally simpler and slower than programs written in Assembly, but it became very successful in the 1980s as the first form of programming for hobbyists.[60] For many users, indeed, the first attempts at programming in simple languages on their home microcomputers and submitting these programs for publication to *Pixel* led to professional activity and opened the way to careers in the computer industry. Reader participation provided particularly important feedback and users' efforts were rewarded, sometimes with an author's job on the magazine. *Pixel* published hundreds of program listings by the end of the decade, when the software became more complex and the capacity for storing media greatly increased. But for nearly a half decade, readers continued to use Pixel's program listings to run new applications and experiment with programming on home computers.

Through the emphasis on software, *Pixel* significantly changed the way computer technology was presented by the press, shifting the focus from hardware (the "machine") to software (the "ghost in the machine"). By publishing program listings, the magazine also facilitated the first step many novices took in programming their home computers, debugging, for instance, the code written by others. This was necessary as the program listings in *Pixel* often had typographical errors, and before the program could run, the user had to experiment with different commands in order to find each mistake and correct it.[61] This was a time-consuming process that required great effort on the part of the user and an exhaustive investigation of the code. The process of typing program listings, correcting possible errors, running applications, writing

[59] Μανούσος, Γράμμα από τον Εκδότη.

[60] For example, the 'Sinclair Programs' magazine published 582 listings from 1982–85. For a complete list, see http://www.users.globalnet.co.uk/~jg27paw4/type-ins/sincprog/sp_name8.htm

[61] See, for example, a mistake in a competition question for submitting the right answer "Και τώρα μπλέξαμε!...," [And now we are in trouble!], *Pixel* 17(1985): 64.

new programs, submitting them to Pixel, or recording new tapes and sharing them with other users or computer stores formed a kind of "circle of life" in software use that instantly summed up quite convincingly the use of computer technology in home computers.

In Greece, the program listings in *Pixel* were not only for games but also included applications one could call "serious." For example, one of the first listings was written for a Word Processor in Basic for the ZX-81 home computer (Fig. 4.4). Although home computers were often considered as complete game consoles, they were often used for tasks such as word processing or filing and calendar scheduling. Thus personal computers soon found their way into small businesses where they were used to perform basic tasks. One author in Pixel considered such an application a wonderful example of why domestic computers were not mere game consoles, but "real" personal computers.[62]

Pixel readers might find listings such as utilities and other, light, business-like applications, which could, under certain conditions, meet the basic needs of micro-business. In response, small software houses and computer stores began to create and market software for the most popular home computers. The magazine's fifth issue had an application that enabled small businesses to manage their warehouse and stock. It was produced by the authorized dealer of Spectravideo in Greece, Elea Ltd., available for free to the users of this home computer.[63] Other popular applications included databases, through which users could organize and manage data. Pixel published several databases in the form of listings. The 19th issue launched a series of articles on the creation of databases by the users themselves.[64]

In its second issue (May–June 1984), *Pixel* initiated a reconstruction of the Greek community of home computer users by setting up a computer club, where amateur users could share knowledge and ideas, helping each other solve the problems they faced. Scholars argue that the institution of computer clubs significantly contributed to the rise and spread of home computers, especially in Britain.[65] But while the British computer clubs were experiencing significant growth at local, national, and academic level, in Greece only a few loose social networks existed without a

---

[62] Μ. Μανδρινός. 1983. Προγράμματα για τον ZX-81 [Programs for **ZX** -81]. *Pixel* 1: 12.

[63] Προγράμματα για Όλους [Programs for all]. *Pixel* 5(1984): 109.

[64] Βάσεις Δεδομένων [Databases]. *Pixel* 19(1986): 114–125.

[65] Leslie G. Haddon. 1988b. *The roots and early history of the British home computer market: Origins of the masculine micro*. PhD thesis, University of London; Skinner, *Technology, consumption and the future*; Leslie Haddon. 1992. Explaining ICT consumption: The case of the home computer. In *Consuming technologies: Media and information in domestic spaces*, ed. R. Silverstone and E. Hirsch, 82–96. London: Routledge; Tove Hapnes. 1996. Not in their machines: How hackers transform computers into subcultural artifacts. In *Making technologies our own? Domesticating technology into everyday life*, ed. Merete Lie and Knut H. Sørensen, 121–150. Oslo/Stockholm/Copenhagen/Oxford/Boston: Scandinavian University Press; Petri Saarikoski. 2005. Club activity in the early phases of microcomputing in Finland. In *History of Nordic computing*, ed. Janis Bubenko, John Impagliazzo, and Arne Sølvberg, 277–287. Berlin: Springer. J. Sumner. 2003. *The mighty microcosm: Home computers and user identity in Britain, 1980–90*. Paper presented to the annual meeting of the Society for the History of Technology, Atlanta, GA, Oct 2003.

ΕΠΕΞΕΡΓΑΣΙΑ ΚΕΙΜΕΝΟΥ

Είναι γνωστά σε όλους μας τα μειονεκτήματα που έχει η γραφομηχανή στο γράψιμο κάποιου κειμένου. Αν γίνει κάποιο λάθος ή παραληφθεί κάποιο γράμμα ή λέξη, είσαι αναγκασμένος να ξαναγράψεις τα κείμενα από την αρχή, κάτι που συνεπάγεται χάσιμο πολύτιμου χρόνου. Άλλο ένα μειονέκτημα της γραφομηχανής είναι ότι μας δίνει μόνο ένα αντίτυπο του κειμένου και έτσι στην περίπτωση που χρειαζόμαστε και άλλα αντίτυπα (δεν είναι λύση η φωτοτυπία) πρέπει να καθίσουμε να γράψουμε το κείμενο πάλι και πάλι απ' την αρχή.

Τα προβλήματα αυτά είχαν σαν φυσιολογική συνέπεια με την εξάπλωση των υπολογιστών να οδηγηθούν οι περισσότερες επιχειρήσεις στην λύση των κομπιούτερ (που εφοδιασμένοι με ισχυρά προγράμματα) έχουν τη δυνατότητα επεξεργασίας κειμένου.

Ένα πρόγραμμα που μπορεί κάλλιστα να μετατρέψει τον ZX-81 σας σε ένα WORD PROCESSOR είναι αυτό που σας παρουσιάζουμε. Το πρόγραμμα είναι γραμμένο ολόκληρο σε BASIC κι έτσι στην αρχή (προτού το περάσω και το τρέξω) μου είχε δημιουργήσει μερικές αμφιβολίες ως προς την αποτελεσματικότητα και την ταχύτητά του. Σας διαβεβαιώ όμως ότι έμεινα έκπληκτος! Η ευελιξία του είναι καταπληκτική και η ταχύτητά του ιδιαίτερα ικανοποιητική. Έτσι πιστεύω ότι με το πρόγραμμα αυτό αποδεικνύεται άλλη μια φορά ότι η BASIC του ZX-81 ενώ δεν μπορεί να πετύχει ικανοποιητικά αποτελέσματα στα video games τα καταφέρνει αρκετά

```
W O R D   P R O C E S S I N G
1:SAVE ON TAPE
2:SEND TO PRINTER
3:WRITE PAGE
4:EDIT PAGE
5:CLEAR PAGE
ENTER OPTION (1 TO 5)?
```

■ C O M P U T E R   GIA OLOYS

TO KATANOHTO PERIODIKO

GIA MIKRO- C O M P U T E R

```
MODE:EDITING              PAGE:?

 10 REM ********************
 11 REM * WORD PROCESSOR *
 12 REM ********************
 20 DIM A$(10,640)
 30 LET B$=""
 40 LET D$=""
 50 LET POS=1
 60 LET PAGE=1
 65 GOTO 160
 70 PRINT "WORDY'S ENTER PROGRAM
NAME-"
 110 INPUT Z$
 115 IF Z$="" THEN GOTO 9050
 120 PRINT "SET UP TAPE DECK THE
N PRESS(N/L)"
 130 INPUT X$
 140 SAVE Z$
 160 CLS
 170 PRINT "
 180 PRINT " W O R D   P R O C E
```

12

Fig. 4.4 Localizing Use. Contrary to the practices of use of microcomputers that we encounter in Western Europe and North America, this type of computer was applied in Greece in several different uses that corresponded to the local characteristics of the Greek sociotechnical environment. Thus, we often find microcomputers processing data in small businesses or used for more "serious" tasks in place of a more expensive IBM compatible. Software for such applications, like a word processor in BASIC for the ZX-81 depicted in the listing, was soon developed. Source: *Pixel* 1 (1983): 12, 13

specific structure, mainly operating in the informal manner of a group of friends. Generally, amateur users did not belong to any form of network whatsoever.[66] The first "official" community network was the one created through Pixel's initiative.

But why create a computer club for home computer users? Some would say to attract more readers. The editor was more explicit: "the scope of creating the computer club is to assemble all the individuals that care about microcomputers, all of us who care about the future."[67] The ideology was consistent throughout the magazine's early years. Computers were not just machines, existing within large organizations, but an important tool in the hands of casual users, who could utilize them at home or at work to improve their lives. Thus, computer clubs aimed to create new networks of communication among users, who previously acted individually without sharing their knowledge and skills. Instead, the computer clubs attempted to circulate technical knowledge, to solve problems of localization such as the "Hellenization" of characters, and to facilitate the sharing of software created or copied by users. As computer shops or small software houses were increasingly resolving these issues, the computer club gradually transformed into a network of software sharing.

Computer stores were the second important factor in shaping an open culture in Greece. In a humorous article in Pixel, the stores were appropriately called, "Pirates S.A." Compared to Western Europe and North America, computer shops in Greece were much more than mere retailers of computers, peripherals, and software. They were also an important channel of information for users about developments in the field, as they maintained direct contact with the booming market of home computers in Britain. Stores often imported their software and hardware directly, since authorized importers and dealers in Greece were almost nonexistent. Even if they did exist, stores had no qualms about arranging parallel imports.[68] In short, the user had two main communication channels for international events: Greek and international computer magazines and computer stores. The stores often employed Greek students studying in the UK to keep them up to date about new releases.[69]

Another important aspect of computer stores' operations was the high level of technical support they provided to customers, compensating for the lack of authorized dealerships in Greece. The range of support included training, demonstrations, and repairs at the customer's home. Many accepted specialized orders for hardware, software, and peripherals.[70] As the manufacturers offered no authorized repair facilities, the third party repair shop sector evolved quickly and was usually incorporated in computer stores, thus enhancing their turnover. With the users seeking the easiest and cheapest way to repair their computers, and the lack of authorized support centers, the computer shops emerged as the only serious alternative. In most cases, the stores

---

[66] Γιατί, άραγε, και λέσχη [Why a computer club?]. *Pixel* 2(1984): 14.

[67] Καραιωσηφόγλου, Τα νέα του Pixel.

[68] For example, PLOT computer shops were parallel importers, not connected to authorized dealers for computers like Spectrum, ORIC ATMOS, Commodore. Νικολάου, Νίκος Λουκίδης: Ο Έλληνας.

[69] Χ. Κυριακός. 1986c. Ο πόλεμος των computer shops [The war of computer shops]. *Pixel* 19: 71.

[70] Φ. Γεωργιάδης. 1986b. Η πρώτη αντιγραφή [First copy]. *Pixel* 25: 128–133.

actually replaced both the authorized dealers and local educational centers, as they provided access to users who wanted to experience microcomputer technology or acquire basic skills.[71]

Greek computer stores' range of activities did not end here. It included creating applications for popular microcomputers on the market. As imported software was limited and prohibitively expensive, a significant number of Greek computer stores recruited young programmers to create cheap applications to meet local needs, such as educational and commercial software applications for small businesses (Fig. 4.5). Greek computer stores in the first half of the 1980s incorporated almost all aspects of computer technology, from importing and marketing machines, software and peripherals, to repairing them, training clients in their use, and building applications on demand and supporting them after purchase. The shops thus emerged as the prime mediators between users and microcomputer technology, a fact that naturally led to the establishment and their support of computer clubs, along the lines of the one formed by *Pixel*. Through these clubs, users learned basic computer skills and shared software that they owned, which had often been copied and if not, they copied it themselves.

Thus stores held a significant pole position for software piracy in Greece. As they were already the major marketers and distributors of commercial software with few if any other distribution channels, several shops began to copy most of the software they sold in the store at lower prices, arguing that their statutory profit should be higher than from marketing imported software. The cost of the copied software was nearly one third of the original price, making the imported software most attractive for the customer and profitable for the store. The practice of copying was so successful that many computer stores began to specialize in pirating computer software, while others sold copies exclusively.[72]

To legalize the practice of copying, computer stores invented the concept of "legitimate copies," whereby the store could sell copies after concluding an agreement with software companies and paying an extra lump sum for copyright. Several shop owners even claimed to have reached such agreements with foreign software companies.[73] The owner of PLOT, one of the most popular computer shops at that time, acknowledged in an interview that shops like his, which chose not to provide copied software, were a minority in the field.[74] He was, however, in the same peculiar position of selling original software to his competitors, who copied and resold it at half the price. He proposed creating an association of computer stores to force the software houses to grant them the right to produce "legitimate copies."[75] Another shop owner repeated the call for legal copies, convinced this solution would

[71] The shop *Computer for you* informed its clients through Pixel magazine that it offered free access to home computers as "many waited in line to use and learn about the microcomputer of their choice," "Ελληνική Αγορά," 9.

[72] Νικολάου, Νίκος Λουκίδης: Ο Έλληνας, "Mr. Chips", 161.

[73] Κυριακός, Οι πειρατές του software, 58.

[74] Νικολάου, Νίκος Λουκίδης: Ο Έλληνας, "Mr. Chips", 160.

[75] Ibid.

Fig. 4.5 Computer Retailers as Mediators. Besides computer magazines like Pixel, computer shops were another important mediator between manufacturers and users. They performed a multifaceted mediating role, as they performed several roles like developing software. The development of software for the most popular home microcomputers regarded both "complete software packages" and custom applications for specific customers. In this advertisement in *Pixel*, a computer store chain "looks for full and part-time developers with experience in home computers and BASIC, to work at their Athens based stores." Source: *Pixel* 13(1985): 56

mutually benefit the stores and software houses that considered cassette piracy a "necessary evil."[76] Producing software copies and selling copiers (Fig. 4.6) had become a key activity for many large computer shops, in the same way that ordinary users were producing copies at home. The open culture meant that software was subject to modification in accordance with user needs and demands. Therefore,

[76] Γεωργιάδης, Η πρώτη αντιγραφή, 128–133.

Fig. 4.6 Sharing Copying Tricks as a Legitimate Practice. As copying and tinkering with software was an accepted and popular practice among users of home microcomputers, programs for such applications (known as copiers) were soon available commercially. Since copying and tinkering practice was legalized within the user community, such programs were sold through official channels like computer stores and advertised in popular magazines like *Pixel*. Source: *Pixel* 17(1985): 25

the equipment and technical knowledge needed for copying became significant advantages for any store wanting to do better than its competitors.[77] The copies were not only of imported software but also domestic products. In one illustrative case, the owner of software house "Micro-Ideas" received serious complaints from angry customers about the unacceptable practice of distributing its products without instructions and packaging. As it turned out, the pirated software was being sold by popular computer stores in Athens.[78]

---

[77] Micro-βιος, Micro Τσιμπήματα [Micro Bites]. *Pixel* 17: 68.

[78] Ibid., 27.

4.5 Conclusion

Home computing in Greece in the early 1980s established a culture for software, encompassing: purchase of software from local shops or abroad and its replication both for games and applications; 'tinkering' with copied software so that the user could acquire countless lives in some game; selling copied software to third parties (even shops) through magazine advertisements or within user clubs, and typing program listings from *Pixel*; correcting these listings and writing new ones which were in turn submitted to the magazine. Gradually, the first software houses were set up for home computers or this role was fulfilled by existing computer stores, which often recruited young members of the hacker community. Thus, the way software was used in home computers in Greece during the 1980s was so multifaceted that it does not resemble the business-focused history of software.[79] In Greece, piracy acquired a different meaning.[80] Home computer use was mediated by Greek computer magazines.[81] In analyzing mediation, I focused on intermediary actors, who operated between producers and consumers to negotiate the form and content of technological products. Such a methodological tool allowed us to pay particular attention to intermediaries' actions at specific junctions.[82] Historical research in particular revealed the various national and regional technological variations when comparing the case of Greece to images of America, IBM or the "global computer."

Pixel magazine played a key role in creating the open culture, by distinctively publishing technical knowledge, forming institutions unprecedented in Greece such as computer clubs, and calling on readers for their (more) active participation in the development of software for the most popular home computers.[83] I tried to show how the magazine incorporated a variety of roles, from propaganda agent of the new home computer technology and communication mediator between users, to shaper of the

---

[79] For example, Martin Campbell-Kelly. 2003. *From airline reservations to Sonic the Hedgehog: A history of the software industry*. Cambridge, MA/London: MIT Press.

[80] On how political, economic, and social factors direct technological developments, see Ceruzzi, *A history of modern computing*.

[81] The press was vital in shaping perceptions on computer technology, being the main means of communication among less experienced users. C.D. Martin. 1993. The myth of the awesome thinking machine. *Communications of the ACM* 36(4): 120–133.

[82] Ruth Schwartz Cowan. 1987. The consumption junction: A proposal for research strategies in the sociology of technology. In *The social construction of technological systems*, ed. Wiebe E. Bijker, Thomas P. Hughes, and Trevor J. Pinch, 261–280. Cambridge, MA: MIT; Ruth Oldenziel, Adri A. Albert de la Bruhèze, and Onno de Wit. 2005. Europe's mediation junction: Technology and consumer society in the twentieth century. *History and Technology* 21: 107–139.

[83] European historians of technology have focused on the role of intermediary actors, who mediate between producers and users of technology. Johan Schot and Adri Albert de la Bruhèze, The mediated design of products, consumption and consumers in the twentieth century, in Oudshoorn and Pinch, *How users matter*, 229–246. For an example of using computer magazines as historical source in the field, see Veraart, *Vormgevers*.

new open culture.[84] The network of small shops selling and repairing computers represented the second mediating actor shaping how users experienced the technology. But the shops were much more than that. Not only did they sell computers, peripherals, and software, they also shaped new trends. Since the shops imported directly from abroad, they were centers of education and information for users, had an active relationship with trade magazines, and formed a microcosm of informatics in Greece.[85]

Computer stores along with *Pixel* shaped the terms of home computer use in Greece, contributing to a culture that rewarded copying (what we would call piracy today in the negative sense of the word) and modification of software (hacking). The culture proudly reserved the title of "hacker" for the advanced user testing his skills, believing that the combination of piracy and hacking had beneficial effects on a relatively technologically underdeveloped society. Both the magazine and the shops believed that piracy and hacking were prerequisites for Greek society's entry into the world of personal computers: the activities allowed the diffusion of computer technology and cultivated the fervor of users for programming.[86] Studying the mediators of computer technology we understand how this technology was established and used.[87]

Bibliography

Adamson, Ian, and Richard Kennedy. 1986. *Sinclair and the sunrise technology: The deconstruction of a myth*. Harmondsworth: Penguin.

Bagnall, Brian. 2005. *On the edge: The spectacular rise and fall of Commodore*. Winnipeg: Variant Press.

Bassett, Ross Knox. 2002. *To the digital age: Research labs, start-up companies, and the rise of MOS technology*. Baltimore: Johns Hopkins University Press.

Bijker, Wiebe E., Thomas P. Hughes, and Trevor J. Pinch (eds.). 1987. *The social construction of technological systems. New directions in the sociology and history of technology*. Cambridge, MA: MIT Press.

Blundell, Gregory S. 1983. Personal computers in the eighties. *BYTE*, January, 166–182.

[84] Christina Lindsay, From the shadows: Users as designers, producers, marketers, distributors, and technical support, in Oudshoorn and Pinch, *How users matter*, 29–50.

[85] On the importance of high-street sales in legitimizing the home computers as a consumer product rather than just a toy for hobbyists, see Adamson and Kennedy, *Sinclair and the Sunrise technology,* and Stan Veit. 1993. *Stan Veit's history of the personal computer: From Altair to IBM, a history of the PC revolution*. Asheville: WordComm.

[86] The importance of hacker cultures in the 1980s was not exclusive to Greece. In the case of Finland, see Petri Saarikoski, and Jaakko Suominen. 2009. Computer hobbyists and the gaming industry in Finland. *IEEE Annals of the History of Computing* 31(3): 20–33.

[87] Robbie Guerreiro-Wilson, Lars Heide, Matthias Kipping, Cecilia Pahlberg, Adrienne van den Bogaard, and Aristotle Tympas. 2004. Information systems and technology in organizations and society (ISTOS): Review essay. In *Tensions of Europe. Network first plenary conference proceedings*, ed. Johan Schot, et al., Budapest, Hungary (CD-ROM). [Also accessible as: *Tensions of Europe Working Paper* http://www.tensionsofeurope.eu/www/en/files/get/Review_IT_Guerreiro.pdf. Accessed 30 Jan 2014]

Campbell-Kelly, Martin. 2003. *From airline reservations to Sonic the Hedgehog: A history of the software industry*. Cambridge, MA: MIT Press.

Ceruzzi, Paul E. 1996. From scientific instrument to everyday appliance: The emergence of personal computers, 1970–77. *History and Technology* 13(1): 1–31.

Ceruzzi, Paul E. 2003 [1998]. *A history of modern computing*, 226. Cambridge, MA/London: MIT Press.

Chposky, James, and Ted Leonsis. 1988. *Blue magic: The people, power, and politics behind the IBM personal computer*. New York: Facts on File.

Cohen, Scott. 1984. *Zap! The rise and fall of Atari*. New York: McGraw Hill.

Cowan, Ruth Schwartz. 1987. The consumption junction: A proposal for research strategies in the sociology of technology. In *The social construction of technological systems*, ed. Wiebe E. Bijker, Thomas P. Hughes, and Trevor J. Pinch, 261–280. Cambridge, MA: MIT Press.

Cringely, Robert X. 1992. *Accidental empires: How the boys of Silicon Valley make their millions, battle foreign competition, and still can't get a date*. Reading: Addison-Wesley.

Dale, Rodney. 1985. *The Sinclair story*. London: Duckworth.

Edgerton, David. 2006. *The shock of the old: Technology and global history since 1900*. London: Profile Books.

Freiberger, Paul, and Michael Swaine. 1984. *Fire in the valley: The making of the personal computer*. Berkeley: Osborne/McGraw-Hill.

Glennie, Paul. 1995. Consumption within historical studies. In *Acknowledging consumption: A review of new studies*, ed. Daniel Miller, 164–203. London/New York: Routledge.

Guerreiro-Wilson, Robbie, Lars Heide, Matthias Kipping, Cecilia Pahlberg, Adrienne van den Bogaard, and Aristotle Tympas. 2004. Information systems and technology in organizations and society (ISTOS): Review essay. In *Tensions of Europe. Network first plenary conference proceedings*, ed. Johan Schot, et al., Budapest, Hungary (CD-ROM). [Also accessible as: *Tensions of Europe Working Paper* http://www.tensionsofeurope.eu/www/en/files/get/Review_IT_Guerreiro.pdf. Accessed 30 Jan 2014]

Haddon, Leslie G. 1988b. *The roots and early history of the British home computer market: Origins of the masculine micro*. PhD thesis, University of London.

Haddon, Leslie. 1990. Researching gender and home computers. In *Technology and everyday life: Trajectories and transformations*, ed. Knut Sørensen and Anne-Jorn Berg, 89–108. Trondheim: University of Trondheim.

Haddon, Leslie. 1992. Explaining ICT consumption: The case of the home computer. In *Consuming technologies: Media and information in domestic spaces*, ed. R. Silverstone and E. Hirsch, 82–96. London: Routledge.

Hapnes, Tove. 1996. Not in their machines: How hackers transform computers into subcultural artefacts. In *Making technology our own? Domesticating technology into everyday life*, ed. Lie Merete and Knut H. Sørensen, 121–150. Oslo/Stockholm/Copenhagen/Oxford/Boston: Scandinavian University Press.

Kornfeld, Lewis. 1997. *To catch a mouse make a noise like a cheese*. Irving: The Summit Publishing Group.

Latour, Bruno. 2005. *Reassembling the social: An introduction to actor-network-theory*. Oxford: Oxford University Press.

Lean, Thomas. 2008. *'The making of the micro': Producers, mediators, users and the development of popular micro-computing in Britain (1980–1989)*. PhD thesis. University of Manchester.

Lean, Thomas. 2014. 'Inside a day You'll be talking to it like an old friend': The making and remaking of Sinclair personal computing in 1980s Britain. In *Hacking Europe. From computer cultures to demoscenes*, ed. Gerard Alberts and Ruth Oldenziel, 49–71. New York: Springer.

Lécuyer, Christophe. 2005. *Making Silicon Valley: Innovation and the growth of high tech, 1930–1970*. Cambridge, MA: MIT Press.

Levy, Steven. 1984. *Hackers: The heroes of the computer revolution*. Garden City, NY: Anchor Press/Doubleday.

Lindsay, Christina. 2003. From the shadows: Users as designers, producers, marketers, distributors, and technical support. In *How users matter: The co-construction of users and technology*, ed. Nelly Oudshoorn and Trevor J. Pinch, 29–50. Cambridge, MA/London: MIT Press.

Lönnblad, H. 1997. Kahden tietokonedemon vertaileva analyysi [A comparative study of two computer demos]. *Musiikin Suunta* 19(2): 28–34. http://www.kameli.net/demoresearch2/

Mackay, Hughie, and Gareth Gillespie. 1992. Extending the social shaping of technology approach: Ideology and appropriation. *Social Studies of Science* 22(4): 685–716.

MacKenzie, Donald A., and Judy Wajcman (eds.). 1985. *The social shaping of technology: How the refrigerator got its hum*. Milton Keynes: Open University Press.

Markoff, John W. 2005. *What the dormouse said: How the 60s counterculture shaped the personal computer industry*. New York: Viking.

Martin, C.D. 1993. The myth of the awesome thinking machine. *Communications of the ACM* 36(4): 120–133.

Mäyrä, F. 2002. Introduction: All your [base are] belong to us. In *Computer games and digital cultures conference proceedings studies in information sciences*, 5–8. Tampere: Tampere University Press.

Misa, Thomas J., and Johan Schot. 2005. Inventing Europe: Technology and the hidden integration of Europe. *History and Technology* 21: 1–19.

Moritz, Michael. 1984. *The little kingdom: The private story of Apple computer*. New York: W. Morrow.

Morton, David L. 2000. *Off the record: The technology and culture of sound recording in America*. New Brunswick: Rutgers University Press.

Nissen, Jörgen. 1993. *Pojkarna vid datorn: Unga entusiaster i datateknikens värld* [Boys in front of computers. Young enthusiasts in the world of computer technology]. PhD thesis, Lynköping Universitet.

Norberg, Arthur L. 2005. *Computers and commerce: A study of technology and management at Eckert-Mauchly Computer Company, Engineering Research Associates, and Remington Rand, 1946–1957*. Cambridge, MA: MIT Press.

Oldenziel, Ruth, Adri Albert de la Bruhèze, and Onno de Wit. 2005. Europe's mediation junction: Technology and consumer society in the twentieth century. *History and Technology* 21(1): 107–139.

Ortiz-Arroyo, D., F. Rodriguez-Henriquez, and C.A. Coello. 2010. The turing-850 project: Developing a personal computer in the early 1980s in Mexico. *IEEE Annals of the History of Computing* 32(4): 60–71.

Oudshoorn, Nelly, and Trevor J. Pinch (eds.). 2003. *How users matter: The co-construction of users and technology*. Cambridge, MA/London: MIT Press.

Pearson, Jamie Parke. 1992. *Digital at work: Snapshots from the first thirty-five years*. Burlington: Digital Press.

Pinch, Trevor J., and Wiebe E. Bijker. 1984. The social construction of facts and artefacts: Or how the sociology of science and the sociology of technology might benefit each other. *Social Studies of Science* 14(August): 399–441.

Polgár, Tamás. 2005. *Freax. The brief history of the demoscene*, vol. 1. Winnenden: CSW Verlag.

Pugh, Emerson W. 1995. *Building IBM: Shaping an industry and its technologies*. Cambridge, MA: MIT Press.

Reunanen, Markku, and Antti Silvast. 2009. Demoscene platforms: A case study on the adoption of home computers. In *History of Nordic computing 2*, IFIP advances in information and communication technology, ed. John Impagliazzo, Timo Järvi, and Petri Paju, 289–301. Berlin: Springer.

Saarikoski, Petri. 2004. *Koneen lumo. Mikrotietokoneharrastus Suomessa 1970-luvulta 1990-luvun puoliväliin* [The Lure of the machine. The personal computer interest in Finland from the 1970s to the mid-1990s]. Nykykulttuurin tutkimuskeskuksen julkaisuja 83. Jyväskylä: Jyväskylän yliopisto.

Saarikoski, Petri. 2005. Club activity in the early phases of microcomputing in Finland. In *History of Nordic computing*, ed. Janis Bubenko, John Impagliazzo, and Arne Sølvberg, 277–287. Berlin: Springer.

Saarikoski, Petri, and Jaakko Suominen. 2009. Computer hobbyists and the gaming industry in Finland. *IEEE Annals of the History of Computing* 31(3): 20–33.

Schot, Johan, and Adri Albert de la Bruhèze. 2003. The mediated design of products, consumption and consumers in the twentieth century. In *How users matter: The co-construction of users and technology*, ed. Nelly Oudshoorn and Trevor J. Pinch, 229–246. Cambridge, MA/London: MIT Press.

Shurkin, Joel N. 2006. *Broken genius: The rise and fall of William Shockley, creator of the electronic age*. London/New York: Palgrave Macmillan.

Skinner, David Ian. 1992. *Technology, consumption and the future: The experience of home computing*. PhD thesis, Brunel University.

Smith, Merritt Roe, and Leo Marx (eds.). 1994. *Does technology drive history? The dilemma of technological determinism*. Boston: MIT Press.

Sotamaa, O. 2005. Creative user-centred design practices: Lessons from game cultures. In *Everyday innovators: Researching the role of users in shaping ICTs*, ed. Leslie Haddon et al., 104–116. Dordrecht: Springer.

Sumner, J. 2003. *The mighty microcosm: Home computers and user identity in Britain, 1980–90*. Paper presented to the annual meeting of the Society for the History of Technology, Atlanta, GA, Oct 2003.

Sumner, J. 2007. What makes a PC? Thoughts on computing platforms, standards, and compatibility. *IEEE Annals of the History of Computing* 29(2): 87–88.

Sumner, James. 2008. Standards and compatibility: The rise of the PC platform. *History and Technology* 28 [=Sumner and Gooday. 2008]: 101–127.

Sumner, James, and J.N. Graeme Gooday (eds.). 2008. *By whose standards? Standardization, stability and uniformity in the history of information and electrical technologies* [*Special issue History and Technology* 28]. London: Continuum International Pub. Group.

Tasajärvi, L., B. Stamnes, and M. Schustin (eds.). 2004. *Demoscene: The art of real-time*. Even Lake Studios & katastro.fi.

Tedlow, Richard S. 2006. *Andy Grove: The life and times of an American business icon*. New York: Portfolio.

Thomas, David. 1991. *Alan Sugar: The Amstrad story*. London: Pan Books.

Thomas, Douglas. 2002. *Hacker culture*. Minneapolis: University of Minnesota Press.

Tomczyk, Michael S. 1984. *The home computer wars: An insider's account of Commodore and Jack Tramiel*. Greensboro: Compute! Publications.

Turkle, Sherry. 1984. *The second self: Computers and the human spirit*. New York: Simon & Schuster.

Turner, Fred. 2006. *From counterculture to cyberculture: Stewart Brand, the Whole Earth Network, and the rise of digital utopianism*. Chicago: University of Chicago Press.

Tympas, Aristotle. 2006. Electronic era technologies, the European experience: Historiographical omissions and ambitions. In *Tensions of Europe network second plenary conference proceedings*, ed. Johan Schot, et al., Lappeenranta, Finland (CD-ROM).

Tympas, Aristotle, Fotini Tsaglioti, and Theodore Lekkas. 2008. *Universal machines vs. national languages: Computerization as production of new localities*. Paper presented at the international conference 'Technologies of Globalization', Darmstadt.

Usselman, Steve. 1993. IBM and its imitators: Organizational capabilities and the emergence of the international computer industry. *Business and Economic History* 22(1): 1–35.

Veit, Stan. 1993. *Stan Veit's history of the personal computer: From Altair to IBM, a history of the PC revolution*. Asheville: WordComm.

Veraart, Frank. 2008a. Basicode: Co-producing a microcomputer Esperanto. *History and Technology* 28: 129–147.

Veraart, Frank. 2008c. *Vormgevers van Persoonlijk Computergebruik: De ontwikkeling van computers voor kleingebruikers in Nederland 1970–1990*. PhD thesis, TU Eindhoven.

Wark, McKenzie. 2004. *A hacker manifesto*. Cambridge, MA: Harvard University Press.

Willison, Robert, and Mikko Siponen. 2008. *Software piracy: Original insights from a criminological perspective*. Paper presented at the proceedings of the annual Hawaii international conference on system sciences, Maui.

Winner, Langdon. 1993. Upon opening the black box and finding it empty: Social constructivism and the philosophy of technology. *Science, Technology & Human Values* 18(3): 362–378.

Woolgar, Steve. 1991. Configuring the user: The case of usability trials. In *A sociology of monsters: Essays on power, technology and domination*, ed. John Law, 58–100. London/New York: Routledge.

Yost, Jeffrey R. 2005. *The computer industry, Emerging industries in the United States*. Westport: Greenwood Press.

Γεωργιάδης, Φ. 1986a. Εισαγωγή στο Hacking [Introduction to hacking]. *Pixel* 23: 103.

Γεωργιάδης, Φ. 1986b. Η πρώτη αντιγραφή [First copy]. *Pixel* 25: 128–133.

Ηλίας Γεωργάκης. 2010. Μείωση εισφορών έως 25 %. *TA NEA*, December 21. http://www.tanea.gr/default.asp?pid=2&ct=3&artid=4609892. Accessed 2010.

Καραιωσηφόγλου, Γ. 1984. Τα νέα του *Pixel* [Pixel's news]. *Pixel* 2: 5.

Καράλης, Κ. 1990. Στα άδυτατης ελληνικότητας. *RAM*, April, 69.

Κυριακός, Χ. 1986a. Οι Hackers αποκαλύπτουν [Hackers reveal]. *Pixel* 27: 76–81.

Κυριακός, Χ. 1986b. Οι πειρατές του software [Software pirates]. *Pixel* 21: 55.

Κυριακός, Χ. 1986c. Ο πόλεμος των computer shops [The war of computer shops]. *Pixel* 19: 71.

Μανδρινός, Μ. 1983. Προγράμματα για τον ZX-81 [Programs for ZX -81]. *Pixel* 1: 12.

Μανούσος, Ν. 1983. Γράμμα από τον Εκδότη [Letter from the Editor]. *Pixel* 1: 3.

Νικολάου, Μ. 1985. Νίκος Λουκίδης: Ο Έλληνας 'Mr. Chips' [Nikos Loukidis: The Greek "Mr. Chips"!]. *Pixel* 15: 158.

Τσουάνας, Ν. 1984. Σπάστε το Manic Miner [Break Manic Miner]. *Pixel* 3: 16.

Τσουάνας, Ν. 1985. Επεμβάσεις: Ξεκλειδώστε το Pole Position [Interferences: Unlock pole position]. *Pixel* 15: 134.

Part II
Bastard Sons of the Cold War: Creating Computer Scences

Chapter 5
Galaxy and the New Wave: Yugoslav Computer Culture in the 1980s

Bruno Jakić

5.1 Introduction

In the world of 1980, Socialist Federal Republic of Yugoslavia was something of an oddity. Being neither a part of the Warsaw Pact nor of NATO, yet still being a communist country, in a highly polarized world, it occupied a unique position among countries, not only politically but also technologically and culturally. The Cold War context had given rise to a high level of technological expertise in urban Yugoslavia, while the government maintained control over the import of digital equipment. In the cultural sense, it followed many contemporary trends with the West, while adding to them a distinct local cultural flavor. As a consequence, the Republic spawned local subcultures that were more than a mere emulation of their Western analogues. One of these subcultures, coming to prominence in the 1980s, was the Yugoslav New-Wave scene, which blended social critique, music, and arts with the use of home computers. While import of digital equipment from the West was strictly controlled by Yugoslavia's communist government, leading to prohibitions on import of various computer models and components in the early 1980s, the prices of Western computers were experienced as the bigger problem – averaging a monthly Yugoslav salary.[1] A specific set of routes and habits towards appropriation of technologies ensued, most interestingly, a home brew home computer industry in Yugoslavia and associated meetings, radio shows, parties, and indeed a distinct subculture revolving around home computer technology.

[1] Economist. 1984. Yugoslavia. In *The world in figures*, 240–242. London: MacMillan. For an impression of daily life in Bosnia and Herzegovina, Croatia and Serbia 1945–1990, see: Edin Veladžić, Goran Miloradović, et al. 2010. *Yugoslavia between East and West; Ordinary people in unordinary country*. Online project EUROCLIO – HIP http://www.cliohip.com. Accessed 24 Nov 2011.

B. Jakić (✉)
Independent researcher, University of Amsterdam, Amsterdam, The Netherlands
e-mail: bruno@ai-applied.nl

G. Alberts and R. Oldenziel (eds.), *Hacking Europe. From Computer Cultures to Demoscenes*, History of Computing, DOI 10.1007/978-1-4471-5493-8_5,

Even if this essay is the result of recent historical research, in a way it is a personal history. The author was born into it: in Sarajevo, Yugoslavia, 1983. He spent the first years of his life in an apartment building in the city center, in which his aunt also lived.[2] This aunt, herself a member of the rock culture of inner-city Sarajevo, was responsible for the author's first experience of a party in 1989; indeed, some of his earliest memories go back to this time.[3] At these parties, among the customary sex, drugs, and rock 'n' roll, home computers were present too. People would play games, show off their software to other participants, and share software, magazines, and schematics. At the time, the author did not realize the depth of this computer enthusiast movement, not having seen or even heard about a computer before. Many years later, in 1990s, as a refugee in Serbia visiting a cousin with a computer engineering degree over the summer holidays, the author discovered a large number of computer magazines from the 1980s, audiotapes containing programs, home computers of different makes, and a willing story teller the cousin's own computer-related experiences during that past decade.[4] The sum of these experiences had awakened a profound interest of the author into the theme. Later reviews of contemporary literature and media research and informal interviews with the participants of this subculture have deepened and solidified the author's knowledge about the subject.[5]

5.2 History of Computing in Yugoslavia

To gain an understanding of the impact of home computing on Yugoslav subcultures, we first need to consider the history of early computing in Yugoslavia, in particular the unique political situation and the position of Yugoslavia during the Cold War.[6]

The geopolitical situation of an independent country not only explains the relatively well-known cultural openness as compared to Soviet-dominated communist

[2] Interview author with Gordana Radević, M.D. in Belgrade, a student of medicine in Sarajevo 1985–1990, July 18, 2010.

[3] Interview author with Rafo Dužnović, Vareš, Bosnia-Herzegovina, Summer of 2009.

[4] Interviews author with Darko and Andrej Šolar, Sombor, Serbia, early 1994 and Novi Sad, Serbia, July 13, 2009.

[5] This chapter has been based on magazines *Galaksija*, *Svet Kompjutera*, *PC Pres*, *Džuboks*, *Polet*, and *Ilustrovana Politika* as well as the online resources and recollections by Zoran Modli, a Yugoslav counterculture icon from the 1980s, (http://www.modli.rs/. Accessed 20 Feb 2011); "Srbima Treba Vremeplov," Interview with Zoran Modli, *Feral Tribune*, Split, Croatia, June 23, 2006; recollections of Dejan Ristanović, Yugoslav 1980s home computing pioneer. http://www.dejanristanovic.com. Accessed 23 Sept 2010; documentary film "Sretno Dijete" about the New Wave in Yugoslavia (Zagreb, Croatia, 2003).

[6] William Zimmerman. 1987. *Open borders, non-alignment and the political evolution of Yugoslavia*. Princeton: Princeton University Press; Sabrina P. Ramet. 2006. *The three Yugoslavias: State-building and legitimation, 1918–2005*. Bloomington: University of Indiana Press.

countries but just as well the lesser known figures of decades of enormous investments in a national armament industry. It was on the basis of this national military-industrial complex that a domestic computer industry could thrive. The combination of these two factors bore fruit in the manufacturing Galaksija and similar computers but also in subcultures feeling free to attribute their own meaning to computers and computerization.

While the Yugoslav communist government had been supported both by the USA and Great Britain as well as the Soviet Union during World War II, diverging political agendas of the new superpower blocks meant a quick end of this support for the dissenting countries. At the (in)famous Yalta conference, held by the Allies at the Livadia Palace near Yalta from the 4th of February 1945, the division of the world in blocks of influence of the respective allied superpowers had been agreed. Yugoslavia was assigned to the "communist" sphere of influence, effectively ending the political and economic support from the West at the end of World War II. At the same time, this also meant that the USSR considered it as its right to administer and organize Yugoslavia in a similar fashion as Poland, Czechoslovakia, Hungary, Romania, and other Soviet satellite states.[7] However, contrary to these countries, Yugoslavia was the only communist state in Europe to have an independent communist party, formed through the resistance against the Axis powers, which was organized and led by that party. Consequently, the Yugoslav communists did not feel much for Soviet administration and leadership and, led by Josip Broz Tito, Yugoslav party chief at the time and formerly a longtime ally of Joseph Stalin of the USSR, resisted Soviet influence in Yugoslav affairs. This led to the Tito-Stalin split of 1948, where Stalin and the Soviet Union not only halted all assistance to war-ravaged Yugoslavia but also expelled Yugoslavia from the Cominform organization (the umbrella organization of worldwide communist parties dominated by the Soviet Union) and considered Yugoslavia a revisionist enemy and a potential invasion target.[8]

Faced with the situation of being isolated, and indeed being threatened by both major superpower blocks, Yugoslav leadership decided to build a military-industrial apparatus that would assure Yugoslavia's self-sufficiency in the field of national defense.[9] A massive effort was launched at the expense of up to two-thirds of the

[7] Zimmerman in 1972 sketched the Yugoslavia's restricted room to maneuver in terms of Rothstein's concept of "small power," bound to short terms policies. William Zimmerman. 1972. Hierarchical regional systems and the politics of system boundaries. *International Organization* 26(1): 18–36, here 30. Robert L. Rothstein. 1968. *Alliances and small powers*. New York: Columbia University Press.

[8] Gary K. Bertsch, and Thomas W. Ganschow. 1976. *Comparative communism: The Soviet, Chinese, and Yugoslav models*, 131–133. San Francisco: W.H. Freeman.

[9] Untypical of Zimmerman's "small power" behavior, Yugoslavia succeeded in creating an international milieu for what Dulić and Kostić refer to as "socialist self-management." It developed such long term policies as a defense industry. Zimmerman, Hierarchical regional systems and the politics of system boundaries, 30. Tornislav Dulić, and Roland Kostić. 2010. Yugoslavs in arms: Guerrilla tradition, total defence and the ethnic security dilemma. *Europe-Asia Studies* 62(7): 1051–1072, here 1052. J. Barryman. 1988. The Soviet Union and Yugoslavia's defence and foreign policy. In *Yugoslavia's security dilemmas—Armed forces, national defence and foreign policy*, ed. M. Milivojević, J.B. Allcock, and P. Maurer, 192–260. Oxford: Oxford University Press.

federal budget that included the building of indigenous tank and aircraft industries; command, communication, and control centers; underground air bases; shipbuilding industries; and a nuclear research program.[10] As the effort concentrated on building many new, independent designs, the progress in many areas was dependent on the capacity to perform complex calculations over shorter periods of time. This included not only factors such as calculations of architectural stresses, ballistic tables, or nuclear simulations but also command-and-control equipments needed to perform modern methods of manufacturing. This need translated itself into lavish grants awarded to academic institutions that indirectly led to well-funded research into automatic computing.[11]

5.3 Research Institutes and Digital Computers

Established in 1948 as the Vinča Institute of Research on the Structure of Matter (Institut za Istragu Strukture Materije Vinča), and subsequently renamed in 1952 to Institute for nuclear sciences Boris Kidrič Vinča (Institut za nuklearne nauke Boris Kidrič Vinča or IBK Vinča for short), this institute was the first to benefit from the defense budget funding.[12] Using the grant and out of the need for advanced computation capabilities, basic conditions were created for building up an indigenous computer manufacturing industry. Due to the break away from the Soviet Union, France was more sympathetic to Yugoslavia. Therefore, a team of experts in mathematics and electrical engineering, led by academician Dr. Rajko Tomović, was sent to Paris to gain a practical understanding of the development of digital computer parts. Upon its return to Yugoslavia in 1956, the team started the design of an entirely new computer in cooperation with Belgrade's Telecommunication and Electronics Institute Mihajlo Pupin (Institut za elektroniku i telekomunikacije Mihajlo Pupin or IMP Beograd for short). This institute was tasked with the development of the computer parts, including all the features found in the contemporary computing machinery, but being produced entirely by local industries, out of local parts, and under local manufacturing methods.[13] This was the initial spark that started digital computing in Yugoslavia.

[10] Glenn E. Curtis. 1990. *Yugoslavia: A country study*. Washington, DC: Library of Congress, Federal Research Division. William C. Potter, Djuro Miljanić, and Ivo Slaus. 2000. Tito's nuclear legacy. *Bulletin of Atomic Scientists* 56(2): 63–70.

[11] The organization and funding of Yugoslav scientific programs with (semi-)military purposes has traditionally suffered from intentional lack of transparency, as indicated by Robert J. Walen, Stevan Dedijer, and Pavle Savić of IBK Vinča. 1953. *O dva bitna uslova za razvitak atomske energije kod nas*. Belgrade. However, the institutes receiving funding from the defense budget were the first to initiate research and production of automatic computers in Yugoslavia.

[12] For the nuclear aspect of this institute, see Potter, Miljanić, and Slaus, Tito's nuclear legacy.

[13] R. Tomović, A. Mandžić, and T. Aleksić, et al. 1960. Cifarski Elektronski Računar CER10 IBK Vinča. *ETAN-1960* 1:305–330.

By 1956, a thaw had occurred in the previously strained political relations with the Soviet Union, caused by the death of Stalin in 1953 and the process of de-Stalinization in the Soviet Union under Nikita Khrushchev. Famously, Khrushchev visited Belgrade in 1955 to apologize for Stalin's policies at the same time shutting down the Cominform organization. Yugoslav-Soviet relations were to freeze again after the Soviet invasions of Hungary in 1956 and the Czechoslovakian Prague Spring in 1968.[14] The intermediate thaw in the relations also implied that military equipment started to be imported – and domestically adapted with indigenous electronics – from the Soviet Union. Moreover, joint computing efforts with the USSR were envisaged, mainly in the fields of building hybrid computers, but only established in the early 1970s.

The pioneering work initiated by IBK Vinča and IMP Beograd in 1956 bore fruit in 1960 when the first Yugoslav digital computer was introduced: CER-10 ("Cifarski Elektronski Računar 10" or "Numerical Digital Computer 10").[15] CER-10 used vacuum tubes, transistor technology, and magnetic core memory and, not unlike other contemporary computers, could be programmed using punched tape (Fig. 5.1). CER was to become a dominant line of domestically produced computers intended for different purposes.[16] Next to the research applications for which these machines were originally intended, many civilian state institutions obtained their own CER computers to perform statistical analyses and business-related calculations, leading to a total of 30 installed digital computers by the end of 1962.[17] In parallel with the developments of multipurpose digital computers, the Institute for Machine-Building and Tools Belgrade (Institut za alatne mašine i alate, IAMA), that would later become the Ivo Lola Ribar Institute of Belgrade (Institut Ivo Lola Ribar or Lola Institut for short), started research into the development of command-and-control devices for industrial processes. Their example was later followed by many companies constituting the electronics industry of Yugoslavia, such as EiNiš (Elektronska Industrija Niš or Electronic Industries Niš) and others.[18] Soon their efforts into the miniaturization of electronics were to be utilized for weapon systems, as Yugoslavia manifested itself as one of the world's major weapons manufacturers and exporters.[19]

---

[14] Marvin Perry, Myrna Chase, and Margaret C. Jacob, et al. 2007. *Western civilization: Ideas, politics, and society*, 860–865. Boston: Wadsworth.

[15] Jelica Protić, and Dejan Ristanović. 2011. Building computers in Serbia: The first half of the digital century. *Computer Science and Information Systems* 8(3): 549–571.

[16] Tomović, Mandžić, and Aleksić et al., Cifarski Elektronski Računar CER10 IBK Vinča.

[17] Vladan Batanović, and Jovan Kon. 2006. *IMP Riznica znanja*, 25–28. Belgrade: M. Pupin Institute and PKS.

[18] Milan Mesarić. 1971. *Suvremena znanstveno tehnička revolucija*. Zagreb: Ekonomski institut.

[19] See: CIA's overview in the annual *World factbook* (Washington, DC: Central Intelligence Agency, 1975).

Fig. 5.1 National Computer Industry in Socialist Yugolavia. CER-10 (Cifarski Elektronski Racunar 10—Numerical Electronic Calculator 10) was the first computer designed and built in the Socialist Federal Republic of Yugoslavia, used from 1961 to 1967. Yugoslavia's geopolitical position at the time, sandwiched between the forces of the NATO on one side and the Warsaw Pact on the other, while being a member of neither and potentially hostile to both, prompted the government to make large-scale investments in the development of domestic military, scientific, and industrial sectors. Domestic computer development was one of the priorities, resulting in a long line of domestically built CER machines. These computers were used for scientific, military, and business purposes over the next 30 years. Operated by highly trained specialists, they were not accessible to ordinary citizens. Source: Image by Dusan Hristovic, in the public domain

5.4 Consumer Society

Meanwhile, the development of the political situation in the world was moving into Yugoslavia's favor. With the condemnation of the Soviet invasion of Hungary, Yugoslavia's relationships with the West significantly improved in the 1960s, while at the same time relationships with the Soviet Union normalized.[20] In 1961, Yugoslavia, together with Egypt and India, was the main initiator of the Non-Aligned Movement that had as a goal to offer an alternative, non-ideological political bloc as a counterweight to the USA and USSR in geopolitical matters. The movement became hugely successful, as many countries controlling strategic resources, such as oil, joined. In cooperation, they were able to exert international influence in favor of their independence from the superpowers. The new political situation on the world stage signified a major increase in economic activity in Yugoslavia and a

[20] Patrick H. Patterson. 2006. Dangerous liaisons: Soviet-Bloc tourists and the Yugoslav good life in the 1960s and 1970s. In *The business of tourism: Place, faith and history*, ed. Philip Scranton and Janet F. Davidson, 186–212. Philadelphia: University of Pennsylvania Press.

subsequent rise of standards of living that was both large and rapid. Yugoslavia was rapidly becoming a consumer society.[21]

As Yugoslavia had a controlled market economy, unlike Soviet Union and its satellite states, the large increase of economic activity lead to a need for automated calculation machines as well as online banking equipment. The manufacturers of the CER series of computers, witnessing a gradual drop in financial backing from the defense apparatus, were looking out for alternative markets. As the accumulation of expertise at the Mihajlo Pupin Institute (IMP) allowed the design of further CER machines, the IMP was from that time on often involved in joint projects with commercial Yugoslav industries to manufacture machines designed by the IBK Vinča and IMP, such as EiNiš and RIZ Zagreb electronics industries.[22] These alliances lead to a highly successful line of CER computers throughout the 1960s, such as the CER-20x and CER-30x series which were sold in high numbers to many Yugoslav companies and served as bookkeeping computers. These series of machines were mostly built using the proven technologies. Yet, in 1967 Yugoslav manufacturers started to employ integrated circuits on a large scale. This reflected the latest developments, as the Yugoslav computer industry, because of the economic prosperity, had gained ground and, despite a late start, was using state of the art, domestically manufactured technologies. Inspired by the IBM unified system approach in the USA, but not cloning it, the newest generations of CER computers, such as CER-203, were utilizing many auxiliary devices such as printers, magnetic tape equipment, plotters, and others. Companies would typically use these machines for market forecasts, bookkeeping, or inventory management.[23] Around the same time, foreign computer manufacturers, including IBM, entered the Yugoslav market with great success, offering top-of-the-line service with their machines.[24] Both domestic and foreign machines were usually employed in specifically organized computing centers and operated by specialists. Unlike the situation at IBM, such centers would not be operated by the computer manufacturer's staff but by company personnel trained by the manufacturer.[25] The widespread use of computers certainly did not harm the Yugoslav industry and economy at large to perform as well as it did during these two decades.

Around 1971, joint projects with Soviet Union and other Comecon nations resulted in the development of new generations of hybrid computer systems, with the design mainly done by Yugoslav and Soviet staff, and the manufacturing performed in the GDR and Czechoslovakia. A case in point was the HRS-100 ("Hibridni Računarski Sistem 100" or "Hybrid Computer System 100") developed by the same

[21] Patterson, Patrick H. 2003. *Consumer culture, the new 'New Class,' and the making of the Yugoslav dream, 1950–1965*. Paper presented at states and social transformation in Eastern Europe 1945–1965. London: The Open University Conference Center.

[22] Protić and Ristanović, Building computers in Serbia.

[23] Ibid.

[24] New Scientist Technology Review. 1971. Yugoslavia Grows Ripe for computer boom. *New Scientist and Science Journal* 51(768): 576.

[25] Yugoslavia Grows Ripe.

Mihajlo Pupin Institute, which had been responsible for the CER line of computers.[26] Yet, the only HRS-100 system known to have been used was deployed at the Academy of Sciences of the Soviet Union since 1971.[27] Another cooperative effort with the Comecon countries was the design and manufacturing of clones of Western computers. Thus the PDP-11/34, produced mainly by the Iskra Delta company for Yugoslavia in a joint venture with DEC of USA, was intended as an affordable competitor on the Yugoslav market for the domestic large computers, the IBM-supplied mainframes and the earlier IBM clones produced by a Comecon consortium under the name of Unified Systems.[28] These machines were often used alongside domestically produced equipment for compatibility purposes, as in the mid-1970s, many large Yugoslav conglomerates such as Energoinvest operated on the international markets and cooperated with large multinational companies in the West.

The positive economic development in Yugoslavia starting in 1960, based on the country's capability to assert its independence through the Non-Aligned Movement, largely contributed to the simultaneous development of a popular consumer culture.[29] Whereas the state leadership in most Warsaw Pact countries forbade cultural expressions which were influenced by the Western consumer society, and subsequently became rather unpopular, the leading League of Communists of Yugoslavia believed in the freedom of cultural expression, as long as taboo themes such as nationalism and separatism were avoided.[30] Consequently, not only the purchasing power but also the cultural life as expressed in film, music, and fine arts would thrive from the early 1960s onwards.[31]

5.5 "New Tendencies"

A striking example of the development in fine arts was the New Tendencies cultural movement, defined by a series of exhibitions and a magazine, *Bit International*. Originating in Zagreb in 1961, New Tendencies took on a significant presence on the international stage in the following years. The idea of independence was very much present in this movement, as its self-declared goals were the demystification and democratization of art by treating of the art process as a scientific and systematic method as opposed to the "stroke of genius" mentality, governing the art markets of the time. Another important issue was the reproducibility of art through

[26] Protić and Ristanović, Building computers in Serbia.

[27] D. Abramovitch. 2005. Analog computing in the Soviet Union. An interview with Boris Kogan. *IEEE Control Systems* 25(3): 52–62.

[28] Nikola Markovic. 2009. E-Potencijali Srbije nr1. *CEPiT E-volucija*, 3–11. Belgrade: Studeni.

[29] Patrick H. Patterson. 2009. Making markets Marxist? The East European grocery store from rationing to rationality to rationalizations. In *Food chains: From farmyard to shopping cart*, ed. Warren Belasco and Roger Horowitz, 196–216. Philadelphia: University of Pennsylvania.

[30] Patterson, Dangerous liaisons.

[31] Petar Janjatović. 1998. *Ilustrovana Enciklopedija Yu Rocka 1960–1997*. Belgrade: Geopoetika.

industrial means and the conversion of the position of the art consumer from mere spectator to participant. Independence was present on a practical level as well, as the New Tendencies expositions featured artists from both sides of the Iron Curtain and from nonaligned nations, which at the time was a rarity. To achieve the stated goals, the movement would, especially since 1968, heavily rely on the use of computers in order to generate visual art and enable mechanical and interactive art and in some cases sound. Works of the movement became defining for the world mainstream after 1965, when the machine-generated patterns and shapes were displayed at the Museum of Modern Art in New York and were received enthusiastically by the audience, to be later used in clothing and other everyday items.[32]

In Yugoslavia's local mainstream, highly modern rock bands came into existence. In urban areas of Yugoslavia rock 'n' roll was the most popular musical expression, while cultural and economic progress had yet to find its way to the rural areas of the country.[33] The economic and cultural development continued almost undisturbed until the late 1970s, with the exception of student and nationalist protests of 1969, which were to a great extent a mirror of the happenings in the West, where in the same year young people collectively came to rebel against authority.[34] While the cultural development in Yugoslavia progressed with a great deal of independence from the state authority, most of it concerned itself with themes common in a consumer society, such as love, growing up, and in some cases even venereal diseases. Due to the cultural and economic focus on consumerism, the general public rarely, if ever, came in contact with computers; those were the machines that were operated by very rare, highly respected, highly skilled experts at enterprises, scientific institutions, and the military; a "normal" person had no business dealing with them. And computers were no object of cultural dissent.

In stark contrast to the USA with its many cultural protest movements, in Yugoslavia in the early 1970s, culture hardly came into view as a vehicle for the expression of dissatisfaction. Standards of living were rising every year and the war and postwar generations saw their quality of life improve constantly and palpably. The country was unique in having a one-party authoritarian government that was, despite its character, very popular. The economic decline set in with the international economic crisis in 1974. Yugoslavia countered the initial decline by increased foreign borrowing and by putting more emphasis on production for export, resulting in the decline being barely perceptible by the population. The steady rise in the standards of living was in danger for the first time since the initial boom in 1950s, and Yugoslav leadership's focus shifted to maintaining the level of wealth with a sizable proportion of foreign credits going to nonproductive sectors, such as public

[32] Margit Rosen. 2011. *A little-known story about a movement, a magazine, and the computer's arrival in art; New tendencies and bit international, 1961–1973*. Cambridge, MA: MIT Press.

[33] Holm Sundhaussen. 2012. *Jugoslawien und seine Nachfolgestaaten 1943–2011. Eine ungewöhnliche Geschichte des Gewöhnlichen*. Wien: Böhlau. See especially the section "Vom Dogmatismus zur Verwestlichung der Kulturszene", 148–151.

[34] Time magazine. 1972. Yugoslavia: The specter of separatism. *TIME Magazine*, February 7, 1972.

services and the consumer expenses.[35] With the economy no longer thriving on heavy industry, the socialist route to modernization ran into crisis. While Western European governments sought to develop post-Keynesian policies, the Yugoslav leadership kept investing, and borrowing, for that purpose. In order to make up for its crumbling legitimacy, the national government decentralized, increasingly depending on a complex equilibrium of the republics states making up Yugoslav republic. After the boom the communist party showed a decade of what Calic calls "Bonapartist reactions."[36]

5.6 Culture Shift and Generation Gap

By late 1979, the rise of the standards of living in Yugoslavia noticeably halted for the first time in more than a decade. The country's decline became plain for all to see. While major reasons for the economic decline may be found in an outdated manufacturing industry and mismanagement of enterprises by a new class of politically appointed bureaucrats, an increasingly unfavorable political situation contributed significantly to the continued unfavorable economic trend.[37] After the death of long-serving Yugoslav president Josip Broz Tito on the 4th of May 1980, the world political situation started to change. A key element in the changing political situation was the waning influence of the Non-Aligned Movement on world affairs and a correspondingly waning influence of Yugoslavia within the Non-Aligned Movement. Added to that, the new policy of the freshly installed Reagan administration in the USA specifically targeted the Yugoslav economy and state as targets for weakening, overthrowing, and incorporation into the Western economic model, trough institutions such as IMF.[38] This was extremely detrimental to an economy relying increasingly on loans and exports. The pressure on the Yugoslav economy was further compounded by the institution of a collective Yugoslav presidency after the death of Tito, that proved very ineffective in combatting the emerging crisis.

At the same time, the young generations of consumers, born in the prosperity of earlier years and used to the combination of increasing standards of living and civil

[35] Central Intelligence Agency. 1990. *World factbook*. Washington, DC: Central Intelligence Agency.

[36] Marie-Janine Calic. 2011. The beginning of the end: The 1970s as a historical turning point in Yugoslavia. In *The crisis of socialist modernity. The Soviet Union and Yugoslavia in the 1970s*, ed. Marie-Janine Calic, Dietmar Neutatz, and Julia Obertreis, 66–86, here 76. Göttingen: Vandenhoeck & Ruprecht.

[37] Harold Lydall. 1989. *Yugoslavia in crisis*, 102–105. Oxford: Clarendon. Calic, The beginning of the end, 79.

[38] "US Policy toward Eastern Europe," National Security Decision Directive NSDD-54 and NSDD-133 (partially declassified in 1990).

freedoms, started to rebel against the older generations which, in their eyes, were mismanaging the country. In 1980, a number of protest movements spontaneously arose, ranging from an environmental movement to movements advocating social reform. Due to the one-party censorship on issues of nationalism and separatism, bottom-up-initiated political reform remained off the agenda.

These protest movements generally consisted of urban youth, many of whom were university students.[39] At the same time, these were also the people who were closely following the cultural development of their peers in the West. Rock 'n' roll did not stop at the borders of socialist countries.[40] Yugoslavia, even more so than the other socialist countries because of its position between the power blocks, had been open to this level of cultural exchange all along. Consequently, Western trends such as punk and *Oi!* music quickly found their way to Yugoslavia, and new music bands came into existence on the platforms of protest and punk. However, as before, the new musical movement had its unique local twist, in its sound, in its message, as well as in its presentation.[41] While the punkers of Great Britain and the USA were very often working-class youth with little education, in Yugoslavia most of the newly formed bands consisted of well-educated university students. Consequently, the music itself was much less harsh, the lyrics much more poetic and multilayered and the presentation often much more "commercial" or "mainstream" than of the Western punk bands. This is why this new style in Yugoslavia is colloquially called New Wave ("Novi Val") of rock, instead of punk. While related to the New-Wave movements in other countries such as USA and UK in their common relationship to the earlier Punk and Rock movements, Yugoslav New Wave was unique both in its local thematic influences and its sound.

Bands rising to fame in this period were the Belgrade-based Idoli, Ljubljana-based Pankrti, Zagreb-based Azra, and Sarajevo-based Zabranjeno Pušenje. While each band had its own distinct style, their unifying element was the fact that all of them provided social commentary on the ever-growing list of social injustices caused by the drop in living standards. These and other bands tied with the first phases of the Yugoslav home computer scene. Idoli, of 1980, is well known for its use of early electronic instruments such as drum computers, as well as programming early home computers for use as music sequencers. Such garage-based bands often had many local admirers who would frequently visit the rehearsals and gigs, which for many people also meant the first contact with computing machinery – other than pocket calculators.

---

39 Predrag Marković, 'Where have all the flowers gone?' – Yugoslav culture in the 1970s, in Calic, Neutatz, and Obertreis, *The crisis of socialist modernity*, 118–133.

40 Sergei Zhuk. 2010. *Rock and roll in the Rocket City: The West, identity and ideology in Soviet Dnepropetrovsk.* Washington, DC: Woodrow Wilson Center Press.

41 Dalibor Misina. 2008. *'Who's that singing over there?' Yugoslav rock-music and the poetics of social critique.* PhD thesis, University of Alberta, Alberta; Thomas Taylor Hammond. 1954. *Yugoslavia between East and West.* Washington, DC: Foreign Policy Association.

5.7 Illegal Imports and the Birth of a Scene

With a more socially engaged youth, through the rise of a protest generation, finding a voice in the magazines ran by The League of Communist Youth of Yugoslavia, experimenting with the unknown, became more popular and common.[42] As much as this had been the case with new musical tastes, drugs, and other experiences youth tended to experiment with, in the early 1980s, this came to include experimenting with home computers.

At this time, a number of problems existed for those who showed an early enthusiasm for the use of home computers. While this enthusiasm was often triggered by witnessing computers at universities, and few university institutes would actually possess an early microcomputer like the Iskradata 1680, or at some friend's place, becoming an owner of a home computer was a different thing altogether. The greatest problem confronting the prospective home computer owners was the price, which could be as high as multiple monthly salaries. At this time, domestic home computer production delivered home computers which were hard to get by, non-compatible with the most available software and usually technologically outdated, so that most people considered a Western-built computer the only realistic option. In addition, the Yugoslav legislative and philosophical tradition of self-reliance was still very much alive, resulting in a situation where import bans for computer equipment remained in place through a good portion of the 1980s. Neither of these reasons, however, was sufficient to deter the well-educated urban youth, which had lost its respect for authority and developed a keen curiosity in the possibilities of the new technology. Only the lucky few could afford to buy a home computer for themselves. The larger part of this small group of computer enthusiasts relied on the culture of collectivism, which was still very much alive in Yugoslavia. Friends from local neighborhoods, used to spending their time together at someone's place anyway, would put the money together to buy home computers abroad and use them together.[43] A common way to obtain a computer for someone living in Sarajevo would be to contact the local black marketeers who were selling imported jeans and other not readily available consumer goods from the West and through their contacts arrange the purchase of a home computer. The machine would either be delivered by them or could be picked up in the Italian city of Trieste, which was frequented by Yugoslav citizens shopping for Western goods, attracted by the much lower prices. For their monetary value, and because they were relatively rare orders, computers were considered more valuable than jeans both by those who transported them and by those who ordered them. Those who ordered them often valued computers more than most things, as they were hard to

[42] Tjebbe van Tijen (ed.). 1989. *Europe against the current: Catalogue on alternative, independent and radical information carriers*. Amsterdam: IISG; Tjebbe van Tijen. 1990. Europa tegen de stroom. *De Gids* 153(6): 466–471; John K. Cox. 2005. *Slovenia: Evolving loyalties*, 77. London: Routledge.

[43] Interviews with Gordana Radević; with Rafo Dužnović; with Darko and Andrej Šolar. Cf note 2, 3, 4.

come by, and owning one represented a unique value in itself.[44] Small private firms in Belgrade would arrange with companies in Germany to deliver the home computers in separate parts, so as to avoid breaking import restrictions. Subsequently, they would assemble these machines by themselves.[45] Most of these machines were Sinclair Z81 or Commodore 64 home computers.

Regardless of these measures, however, home computer ownership and programming remained the activity of a small but highly dedicated group. If not through personal connections, these people would communicate through classified advertisements in the newspapers and meet to exchange software and experiences.

5.8 Galaksija, Computers in Your Home, Revolution

The slow but steady rise of a home computer scene in Yugoslavia, with its ties to both the counterculture and academia, produced a number of inspired and capable technology enthusiasts. While this scene was never formally exclusive, most participants were members of the "in-crowd" – university students with sharp opinions that conflicted with those of the established majority and always ready to express their opinion, usually following the latest trends in underground music and almost exclusively coming from the urban centers of the nation, which constituted a minority of the total population of Yugoslavia.

Among the best known of these enthusiasts was Voja Antonić, a young electrical engineer at the time. As home computers had the tendency to be rather expensive and difficult to import, Antonić found a way to save parts and money. Reading an application manual for the RCA CDP1802 CPU during a holiday in early 1983 in Risan, he came across a method to generate computer graphics by utilizing software on a CPU, as opposed to using a dedicated graphics card. Since the single most expensive component of the home computers at that time was the graphics card, Antonić immediately recognized the potential of generating graphics trough software and make computers cheaper and, therefore, more accessible. Even before he came back from his holiday he had completed a schematic of a computer system that did away with the graphics card. Thus Antonić not only reduced the price of components but also simplified the design.

Around the same time, Dejan Ristanović, a computer enthusiast and part-time journalist, had published an article on the computational properties of the Rubik's cube in the magazine *Galaksija*, something of a popular science type of magazine published in Yugoslavia at the time. One of the readers of his article sent a letter to the editor, asking whether they could make a special publication about computing

---

[44] Interview author with Gordana Radević (cf note 2); interview author with Zdravko Jakić, Amsterdam, Netherlands, September 19, 2010.

[45] Interview author with Djordje Jovanović, co-owner of such a small firm in 1984, Belgrade, Serbia, July 24, 2009.

machinery.[46] Ristanović at the time never figured that there would be a large enough market. The magazine editors decided otherwise and entrusted Ristanović with preparing a special edition of the magazine titled *Računari u vašoj kući* (or *Computers in your home*), dealing with home computers, their programs, applications, and similar subjects. As Ristanović was preparing the special edition,[47] according to his own words,[48] Antonić was looking for a place to publish his – now tested – diagrams for a build-it-yourself cheap home computer. His first thought had been to publish in the popular science *SAM Magazine* in Zagreb, but due to previous bad experiences he decided to look elsewhere. The magazine *Galaksija* being too general to publish computer diagrams in the news of the preparation of a special edition reached Antonić by coincidence through an informed friend. Ristanović and Antonić soon connected and dedicated a major part of the special edition to the diagrams and detailed instructions of how to build their own computer using off the shelf parts that could be found in every electronics store or legally ordered from abroad.[49]

Both the special edition of the magazine, as well as Antonić's home computer, by now named "Galaksija" ("The Galaxy"), appeared to spark a true home computing revolution. The magazine had an initial circulation of 30,000 copies. No one had expected that due to the demand, multiple reprints would have to be issued until a staggering total of 120,000 copies was distributed. Antonić and Ristanović had estimated the number of home computers people would build by themselves, by the "ridiculously optimistic" guess of 1,000. In the end about 8,000 people ordered the build-it-yourself part kits from Antonić,[50] with an estimated total of 11,000 people building their own "Galaksija" home computer. These were huge numbers, and in a matter of months home computing moved from an activity practiced by a small group of hard-core enthusiasts to something of a minor mass phenomenon. Still, despite the increasing popularity of home computing, the demographics of the socially active New-Wave youth and home computer enthusiasts greatly overlapped. And it showed on the machines in a surprising way. The "Galaksija" computers, all identical by the design of their electronics, were delivered without a casing. As a result, most "Galaksija" computers looked different, some were without even a case. In the hands of the creative youth assembling them, many were fitted with quite creative and artistic cases, a feature that would not be repeated in the PC industry until a decade later. Even the innards of the machine reflected a social commitment characteristic of the scene. The "Galaksija" used audiotape as its main storage system, just like other contemporary home computers. Unlike those, "Galaksija" failed to support automatic running of a program after it had been loaded from the tape. The user would have to type the "RUN" command in order to start a program. This was done on purpose, to prevent anyone from creating copy

[46] Dejan Ristanović, http://www.dejanristanovic.com/rac1.htm. Accessed 23 Sept 2010.

[47] Protić and Ristanović, Building computers in Serbia.

[48] Voja Antonić. 1983. *Galaksija*. http://www.paralax.rs/pr83.htm. Accessed 17 June 2010.

[49] Ratko Bošković. 1984. Kako je rodjena Galaksija. *Magazine Start*, February, 25–26.

[50] Protić and Ristanović, Building computers in Serbia.

Fig. 5.2 Galaksija designer, Voja Antonic, in a Yugoslav Homebrewing Scene. The Galaksija home computer was designed and prototyped by Voja Antonic (*right*), who was well known in Yugoslavia at the time as an electronics engineer and science publicist. Antonic is photographed here testing one the first Galaksija's with a friend. The design and schematics for the computer were published in the *Racunari u vasoj kuci* (*Computers in your home*) magazine in late 1983. So was a list of parts, which could either be bought in most electronic stores or ordered as a kit. From the very start, Antonic's vision was to create an affordable computer that would both educate ordinary people about how computers work by having the experience of assemble assembling one as well as let them explore the potential of computers and software. Many users went on to share self-made computer programs and games for the machine through a variety of channels. Source: Image from personal collection Voja Antonic, under Creative Commons license

protection on their software. The design of the system encouraged the sharing of software, as the users, after the program was loaded, also could view and edit the program instead of just running it. The inner design of the machine extended the conviction that computing technology and software should be free and available to anyone, adhered to by the designer Antonić, publisher Ristanović, and also Zoran Modli[51] who was to play his part in the development of the scene (Figs. 5.2 and 5.3).

5.9 Ventilator 202

By that, for home computing in Yugoslavia was very important, in 1984, the host of the already iconic radio show Ventilator 202 ("Electric fan 202") on Radio Beograd 202, Zoran Modli, introduced something very new to this stronghold of the New Wave. On top of the usual airplay of the current hits intermixed with demo tapes of various New-Wave bands, many of whom would go on to become

[51] Ibid. Recollections of Zoran Modli. http://www.modli.rs/. Accessed 20 Feb 2011.

Fig. 5.3 Do-it-yourself Galaksija. Galaksija home computers were usually self-assembled by their users and did not come with a computer case. Sometimes parts were used that were compatible but not specified in the original design. While recommendations for computer case design were supplied in the original design documentation, some users chose not to use a case for the computer at all, as seen here on the image on the *top*. Other users customized their Galaksija cases to reflect their individual preferences, like the design shown in the image on the *bottom*, giving expression to their individuality through yet another medium. Of the approximately 10,000 Galaksija computers assembled, most acquired distinct looks, created by their users. Source: Courtesy Old-computers.com

famous, he would broadcast tape recordings of software programs for different home computers his listeners owned, most importantly the "Galaksija." All this was mixed with some foreign hits and often with interviews with experts from different fields of technology giving their view on the new developments. Himself a professional aviator (commercial airline pilot), radio personality and amateur musician, and one of the recognized front men of the New-Wave movement, he gained an interest in home computing machinery as early as 1979 and saw in it a way to give the power of technology to the "ordinary guy on the street." The first computer-related broadcast consisted of playing the application "Paginator" for the Spectrum Z81 in the late evening of an autumn day in 1983.[52] Soon, however, his listeners started sending in copies of tapes of the computer programs they owned for different platforms, and the computer programs segment became a fixed item in his radio show. Zoran would announce what was going to be played, and for which platform, and the ready listeners could then turn on their recording equipment and record the computer program.

Almost overnight the initiative became immensely popular. Within months from the first computer program broadcasts, people were actually writing software with the specific idea to share it with the entire nation through the broadcasts of Ventilator 202. A number of games, such as a flight simulator and an action-adventure were written specifically for the show, the latter in an iterative way with different programmers actually adding missions to the game and resubmitting it. Next to the games, a number of productivity programs aimed at helping the, high school and university, students to better prepare their lessons were distributed, as well as an early form of electronic journals and magazines. The latter were particularly interesting, because different associations, often music related, describing the party venues, upcoming events, but also discussing the political and social situation, could send in the audiotapes with their electronic journals on a regular basis and have large distribution numbers at virtually no cost and without any state censorship.[53]

5.10 New Kids on the Block

While the economic and social situation continued to gradually deteriorate, starting in late 1984 the restrictions on import of foreign computing machinery were gradually relaxed to the point of annulment by the Yugoslav collective presidency. By the second half of 1985, the prices of foreign home computers had reached quite acceptable levels, which, combined with an already established scene, fueled a relatively large adaptation of home computers. They became commonplace in urban areas. At the same time, the domestic computer manufacturers, especially those who had experience with miniaturization of computers for command-and-control and

[52]Zoran Modli. 2011. *Ventilator 202 recollections*. http://www.modli.rs/radio/ventilator/ventilator.html. Accessed 20 Feb 2011.

[53]Antonić, *Galaksija*.

military purposes, realized the potential of the new market and came with special offers. One of the most popular domestically built machines was mass produced version of Galaksija. It was for a large part purchased by schools and universities, some of which, on an elementary school level, used these machines to educate their students about computers; that was in late 1984! While there was no coherent policy on the federal level, at this time in Yugoslavia the individual republics had established computer education projects in primary education. By law, the educational institutions were obliged to buy domestically produced machines, both to remain independent of foreign influence, and to stimulate the fledgling home computer industry in Yugoslavia. In the market were such machines as the Galeb and Orao produced by PEL Varaždin or the Lola-8 machine produced by Ivo Lola Ribar Institute.[54] The Ivo Lola Ribar Institute, known for building command-and-control and military computers, came with the offering of Lola-8 home computers in 1985, which were mostly used in educational institutions. The market preferred the Western-made machines due to compatibility with the available software and games, lower price, and better availability of the Western-produced machines after the import bans had been lifted – most domestically fabricated home computers were not available in the stores – and the poor computing power of the domestically produced machines.[55] The interesting thing about Lola-8 home computer is that the first editions had a keyboard completely orthogonally laid out rectangular key caps. This was done as a result of using standard command-and-control keyboard components that needed to minimize the entry of environmental dirt into the system. This clearly revealed the military and industrial origins of the machine. In addition to the rectangular keyboard, Lola-8 was mostly built from components that were used in industrial process controllers and mobile military computers produced by Ivo Lola Ribar Institute. Later models, known as Lola-8a, were equipped with regular Qwerty keyboards.[56] Many other domestic manufacturers had entered the market by the late 1980s, meeting only with limited success for the same reasons as those for the relatively low adaptation of the Lola-8 machine – very limited availability in stores, incompatibility with vast software stores for foreign-produced machines, a higher price than the Western-produced competition, and lower computing power.

In contrast with home computer enthusiasts in the West who had to deal with a slightly geek stigma, in Yugoslavia at the time, an average home computer enthusiast was a socially popular person, organizing parties and being generally looked up to by his peers. It was therefore, as mentioned in the introduction, a very common thing to see a home computer fulfilling a role at some house party as a device of entertainment or competition. Different partygoers would bring their own software, or the software they just obtained, and show off their computer skills. The beer-drinking

---

[54] Protić and Ristanović, Building computers in Serbia.

[55] Cox, *Slovenia*; interviews author with Darko and Andrej Šolar; Wikipedia contributions by Aleksandar Šušnjar. http://en.wikipedia.org/wiki/History_of_computer_hardware_in_the_SFRY. Accessed 21 Feb 2011.

[56] Protić and Ristanović, Building computers in Serbia.

contests, common at such parties, were sometimes less important than programming contests.[57]

While home computers and the subculture within which they existed became increasingly mainstream, the political and economic situation in Yugoslavia kept deteriorating. Interestingly, when, under the influence of nationalism, in the late 1980s signs started appearing that Yugoslavia might disintegrate, it was the same protest culture of, meanwhile very popular, bands and computer enthusiasts that most vocally protested a possible breakup. The subculture was now in a position of generally supporting the Yugoslav federation and the idea that while the society needed to be reformed, it did not need to be destroyed. Unfortunately, since the support from the, larger, rural areas was in favor of the nationalist option, and with the traditional dislike on the part of the rural dwellers for the urban people, this often only intensified the nationalist sentiment and the downfall of Yugoslav economy.

With the downward spiral in society and economy well underway, the beginning of the 1990s brought not only the end of the Socialist Federal Republic of Yugoslavia in a series of what would ultimately become bloody wars but also the end of the once vibrant New Wave and home computer scene. Many who participated in both movements went on to graduate during the 1980s and become prolific electric and computer engineers, who, at the breakout of Yugoslav wars, emigrated en masse to the West where their skills were met with appreciation. Indeed, many of this generation went on to fulfill highly placed jobs at large Western corporations such as IBM and Sun Microsystems. In what would later become Serbia alone, about 350,000 skilled graduates left the country between 1991 and 1993. Another part of the scene stayed and continued to make music while intensifying their political engagement. This occurred, however, on the level of their newly formed republics, as Yugoslavia already had disintegrated. Most notable is the Serbian movement against the Slobodan Milošević regime, OTPOR ("Resistance"), which largely consisted of university students and often was led and supported by former members of the New-Wave underground. New generations of protesters quickly found that using the technology, as the prolific Modli had realized a decade earlier, to spread their message electronically and to organize – this time using the Internet instead of a radio show and radio over the Internet – gave them the power to be heard by the world and to be feared by the regime. Notable is the example of the Belgrade-based radio station B92 that cooperated with the Amsterdam, Netherlands, based Internet access providers XS4ALL, and De Digitale Stad to provide their radio streams over the Internet since 1996. After their FM operations had been shut down by the Milošević regime in 1998, and also during the bombing of Yugoslavia by NATO in 1999, B92 continued to broadcast over their Internet lines. Those broadcasts were then rebroadcasted by the BBC World Service by satellite, with small independent radio stations in Serbia picking up the signal and broadcasting it locally again over FM.[58] That

---

[57] Interviews author with Gordana Radević; with Rafo Dužnović; with Darko and Andrej Šolar, note 2, 3, 4.

[58] Marie-José Klaver. 1998. De digitale vluchtweg. *NRC Handelsblad*, October 29. CFJE. 1999. CFJE Joins Campaign to support Radio B92 in Belgrade. *CJFE News Release*, March 26, 1999; Marie-José Klaver. 1999. Boem, boem uit de chatroom. *NRC Handelsblad*, May 17.

generation has managed to be instrumental in the ousting of Milošević, yet their use of computing machinery was in that sense clever yet purely utilitarian, as it did not arise from an enthusiasm about the possibilities.

5.11 Conclusion

Having reviewed the research materials for this paper, and combining the literature with personal recollections of participants in the events that unfolded some 30 years ago, publications and personal experiences, it is hard to escape the conclusion that the development of computing in Yugoslavia in general, and specifically of the home computing in the 1980s, has indeed had a local flavor distinct from the developments in other countries at the time. As the Cold War paradigm, in which Yugoslavia found itself only shortly after its creation, had prompted an indigenous development of different technologies including computing machinery, it also gave rise to a technologically advanced culture, in which science and technology were promoted both by the government and by individuals with distinctly technology-oriented hobbies and interests. While there were always external influences with regard to the knowledge about the field of computing technology, for instance with France in the early days of computer development in Yugoslavia, major contributions were made by local researchers and industries. This led to the creation of what was for a significant period of time a competitive local computer industry, performing domestic research, development and production of computing machines, and associated knowledge. With the advent of more accessible computer technologies and the rise of a protest music scene in Yugoslavia, young people combined their new tastes in music and sympathetic rebellion with the use of home computers for leisure, communication, personal development, and peer competition. In this way, they appropriated what were initially hallmarks of Western culture creating a distinct local narrative. With the disintegration of Yugoslavia and subsequent wars, sanctions, emigrations, and open violent protests, the heritage of this scene remains only marginally visible in the new countries that used to form Yugoslavia. No special scenes exist today for computer technology enthusiasts that would be distinct from those in the USA or most other places in the world, and the skills which used to have a wider social meaning now find almost exclusively only professional appreciation.

Bibliography

Abramovitch, D. 2005. Analog computing in the Soviet Union. An interview with Boris Kogan. *IEEE Control Systems* 25(3): 52–62.

Antonić, Voja. 1983. *Galaksija*. http://www.paralax.rs/pr83.htm. Accessed 17 June 2010.

Barryman, J. 1988. The Soviet Union and Yugoslavia's defence and foreign policy. In *Yugoslavia's security dilemmas – Armed forces, national defence and foreign policy*, ed. M. Milivojevic, J.B. Allcock, and P. Maurer, 192–260. Oxford: Oxford University Press.

Batanović, Vladan, and Jovan Kon. 2006. *IMP Riznica znanja*. Belgrade: M. Pupin Institute and PKS.

Bertsch, Gary K., and Thomas W. Ganschow. 1976. *Comparative communism: The Soviet, Chinese, and Yugoslav models*. San Francisco: W.H. Freeman.

Bošković, Ratko. 1984. Kako je rodjena Galaksija. *Magazine Start*, February, 25–26.

Calic, Marie-Janine. 2011. The beginning of the end: The 1970s as a historical turning point in Yugoslavia. In *The crisis of socialist modernity. The Soviet Union and Yugoslavia in the 1970s*, ed. Marie-Janine Calic, Dietmar Neutatz, and Julia Obertreis, 66–86. Göttingen: Vandenhoeck & Ruprecht.

Central Intelligence Agency. 1990. *World factbook*. Washington, DC: Central Intelligence Agency.

Cox, John K. 2005. *Slovenia: Evolving loyalties*. London: Routledge.

Curtis, Glenn E. 1990. *Yugoslavia: A country study*. Washington, DC: Library of Congress, Federal Research Division.

Dulić, Tornislav, and Roland Kostić. 2010. Yugoslavs in arms: Guerrilla tradition, total defence and the ethnic security dilemma. *Europe-Asia Studies* 62(7): 1051–1072.

Economist. 1984. Yugoslavia. In *The world in figures*, 240–242. London: MacMillan.

Hammond, Thomas Taylor. 1954. *Yugoslavia between East and West*. Washington, DC: Foreign Policy Association.

Janjatović, Petar. 1998. *Ilustrovana Enciklopedija Yu Rocka 1960–1997*. Belgrade: Geopoetika.

Klaver, Marie-José. 1998. De Digitale Vluchtweg. *NRC Handelsblad*, October 29.

Klaver, Marie-José. 1999. Boem, boem uit de chatroom. *NRC Handelsblad*, May 17.

Lydall, Harold. 1989. *Yugoslavia in crisis*. Oxford: Clarendon.

Markovic, Nikola. 2009. E-Potencijali Srbije nr1. *CEPiT E-volucija*, 3–11. Belgrade: Studeni.

Marković, Predrag. 2011. 'Where have all the flowers gone?' – Yugoslav culture in the 1970s. In *The crisis of socialist modernity. The Soviet Union and Yugoslavia in the 1970s*, ed. Marie-Janine Calic, Dietmar Neutatz, and Julia Obertreis, 118–133. Göttingen: Vandenhoeck & Ruprecht.

Mesarić, Milan. 1971. *Suvremena znanstveno tehnička revolucija*. Zagreb: Ekonomski institut.

Misina, Dalibor. 2008. *'Who's that singing over there?' Yugoslav rock-music and the poetics of social critique*. PhD thesis, University of Alberta, Alberta.

Modli, Zoran. 2011. *Ventilator 202 recollections*. http://www.modli.rs/radio/ventilator/ventilator.html. Accessed 20 Feb 2011.

New Scientist Technology Review. 1971. Yugoslavia Grows Ripe for computer boom. *New Scientist and Science Journal* 51(768): 576.

Patterson, Patrick H. 2003. *Consumer culture, the new 'New Class,' and the making of the Yugoslav dream, 1950–1965*. Paper presented at states and social transformation in Eastern Europe 1945–1965. London: The Open University Conference Center.

Patterson, Patrick H. 2006. Dangerous liaisons: Soviet-bloc tourists and the Yugoslav good life in the 1960s and 1970s. In *The business of tourism: Place, faith and history*, ed. Philip Scranton and Janet F. Davidson, 186–212. Philadelphia: University of Pennsylvania Press.

Patterson, Patrick H. 2009. Making markets Marxist? The East European grocery store from rationing to rationality to rationalizations. In *Food chains: From farmyard to shopping cart*, ed. Warren Belasco and Roger Horowitz, 196–216. Philadelphia: University of Pennsylvania Press.

Perry, Marvin, Myrna Chase, Margaret C. Jacob, et al. 2007. *Western civilization: Ideas, politics, and society*. Boston: Wadsworth.

Potter, William C., Djuro Miljanić, and Ivo Slaus. 2000. Tito's nuclear legacy. *Bulletin of Atomic Scientists* 56(2): 63–70.

Protić, Jelica, and Dejan Ristanović. 2011. Building computers in Serbia: The first half of the digital century. *Computer Science and Information Systems* 8(3): 549–571.

Ramet, Sabrina P. 2006. *The three Yugoslavias: State-building and legitimation, 1918–2005*. Bloomington: University of Indiana Press.

Rosen, Margit. 2011. *A little-known story about a movement, a magazine, and the computer's arrival in art; New tendencies and bit international, 1961–1973*. Cambridge, MA: MIT Press.

Rothstein, Robert L. 1968. *Alliances and small powers*. New York: Columbia University Press.

Sundhaussen, Holm. 2012. *Jugoslawien und seine Nachfolgestaaten 1943–2011. Eine ungewöhnliche Geschichte des Gewöhnlichen*. Wien: Böhlau.

Tomović, R., A. Mandžić, T. Aleksić, et al. 1960. Cifarski Elektronski Računar CER10 IBK Vinča. *ETAN-1960* 1: 305–330.

van Tijen, Tjebbe (ed.). 1989. *Europe against the current: Catalogue on alternative, independent and radical information carriers*. Amsterdam: IISG.

van Tijen, Tjebbe. 1990. Europa tegen de stroom. *De Gids* 153(6): 466–471.

Veladžić, Edin, Goran Miloradović, et al. 2010. *Yugoslavia between East and West; Ordinary people in unordinary country*. Online project EUROCLIO – HIP http://www.cliohip.com. Accessed 24 Nov 2011.

Walen, Robert J., Stevan Dedijer, and Pavle Savić of IBK Vinča. 1953. *O dva bitna uslova za razvitak atomske energije kod nas*. Belgrade, Yugoslavia.

Zhuk, Sergei. 2010. *Rock and roll in the Rocket City: The West, identity and ideology in Soviet Dnepropetrovsk*. Washington, DC: Woodrow Wilson Center Press.

Zimmerman, William. 1972. Hierarchical regional systems and the politics of system boundaries. *International Organization* 26(1): 18–36.

Zimmerman, William. 1987. *Open borders, non-alignment and the political evolution of Yugoslavia*. Princeton: Princeton University Press.

Chapter 6
Playing and Copying: Social Practices of Home Computer Users in Poland during the 1980s

Patryk Wasiak

6.1 Introduction

This chapter discusses how private users domesticated home computers in socialist Poland during the late 1980s and which social actors shaped computer consumer culture.[1] Entrepreneurs operating in the informal economy based on international networks and state-owned retail stores provided potential users indirect access to Western Europe's home computer market. In this way, Polish customers were able to purchase imported hardware platforms that were popular in Western Europe along with the software. The dissemination of imported technology and knowledge shaped the appropriation of scripts for computer use and the development of the local "demoscene" as did advocates of the Polish computerization movement.

My study covers the development of Poland's computer culture in the brief but dynamic period from 1985 to 1989. In 1985, dedicated "computer bazaars" appeared alongside pioneering computer magazines. Both helped popularize home computers among young people. Neither political dissidents nor the fall of the communist regime in 1989 significantly changed computer user practices.[2] The transformation

---

[1] This chapter was written with the support of the Andrew W. Mellon Foundation Fellowship at the Netherlands Institute for Advanced Study in the Humanities and Social Sciences and a research grant from the Foundation for the History of Technology. I would like to express my gratitude to Gerard Alberts, Ruth Oldenziel, Markku Reunanen, and Antti Silvast for valuable comments on my manuscript.

[2] Home computers were very rarely used for editing samizdat magazines. One well-known case was when a ZX Spectrum helped to locally scramble the state TV signal and enabled pirate broadcasting of a Solidarity statement lasting a few minutes. Reported online at http://w.icm.edu.pl/tvS/tvs.htm. Accessed 20 Dec 2010. For an overview of computer crime stories see Buck BloomBecker. 1990. *Spectacular computer crimes: What they are and how they cost American business half a billion dollars a year!*. Homewood: Dow Jones-Irwin.

P. Wasiak (✉)
Institute for Cultural Studies, University of Wrocław, Wrocław, Poland
e-mail: patrykwasiak@gmail.com

G. Alberts and R. Oldenziel (eds.), *Hacking Europe. From Computer Cultures to Demoscenes*, History of Computing, DOI 10.1007/978-1-4471-5493-8_6,

of computer consumer culture only occurred after a copyright protection law was imposed in 1994. The prohibitively expensive IBM PC MS-DOS standard computers were found in some companies and institutions. The first popular hardware platform of 8- and 16-bit home computers in the mid-1980s was the ZX Spectrum, only to be quickly replaced by the Atari XE and Commodore 64 before the Commodore Amiga and the less popular Atari ST took over. By the mid-1990s, the PC standard dominated the computer market. Two Polish computers were produced in small quantities (the TRS-80 clone Meritum and the ZX Spectrum clone Elwro Junior) for a few schools. Just like machines from other socialist countries, they failed to play any significant role in the domestication of home computers.

I focus on the social space where manufacturers, retailers, mediators, and users negotiated scripts using technological artifacts in what has been called the "mediation junction."[3] This concept originally described the mediation technologies between producers and consumers, emphasizing the role of users as coproducers of technology. Steve Woolgar has discussed the role of computer technology designers in "configuring the user."[4] Thus far, social studies of technology have only sporadically recognized the role of home computer users such as in Christina Lindsay's case study of TRS-80 users.[5] My analysis uses printed sources such as the popular press, computer magazines, computer hobbyists' interviews, and memoirs, along with reader surveys in computer magazines like the Polish *Bajtek*. Its survey showed that of computer users, 97 % were male, 70 % were aged between 12 and 17, and 60 % lived in large cities.[6] According to *Komputer* magazine's reader survey, 41 % bought imported home computers abroad, 34 % bought them with local currency mostly at computer bazaars, and 25 % in Pewex or Baltona retail stores.[7]

While the state-owned media distinguished between the negative "capitalist" and positive "socialist," popular opinion subverted this, employing the term "Western" for goods brought from West Germany or the USA as positive, modern, and fashionable.[8] The term "Western" was more widely used in the communist period than

---

[3] Madeleine Akrich. 1992. The de-scription of technical objects. In *Shaping technology/building society: Studies in sociotechnical change*, ed. Wiebe E. Bijker and John Law, 205–224. Cambridge, MA: MIT Press; Ruth Oldenziel, Adri Albert de la Bruhèze, and Onno de Wit. 2005. Europe's mediation junction: Technology and consumer society in the twentieth century. *History and Technology* 21(1): 107–139.

[4] Steve Woolgar. 1991. Configuring the user: The case of usability trials. In *A sociology of monsters: Essays on power, technology and domination*, ed. John Law, 57–102. London/New York: Routledge.

[5] Christina Lindsay. 2003. From the shadows: Users as designers, producers, marketers, distributors and technical support. In *How users matter: The co-construction of users and technology*, ed. Nelly Oudshoorn and Trevor J. Pinch, 29–50. Cambridge, MA: MIT Press.

[6] "About 5,000 respondents," *Bajtek* (June 1989): 4. Because these were predominantly male, I will refer to single users as "he."

[7] *Komputer* (February 1988): 8.

[8] "Nylon curtain" is the metaphor invoked to describe the flow of cultural phenomena across the Iron Curtain: Gyorgy Péteri (ed.). 2006. *Nylon curtain. Transnational and transsystemic tendencies in the cultural life of state-socialist Russia and East-Central Europe*, TSEECS no. 18. Trondheim: TSEECS.

"European" or "American."[9] Not only popular culture but also primarily music and movies from the West were highly regarded by Poles in the era. Virtually all fast-moving consumer goods and material artifacts manufactured in the West were regarded as superior to domestic products, and its possession and consumption was recognized as a significant indicator of both material and cultural capital. Consumer electronics in the 1980s like VCRs, satellite TV receivers, and home computers provided users with access to cultural goods such as movies and computer games produced in Western Europe and the USA which were previously unavailable in the Soviet Bloc.[10] In such a context, computer culture was appealing as a consumption of "Western" material artifacts which at the same time provided user with interesting practices such as programming and playing computer games.

6.2 Private Importers

Monographs on technology transfer across the Iron Curtain usually focus on the policies of state actors like the Coordinating Committee for Multilateral Export Controls (COCOM).[11] The role of non-state actors in the transfer of domestic electronics through the Iron Curtain is still not recognized. The COCOM embargo was not strict in the 1980s, when personal and home computers became popular and obtaining an export license was a mere formality. Moreover, 8-bit home computers were excluded from the list. In the final decade of the Cold War, more and more computers were imported to socialist countries especially Poland and Hungary, where the cross-border flow of people and commodities was relatively easy.

The communist regime in Poland was led by General Wojciech Jaruzelski, who had crushed the Solidarity movement in the early 1980s by imposing Martial Law. Declared on December 13, 1981, this law would only last for a year and a half. The growing social conflict between communist authorities and the underground Solidarity would ultimately lead to the collapse of the communist regime in1989. The 1980s saw a deepening economic crisis, growing shortages of consumer goods,

---

[9] See Gyorgy Péteri (ed.). 2010. *Imagining the West in Eastern Europe and the Soviet Union*. Pittsburgh: University of Pittsburgh Press.

[10] Almost all domestic electronics were brought to Poland from Western Europe. Despite frequent travels to USA, the import of home media electronics was rare due to the incompatibility of the American NTSC analog television system with PAL and SECAM used in Europe and differences in voltage.

[11] For technology transfer during the Cold War, see Gary K. Bertsch (ed.). 1988. *Controlling East–West trade and technology transfer: Power, politics, and policies*. Durham: Duke University Press; Frank Cain. 2005. Computers and the Cold War: United States restrictions on the export of computers to the Soviet Union and Communist China. *Journal of Contemporary History* 40(1): 131–147; Michael Mastanduno. 1992. *Economic containment: CoCom and the politics of East-West trade*. Ithaca: Cornell University Press; Paul N. Edwards. 1996. *The closed world: Computers and the politics of discourse in Cold War America*. Cambridge, MA: MIT Press.

and hyperinflation. The crisis was somewhat eased by the possibility of foreign travel, with strict restrictions only applied to political dissidents. By 1983, numerous Poles used the restored opportunities for foreign travel to work illegally in West Germany, the UK, Sweden, and the USA. Due to an extremely high black market exchange rate for convertible currency, even small sums earned abroad were worth a fortune in Poland. In the 1980s, paradoxically Poles could travel to West Berlin far more easily than GDR citizens. It was customary for them to bring back consumer goods as gifts or items for sale on the domestic black market.

These circumstances led to a flourishing informal economy and the domestication of consumer goods.[12] Aside from coffee and chocolate, which are difficult to obtain in Poland at the time, commodities such as clothes and consumer electronics were symbols of high social status. With a little luck and a long time standing in line, Poles could buy a Polish or Soviet TV set, radio, or tape recorder in a retail store, but VCRs and home computers were produced in small quantities and unavailable through the official distribution outlets in the early 1980s. Private import was the only way to acquire such commodities. The presence of these objects in households, where they were shown to relatives and friends, increased their popularity. The ensuing demand was met by trade tourists traveling abroad to import consumer goods. Entrepreneurs established profitable trade routes to other socialist and capitalist countries. West Germany, and especially West Berlin, was the most popular destination for Poles' trade travels.[13] This was described in the official press as black market "economic pathology":

> During a tourist excursion to Hamburg, an individual buys a single ZX Spectrum 2 for 120 DM. He brings it to the domestic bazaar to earn 250,000 zł. From hand to hand, no formalities, no efforts. According to the black market currency exchange rate, the person could earn 190,000 zł, a fourfold profit. Even if one needs to subtract the cost of the tour, such travel brings a substantial profit.[14]

To quote the 1986 Customs Office report, imports of 4,590 home computers were declared by private individuals at Warsaw airport. In 1987, the average Polish citizen earned about 30,000 zł per month: a home computer was the equivalent of several months' salary. The disproportion made private import extremely profitable.

Some home computers, for instance, Commodore 64 and Amiga, arrived equipped with locally appropriated European keyboards. The popularity of two

[12] Case studies of consumerism in socialist countries can be found in Susan E. Reid, and David Crowley (eds.). 2000. *Style and socialism. Modernity and material culture in post-war Eastern Europe*. Oxford/New York: Berg Publishers; David Crowley, and Susan E. Reid (eds.). 2002. *Socialist spaces: Sites of everyday life in the Eastern bloc*. Oxford/New York: Berg Publishers.

[13] The impact of trade tourism on consumer culture in Poland is discussed in Ursula Weber. 2002. *Der Polenmarkt in Berlin: zur Rekonstruktion eines kulturellen Kontakts im Prozeß der politischen Transformation Mittel- und Osteuropas*. Neuried: Ars Una; Małgorzata Irek. 1998. *Schmugglerzug Warschau-Berlin-Warschau: Materialien einer Feldforschung*. Berlin: Das Arabische Buch.

[14] Jerzy Szperkowicz. 1987. Skąd się biorą komputery? [Where computers came from?] *Horyzonty Techniki*, special issue *64 strony o komputerach* (*64 pages on computers*), 34.

specific keyboards illustrates the transnational trade routes of Polish workers and trade tourists. The most popular were the UK standard QWERTY keyboard with a £ sign and the German QWERTZ with German diacritics. The latter was perceived as cumbersome and computers with such keyboards were slightly cheaper.

6.3 Computer Bazaars

The economy of shortages in state socialist Poland produced an informal economy.[15] Consumer electronics brought in by trade tourists were sold at bazaars, which were a substitute for a free market, based on the rule of supply and demand. In the early 1980s, these bazaars were the main source of imported hardware and pirate software. In 1986, one observer described the largest Polish computer row in "The Persian bazaar" in Warsaw thus:

> There is a wide range on offer at the Warsaw bazaar. There is everything from microcomputers and peripherals through software to services like repairs and hardware modifications. There is no problem with the availability of literature. [...] Among computers for sale the most popular are ZX Spectrum and Commodore 64. [...] Certainly, software is also available.[16]

The bazaars also provided the services needed for the daily use of technological artifacts.[17] Aside from bazaars, pirate software was massively copied in numerous "computer studios" – small privately owned shops, which also distributed software through mail order. The first dedicated "computer bazaar" was established in Warsaw's Grzybowska Street in 1985 at the initiative of the computerization movement and *Bajtek* magazine in an effort to "civilize the computer market." In technology enthusiasts' view, computer bazaars should be sites where computer users, instead of entrepreneurs, could sell their old computers and peripherals for fair prices. Software would be exchanged on a nonprofit basis. In reality, peddlers moved in from other bazaars and quickly took over the supply of hardware and pirate software. The computer movement had not anticipated such practices and would later criticize these bazaars in computer magazines and the popular press for being breeding grounds of shady and unfair economic activities, even as sources of pirate software.[18]

---

[15] Alejandro Portes, Manuel Castells, and Lauren A. Benton (eds.). 1995. *The informal economy: Studies in advanced and less developed countries.* Baltimore: Johns Hopkins University Press; Janine Wedel (ed.). 1992. *The unplanned society: Poland during and after communism.* New York: Columbia University Press.

[16] Roman Poznański. 1985. Informatyka na Perskim [Informatics on the Persian Bazaar]. *Bajtek*, October, 24–25.

[17] One popular modification was tuning TV sets produced in Poland and the Soviet Union from SECAM to PAL signal system to work with home computers and VCRs bought in Western Europe.

[18] After numerous appeals, *Bajtek* finally withdrew its patronage from the Warsaw bazaar in 1989 due to mass piracy and shady businesses. The decision had minimal impact.

Dedicated computer bazaars did play a significant role in disseminating computer entertainment and developing social networks among users. Dealers in pirate software primarily offered computer games, which after all were more popular than spreadsheets, word processors, and programming language compilers. Software peddlers from bazaars and owners of "computer studios" offered potential clients the opportunity to try new games on the spot. Game reviews and advertisements cut from foreign computer magazines were exhibited on stands with pirate software.[19] At the same time, such sites also played a significant part in disseminating knowledge. You could buy photocopies of English original or homemade translations of hardware manuals and textbooks at various levels of proficiency. Imported computers included manuals in English or German, languages most Poles did not know, since they were usually obliged to learn Russian at school. This factor shaped the demand for computer knowledge in Polish and led to the mass production of bootleg translations of manuals as well as the authorship of such books by Polish authors.[20]

Smaller computer bazaars were established during the late 1980s in most Polish cities. These survived until 1995, when the police started regular anti-piracy raids as a result of the Copyright Protection Act. Computer bazaars played a pioneering role, and after 1989, they evolved concurrently with the growing industry of legal software retailers.[21]

6.4 Pewex and Baltona Retail Stores

During the late 1980s, Pewex and Baltona state-owned dollar retail stores offered consumer electronics along with other Western consumer goods because of their growing popularity. This so-called internal export aimed to collect hard currency from citizens to pay back Western loans from the 1970s, which was a matter of urgency for Poland's economy in the 1980s. Pewex was a counterpart of the better-known East German Intershop, where you could also purchase home computers. Both companies chose the Atari XE as their hardware platform. A market failure in Western Europe, the XE model was introduced to Eastern Europe with an extensive marketing campaign and at a relatively low price.[22] Atari computers became very

---

[19] Pirate software was also distributed through a mail-order system. In catalogues of pirate software available in Poland, games constituted about 70 % of the programs. A list of catalogs is available on http://atarionline.pl. Accessed 20 Dec 2010.

[20] A large list of publishers' bootleg brochures and books is available at http://atarionline.pl. Accessed 20 Dec 2010.

[21] Currently computer bazaars only exist in Warsaw. New and used hardware and legal software is offered there cheaper than in retail stores and pirate games are available.

[22] Interview with Wencel, Lucjan. 1986. Head of cooperation with Eastern Europe at Atari. *Komputer* (August): 11–12. Atari was the only home computer manufacturing company which had a marketing campaign in Poland before 1989. Atari computers were also distributed in Hungary, GDR, and Yugoslavia. Commodore International Ltd. officially entered the Polish market in 1991:

popular among Poles for two reasons. Both retail stores' networks were considered sources of the best brands of Western consumer goods. Poles tended to perceive anything sold there not merely as good quality but also as a luxury item. Pewex in cooperation with state-owned company Karen was the first retailer in Poland to provide warranty services for their computers.[23] Both companies developed marketing strategies such as the first full-page color advertisement for a home computer published in *Bajtek*, featuring an Atari 130XE with the slogan "Atari – computer for a Christmas gift" and a small Pewex logo.[24] Atari was sold in Pewex at the same price as the Commodore C-64 in computer bazaars but became more popular despite a smaller choice of software. As both retail chains wanted to increase their profits, the computers were marketed primarily as game platforms – probably perceived as the most attractive script for potential consumers – and offered with a games package.[25]

6.5 Computerization Movement

The computerization movement played an equally significant role as intermediary in expanding computer use.[26] The broad coalition included the Polish Association of Informatics (Polskie Towarzystwo Informatyczne, or PTI, founded in 1982), activists from the Association of Polish Socialist Youth (Związek Socjalistycznej Młodzieży Polskiej, ZSMP), and journalists from *The Young Technician* (*Młody Technik*) magazine involved in the popularization of technology.[27] Their aim was to lobby among party decision-makers to increase investments for disseminating computer technologies and promoting computers to ordinary citizens:

> We are convinced that a country unable to develop autonomous systems for gathering, processing and making available information could not become a rightful member of modern civilized community. We seek public understanding of the necessity for state patronage over applications of informatics.[28]

"Nareszcie w Polsce" (Finally in Poland), *Commodore & Amiga* (February 1992), 2. There is no evidence of any other computer manufacturers interested in the Polish market before 1989; obviously, computer magazines would have welcomed such information.

[23] Interview with Wiesław Migut, Head of Atari computers marketing branch in foreign trade for the company Karen, *Komputer* (August 1986): 12.

[24] *Bajtek* (November 1986): 24.

[25] As proof of the continuing popularity of *the* platform, an active Polish community of retro Atari XE users exists to this day: http://atarionline.pl. Accessed 20 Dec 2010.

[26] Rob Kling, and C. Suzanne Iacono. 1995. Computerization movements and the mobilization of support for computerization. In *Ecologies of knowledge. Work and politics in science and technology*, ed. Susan Leigh Star, 119–153. Albany: State University of New York Press.

[27] *Młody Technik* was a very popular Polish magazine on hobby electronics and tinkering, which aimed to promote technical culture – a counterpart of the Soviet *Tekhnika Molodezhi.*

[28] *TPI Bulletin* 10 (1982). http://www.cs.put.poznan.pl/archiwumpti/. Accessed 20 Dec 2010.

PTI members tried to achieve their goals by participating in numerous bureaucratic advisory committees. They also promoted the dissemination of computer technology in media interviews, like in *The People's Voice* (the press organ of the PZPR – the Polish United Workers' Party), the ruling communist party, and computer magazines. PTI experts presented computerization as a crucial agent of social development, indeed as a silver bullet to increase the efficiency of a planned economy in decline. Combining computerization with the vision of socialist modernization, they sought to influence high-ranking party leaders and simultaneously promote responsibility among computer users. The chairman of PTI appealed with typical communist propaganda:

> The computer hype concerns only entertainment informatics. Computer toys are merely an unimportant episode and the cheapest method in the communion with the West. [...] To achieve the real, not merely spectacular, benefit from the dissemination of informatics, intellectual and material concentration of efforts should come soon.[29]

Officially, computerization in Poland was called "The game for tomorrow" ("Gra o jutro"). Young people were encouraged to use computers exclusively for "serious purposes" instead of entertainment. For instance, an editorial in *Bajtek* in 1989 criticized computer entertainment for its failure to increase "the actual output of national economy."[30] Young users were supposed to improve their knowledge of computers and programming skills to help computerize companies where they would work as adults. Appeals voiced in this tone had virtually no impact on the domestication of home computers. One success of the computerization movement was the implementation of a computer education program based on obligatory programming courses in LOGO and BASIC in selected schools; however, due to the lack of funds and trained teachers, the project had a rather limited social impact.[31]

6.6 Computer Magazines

The most influential Polish computer magazine in the late 1980s was *Bajtek*. The title was an intentional reference to the term "byte" and the American magazine *Byte*. Established in 1985, *Bajtek* targeted current and potential young users of home computer and was modeled after the English-language magazines *Your Computer* and *Compute!* The second Polish magazine, *Komputer*, established in

[29] "Rzecz głęboko matematyczna, rozmowa z Władysławem M. Turskim, prezesem PTI" (About mathematics, Interview with Marian Turski, chairman of PTI), *Życie gospodarcze* (April 4, 1986): 39.

[30] Waldemar Siwiński. 1989. Poza priorytetem [Outside the priority]. *Bajtek*, March, 2.

[31] Maciej M. Sysło, and Anna B. Kwiatkowska. 2008. The challenging face of informatics education in Poland. In *Informatics education – Supporting computational thinking*, ed. Roland T. Mittermeir and Maciej M. Sysło, 1–18. Berlin/Heidelberg: Springer.

1986, with a similar format to *Byte* and *Chip*, addressed a readership interested in using computers in their professional careers. *Bajtek* was popular among the Polish youth and played an important role in disseminating computer knowledge. Published under the auspices of ZSMP, *Bajtek* became a major media channel for the computerization movement. Its first issue in 1985 clearly stated the goals of the coalition:

> *Bajtek* is a popular magazine dedicated to all issues linked with information processing. Our aim is to help everyone who owns, or would like to own a computer. There is no point in talking about the significance of development of microcomputer technologies for all societies. [...] We would like only to add that this cause is CRUCIAL FOR THE PROSPEROUS FUTURE OF OUR COUNTRY. Our ambition is to fight against computer illiteracy. We seek the help of all who have some experience in fighting for the cause of informatics.[32]

Every issue began with a similar propaganda editorial. A section entitled "The game of tomorrow" included interviews with computer experts, scientists, or professionals who were using computers. Sometimes there were enthusiastic reports on computerization in the Soviet Union. However, that was the only political part of *Bajtek* and the rest of the content resembled Western computer magazines. The news section featured information from Silicon Valley and the Far East. There were sections dedicated to Spectrum, Atari, and Commodore hardware platforms including entry-level information on computer use, programming courses, software listings in BASIC, and blueprints for hardware hacking. Type-in listings were published with extended comments mostly for educational purposes; readers were encouraged to modify programs to understand the principles of programming. The opportunity to learn programming skills was acknowledged by many user testimonials. "I started with playing games. [...] First, I was learning BASIC commands. Then *Bajtek* came along. I was typing listings of programs published in *Bajtek* and *Komputer* and this way I learned how to program."[33]

There was also a section on computer games called "What's going on?" ("Co jest grane?"). Aside from reviews of new titles and a top-ten list, the section featured numerous instructions on how to modify games to get unlimited lives, and similar cheats. The editors sought to encourage children to understand how programs were structured. They expected that after a short period of fascination with computer games, children would turn into "serious" computer users. Publishing tutorials of game modifications could be perceived as a form of offering entry-level programming courses.

A group of young informatics students edited *Bajtek* and wrote most of its content while providing unlicensed translations of articles from foreign magazines. The editorial team encouraged readers to send in their own programs and hardware hacking blueprints to the "Do It Yourself" ("Zrób to sam") section. Such content,

---

[32] *Bajtek* (September 1985): 2.

[33] Interview with Marcin Kozieł, *Commodore & Amiga Fan* (December 2009): 14. http://ca-fan.pl. Accessed 20 Dec 2010.

submitted by more experienced users, was often published. Klaudiusz Dybowski, who later became an activist in Commodore users' circles, recalls:

> In mid-1985 I got *Bajtek* for the first time. After reading it, I decided to write to the editorial team to boast about my "hardware hacking" achievement: the signaling device for Datasette tape recorder […]. My article was approved and I was invited to an editorial meeting. […] A decision was made and I became a member of *Bajtek*, responsible for Commodore 64.[34]

Most published blueprints had more practical purposes. Due to the high costs and shortage of peripherals, interfaces, and connecting cables, homemade peripherals and hardware modifications were popular in Poland. The frequency of articles instructing how to make a hardware modification with little knowledge of soldering illustrates the popularity of such practices.[35] *Bajtek* also published content for potential users, with advice on the choice of computers depending on personal interests and needs. Every issue published the price list of computers available in Poland, along with current prices in West Germany and the UK. The topic of mass software piracy was often discussed, the editors claiming that nothing could be done in the absence of proper copyright protection legislation and legal software retailers. Despite such discussions, every issue contained dozens of classified advertisements for computer studios.

Bajtek's editors never stopped expressing their aim to promote "serious" scripts despite the proportion of the magazine devoted to computer games. This was the most popular section as in a 1988 reader survey, 60 % of respondents claimed they read it regularly.[36] Shortly after 1989, confronted with the harsh rules of the free market, *Bajtek* had to become profitable. The editorial team simply established *Top Secret*, a new commercial title, and the first Polish computer games magazine. It became very popular in the early 1990s and played a significant role in gaming culture. At the same time *Bajtek* quickly lost its popularity to new magazines targeting users of specific platforms, especially Amiga.[37]

6.7 Communist Sanctioned Computer Clubs

The computerization movement promoted computer clubs in order to provide young people easy access to computers and programming courses. Such clubs were mostly established under the auspices of ZSMP, local housing associations,

[34] Interview with Klaudiusz Dybowski, *Commodore & Amiga Fan* (November 2008): 10. http://ca-fan.pl. Accessed 20 Dec 2010. Later Dybowski became editor in chief of *Commodore & Amiga*, a popular magazine published from 1992 to 1995. In the 1990s, computer magazines contained a considerable amount of hints for software use, programming tutorials, and advice on graphics, music, and DTP, written by hobbyists, not professional journalists.

[35] One ingenious practice of hardware hacking is rigging a joystick from easily available parts of electronic devices and gear levers. Interview with Waldemar Czajkowski by "V-12/Tropyx," January 12, 2010, www.riversedge.pl. Accessed 20 Dec 2010.

[36] *Bajtek* (June 1989): 4.

[37] The last issue of *Bajtek* was published in October 1996. *Komputer* had vanished in 1990.

state-owned companies, and schools. According to the Central Office of Statistics, in 1993, at a total of 3,792 state-sponsored cultural centers, 842 had computer clubs and 422 with computer rooms. The clubs totaled 15,283 members, including 11,499 children under 15.[38] Computer enthusiasts' testimonials show that computer clubs were often children's first contact with computers. The political framework of computerization that came with socialist state funding was demonstrated by the emphasis on "serious" scripts for computer use in information about club activities. Numerous clubs advertised their activities in *Bajtek* to attract new members:

> As "dissemination of informatics" we understand all activities which aim to familiarize youth (but not only them!) with the principles and the architecture of computers, learning of programming, etc. We emphasize such forms of activity because we know about some "clubs" where microinformatics is disseminated with the help of computer games. Of course, we are also staging such events, but these are marginal to our activity.[39]

Theoretically, most clubs primarily offered courses in handling computers and programming, LOGO and BASIC being adopted as the most suitable languages for young people. In practice, however, things were rather different. In some clubs, computer games were a form of recreation allowed during pauses between courses or as a prize for solving programming tasks. One user remembered how easily he adapted to both scripts of computer use:

In 1988, the authorities of Nowe Miasto housing district in Rzeszów decided it was time to undertake informatics education of the youth. The local culture center was full; the interest in proposed courses outgrew expectations of the authors of this idea. […] I also remember how we were waiting for pauses between courses. Not because we were not interested in them but we were just waiting to play *Bomb Jack, Batman,* and *Yie Ar Kung-Fu*.[40]

The year 1989 and the fall of the communist regime marked the end of the computer clubs. ZSMP was disbanded and local, state-owned companies withdrew most of their support due to financial difficulties. Also, users' interest in clubs declined. With the prices of hardware dropping and wages increasing, far more potential users could afford a computer of their own. No longer were crowded clubs the exclusive sites of access to computers. By the 1990s, there was no mention of computer clubs in computer magazines.

---

[38] Computer clubs in schools are not included here. *Kultura w 1993 r.* (Warszawa: Główny Urząd Statystyczny, 1994), 188–189. Data for previous years is not available. Given the severe cutbacks in funding cultural centers in the early 1990s, the centers counted in 1993 probably existed before 1989.

[39] Klaudiusz Dybowski, and Michał Silski. 1986. Maniak. *Bajtek*, May–June, 30.

[40] Arti. C&A Fan – złedobregopoczątki. *Commodore & Amiga Fan* (August 2009): 27.4. http://ca-fan.pl. Accessed 20 Dec 2010.

6.8 Social Networks, Gaming Culture, and Sneakernets[41]

Popular books on computer games tend to present gaming as the natural route towards domestication of home computing.[42] The literature describing how social actors were responsible for the process is limited. In Poland, intermediaries in technology and social networks significantly shaped the popularity of computer games. Two main actors at the mediation junction stimulated the use of computers to play games: First, *Bajtek* offered readers attractive reviews of new games available in Poland along with color screenshots. Second, retailers of pirate software at computer bazaars actively promoted gaming scripts.

According to user testimonials, the first opportunity to see and touch a real home computer was through social networks. "I was about 10 when my grandma took me to a party at her friend. Her son owned a Commodore 64. I went crazy. It was love at first sight."[43] In a 1988 *Komputer* reader survey, of the readers not owning a computer, 60 % responded that a friend gave them the opportunity to access a computer. Only 17 % said they gained access through a computer club and 12 % through their workplace.[44] Users indicated that playing games was the first script of computer use learned during accessing a home computer owned by a relative or a friend.

Physically I was able to touch this "wonder" which belonged to a friend of my parents. He was relatively rich and probably bought the Atari merely as a curiosity. He used the computer to get rid of me and my brother during family visits. I was about 12 then. I scored most of classic games, for instance, *River Raid* and *Montezuma's Revenge*.[45]

Such contacts played a significant role in mediating future scripts for computer use and peer social networks influenced the choice of hardware. One Atari user described how he became adept even before owning one:

> I liked mostly going "for a computer" to my colleagues – owners of the toy with Fuji mountain in a logo. I was a frequent guest at the homes of owners of this hardware and I "chopped" games with hypnotic fascination. It was clear that if I was going to have a computer it MUST be an Atari.[46]

---

[41] Polish gaming culture in the late 1980s was vividly portrayed in *Retro Gamer*, a popular retrocomputing magazine: John Szczepaniak. With fire and sword. *Retro Gamer* no. 22 (YEAR): 14–15.

[42] See Steven Kent. 2001. *The ultimate history of video games: From Pong to Pokemon and beyond: The story behind the craze that touched our lives and changed the world.* New York: Three Rivers Press; Diane Carr, David Buckingham, Andrew Burn, and Gareth Schott. 2006. *Computer games. Text, narrative and play*. Cambridge: Polity Press.

[43] Benedykt Dziubałtowski interview with Paweł Zgrzebnicki, May 7, 2009. http://www.ppa.pl/. Accessed 20 Dec 2010.

[44] *Komputer* (February1988): 8.

[45] Karol Wiśniewski interview with Dariusz Bartoszewski, January 7, 2008. http://atarionline.pl. Accessed 20 Dec 2010.

[46] "Kaz" Interview with Michał Brzezicki March 28, 2009. http://atarionline.pl. Accessed 20 Dec 2010. The phrase "chodzić na komputer" literally meant "going for a computer" and was used to describe visits to gain access to a computer at someone else's home. "Rąbać" literally means "to

Users in the peer group were the crucial mediators of technology.[47] Choosing the same home computer as one's colleagues was practical since social networks were the most important source of software. Conversely, home computers shaped the social identity of young users. A journalist reporting on young computer aficionados at a Warsaw computer bazaar described the identities taking shape:

> Mostly primary and secondary school children are here. [...] They know everything: what, where, and how, how much it costs and if it is modern. [...] They know how to use computers; they are knowledgeable about technical details. Moreover, they are building closed clans of "Atarians" ("atarowcy"), "Spectrumians" ("spektrumowcy"). Their free time is dominated by computers. [...] Contact with a computer is a substitute for the family, peer group, friends.[48]

While the writer worried that the computer was perilously breaking down social networks among the youth, in fact, home computers were forming new social identities based on the various hardware platforms. Shared gaming as a cultural and social practice could strengthen existing social networks:

> My first computer was Atari 65 XE bought at Pewex. I couldn't sleep at all when I was aware that the object of my desire was just a few meters away. I borrowed some cassettes from my colleagues and I was simply playing all the time for a few weeks. [...] My colleague A.G. had similar interests. We were attending the same secondary school; our apartment buildings were located opposite each other. Instead of attending school lessons, I was just going to his place on mornings and, well, we were just... creating.[49]

Several computer games had a two-player option enabling competition, which was obviously popular considering the classified advertisements in computer magazines. Most sellers of 8-bit computers offered two joysticks, further peripherals, and hundreds of games. Gamer contacts built up networks to exchange tapes and disks with software, so-called Sneakernets:

> At the beginning I was exchanging games with my friend who dragged me into the C64-atmosphere. After a while we exchanged all software we possessed and we simply haven't got any new games.[50]

A 1991 *Top Secret* reader survey reveals the social and economic practices linked with software distribution. The provenance of software could be a friend, indicated by 85 % of respondents; a computer shop (a "computer studio"), 60 %; a computer bazaar, 50 %; school (copying games from schoolmates), indicated by

---

chop." In Polish computer jargon, it was a popular term for intensive computer gameplay with joysticks.

[47] The role of users as coproducers of technology was briefly mentioned by Lindsay, From the shadows, 37–40.

[48] Marek Jędrzejewski. 1987. Gdykomputer jest bożkiem [When a computer becomes an idol]. *Argumenty*, September 27, 12.

[49] "Kat" interview with Michał Brzezicki, March 28, 2009. http://atarionline.pl. Accessed 20 Dec 2010.

[50] "V-12/Tropyx" interview with Waldemar Czajkowski, January 12, 2010. www.riversedge.pl. Accessed 20 Dec 2010.

10 %; or "the West," 10 %.[51] The survey shows how universally the distribution of pirate software relied on personal networks. Sneakernets operated alongside the commercial software piracy market. It was customary to distribute newly acquired games among close colleagues: "In those days we hadn't even thought about "copyrights," we were copying games from each other. A mine of software was the computer bazaar at Grzybowska Street."[52] The 10 %, claiming their games were from the West, brought software from personal trips; downloaded from Bulletin Board System nodes, which became popular in Poland around 1989; or used personal networks in the demoscene.

Some users went further and experimented with programming, thus breaking away from gaming and using a novel script. Paweł Sołtysiński, a pioneer of the Polish demoscene, better known by his alias Polonus, described a typical trajectory of changing scripts:

> At the beginning there was a massive fascination with computer games. [...] People were just playing, playing, and copying games, and then still playing, and playing. Fortunately, some people were able to break away from the closed circle of "playing and copying." They started programming on their own. They succeeded in making the first Polish demos, educational and other kinds of software.[53]

Gamers succeeded in learning to program by experimenting with game modifications and copy protection removal. Fundamental programming in BASIC and higher-level languages could be acquired through experiments with simple listings in *Bajtek*. However, game modifications could not be achieved with higher-level languages alone. Modifying computer games required basic knowledge of machine code, which could be learned from an experienced colleague, special articles in *Bajtek*, or bootleg photocopies of programming textbooks available in computer bazaars. Such was the knowledge required for the practical purposes of distributing games among colleagues and which could be used later in new cultural contexts when one entered the demoscene.

6.9 User Groups

Social user networks and Sneakernets sometimes evolved into formalized user groups customarily called "computer clubs" – but not to be confused with the state-sponsored clubs discussed previously. The phenomenon of computer user groups was analyzed by Frank Veraart in the case of the Dutch Hobby Computer Club

[51] There were 1,680 responses. *Top Secret* (April–May 1991): 5. Assuming that habits do not change overnight, not even with the transition of 1989, the survey is also relevant for the 1980s.

[52] Krzysztof Ziembik interview with Maciej Wiewiórski, January 10, 2010. http://atarionline.pl. Accessed 20 Dec 2010.

[53] Paweł Sołtysiński. 1992. Na dobry początek... [To make a good start...]. *Kebab*, January, 2.

(HCC).[54] In Poland, the first user groups were established in the mid-1980s mostly initiated by private users seeking contact with users outside their local social milieu. Each group had one specific hardware platform, and in Poland, the popular platforms were the Atari XE, the Commodore C64, the Sinclair ZX Spectrum, and later the Commodore Amiga and Atari ST. The largest user group in the late 1980s was "Commodore Clan Komoda," counting 2,374 registered members in 1989.[55]

User groups collected software libraries, publications, and periodicals, making them available to all members. *Bajtek* offered user groups the space to introduce themselves. Here is the list of activities of "Klub Użytkowników Atari" (Atari User Club) from Cracow:

- Subscription to Western computer magazines: *Compute*, *Antic*, *A.N.A.L.O.G.*, *l'Atarien*, *Atari User*, *Atari Connection*, *A–Z of Personal Compute!*
- Organization of warranty services for Atari computers in cooperation with Pewex, the official Atari retailer
- Publishing a book on Atari BASIC and plans for a textbook with commands for the 6502 processor
- Collection of about two thousand programs[56]

The larger clubs were not just providing a platform for social activities and sharing know-how among members. They could also become important mediatory institutions, promoting a particular model of hardware by providing services and software to attract new users and potential club members. For some members, user groups were merely convenient providers of free software. Others added their programs to the software library and spread their amateur software in the public domain. User groups also organized copy-parties where attendees copied software on a nonprofit basis. Similar events were later organized among members of the demoscene.

The Dutch HCC, according to Veraart, was shaped with knowledge about clubs in the UK and the USA.[57] Similar factors may have influenced user group culture in Poland. *Bajtek* user groups claimed that, aside from ordering Western computer magazines, they had direct contact with clubs in Western Europe, the USA, and even Australia. *Komputer* regularly published HCC activities based on the editors' personal contacts. Brief reports about clubs in Western and socialist countries were

---

[54] Frank Veraart. 2008c. *Vormgevers van Persoonlijk Computergebruik: De ontwikkeling van computers voor kleingebruikers in Nederland 1970–1990.* PhD thesis, TU Eindhoven.

[55] Marek Pampuch, "PASSA C64 TRWA (I)," *Horyzonty Techniki* (April 1989). http://filety.net/. Accessed 10 Jan 2012. This number could not be compared with the 68,000 members of HCC in 1988, Frank Veraart. 2011. Losing meanings: Computer games in Dutch domestic use, 1975–2000. *IEEE Annals of the History of Computing* 33(1): 52–65.

"Komoda," literally "chest of drawers," was an affectionate name for C-64, a counterpart of the English "Commy."

[56] *Bajtek* (February 1986): 27.

[57] Frank Veraart. 2008a. Basicode: Co-producing a microcomputer esperanto. *History and Technology* 28: 129–147, 132.

published in both magazines.[58] Contact with foreign clubs probably played a rather symbolic role in providing members with the awareness that they belonged to a global technical culture.[59]

The founder of the first Polish Amiga user group claimed that his club was based on Commodore Clan Komoda:

> We thought of establishing the Amiga Commodore Club for our convenience. In 1988 in Poland there were about 100, maybe 200 owners of an Amiga. The possibilities of communication among us were limited. If you wanted to have new games, you had to get the train and travel far away, sometimes to the other end of the country, in order to copy them. We concluded that if we would establish a club, other users would travel to us, and we would be relieved from the need of uncomfortable travels. [...] We were deeply inspired by the club of C-64 users excellently run by Marek Pampuch.[60]

Accounts show that the user groups aimed to provide members with software and knowledge, rather than a strong social identity. User groups were therefore often short-lived and disappeared completely in the early 1990s when computer bazaars and computer studios took over their role as software source. Knowledge was provided by new computer magazines devoted to specific platforms, especially Amiga, the most popular home computer at this time. Unlike HCC, Polish user groups never became long-lasting social structures beyond the small group of founders and activists, who later moved away to work on the editorial teams of the new computer magazines.[61] Earlier, the platforms had provided users with an identity and an opportunity for social activities. The user groups were less successful in this role. For offering identity, the platforms were replaced by the demoscene, which reached its peak in the first half of the 1990s.

6.10 The Demoscene

Hacker culture appears to have taken on specific European forms in the "cracking scene" and the "demoscene."[62] The computer-oriented subcultures, sometimes referred to as just "the scene," grew quickly during the mid-1980s in West Germany, the

[58] *Bajtek* regularly published letters from other socialist countries, in which hobbyists praised the magazine, emphasizing its role as source of knowledge for shaping local club activity.

[59] Kristen Haring mentioned similar phenomena among ham radio users, where contacts with remote locations were highly desirable; see Kristen Haring. 2007. *Ham radio's technical culture*. Cambridge, MA: MIT Press.

[60] Benedykt Dziubałtowski interview with Marek Hyla, September 7, 2007. http://www.ppa.pl/. Accessed 20 Dec 2010.

[61] For example, Marek Pampuch became editor in chief for the Polish edition of German *Amiga Magazin* in 1992.

[62] Only recently have scholars started researching specific European forms of hacker culture like the "cracking scene" and "the demoscene." Tamás Polgár. 2008. *The brief history of the computer demoscene*. Berlin: CSW Verlag. Markku Reunanen. 2010. *Computer demos – What makes them tick?* Licentiate thesis, Helsinki University of Technology. Markku Reunanen, and Antti Silvast. 2009.

Netherlands, and Scandinavia. Young gamers with programming experience took the appropriation of home computers a step further. They started to "crack" games – that is, make software modifications to remove copy protections and provide players with cheats, like "unlimited lives." Modified software would then be spread among computer users in the neighborhood, to groups in other regions, and even in other countries. The technique was to mount a "crack intro" onto the modified game, a short visual presentation with messages to other members of "the scene." It was around the Commodore C64, the most popular home computer in Western Europe, that the most vibrant subculture appeared. In the late 1980s, "crack intros" evolved into demonstration programs, "demos": independent audiovisual presentations written as executable files. The mark of distinction in creating these artifacts was to compete for the highest efficiency in programming the most spectacular graphic and sound effects. A form of journalism specific to the scene cemented the subculture. Hundreds of "papermags" and electronic "diskmags," or "zines," were published and spread through private mailing lists.[63] From the beginning, members of the subculture perceived it as an international community in which nationalities played a minor role. Theoretically, every talented C-64 user with advanced knowledge of programming or creativity in computer graphics and music could join. This openness greatly facilitated the spread of the subculture in Europe. Contrary to the user groups' heterogeneous activities, the demoscene was homogeneous, with a set of codified customs and practices. Members of "the scene" were supposed to regularly spread copies of games with their crack intros, release their own demos, and publish diskmags.

In Western Europe, the scene began with peer groups in local, social networks. In Poland, most early sceners made further contacts during visits to computer bazaars, some of which resulted in the creation of local scene groups:

> My first computer was a Commodore Plus/4. [...] It was a decent computer due to an implemented machine code monitor. This simply lured me to do something in assembler. Later I learned about a computer bazaar in Warsaw. I decided to go there. At the bazaar I met a group called KLC who were working on Commodore Plus/4. Those were cool people; it was great to talk with them. We copied software and exchanged experiences in programming.[64]

Easy access to Western cracked software, along with opportunities to meet other users with similar interests, led to the growing popularity of "demoscene" activities in the late 1980s. According to a detailed online database of C-64 scene activity, 11

Demoscene platforms: A case study on the adoption of home computers. In *History of Nordic computing* 2, IFIP advances in information and communication technology, ed. John Impagliazzo, Timo Jarvi, and Petri Paju, 289–301. Berlin: Springer; Antti Silvast, and Markku Reunanen. 2014. Multiple users, diverse users: The appropriation of the personal computer by the demoscene hackers. In *Hacking Europe. From computer cultures to demoscenes*, ed. Gerard Alberts and Ruth Oldenziel, 151–163. New York: Springer.

[63] A list of software artifacts from the scene is available on www.pouet.com website. Accessed 20 Dec 2010. At least 700 issues of magazines were published in Poland; most are available at the website www.filety.net. Accessed 20 Dec 2010.

[64] Interview with Polonus, *Włócznia Wschodu* no. 2 [The Spear of the East], 1990, no. 2, http://nonane.c64.org/csdb/. Accessed 20 Dec 2010.

groups with 33 members were active in Poland before January 1, 1990, and 118 software artifacts: crack intros, demos, and diskmags were produced during that period.[65] In Western Europe, there were thousands of sceners and many thousands of software products, but in Eastern Europe, only the Hungarian sceners' activities in the late 1980s could compare in volume to the Polish.[66]

The first crack intros and demos appeared in 1988, published by groups from Warsaw and the port city of Szczecin. Along with imported pirate software, early demos were brought to computer bazaars where you could get information about the demoscene as a social phenomenon and learn new programming techniques. Polish groups adopted English names and their members used aliases. The most significant groups founded in the late 1980s were called Quartet Inc., The Housebreakers, and World Cracking Federation.[67] Members of the Polish demoscene continued to use the term "the world scene" to refer to well-known groups from Western Europe and their software artifacts circulating in Poland. One early Polish scener with the alias TG JSL recalled: "We were watching demos to see who invented something new and who was active on the scene in Europe. Of course, as a coder, I was looking inside to see how the demos were made."[68]

To be a member of the demoscene, aside from knowledge about production and distribution of software objects, one needed to be proficient in machine code programming. "Fun begins when one trespasses the barrier of games and BASIC, and enters into the world of machine code and everything linked with it: demos, cracks etc."[69] Information on learning the tricks was scarce in computer magazines. The first tutorial on machine code in *Bajtek* was not published till 1989, more as a response to the growing popularity of demoscene practices. Sołtysiński mentioned social learning through sharing experiences with other users, but some sceners learned it themselves.

Everything I liked (copy protections, intros, demos) was written in 100 % machine code. It was necessary to learn it, so I started this on my own. I was learning to crack copy protections. If someone from my neighborhood traveled to West Germany, I would ask for current issues of *64'er*, *INPUT64* and *Magic Disk*. We also had single issues of American *Compute!* and *Compute!'s Gazette*.[70]

---

[65] Commodore Scene Database, http://nonane.c64.org/csdb/. Accessed 11 Dec 2011. There were similar groups working on ZX Spectrum and Atari but no detailed sources for those platforms.

[66] Appropriation of computers in Hungary during the 1980s was briefly described in Polgár. *The brief history of the computer demoscene*, 92–95.

[67] It is worth noting other ingenious names of Polish groups like International Cracking Service, Slaves of Keyboard, and Crazy Boys Software.

[68] TG JSL stands for The Great Jarek Software Limited. Author's e-mail correspondence with J. H., November 23, 2010.

[69] Maciek Szlemiński. 1993. Polska scena C-64 teraz i kiedyś [Polish C-64 scene: Past and present]. *Commodore & Amiga*, July, 36.

[70] Interview with "Silver Dream," *Commodore & Amiga Fan* (December 2009): 75. http://ca-fan.pl/. Accessed 20 Dec 2010.

Polish sceners established contact with Western groups through private addresses published in demos and diskmags.[71] "We were surprised because we even received some responses. When we saw the quality of Western demos, we were depressed by our own productions."[72] Rare in the late 1980s, the number of contacts grew in the early 1990s, when some Polish sceners joined Western international groups, and interviews with foreigners were published in Polish diskmags. Polish texts featured in well-known international publications, and finally a few elite Polish groups, were included in international "charts," regular rankings of groups based on readers' votes. Sołtysiński joined the well-known groups Science 451 and Padua:

> I realized that I was the only coder in Quartet doing exciting things. It was 1989 when I made my first music editor called Voice tracker. That was my ticket to join Science 451. Living in Szczecin, I could visit people in Berlin but not in Sweden (where most S451 members were living). So I easily searched one group in Berlin, someone tipped me off - maybe Padua? I wrote a letter, they became aware of who I was, and I joined the group.[73]

Poles effectively established contact with demoscene members abroad, receiving software objects, and joining West European groups. Their interest in other East European countries was minimal except for the scene in Hungary, which was perceived as part of "the world scene." Poland did play a mediating role in shaping computer practices in Russia in the 1990s. The eastbound dissemination involved pirate software with Polish crack intros rather than demoscene content:

> Software was not a big problem either – traders traveled to the socialist European block, countries like Czechoslovakia and Poland, where cracking groups already existed, […] and programs were easy to get hold of. The first Polish demos reached Russia that way. As far as I know, in the early 1990s some Russian coders decided that they were better than the Polish, so they made their own demos.[74]

6.11 Conclusion

In the 1980s, Polish users appropriated home computers in the social, political, and economic realities of the Soviet Bloc, part of which was a significant informal economy. Poland's computerization movement, in its efforts to cope with the political framework, offered contradictory scripts and promoted attractive domestically produced home computers and scripts. The years between 1985 and 1989 were crucial for home computing developments in Poland. Initially a high-tech luxury

---

[71] Polgár stated that in communist Hungary, it was forbidden to send diskettes abroad, but crackers were somehow able to evade this restriction, Polgár, *The brief history of the computer demoscene*, 95. I have not found any such regulation in socialist Poland.

[72] Interview with Polonus, *Inverse* no. 10 (2002), http://nonane.c64.org/csdb/. Accessed 10 Jan 2012.

[73] Ibid.

[74] Konstantin Elfimov. 2008. Brief history of Russian Speccy demoscene and the story of Inward. *Mustekala Kulttuurilehti* [online journal]. http://www.mustekala.info/node/35580. Accessed 30 Jan 2014.

gadget, the home computer soon became an entertainment platform and, to use Sherry Turkle's phrase, "a second self."[75] Still a status symbol, the home computer did not become an everyday affordable object till the 1990s.

A young potential user, whose parents could afford his dream machine, might become a devoted gamester, a frequent visitor to computer bazaars, and proficient in "playing and copying."If on top of that he managed to learn machine code, he would evolve into a hacker: a member of the demoscene. The ease and selectiveness shown by young users in coping with the high threshold to access the technology and limited scripts are remarkable. Young people could visit a computer bazaar, an offshoot of the socialist economy of shortages, to obtain new software. They could read computer magazines adorning program listings with messages that typing those programs helped to strengthen the socialist economy. Having read those listings, they would reject the political messages then check the game review section to prepare for their next visit to the bazaar. They could select and shape an identity.

The domestication of the home computer in state socialist Poland was definitely a cross-border phenomenon as its dissemination was based on importing cultural trends, material objects, and information from "the West." Developments in domestic electronics depended on the cultural distinction between "socialist" and "Western" objects. It would be useful to include such categories in further studies of the cross-border domestication of technologies in postwar Europe.

Potential users could choose to be either an Atari or a Commodore user – in both cases implying strong loyalty to American consumer electronics brands. No official presence of the companies was required; for computer users, both brands were just "Western." If a user defined himself as a hacker, or to be more specific "a scener," he shaped his own identity as a member of an international informal community established only a few years earlier in West Germany. The image of young Poles owning a home computer demonstrates that users actively participated in socially constructing home computer technology.

Bibliography

Akrich, Madeleine. 1992. The de-scription of technical objects. In *Shaping technology/building society: Studies in sociotechnical change*, ed. Wiebe E. Bijker and John Law, 205–224. Cambridge, MA: MIT Press.

Bertsch, Gary K. (ed.). 1988. *Controlling East–West trade and technology transfer: Power, politics, and policies*. Durham: Duke University Press.

BloomBecker, Buck. 1990. *Spectacular computer crimes: What they are and how they cost American business half a billion dollars a year!*. Homewood: Dow Jones-Irwin.

Cain, Frank. 2005. Computers and the Cold War: United States restrictions on the export of computers to the Soviet Union and Communist China. *Journal of Contemporary History* 40(1): 131–147.

Carr, Diane, David Buckingham, Andrew Burn, and Gareth Schott. 2006. *Computer games: Text, narrative and play*. Cambridge: Polity Press.

[75] Sherry Turkle. 1984. *The second self: Computers and the human spirit*. New York: Simon & Schuster.

Crowley, David, and Susan E. Reid (eds.). 2002. *Socialist spaces: Sites of everyday life in the Eastern bloc*. Oxford/New York: Berg Publishers.

Dybowski, Klaudiusz, and Michał Silski. 1986. Maniak. *Bajtek*, May–June, 30.

Edwards, Paul N. 1996. *The closed world: Computers and the politics of discourse in Cold War America*. Cambridge, MA: MIT Press.

Elfimov, Konstantin. 2008. Brief history of Russian Speccy demoscene and the story of Inward. *Mustekala Kulttuurilehti* [online journal]. http://www.mustekala.info/node/35580. Accessed 30 Jan 2014.

Haring, Kristen. 2007. *Ham radio's technical culture*. Cambridge, MA: MIT Press.

Irek, Małgorzata. 1998. *Schmugglerzug Warschau-Berlin-Warschau: Materialien einer Feldforschung*. Berlin: Das Arabische Buch.

Jędrzejewski, Marek. 1987. Gdykomputer jest bożkiem [When a computer becomes an idol]. *Argumenty*, September 27, 12.

Kent, Steven. 2001. *The ultimate history of video games: From Pong to Pokemon and beyond: The story behind the craze that touched our lives and changed the world*. New York: Three Rivers Press.

Kling, Rob, and C. Suzanne Iacono. 1995. Computerization movements and the mobilization of support for computerization. In *Ecologies of knowledge. Work and politics in science and technology*, ed. Susan Leigh Star, 119–153. Albany: State University of New York Press.

Lindsay, Christina. 2003. From the shadows: Users as designers, producers, marketers, distributors and technical support. In *How users matter: The co-construction of users and technology*, ed. Nelly Oudshoorn and Trevor J. Pinch, 29–50. Cambridge, MA: MIT Press.

Mastanduno, Michael. 1992. *Economic containment: CoCom and the politics of East–West trade*. Ithaca: Cornell University Press.

Oldenziel, Ruth, Adri Albert de la Bruhèze, and Onno de Wit. 2005. Europe's mediation junction: Technology and consumer society in the twentieth century. *History and Technology* 21(1): 107–139.

Péteri, Gyorgy (ed.). 2006. *Nylon curtain. Transnational and transsystemic tendencies in the cultural life of state-socialist Russia and East-Central Europe*, TSEECS no. 18. Trondheim: TSEECS.

Péteri, Gyorgy (ed.). 2010. *Imagining the West in Eastern Europe and the Soviet Union*. Pittsburgh: University of Pittsburgh Press.

Polgár, Tamás. 2008. *The brief history of the computer demoscene*. Berlin: CSW Verlag.

Portes, Alejandro, Manuel Castells, and Lauren A. Benton (eds.). 1995. *The informal economy: Studies in advanced and less developed countries*. Baltimore: Johns Hopkins University Press.

Poznański, Roman. 1985. Informatyka na Perskim [Informatics on the Persian Bazaar]. *Bajtek*, October, 24–25.

Reid, Susan E., and David Crowley (eds.). 2000. *Style and socialism. Modernity and material culture in post-war Eastern Europe*. Oxford/New York: Berg Publishers.

Reunanen, Markku. 2010. *Computer demos – What makes them tick?* Licentiate thesis, Aalto University School of Science and Technology, Helsinki.

Reunanen, Markku, and Antti Silvast. 2009. Demoscene platforms: A case study on the adoption of home computers. In *History of Nordic computing 2*, IFIP advances in information and communication technology, ed. John Impagliazzo, Timo Jarvi, and Petri Paju, 289–301. Berlin: Springer.

Silvast, Antti, and Markku Reunanen. 2014. Multiple users, diverse users: The appropriation of the personal computer by the demoscene hackers. In *Hacking Europe. From computer cultures to demoscenes*, ed. Gerard Alberts and Ruth Oldenziel, 151–163. New York: Springer.

Siwiński, Waldemar. 1989. Poza priorytetem [Outside the priority]. *Bajtek*, March, 2.

Sołtysiński, Paweł. 1992. Na dobry początek… [To make a good start…]. *Kebab*, January, 2.

Sysło, Maciej M., and Anna B. Kwiatkowska. 2008. The challenging face of informatics education in Poland. In *Informatics education – Supporting computational thinking*, ed. Roland T. Mittermeir and Maciej M. Sysło, 1–18. Berlin/Heidelberg: Springer.

Szlemiński, Maciek. 1993. Polska scena C-64 teraz i kiedyś [Polish C-64 scene: Past and present]. *Commodore & Amiga*, July, 36.

Szperkowicz, Jerzy. 1987. Skąd się biorą komputery? [Where computers came from?] *Horyzonty Techniki*, special issue *64 strony o komputerach* (*64 pages on computers*), 34.

Turkle, Sherry. 1984. *The second self: Computers and the human spirit.* New York: Simon & Schuster.

Veraart, Frank. 2008a. Basicode: Co-producing a microcomputer Esperanto. *History and Technology* 28: 129–147.

Veraart, Frank. 2008c. *Vormgevers van Persoonlijk Computergebruik: De ontwikkeling van computers voor kleingebruikers in Nederland 1970–1990.* PhD thesis, TU Eindhoven.

Veraart, Frank. 2011. Losing meanings: Computer games in Dutch domestic use, 1975–2000. *IEEE Annals of the History of Computing* 33(1): 52–65.

Weber, Ursula. 2002. *Der Polenmarkt in Berlin: zur Rekonstruktion eines kulturellen Kontakts im Prozeß der politischen Transformation Mittel- und Osteuropas.* Neuried: Ars Una.

Wedel, Janine (ed.). 1992. *The unplanned society: Poland during and after communism.* New York: Columbia University Press.

Woolgar, Steve. 1991. Configuring the user: The case of usability trials. In *A sociology of monsters: Essays on power, technology and domination*, ed. John Law, 57–102. London/New York: Routledge.

Chapter 7
Multiple Users, Diverse Users: Appropriation of Personal Computers by Demoscene Hackers

Antti Silvast and Markku Reunanen

7.1 Introduction

The demoscene is a technically oriented community that emerged in Europe in the 1980s. Concurrently with the growing popularity of the home computer, the members of the demoscene wanted to distance themselves from the common uses of computers such as productivity or gaming. Instead of utility or entertainment, their interest lay in creative experimentation, comparable to the original MIT hackers or the Lévi-Strauss-inspired concept of "tinkering" used by Turkle.[1] They formed an international community, eventually called "the demoscene" or just "the scene," once it became aware of its existence. The main artifacts of the demoscene are demos that showcase the programming and artistic skills of their creators. Simply put, a demo is a computer program that displays a series of real-time visual effects combined with a soundtrack.[2]

---

[1] Steven Levy. 1984. *Hackers: Heroes of the computer revolution*. Garden City, NY: Anchor Press/Doubleday. Sherry Turkle. 1984. *The second self: Computers and the human spirit*. New York: Simon & Schuster.

[2] Petri Saarikoski. 2004. *Koneen Lumo: Mikrotietokoneharrastus Suomessa 1970-luvulta 1990-luvun puoliväliin* [The Lure of the machine. The Finnish microcomputer hobby from the 1970s to mid-1990s], Nykykulttuurin tutkimuskeskuksen julkaisuja 83, 190–206. Jyväskylä: Jyväskylän yliopisto; Anders Carlsson. 2009. *The forgotten pioneers of creative hacking and social networking – Introducing the demoscene*. Paper presented at the Re:live: Media Art Histories. Conference proceedings, Melbourne, 16–20; Antti Silvast, and Markku Reunanen. 2010. The demoscene – An overview. Editorial for the *Rhizome* special issue on the demoscene, May 17.

A. Silvast (✉)
Department of Social Research, University of Helsinki, Helsinki, Finland
e-mail: antti.silvast@helsinki.fi

M. Reunanen
Department of Media, School of Arts, Design and Architecture,
Aalto University, Espoo, Finland
e-mail: markku.reunanen@aalto.fi

G. Alberts and R. Oldenziel (eds.), *Hacking Europe. From Computer Cultures to Demoscenes*, History of Computing, DOI 10.1007/978-1-4471-5493-8_7,

The demoscene has flourished mostly in Western and Northern Europe, with some activities scattered around other parts of the globe. Other main locations where home computers were available and commonplace, such as the United States or Japan, had equally enthusiastic user communities striving to display their skills, but they assumed different forms, such as the hacker or otaku culture.[3] Soon turning 30, the scene is still a predominantly male community in which women might feature but not necessarily receive recognition. There has not been much research on the social class of its members, but most probably they represent the middle class.[4]

So far, most studies dealing with the demoscene could be called descriptive. Many authors have charted the most visible practices and artifacts but mostly omitted major factors such as the wider cultural perspective, the emotional dimension, and the diversity of the community. In general, you could say that most of the writings start with a broad overview of how the scene was born and then move on to describe a range of demos, groups, and parties. The doctoral theses written by Nordli, Saarikoski, and Botz serve as counterexamples, where the community is placed in a wider context of gender studies, cultural studies, or media art.[5] A comprehensive bibliography of demo-related publications is available online on the *Demoscene Research* page (http://www.kameli.net/demoresearch2/).

We aim to continue these efforts by placing the demoscene in a wider perspective. Our particular interest lies in the appropriation of the personal computer by the demoscene members. Motivated by international discussions on the diffusion of technologies and our previous published article, we propose that the demoscene is not just a group of "end-users" that deploys technology as envisioned by its producers.[6] Instead, in order to demonstrate how greatly the demoscene hackers are involved with the appropriation of the computer, we focus on two theories: the concept of "scene" denoting the thematically focused and self-expressive character of the demoscene and demosceners and the concept of "script" highlighting the diverse and original practices of use that these people construct for personal computers.

In order to research the phenomena, we conducted a study of texts produced by the community. As one of its earliest communication media, the demoscene created disk magazines, or diskmags for short, electronic magazines which were circulated

[3] Douglas Thomas. 2002. *Hacker culture*. Minneapolis: University of Minnesota Press.

[4] Markku Reunanen. 2010. *Computer demos – What makes them tick?* Licentiate thesis, Aalto University, School of Science and Technology, Helsinki, 24–26, 48.

[5] Hege Nordli. 2003. *The net is not enough: Searching for the female hacker.* Trondheim: Norwegian University of Science and Technology; Saarikoski, *Koneen Lumo*; Daniel Botz. 2011. *Kunst, Code und Maschine – Die Ästhetik der Computer-Demoszene* [Art, code and machine – The aesthetic of the computer demoscene]. Bielefeld: Transcript Verlag.

[6] Everett M. Rogers. 2003. *Diffusion of innovations*, 5th ed. New York: Free Press; Turo-Kimmo Lehtonen. 2003. The domestication of new technologies as a set of trials. *Journal of Consumer Culture* 3(3): 363–385; Nelly Oudshoorn, and Trevor J. Pinch. 2003. How users and non-users matter. In *How users matter: The co-construction of users and technology*, ed. Nelly Oudshoorn and Trevor J. Pinch, 1–28. Cambridge, MA: MIT Press; Markku Reunanen, and Antti Silvast. 2009. Demoscene platforms: A case study on the adoption of home computers. In *History of Nordic computing 2*, IFIP advances in information and communication technology, ed. John Impagliazzo, Timo Järvi, and Petri Paju, 289–301. Berlin: Springer.

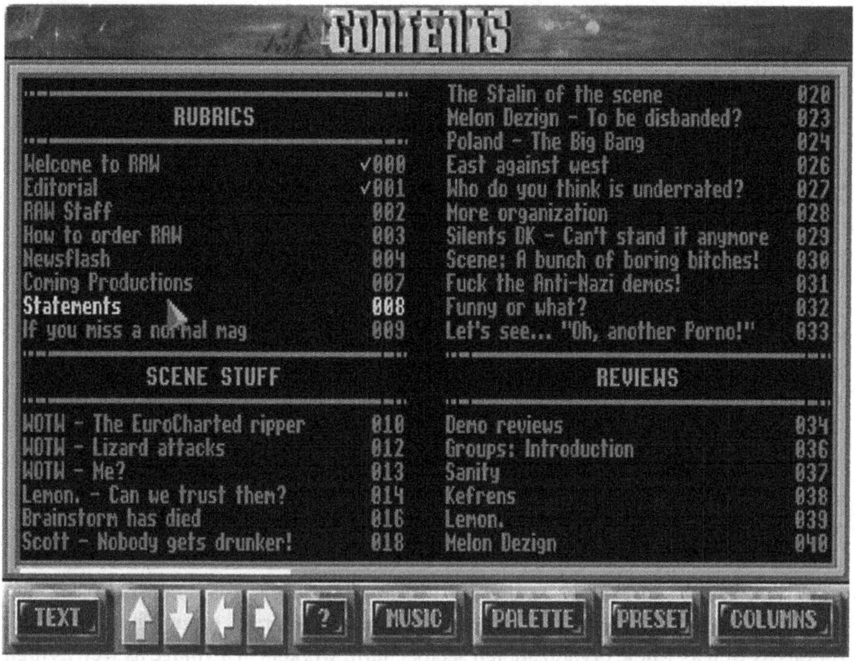

Fig. 7.1 Creating the Scenes through Diskmag. R.A.W. #6, 1993—a typical diskmag contents page

on diskettes by regular mail. Similar commercial publications had appeared as early as 1981, but the demoscene changed the concept significantly to fit its own needs and style. For an example of what diskmags look like, see Fig. 7.1. These magazines were a direct means of debating social relationships, practices, as well as technology, such as hardware and software. To say it short, all that is fundamental to the demoscene.[7] Whereas some diskmags, such as *Sex'n'Crime*, were published by game companies, most were produced, edited, and disseminated by sceners themselves. The "insiders only" nature of these publications meant that the attitudes and views were hardly ever toned down. The magazines were typically written in English and circulated among international audiences early on.[8]

To represent different eras and the scenes of various computer platforms, we chose five diskmag publications as our source material: *Sex'n'Crime* (published on the Commodore 64, 1989–1990), *Zine* (Commodore Amiga, 1989–1991), *R.A.W.* (Commodore Amiga, 1991–1996), *Imphobia* (IBM PC, 1992–1996), and *Hugi* (IBM PC and online, 1998–). Similar diskmags exist in several languages, but all of our material was written in English. In addition, whereas some of this material concerns national issues—for example, demo production in Finland or anti-piracy in Belgium—most of it pays little attention to nationality. Out of a total of 54 issues,

[7] Reunanen and Silvast, Demoscene platforms.

[8] Reunanen, *Computer demos*, 71.

we collated around 200 stories, including articles, interviews, editorials, and reader feedback, selecting relevant quotations from each story in order to observe the scripting taking place inside the community.

7.2 Technology Appropriation Within a Scene

When considering the adoption of technology that took place in the demoscene, our starting point was the theory of *diffusion of innovations* by Everett M. Rogers. Rogers emphasized two key subjects: by *innovation* he understood "an idea, practice, or object perceived as new by an individual or other unit of adoption"; and by diffusion "the process in which an innovation is communicated through certain channels over time among the members of a social system."[9] The underlying idea of this somewhat technical description is straightforward: innovations, that is, new ideas, practices, or objects, are first communicated to and then adopted, rejected, or reinvented little by little by the communities that deploy them on a daily basis.[10]

As Rogers sought a generic framework for innovations and their diffusion, he consequently looked at an extensive range of users. According to his empirical cases and examples, the users of technology can be individuals or informal groups, formal organizations as well as whole organizational sectors, farm workers in a village as well as high schools, medical doctors, or all the consumers in the United States.[11] While such generic frameworks are of great importance, they can also be problematic: when operating at the level of such "social systems" or "communities" in the broadest possible sense, perhaps we lose some of the particular traits of specific user groups. Can a community ever be considered uniform, discarding the actual diversity of its members? And can we presume that people simply belong to a professional or other community, disregarding the continuous efforts required to keep a social group focused and coherent?

A concept not included in Rogers's vocabulary (who preferred to speak of social systems or communities), but relevant to this study, is a *scene*. According to the sociological analysis of post-traditional community building by Michaela Pfadenhauer, a scene has the following characteristics:

> a) [A scene] does not constitute itself due to common life circumstances (such as milieus) or professional interests of the participants, b) [it] features a significantly marginal degree of obligation and binding character, c) [its] structure is not in principle selective and excluding and calculated for an exclusive set of participants but which nonetheless d) [it] acts as a thematically focused community-building forum for experience and self-stylization.[12]

---

[9] Rogers, *Diffusion of innovations*, 36, 35.

[10] For further developments in the context of ordinary technological "trials," see Lehtonen, The domestication of new technologies as a set of trials, 363–385.

[11] Rogers, *Diffusion of innovations*, 24.

[12] Michaela Pfadenhauer. 2005. Ethnography of scenes: Towards a sociological life-world analysis of (post-traditional) community-building. *Forum: Qualitative Sozialforschung/Forum: Qualitative Social Research* 6(3): 1–15.

While scenes are often discussed in relation to music, clothing, or consumption styles, the concept also explains the technology users' scenes—in fact, perhaps due to the popularity of the concept in media, also the demosceners adopted the term. In our case, the concept of a scene enables us to focus on specific technology users who are bound together by common interests, rather than, for example, their region, profession, or other position in life. Another useful feature of a scene is its emphasis on the *ways* these communities are built. Scenes, according to Pfadenhauer, are a matter of constant negotiation. The boundaries of the scene and its common styles and themes are not self-explanatory: instead, the sceners themselves have to produce knowledge related to the orientation of the scene and the skills required from a worthy member. To analyze a scene, therefore, it makes sense to go where the communication is taking place: to those debates through which the members of the scene are enacting the possibilities of the personal computer and its users.

7.3 Scripting Technology

In the past 20 years, various works of Science and Technology Studies (STS) have discussed the concept of a technological *script*.[13] Scripts, by definition, are assumptions about the potential uses of technology: they attribute "specific competencies, actions and responsibilities to users and technological artifacts."[14] By another definition, a script is a framework related to technology that defines specific kinds of actions, specific kinds of actors, and "the space in which they are supposed to act."[15]

A well-known early application of the notion of script is found in a study by Steve Woolgar.[16] Woolgar discusses technological scripts in relation to engineers and designers of microcomputers, concluding that the design phase of technology always limits how technologies can be interpreted and used by different social groups. In this article, we apply the concept of "script" to study how technology

[13] Steve Woolgar. 1991. Configuring the user: The case of usability trials. In *A sociology of monsters: Essays on power, technology and domination*, ed. John Law, 57–100. London/New York: Routledge; Madeleine Akrich. 1992. The de-scription of technical objects. In *Shaping technology/buildingsociety: Studies in sociotechnical change*, ed. Wiebe E. Bijker and John Law, 205–224. Cambridge, MA: MIT Press; Madeleine Akrich, and Bruno Latour, A summary of convenient vocabulary for the semiotics of human and nonhuman assemblies, in Bijker and Law, *Shaping technology/building society*, 259–264; Oudshoorn and Pinch, *How users matter*. For a more recent development concerning the active figuration of technology by their users and their designers, see Sampsa Hyysalo. 2009. Figuring technologies, users and designers – Steps towards an adequate vocabulary for design–use relation. In *Use of science and technology in business: Exploring the impact of using activity for systems, organizations, and people*, ed. Frans Prenkert, Enrico Baraldi, Håkan Håkansson, and Alexandra Waluszewski, 291–313. Bingley: Emerald Publishing Group.

[14] Oudshoorn and Pinch, *How users matter*, 9.

[15] Akrich, The de-scription of technical objects, 208.

[16] Woolgar, Configuring the user, 57–102.

users themselves view the capabilities of users and technological artifacts and thus reconfigure and reinvent technologies.[17]

In the following analysis, we focus on the technological scripts that have been produced for the personal computer by the demoscene hackers. These scripts are divided in two to highlight their individual characteristics. Firstly, we study how demosceners construct the practices of using computers in different situations. Secondly, we underline how new personal computers are also understood by sceners as "scripting" those computing skills that their owners have.

Our basic assumption here is that being in the demoscene is not only about learning to program or create digital art. It is also a matter of adopting a specific disposition concerning technology. This disposition determines how sceners apply their computing skills, present themselves, compete with each other, and take a stance on other sceners. As we will discuss, these observations lead to relevant conclusions that help to understand the computer hobbyist culture in general, as well as user communities' technological scripts.[18]

7.4 Me and My Scene

The Scene as a Stage

Originally, the concept *scene* literally meant the same as a stage. In her article on scenes and community building, Pfadenhauer quotes the following definition that directly mirrors this aspect of a scene:

> (T)he word "scene" reflects an emergent urban psychological orientation – that of a person as "actor", self-consciously presenting him—or herself in front of audiences.[19]

As far as the demoscene hackers' communications in our source material are concerned, the definition seems accurate. "The demoscene" and "the demosceners" were ongoing subjects of debate throughout two decades from 1989 to 2009 and also across various computing platforms, from the Commodore 64 to the Commodore

[17] For a corresponding study of a personal computer, see Christina Lindsay, From the shadows: Users as designers, producers, marketers, distributors, and technical support, in Oudshoorn and Pinch, *How users matter*, 29–50. In other cases, such "re-figurations" by users have also reflected back to the level where technologies are designed by their producers, see Hyysalo, Figuring technologies. Our study, possibly due to the limitations of the source material, could not unfortunately observe similar examples.

[18] Alf Rehn. 2001. *Electronic Potlatch – A study on new technologies and primitive economic behaviors*. Stockholm: Royal Institute of Technology; Alf Rehn. 2004. The politics of contraband – The honor economies of the Warez Scene. *Journal of Socio-Economics* 33(3): 359–374; Jukka Vuorinen. 2007. Ethical codes in the digital world: Comparisons of the proprietary, the open/free and the cracker system. *Ethics and Information Technology* 9(1): 27–38.

[19] John Irwin. 1977. *Scenes*, 23. London: Sage, quoted in Pfadenhauer, Ethnography of scenes, 3.

Amiga and the IBM PC. A notable turn can be observed in the texts of the early 1990s, when the community's self-awareness began to grow, which led to a clearer separation between the scene and other computer enthusiasts.[20]

Nonetheless, recognizing the scene as a "psychological orientation" can only be a starting point. In a practical sense, presenting oneself to others involves more than individual adopting an attitude. Self-presentation is also a social practice and as such, requires discipline and recognition by peers: one should be able to express oneself confidently to others while not appearing pretentious. In the discussions on what constitutes a good display of skill, demosceners seem to be highly aware of this aspect, starting with a fundamental issue: how should you include your name in a demoscene production?

At basic level, people add their names to their work in order to make themselves known among their peers. As the writer below reflected in 1989 in a Commodore 64 diskmag, the activities of the game cracking scene, which was the forerunner of the demo scene, started out as tinkering for tinkering's sake. Subsequently, the writer found it logical that people included their names in the cracks:

> Ever since people used their computer, they acted in big waves. In the beginning some people just cracked a game for fun. Later everyone started putting his name in his cracks so everyone could see how good he was. (Sex'n'Crime #3, 1989)

According to this short quotation, there is a direction from including your name in the crack and being seen as "good." In another text from the same period on the Commodore Amiga, a member of a newly formed cracking group states: "We aim to be a major force on the cracking scene in Europe and to be able to deliver the highest quality-wares to our contacts" (Zine#1, 1989). It is as if "being good" would again be a case of confidently announcing it to others.

Other members of this scene, however, do not just look at such announcements. They see a piece of work which they might admire or not. If one wants to be good or even better than others, it must therefore be proved. This happened to one commentator: according to his story in a 1990 Commodore 64 magazine, a particular scener "once again proved that he is superior to all other so-called crackers. He put the 210 files of 'Curse of Ra' into only 3 files and packed it down to approx. 350 blocks. This is yet another world-record!" (Sex'n'Crime#21, 1990). The background to his story is a competition to see who can make the smallest possible game file and thereby create a world record. As we can see, one sentence and its deployment of three figures—210 files, 3 files, and 350 blocks, respectively—is all that it takes for the record to be proven. While the details about the competence of this scener are certainly not self-explanatory to an outside reader, they were very meaningful to the writer.

On the other hand, if the claim of "being good" is not substantiated, the scener might face marked hostility from others. In fact, claiming to be something and exhibiting something else was viewed as misbehavior and reflected over and over

[20] Reunanen, *Computer demos*, 29–30.

again in the source material. In the text below, a scener expresses his feelings about such negligence when viewing a new demo:

> Another thing is all this shit about inventing new routines. I saw a demo from a group that claimed to have invented a new raster line style. The only difference I saw, was that they consisted of extremely ugly colors. That's stretching the limit if you ask me. (Sex'n'Crime #3, 1989)

Similar examples of "stretching the limit" of claiming to be good are so significant to the sceners that they have invented their own word for it: someone who is a "wannabe" is often referred to as a *lamer*.

Winners vs. Losers

For the demosceners, the concept lamer is a way of classifying people. It is the opposite category of the elite, "something only a few people are because of outstanding deeds and great fame" (R.A.W. #4, 1992). But lamer is also more than a fixed category of people. In disk magazines, lamer is constantly defined in relation to the practices that supposedly belong to the scene. It would seem, therefore, that the features of a lamer cannot be defined conclusively: instead, lamers have to be actively discussed by the demoscene in order to keep the concept alive.

One scener, for example, wrote: "I personally think a lamer is a wannabe, trying to be better than he really is. In the past, lamers used demo-makers to do some lame shit and spread it, just to let other people know they were alive" (Sex'n'Crime #9, 1989). "Lamers," according to the text, announce that they "are alive" but at the same time do not demonstrate that they are competent users of the personal computer. To the writer, this is proved by the fact that lamers are using "demo-makers": software tools that accordingly do not require programming skills but can be used to produce demos. Similarly, for another writer who comments on the "definition of a typical Amiga freak and a lamer," the issue is that "lamers would like to be famous. But he isn't (sic) because he can't do anything" (Zine #2, 1989).

In summary then, a lamer does not know how to use a computer for purposes seen as serious by demoscene hackers. Regarding the concept of technological script, lamers are end-users trying to appropriate demoscene scripts while lacking the necessary technical skills. In some source material, a lamer is explicitly a computer gamer: "[lamers] use only their Amigas to play games" (Zine #2, 1989) or he is a "person who uses his computer only to play games" (Imphobia #1, 1992). Moreover, according to this same article, lamers may try to cheat their way to fame by buying demos or "ripping" (in practice, stealing) other authors' music and graphics.

There is also more to the enactment of a lamer than his lack of skill. A lamer lacks other specific but different modalities: interest and appreciation. One writer on the IBM PC characterizes the group this way: "the people with no interest in the scene and in demos, scene music, and graphics whatsoever–the, I write and mean the word honestly, LAMERS" (Hugi #19, 2000). The following quote shows that not only does the writer disrespect "lamers" and their competencies; much worse, he thinks that lamers are not treating demosceners with enough respect for their dedication and their creativity. He reflects on an experience from the computer events called parties:

> Also, the atmosphere is spoiled when a party consists of 85-90% lamers - the feeling is just not the same when you know that the guy next to you really thinks you're some kind of a weirdo, bothering about something as antique as Amiga, bothering to make productions for free, for the fun of it, though that is what being creative is all about—but he doesn't know, does he? (Hugi #19, 2000)

The word "lamer" therefore seems to have several social uses for the sceners. The notion not only pinpoints those people who lacked the skills, it also seems to identify who the elite demosceners actually were. According to one writer, the lamer was once indeed even a "proud word" for "what's the point in being elite if there are no lamers?" (R.A.W. #6, 1993).

However, it should be noted that during the last 10 or 15 years, the word has started falling out of use. The heated discussions and group wars of the late 1980s and the early 1990s have cooled down significantly, and the general tone of the more recent publications is notably more laid-back. In spite of such increasingly relaxed attitudes, it is evident that the original mindset has by no means vanished, even if it is not brought forward as aggressively as before.

Thus, the script for using personal computers in the demoscene is one consisting of competition, recognition of skill, self-assertion, and hierarchy. As harsh as it may sound, such factors color most of the community's practices, as reflected in the examples above. Competition does not take place merely under the hood but is made totally visible and explicit through mechanisms such as ranking lists, competitions, and online/off-line discussions. Competition is also accepted as a natural part of being in the scene, hardly ever questioned or criticized. Similar evidence from comparable communities, such as different generations of hackers and the warez scene, suggests that technologically oriented, dominantly male communities often share the same features.[21]

7.5 Me and My Computer

The relationship between technological innovations and users that appropriate them is a multidimensional issue, which applies to demoscene enthusiasts as well.[22] From a purely practical perspective, new computers, upon arriving in the market, enable more advanced self-expression, higher quality graphics, and better music and, therefore, should be desirable. Yet this is hardly the case when you look into the discussions of the demoscene hackers. Regardless of the scene members' technical

[21] Levy, *Hackers*, 115–118; Thomas, *Hacker culture*, xvi; Rehn, The politics of contraband, 359–374.

[22] E.g., Oudshoorn and Pinch, *How users matter*.

competence, the adoption process consists of several stages that correspond to the model proposed by Rogers: *innovators* try out new platforms, influential *early adopters* make them acceptable, until the *early majority* and eventually the *late majority* follow. *Laggards* will trail behind, possibly resisting the change altogether (it should be noted that Rogers' concept of a "laggard" is not to be taken as derogatory). This adoption process by the demoscene members is markedly emotional, as illustrated by the following quotes:

> OK, you'll be able to do much better and faster routines, but everybody knows that you're not one of the best coders then, you just have got one of the best Amigas! So nobody will be that impressed by your work. (R.A.W. #6, 1993)
>
> With Windows'95 taking over the PC platform, where is the demo scene to migrate to? Should we comply and write Win'95 *compatible* demos (AGHHHHH!) Should we search new frontiers like Linux or OS/2? Or should we change the rules so that each group has to write his own small little demo operating system. (Imphobia #11, 1995)

In addition to the aforementioned high appreciation of skill, there are other influential factors: the unwillingness to change the status quo and nostalgia. The skills painstakingly acquired on one platform would need to be relearned on another, and at the same time, the emotional bond between the user and the familiar computer or operating system would need to be broken.[23]

High emotional involvement between people and home computers was observed by Sherry Turkle already in 1984, when microcomputers had not yet become commonplace. She calls the emotional bond "the holding power of the computer." A crucial factor in the relationship is *mastery*, the feeling of being empowered and in control.[24] Likewise, the relationship between the demoscene member and his/her computer goes far beyond the tool level. Letting the old computer go would mean insecurity—losing the mastery.

At the same time, demoscene members are a part of a community, which has its own common orientations. The members do not make purely individual decisions about how they use their computer. The community as a whole needs to react to a changing technological landscape in some way: it cannot change the external world, only its own dispositions. While some of these dispositions persisted in our materials as we have shown, it was clear that the demoscene's assessments concerning new platforms were also adjusted over time. According to previous studies, the scene will eventually adapt to new computer platforms because of practical reasons, regardless of the amount of initial resistance.[25] Likewise, the initial script of a computing platform will change radically over time during its life span from novelty to obsolescence. What starts as a viable computer eventually ends up a relic, only remaining in existence thanks to the commitment of its users.[26] The demoscene, a

---

[23] For more discussion on computer "platform wars," see Saarikoski, *Koneen Lumo*, 128–137.

[24] Turkle, *The second self*, 50–76.

[25] Reunanen and Silvast, Demoscene platforms; Reunanen, *Computer demos*, 100–102.

[26] Lindsay, From the shadows.

community centered on skills, can be an ideal site for deploying such relics against their—perceived—irrelevance in the world external to the scene.

Finally, to better understand the traits of the demoscene, we should also reflect on the relevance of not only the users but also the "non-users" of new technologies in this scene.[27] For various reasons, a person might willingly or unwillingly refuse to adapt to a new platform and thus become a laggard, according to Rogers's terminology. In an extreme case he might even leave the community altogether. In our source material, there were few examples of such quitting—just one person reported about a demoscene "break" which he used to party with his friends and ride his motorcycle (Raw #1, 1991). Hence, in this case, non-use was framed as a matter of not engaging with computing at all. But on a more general level, resistance to new platforms through their non-use evokes interesting interpretations, such as the generation gap between sceners of different ages, loss of sense of community around particular platforms, attitudes towards the tech industry and its practices of using personal computers, and boundaries of the scene, to name a few.

In summary, demoscene computers and skills cannot be treated in isolation but rather define each other on several levels. An ideal demoscene computer should not be "too old" for serious tinkering by the user, nor be "too advanced" as otherwise its tinkering will not—perceptibly—require serious computing skills. A computer that is "old" has an aura of mastery, but its user also runs the risk of being a laggard and, therefore, losing touch with the rest of the community that has already moved on. Resolving this tension is an inherent part of the scripting of the personal computer by the demosceners.

7.6 Conclusions

We studied a group of specific technological scripts: the ways that a group of computer users, the demoscene hackers, view their own competence, social relationships, and technical objects. The results illustrate that the adoption of the personal computer by the community is by no means a simple process. In fact, the predominant script of the computer—such as those communicated through advertising and the computer gaming industry—is heavily questioned and filtered through the demoscene's own orientations. These users' scripts were rich and diverse and covered varied aspects of computer use: indeed, they involved not only the potential uses of technology as envisioned by designers and engineers but also specific skills, knowledge, interests, self-expression, and even how the users enact their social relationships.

We concentrated on two aspects of the demoscene's adoption of computers: the construction that defines specific computer users as winners (elite) or losers (lame) and how a scener's skills are shaped by the possibilities of his computer and how the possibilities of the computer are in turn shaped by the skills. Even a new platform

[27] Oudshoorn and Pinch, *How users matter*.

can be used in an acceptable way, and, likewise, the lack of skill is reprehensible in spite of nostalgia or status quo. To us, such attitudes—"scripted" in detail by the sceners themselves—represent an interesting addition to the knowledge that pertains to the appropriation of the personal computer in its local uses.

When considering possible directions for further work, researchers could study the gendered nature of the demoscene script. Gendered issues are frequently mentioned in the source material: indeed, many texts state explicitly that the demoscene is a predominantly male hobby. The reasons for the lack of female sceners are reflected in some articles as well as in disk magazine interviews with women involved in the demoscene. An analysis of these texts would be an interesting contribution to the debates on the gendered nature of computer hacking. The generally male script of computing, combined with the male script of the scene, can make it extremely difficult for women to enter the circles as equal members.

Disk magazines proved to be a valuable source for our study. Their contemporary nature and the sheer volume of text—thousands of issues each with dozens of articles—would be sufficient for several studies with different viewpoints. One possibility would be to differentiate more between the various kinds of material in the diskmags: articles, editorials, interviews, reviews, and reader feedback. The wide range of computer users and uses are portrayed in these articles. Furthermore, the social diversity of the demoscene could be documented in more depth by subsequent studies, taking into account not only the various computer platforms and the temporal developments related to the scene but also national and gendered particularities of the different *demoscenes*.

Acknowledgements We acknowledge Gerard Alberts's and Patryk Wasiak's comments. We would also like to thank the contributors of our online demoscene research bibliography, *Demo Research*, who made the gathering of the rich research literature possible. We acknowledge the funding provided by the Kone Foundation for the *Kotitietokoneiden aika ja teknologisen harrastuskulttuurin perintö* project.

Bibliography

Akrich, Madeleine. 1992. The de-scription of technical objects. In *Shaping technology/building society: Studies in sociotechnical change*, ed. Wiebe E. Bijker and John Law, 205–224. Cambridge, MA: MIT Press.

Akrich, Madeleine, and Bruno Latour. 1992. A summary of convenient vocabulary for the semiotics of human and nonhuman assemblies. In *Shaping technology/building society: Studies in sociotechnical change*, ed. Wiebe E. Bijker and John Law, 259–264. Cambridge, MA: MIT Press.

Botz, Daniel. 2011. *Kunst, Code und Maschine – Die Ästhetik der Computer-Demoszene* [Art, code and machine – The aesthetic of the computer demoscene]. Bielefeld: Transcript Verlag.

Carlsson, Andres. 2009. *The forgotten pioneers of creative hacking and social networking – Introducing the demoscene*. Paper presented at the Re:live: Media Art Histories. Conference proceedings, Melbourne.

Hyysalo, Sampsa. 2009. Figuring technologies, users and designers – Steps towards an adequate vocabulary for design–use relation. In *Use of science and technology in business: Exploring the impact of using activity for systems, organizations, and people*, ed. Frans Prenkert, Enrico Baraldi, Håkan Håkansson, and Alexandra Waluszewski, 291–313. Bingley: Emerald Publishing Group.

Irwin, John. 1977. *Scenes*, 23. London: Sage.
Lehtonen, Turo-Kimmo. 2003. The domestication of new technologies as a set of trials. *Journal of Consumer Culture* 3(3): 363–385.
Levy, Steven. 1984. *Hackers: Heroes of the computer revolution*. Garden City, NY: Anchor Press/Doubleday.
Lindsay, Christina. 2003. From the shadows: Users as designers, producers, marketers, distributors, and technical support. In *How users matter: The co-construction of users and technology*, ed. Nelly Oudshoorn and Trevor J. Pinch, 29–50. Cambridge, MA: MIT Press.
Nordli, Hege. 2003. *The net is not enough: Searching for the female hacker*. Trondheim: Norwegian University of Science and Technology.
Oudshoorn, Nelly, and Trevor J. Pinch. 2003. How users and non-users matter. In *How users matter: The co-construction of users and technology*, ed. Nelly Oudshoorn and Trevor J. Pinch, 1–28. Cambridge, MA: MIT Press.
Pfadenhauer, Michaela. 2005. Ethnography of scenes: Towards a sociological life-world analysis of (post-traditional) community-building. *Forum: Qualitative Sozialforschung/Forum: Qualitative Social Research* 6(3): 1–15.
Rehn, Alf. 2001. *Electronic potlatch – A study on new technologies and primitive economic behaviors*. Stockholm: Royal Institute of Technology.
Rehn, Alf. 2004. The politics of contraband – The honor economies of the Warez scene. *Journal of Socio-Economics* 33(3): 359–374.
Reunanen, Markku. 2010. *Computer demos – What makes them tick?* Licentiate thesis, Aalto University, School of Science and Technology, Helsinki.
Reunanen, Markku, and Antti Silvast. 2009. Demoscene platforms: A case study on the adoption of home computers. In *History of Nordic computing 2*, IFIP advances in information and communication technology, ed. John Impagliazzo, Timo Järvi, and Petri Paju, 289–301. Berlin: Springer.
Rogers, Everett M. 2003. *Diffusion of innovations*, 5th ed. New York: Free Press.
Saarikoski, Petri. 2004. *Koneen Lumo: Mikrotietokoneharrastus Suomessa 1970-luvulta 1990-luvun puoliväliin* [The Lure of the machine. The Finnish microcomputer hobby from the 1970s to mid-1990s], Nykykulttuurin tutkimuskeskuksen julkaisuja 83. Jyväskylä: Jyväskylän yliopisto.
Silvast, Antti, and Markku Reunanen. 2010. The demoscene – An overview. Editorial for the *Rhizome* special issue on the demoscene, May 17.
Thomas, Douglas. 2002. *Hacker culture*. Minneapolis: University of Minnesota Press.
Turkle, Sherry. 1984. *The second self: Computers and the human spirit*. New York: Simon & Schuster.
Vuorinen, Jukka. 2007. Ethical codes in the digital world: Comparisons of the proprietary, the open/free and the cracker system. *Ethics and Information Technology* 9(1): 27–38.
Woolgar, Steve. 1991. Configuring the user: The case of usability trials. In *A sociology of monsters: Essays on power, technology and domination*, ed. John Law, 57–100. London/New York: Routledge.

Part III
Going Public: How to Change the World

Chapter 8
Heroes Yet Criminals of the German Computer Revolution

Kai Denker

When in 1984 Herwart "Wau" Holland and Steffen Wernéry announced their "hack" of Germany's *Bildschirmtext* (Btx,[1] an interactive teletext system), they rattled the operator, *Deutsche Bundespost* (DBP, Germany's Federal Mail), who had promoted Btx as a secure and reliable technology for business and homes. Btx had failed to meet the DBP's initial high expectations, and although some banks and companies started using the system, home consumers were reluctant to adopt it. Hackers succeeded in manipulating electronic mail and tracing passwords. By denying the flaws, DBP ignored the hackers' contribution in tracing bugs in the system. According to Holland and Wernéry, the DBP's arrogant behavior provoked them to publicize their "hack." In November 1984, the hackers found the password for *Hamburger Sparkasse* (HASPA, Hamburg's savings bank) and by manipulating its Btx account with DBP, transferred DM 135,000 to their own account in just one night. The next day, they held a news conference to announce this "bank robbery" to Hamburg's data protection commissioner. Exposed, DBP tried to blame the debacle on the hackers. Yet, the media cheered for Holland and Wernéry.

[1]The *Deutsche Bundespost* modeled Btx on the UK system *PRESTEL* and the French *Minitel*, which both had been designed and rolled out in their respective countries during the late 1970s. PRESTEL has also been the inspiration for the system *Viewtron* which has been offered by the companies *Knight-Ridder* and *AT&T* in the USA between 1983 and 1986. Like eventually Btx and PRESTEL, Viewtron failed to meet the expectations and is now regarded as an economical failure. However, their common screen-oriented design patterns—from 24 characters in 40 lines up to simple, yet colorful graphics—survived in the different teletext systems. Developed as standard for teletext informations broadcasted over television signals in the UK in the 1970s, European and American television companies adopted it in different incarnations during the 1980s—as World System Teletext (WST) in the USA and as Videotext in Germany, for instance. Again while Videotext soon gained momentum in Europe where it is still popular today, only a few WST services took root in the USA.

K. Denker (✉)
Department of Philosophy, Technische Universität Darmstadt, Darmstadt, Germany
e-mail: denker@phil.tu-darmstadt.de

G. Alberts and R. Oldenziel (eds.), *Hacking Europe. From Computer Cultures to Demoscenes*, History of Computing, DOI 10.1007/978-1-4471-5493-8_8,

Four years later the climate had changed. When arriving in France for a conference in 1988, Wernéry was arrested for computer crimes. In 1986/87, when a bug in VAX computers used by public authorities like NASA and research companies was discovered, hackers exploited the bug to log on and access the computers of research facilities and companies throughout Europe. The companies alleged that some hackers had copied and destroyed data on over 100 computers. But when they got way over their head in their hacking activities, they anonymously contacted *Chaos Computer Club* (CCC) for help.[2] Holland had founded this hacker computer organization in 1982 and Wernéry soon became the Club's spokesperson. When the Club notified Germany's Federal Office for the Protection of the Constitution, it ignored the warnings. Nevertheless, a preliminary investigation was started to find out the hackers' identity. The incident raised interest outside Germany, and Wernéry was one of the suspects. This time, the media did not applaud him. Instead, the notion that hacking was an actual criminal act had taken hold, resulting in state repression and increasingly harsh media reactions.

The representational shift from hackers being some kind of consumer protection activists to becoming criminals occurred in a surprisingly short space of time. Legal discourses that initially took hacking into consideration subsequently marginalized it as a hobby that had to be restricted in order to protect society at large. To analyze these developments, I trace the beginnings of hacking to a counterculture and its ambivalent connections between public and legal discourses that highlighted the USA's hacking roots and computer crimes.

The chapter discusses German computer countercultures in the 1980s in general and the Club's early days in particular. Firstly I explain how the Club started and its concept of hacking. Then I consider the "Btx hack" in order to examine the Club's self-representation of *hacktivism*—a portmanteau term combining "hacking" and "activism"—as a leftist progressive idea and to trace its criminalization in the public arena. I analyze criminalization by exploring computer crime legislation in the mid-1980s, when hackers were first considered consumer protection activists before being regarded or ignored as mere hobbyists or even as criminals—an image then emerging in the USA. I will summarize my findings in relation to their impact on hacktivism as a more and more institutionalized movement.

In contrast to the widely discussed American hackers, there is little literature dealing with their German counterparts.[3] Moreover, such biased accounts are often written by hacking activists looking for their own roots. This is especially true for the literature on the German hacker culture of the 1980s, when most hacker journals

[2] I will refer to the *Chaos Computer Club* as "the Club" subsequently.

[3] An example of literature on American hackers is by, Steven Levy. 1984. *Hackers: Heroes of the computer revolution.* Garden City, NY: Anchor Press/Doubleday. There are many hints suggesting that the German hacker culture had access to a rich number of manifests, statements, etc. of American hackers that circulated through international networks. However, in the German press, one finds only a few references to such, American journals like *TAP,* novels like John Brunner. 1975. *Shockwave rider.* New York: Harper & Row and William Gibson. 1984. *Neuromancer.* New York: Ace Books, and science-fiction films like John Badham's *War Games* (1983) for instance. While all these suggest that hacker connections were strong, most can only be found ex post.

and statements appeared. The Club's journal *Datenschleuder*, published since 1984, serves as the main source for this chapter. In addition to technical specifications and findings, this journal contains political statements on hacktivism and new technological developments.[4] Moreover, I use the protocols of the *Bundestag* and its Committee on Legal Affairs to analyze hackers' criminalization.[5] There are also many articles in secondary research dealing with legal or market issues.[6]

---

[4] Most issues of *Datenschleuder* can be found on the Club's website, Last accessed 26 Apr 2011, http://ds.ccc.de/. However, some early issues are not available online, but can be found in local hackers' archives. Some of the journal's articles have been republished in the *Hackerbibel* and *Chaos Computer Buch.* Wau Holland, et al. (eds.). 1985. *Die Hackerbibel.* Löhrbach: Pieper Werner Medienexp.; Jürgen Wieckmann (ed.). 1988. *Das Chaos Computer Buch. Hacking made in Germany.* Reinbek bei Hamburg: Wunderlich. In addition to radio recordings accessible through the Club's media archive. Accessed 30 Apr 2011, http://media.ccc.de/, a biography on the Club's co-founder Wau Holland written by Daniel Kulla. 2003. *Der Phrasenprüfer. Szenen aus dem Leben von Wau Holland.* Löhrbach: Pieper and the Grüne Kraft; which, as an example of activist literature, appears rather hagiographic, and articles on the Club's history, for example Thomas Ammann. 1988. Nach uns die Zukunft. Aus der Geschichte des Chaos Computer Clubs. In *Das Chaos Computer Buch. Hacking made in Germany*, ed. Jürgen Wieckmann, 9–31. Reinbek bei Hamburg: Wunderlich.

[5] *Bundestag, Bundesrat,* and *Drucksachen* protocols (parliamentary documents) are available on http://www.bundestag.de/. Accessed 30 Apr 2011. Rather than considering laws as the very essence of criminalization, I treat them as the concrete expression of an underlying discourse that can be studied in these protocols.

[6] For example, studies published in the *Btx-Reihe* series of the *Studiengruppe Bildschirmtext*: one volume dealt with Btx from a behavioral science perspective written by Ludwig Wiesenbauer. 1983. *Verhaltenswissenschaftliche Grundlagen der Bildschirmtextbenutzung*, Schriftenreihe der Studiengruppe Bildschirmtext. Gröbenzell: Fischer, followed by studies in human resources management, for example, Dirk Stolte. 1983. *Personalsuche und Personalvermittlung mit Bildschirmtext*, Schriftenreihe der Studiengruppe Bildschirmtext. Gröbenzell: Fischer; on banking by Christoph Warnecke. 1983. *Bildschirmtext und dessen Einsatz bei Kreditinstituten*, Schriftenreihe der Studiengruppe Bildschirmtext. Gröbenzell: Fischer; or consumer research by Rolf Ulrich Kaps. 1983. *Die Wirkung von Bildschirmtext auf das Informationsverhalten der Konsumenten*, Schriftenreihe der Studiengruppe Bildschirmtext. Gröbenzell: Fischer. The latter publication was accepted as dissertation. Btx was accepted as field of research in universities. For example, the Ruhr-Universität Bochum set up a project group Bildschirmtext which published analyses of group discussions: Helmut Kromrey, et al. 1984. *Bochumer Untersuchung im Rahmen der wissenschaftlichen Begleitung des Feldversuchs Bildschirmtext Düsseldorf/Neuss.* Bochum: Ruhr-Universität. Some monographs compare it to its French counterpart, Minitel. For instance, Rudolf Pospischil. 1987. *Bildschirmtext in Frankreich und Deutschland: Grundlagen u. Konzeptionen.* Nürnberg: Verlag der Kommunikationswissenschaftlichen Forschungsvereinigung; or Manfred Friesinger. 1989. *Bildschirmtext in Frankreich.* München: Fischer. Btx is often forgotten as a mere predecessor of the Internet. For Btx's legal problems, see Wolf-Dieter Kuhlmann. 1985. *Rechtsfragen des Bildschirmtext-Staatsvertrages vom 18. März 1983.* PhD thesis, Universität Bochum; Hans-Peter Bach. 1985. *Verfassungsrechtliche Grundfragen von Bildschirmtext.* PhD thesis, University of Mainz; and Bernd M. Traut. 1987. *Rechtsfragen zu Bildschirmtext.* München: R. Fischer. For a more recent discussion of German computer laws see Ralf Dietrich. 2009. *Das Erfordernis der besonderen Sicherung im StGB am Beispiel des Ausspähens von Daten, [Para] 202a StGB: Kritik und spezialpräventiver Ansatz.* PhD thesis, Universitat Tübingen.

8.1 Organizing Chaos Computer Club

While never the only hackers' organization in Germany, the Club has been the biggest and undoubtedly the most influential computer club since its establishment in spring 1984. Among hackers, the Club succeeded in becoming the dominant group, already attracting attention from the media and officials in the 1980s, when hacking attacks, computer crimes, or critical reflection of the new and emerging computer technology became newsworthy.

In his 1988 article on the Club's history, Thomas Ammann argues that the movie *War Games* and an interview with the American hacker Richard Cheshire inspired hacking in Germany.[7] In the movie, influential with young computer enthusiasts at that time, an artificially intelligent machine takes control of thermonuclear weapons and plans to start a war. A young hacker tries to stop the machine but fails. Finally, the machine concludes "What a strange game! The only winning move is not to play" and then decides to cancel the war. In the interview Cheshire gave the journal *Der Spiegel* in 1983, he explained some technologies displayed in the movie and confirmed that American hackers actually used them. Ammann suggested that German hackers identified themselves with what was depicted in the movie as Cheshire did. According to their interpretation, the movie emphasized the dangers of a networked computing era.

Ammann introduced Holland as a charming but behind-the-times hippie who irritated his left-wing peers through his enthusiasm for the technology and its potential.[8] Holland's enthusiasm was indeed quite ambivalent: in an early article in the newspaper *die tageszeitung* (*taz*) in 1981, he criticized computer technology as an instrument both of homeland security and for economizing the workplace by replacing recalcitrant employees with for never striking computers. Still, he believed meaningful things were possible with microcomputers that did not need centralized mainframes. He requested what he called his fellow computer freaks to end the scurrying and to meet him at *taz* headquarters to discuss issues like data laws, copyrights, and encryption.[9] Holland sought to question the very idea of security and a safe society to show that "there are no guarantees."[10] Holland also wanted to carry out "therapy" on the German security fetish and "rotten peace" with what he called a strategy of "positive chaos." Although Kulla was obviously sympathetic, his

[7] Ammann, Nach uns die Zukunft; see also: "Zack, bin ich drin in dem System," interview with Richard Cheshire in *Der Spiegel* 46(1983), 222.

[8] The connections to Adorno and Horkheimer's concept of administration and ideas in the 1968 era are evident. While Holland's references to leftist theories are obvious, they are still poorly investigated. Presumably, he read Herbert Marcuse's *One-dimensional man*. Boston: Beacon Press (1964), Theodor W. Adorno, and Max Horkheimer's *Dialectic of enlightenment*. New York: Seabury Press (1972) and Max Horkheimer's *Critique of instrumental reason*. New York: Seabury Press (1974), and Hans Magnus Enzensberger's. 1970. Baukasten zu einer Theorie der Medien. *Kursbuch* 20(1970): 159–186, which greatly influenced him. See Kulla, *Der Phrasenprüfer*, 20.

[9] *die tageszeitung* (September 1, 1981), 2.

[10] Kulla, *Der Phrasenprüfer*, 26.

account provides an insight into Holland's political philosophy: in a technically evolving world, one must fight order through chaos and humor. Thus, Holland's political agenda occupied a space between computer technology's democratization and popularization and its somewhat anarchistic appropriation. Indeed, his agenda has many features similar to the entanglements of home computing technology and countercultures in other European countries during the 1980s.[11] Finding himself in an instrumental-rational world, Holland tried to mobilize chaos and humor as well as ethics to fight it. After studying electrical engineering, computer science, and political science, he began working in leftist bookstores and at an alternative software company.[12] Both Ammann and Kulla suggest that Holland had a "typical" but hard-line post-1968 mindset and thus held anti-capitalist, anti-statist, and somewhat anti-American opinions.[13] However, it was not easy for him to find a place in the leftist political spectrum. While communists agreed to technocratic Soviet projects, he felt 1980s environmentalists fought technology with garlic, the cross, and holy water.[14] Most countercultural movements in Germany at that time adopted a technology-skeptic attitude expressed by the highly influential Frankfurt School and were reluctant to embrace technophiles. Holland had no natural audience on the left but had to create one himself.[15] In the early 1980s, a few computer clubs existed in Germany, but the charismatic Holland decided to establish his own group in line with his critical enthusiasm for computer technology. He invited others to meet at *Schwarzmarkt*—an alternative bookstore in Hamburg. The group meeting at *Schwarzmarkt* developed into a regulars' table, where Holland and Wernéry met for the first time in November 1983. As Holland had set up the meeting just by announcing it in *taz*, he also founded the Club simply by announcing the organization at the end of 1982. However, the Club remained a more or less inactive gathering of like-minded computer enthusiasts.[16]

Holland's next project was *Datenschleuder*. After a rather unsuccessful attempt at starting a hackers' journal on floppy disks in Berlin in 1981, he announced the establishment of *Datenschleuder* in *taz* in 1984, receiving 100 advance orders for a journal that did not yet even exist.[17] Since he had announced it, he then had to

---

[11] For example, Bruno Jakić analyzes the entanglements of home computing with New Wave music in Yugoslavia. Bruno Jakić. 2014. Galaxy and the new wave: Yugoslav computer culture in 1980s. In *Hacking Europe. From computer cultures to demoscenes*, ed. Gerard Alberts and Ruth Oldenziel, 107–128. New York: Springer.

[12] Kulla, *Der Phrasenprüfer*, 16.

[13] See, Ibid., 37 and Ammann, Nach uns die Zukunft, 24. Kulla speaks of counter control and inverse panopticism (p. 29) that formed a crucial part of the Club's agenda. Ammann gives another example: after Chernobyl, the Club discussed building its own surveillance system for radioactivity. With home computers, everyone could measure and analyze local radioactivity and would not have to rely on public information services.

[14] Kulla, *Der Phrasenprüfer*, 20. As I will discuss below, the Green party turned out to be a prototype of these concerns.

[15] Ibid., 16.

[16] Ibid., 22.

[17] The number of 100 advance orders is mentioned in the first *Datenschleuder*. Kulla, however, mentions 800. Ibid., 26.

deliver. He made the first *Datenschleuder* rather hastily. It consisted of a two-sided DIN A4 sheet, the close type giving the impression of the chaos Holland had imagined. The hackers' new organ sought to provide information about new hacks, security vulnerabilities, technical specifications for the broadband communications networks Btx and *Datex-P* network, and government protocols for shutting down telecommunication in case of war or emergencies.[18]

Furthermore, Holland published an ironic acceptance test for aspiring members: to become a member of the Club, you had to program a *quine*.[19] This is hacking culture at its best—a *quine* is a rather useless program, not thought of by the designers of a particular programming language. Its possibility is an unintentional effect in programming languages. Thus, the challenge combines two aspects of hackerism—playing with computer technology as an end in itself and judging others by their technical skills.[20] While we find an ironic elitism in the acceptance test, Holland invited everyone to copy and redistribute *Datenschleuder*. It soon became his printed bullhorn and a popular organ for hackers in Germany.

8.2 The Conscience of Hackers

Holland had a technophile mindset, yet also shared the left-wing sentiment that criticized new technology. We have to examine the first issues of *Datenschleuder* in order to understand Holland's motivation and see how his leftist ideas had created a small, chaotic computer club.

In addition to the challenge for joining the Club, the first issue informed readers about the Club's principles and projects for the near future. The publication also contained an overview of the hardware for hacking (modems, Btx decoders, and microcomputers), some ironic remarks about DBP, and finally a hackers' hymn written by Cheshire Catalyst, editor of American TAP Magazine. Holland wanted a "galactic association without any fixed structure" that fought for new rights.

> We realize — as far as possible — the 'new' human right of at least world-wide free, unrestricted, and uncontrollable information exchange (freedom to the data) between every human being and other intelligent creatures without exception.[21]

---

[18] *Datenschleuder* 1 (1984).

[19] A *quine* is a program whose output equals its own program code. This means the program refers to itself in a way that it keeps reproducing itself. Kleene's recursion theorem, part of the theoretical foundation of programming, proves the existence of quines in every sufficiently strong programming language, but it can be tricky to program them. It is not possible to simply include the human readable programming language and print it on screen. You have to "calculate" the code by playing with the text processing features of the programming language.

[20] As Patryk Wasiak shows in his analysis of the Polish demoscene, judging each other on technical skills is a common phenomenon in hacker (and cracker) groups. Patryk Wasiak, Playing and copying: Social practices of home computer users in Poland during the 1980s, in Alberts and Oldenziel, *Hacking Europe*, 129–150.

[21] *Datenschleuder* 1 (1984).

Being a self-declared vanguard, the Club intended to enlighten readers about the new era's dangers and opportunities. These rather abstract ideas included an agenda to design and publish a construction guide for a universal but cheap modem. Furthermore, the agenda included the announcement to set up publicly accessible *Computer Bulletin Board Systems* (BBS), obtained and published information about the telephone system, and finally provided tips for dealing with "the brave new world in the year of big brotherhood."[22] This was a blatant reference to Orwell's novel, which had had an enormous influence on Holland and the hacker movement. Emerging, increasingly centralized, and opaque information technologies could serve as the surveillance infrastructure needed by big and not-so-big brothers. In the journal's third issue, BBS were discussed, with a clear warning that the government listened to, read, and collected any data it could get.[23] The agenda related to many post-1968 ideas: the struggle against centralized and opaque systems—technological as well as political.

After the second issue of *Datenschleuder* discussed German BBS in April 1984, the authors continued to reveal passwords, tuned into electronic mail systems like TELEBOX and systems like Btx, and mocked advice to choose sufficiently strong passwords as well as totally inexperienced readers who incessantly posed greenhorn questions.[24] They explained commonly used abbreviations, again with a grain of salt. Furthermore, their *Chaos Team* kept criticizing DBP, public authorities, and computer firms for their lax security handling, data privacy violations, and neglect of consumer protection.[25] In the fifth and sixth double issue, the authors defined hacking as actions in the tradition of Greenpeace and Robin Hood, "Robin Data."[26]

In short, Holland did not find "hacktivists" when he came to Hamburg in the early 1980s. In an atmosphere open to technology and simultaneously anxious about opaque, centralized systems, he managed to realize his ideas by creating a Club of politically aware techno-nerds, the *Chaos Computer Club*. The Club, still quite small when the first *Datenschleuder* was published, already considered itself a vanguard, not of hackerism but of a politically vague, yet lively and eager *hacktivism*.

---

[22] Ibid.

[23] *Datenschleuder* 3 (1984), 1.

[24] *Datenschleuder* 4 (1984), 1.

[25] *Datenschleuder* 3 (1984), 2.

[26] *Datenschleuder* 5 + 6 (1984) 1 and Ammann, Nach uns die Zukunft, 20.

8.3 Going Public and Acting Up

Discussing the implications and challenges of the new era automatically stressed the need to go public. Club members did not just organize their own gatherings but visited mainstream conferences on data security and protection.[27] In November 1984, Holland lectured at the eighth data protection conference DAFTA. Here, he presented a way to open Btx decoder boxes without breaking the seal, along with other security flaws. His presentation, cited in a television report on the conference, impressed a data protection commissioner so much that he concluded "whoever uses Btx in the years to come, should be punished for stupidity."[28] Holland explained his own agenda to telecasters as "protecting not the data, but the people from the data."

The Club members were also keen to establish contact with political parties. In 1986, they were asked to give their expert opinion on the introduction of computer technology in the Green party's *Bundestag* offices. Having once again encountered assessments of computers as a mere instrument of power and economizing there, they tried to appease the skeptics by emphasizing attempts to find a low-threshold "alternative" way of appropriating computers in the Green parliamentary group. In the end, the Greens rejected the suggestions. Instead, they stuck to their old policy, becoming the only party to refuse to participate in a test run of a database system for parliamentary protocols and prints a few years later.[29]

The episode sheds light on the Club's failure to win over the left and the alternative movement to their ideas. Members remained aloof from leftist discourses on efficiency, employment rights, environmental protection, peace, and fighting authority and power. At the same time, leftist groups were disenchanted. In 1985, a group named "Black & White against the Computer State" questioned polemically where the promised chaos was.[30] They believed that instead of fighting the Orwellian Big Brother state, the hackers had turned out to be techno-maniacs who had more in common with data protection commissioners than with leftist computer critics. The hackers were the "truffle pigs of the electronics industry."[31]

Nevertheless, the Club's agenda attracted other computer enthusiasts who were open to politics and also had quite an impact on data protection circles. This was still an internal, self-referential discourse without resonance in the leftist movement. The same is true for the political mainstream: although Holland and Wernéry

[27] The literature often fails to substantially address the importance of conferences for such groups. However, Gabriella Coleman shows that face-to-face interactions form crucial part of hacktivism. Gabriella Coleman. 2010. The hacker conference. *Anthropological Quarterly* 83(1, Winter): 47–72.

[28] Ammann, Nach uns die Zukunft, 18. The video recording can be found at http://chaosradio.ccc.de/doc001.html. Accessed 21 Apr 2011.

[29] Ammann, Nach uns die Zukunft, 25; Kulla, *Der Phrasenprüfer*, 40.

[30] The original German name of the group is Schwarz & Weiß gegen den Computerstaat. "Wo bleibt das Chaos?" *die tageszeitung* (February 22, 1985).

[31] Ammann, Nach uns die Zukunft, 23f.

as the Club's de facto spokespersons managed to appear on prime-time news broadcasts, they were little noticed and mostly as esoteric and exotic nerds. Hackers received media attention for tapping and hacking but not for their political agenda.[32] Thus, Holland and Wernéry had to find an opportunity to arouse public interest for a topic in which they could present themselves as experts. In 1984, an opportunity to hack Btx arose when Holland and Wernéry obtained HASPA identification codes.

8.4 Hacking Germany's Bildschirmtext

To understand the impact of the Btx hack on hackerism and computer crime legislation, we must appreciate Btx's relevance in the early 1980s. While its market penetration had failed to meet expectations by far, the media and politicians presented the system as an icon of modern telecommunications and the dawn of the information society. As a centralized public service system, for hackers it was the epitome of large, centralized, and opaque information technology. In Btx, antagonisms of information technology were seen that corresponded to the antagonisms in the political sphere: on the one hand, one could meet technocratic-minded politicians advocating business applications and an alternative, technology-skeptic counterculture on the other. While the public may have been reluctant to adopt Btx in those years, techno-enthusiasts were not.

Unlike today's Internet, Btx distinguished subscribers and content providers. While subscribers' terminal devices were only able to download and render pages, providers had terminal devices with editing functionality. Btx pages were stored in database servers, while companies intending to provide dynamically generated content, e.g., for banking applications, could connect their own infrastructure to Btx via broadband technology. In comparison, subscriber devices were rather simple. They could download and render pages and offered functions for using Btx's micropayment system. The Club appropriated the feature by publishing a donation page billing DM 9.99 per visit. Members found it was tempting to access the page on publicly accessible Btx terminals found in stores and post offices to advertise and demonstrate the new system. By experimenting, Club members discovered that subscriber and most provider devices were actually the same hardware, while the latter had two additional buttons for editing. They figured out how to turn a much cheaper subscriber device into a provider device by drilling two holes in the case and installing the missing buttons.[33]

Btx was introduced in an atmosphere of leftist skepticism about large, anonymous, and opaque technical systems that were already in the public's mind such as

[32] Ibid., 20.

[33] *Chaos Radio Express* no. 161, network podcast produced by Tim Pritlove, available at http://chaosradio.ccc.de/cre161.html. Accessed 30 Apr 2011.

the antinuclear movement's run against risky technology and the resistance to the 1981 population census that finally led to the novel basic right of *informational self-determination*. While these circumstances alienated large groups of potential buyers, they were tempting for hackers, who saw themselves as vanguards of the new information society. Since Btx was controlled by DBP, which hackers considered their secret enemy, the Club tried to draw public attention to flaws in Btx. At the time, Club members used to trigger skirmishes with DBP because it had government monopoly on telecommunication, controlled access to the telephone system, and authorized the hardware that was allowed to be connected to the telephone jack. DBP determined telephone charges and could constrain services. For example, it used to be illegal to connect a modem that had not been approved by the DBP's engineering office. Since only a few very expensive modems had been accredited in the early 1980s, many users who tried to save money with imported hardware found themselves being investigated. They were accused of installing and maintaining a disallowed telecommunication device.[34] However, this was no deterrent for a real hacker: a do-it-yourself guide for a cheap modem was published in *Hackerbibel*.[35] The "Datenklo" modem was designed as an acoustic coupler, not connected to telephone jacks but to telephone receivers.[36] Even such an unaccredited acoustic coupler without an electric connection to the telephone jack was illegal.

8.5 Revealing the Gaps in Btx

Let us turn back to the Club's activities. After members obtained HASPA identification codes, they managed to access the Club's donation page and charge the bank. For every access, the Btx system charged the bank DM 9.99 and credited the Club. On November 18, 1984, after 13,500 automatically performed accesses, the Btx system entered about DM 135,000 on the Club's credit side. The following Monday, Holland and Wernéry pressed charges against themselves with Hamburg's data privacy commissioner and reported their act at a media conference.[37] Wernéry explained that they had learned about the bank's codes by exploiting the entire memory of a Btx page. They triggered the remote system's software to reveal its memory contents randomly as clutter on screen where identity codes could be found.

Legally, it was only a misdemeanor. Hence, the bank decided not to sue Wernéry and Holland but lauded them for revealing a risky security vulnerability in the Btx system. The bank manager blamed DBP instead for falsely assuring Btx's security. Now, DBP was forced to recognize there had been a glitch in the system that could

---

[34] *Gesetz über Fernmeldeanlagen* (Telecommunication Devices Act) of 1892, revised in 1977 and 1986, defined this punishable act as an infringement.

[35] Holland, *Die Hackerbibel*, 95. The name "Datenklo" is explained on p. 98.

[36] The components for this connection originated from a plumbing sleeve which gave the modem its name: "klo" is a German colloquial term for toilet.

[37] Ammann, Nach uns die Zukunft, 18.

be triggered by exploiting the pages memory. Its officials denied, however, that such a glitch could be used to acquire bank codes. While the hackers' testimony stood against the DBP's claim at the time, it was and still is hard to decide whether the hack was actually feasible in theory and practice.

However, since the Club indisputably had knowledge of the identification codes, embarrassed DBP was at a loss to explain the incident. While initially recognizing the glitch, DBP finally blamed HASPA of leaking their codes to the hackers. In a mailing to its employees, it accused the bank of carelessness regarding their own data. The letter was reprinted in *Hackerbibel,* ridiculing DBP.[38]

Soon, the Committee on Posts and Telecommunications in the *Bundestag* reviewed Btx security. On December 5, 1984, the committee discussed the implications of the hack as the last item on its agenda. The chairman demanded a briefing on Btx's data privacy due to an "incident in Hamburg whereby HASPA identification codes were revealed to a computer club."[39] In his response, a DBP official explained that no one knew for sure how the computer club had acquired the identification codes. Surely, these codes had not been discovered through software glitches in the Btx system, he argued. Investigations showed that the bank had been careless by entering the codes during a demonstration in public, where the codes had been tapped. DBP rejected virtually every one of the hackers' claims: the connection device for Btx could neither be opened without anyone noticing—as a matter of fact, Holland had demonstrated this in front of cameras earlier that year—nor were the identification codes and password saved in the same place. Although DBP admitted a software glitch had existed, its officials denied the possibility of abusing it. Finally, the committee agreed that DBP had reported this incident clumsily to the public, since it had acknowledged a bug without insisting on its innocuousness, hence causing a major drawback to the proliferation of Btx.[40]

However, DBP did not actually deny the possibility of entering foreign identification codes to access pages automatically and transfer money from one Btx account to another. Even if Wernéry and Holland had obtained identification codes in another way, they managed to transfer the money. A transfer of such a large amount could not be concealed. A real, malevolent attacker could have succeeded in tapping a larger number of identification codes to debit many accounts with small amounts. This would have been a mere misdemeanor and arguably a large number of small amounts could have remained unnoticed. It is obvious that Wernéry and Holland intentionally planned their coup in such a way that they could easily deny bad faith

[38] "Btx ist sicher! Computer-Club profitiert vom Leichtsinn einer Sparkasse," ("Btx is secure! Computer-Club benefits from a bank's recklessness") *BPM-Information für alle Beschäftigten der DBP* (December 12, 1984), reprinted in Holland, *Die Hackerbibel*, 43.

[39] The German protocol reads "Anlaß dafür sei der kürzlich bekannt gewordene Vorfall in Hamburg, wo die Kennung der Hamburger Sparkasse einem Computer-Club bekannt wurde," Parliamentary Archives (PA-DBT 3115 A 10/15), Prot. 17, 10. Protocols of this Archive are subsequently referred with session and page number.

[40] Ibid., 13.

as well as attract public interest. Likewise, DBP's clumsy behavior played into their hands. Officials were just too eager to defend themselves.

Holland and Wernéry's calculation paid off: many newspapers and magazines, from the right-wing populist tabloid *Bild* and the conservative *Frankfurter Allgemeine Zeitung* to left-wing newspapers like *taz*, reported on serious data protection issues within Btx. While *taz* published an article written by Holland, the centrist newspaper *Die Zeit*, for instance, compared the hackers to the German allotment movement, whose members had tried to escape from a "dominance of machines."[41] In *Die Zeit*, Thomas von Randow was frank in his view:

> It is a wonder that the *Btx* hackers' little games have been harmless so far. After all, they exposed the plaintiveness of the *Bildschirmtext* design with a clarity that leaves nothing to the imagination. […] All this should have been a warning for *Bundespost*, before its favorite child *Bildschirmtext* got a slap in the face through the bank trick early last week. […] A program that needs so much reworking is f…ed up beyond all repair.[42]

The magazine *Der Spiegel* listed more of the flaws that the hackers had found in *Btx*.[43] Even the tabloid *Bild* cheered for the computer enthusiasts, while usually reporting from a law-and-order point of view on computer crimes.[44] The hack raised interest within other hacker groups[45] and in two of Germany's public service television news.[46] Newspaper articles and television reports depicted Holland's and Wernéry's hack as a contribution to data privacy activism. The hack had obviously touched a common conception of new information technology among journalists and presumably with the public at large: while the new possibilities were fascinating, as reports from technology trade shows illustrated, the vision of large systems controlled by a few organizations—at that time the state in the case of DBP—was unsettling. Although it may not have been a common critique as information technology was still a niche topic, the media coverage expressed general discomfort with information technology during the 1980s.

---

[41] Bildschirmtext im Schwachstellentest. *die tageszeitung*, December 22, 1984; Thomas von Randow. 1984. Ein Schlag gegen das System. Ein Computerclub deckt Sicherheitslücken im Btx-Programm der Post auf. *Die Zeit* 49, November 30.

[42] Ibid. My translation.

[43] Lustige Spielchen. *Der Spiegel* 48(1984), 241.

[44] *Bild* (November 20, 1984).

[45] As Nevejan and Badenoch show, the hack was widely discussed in hacker groups outside Germany as well. Holland and Wernéry were invited to speak at a hacker gathering in Amsterdam. Caroline Nevejan, and Alexander Badenoch. 2014. How Amsterdam invented the Internet: European networks of significance, 1980–1995. In *Hacking Europe. From computer cultures to demoscenes*, ed. Gerard Alberts and Ruth Oldenziel, 189–217. New York: Springer. Even today, the Btx hack forms a crucial part of the Club's self-representation.

[46] A video recording of the *heute journal* reporting on the hack can be found at http://chaosradio.ccc.de/doc002.html in German. Accessed 27 Apr 2011.

8.6 Consumer Protection vs. Hacker Ethics

While Club members loved experimenting with hardware to explore its capabilities, DBP aimed to design ready-made end-user devices by anticipating some sort of ordinary user behavior.[47] Its officials considered young computer enthusiasts' experiments "untypical behavior." Here, DBP's approach and the Club's identity were in conflict: Holland sought to enable people to manage their data independently, to fight "the big brotherhood" and become citizens of the new era. DBP, in contrast, had designed, planned, and controlled their system with a more or less passive role in mind for consumers at the end of the economic chain.

The Club's point of view corresponded with the hacker ethics coined by Steven Levy in his influential book *Hackers. Heroes of the Computer Revolution.* He described a "hands-on" philosophy, in which all information and every piece of hardware should be accessible to everyone:

> The best way to promote this free exchange of information is to have an open system, something which presents no boundaries between a hacker and a piece of information or an item of equipment that he needs in his quest for knowledge, improvement, and time on-line. The last thing you need is a bureaucracy. Bureaucracies, whether corporate, government, or university, are flawed systems, dangerous in that they cannot accommodate the exploratory impulse of true hackers. Bureaucrats hide behind arbitrary rules (as opposed to the logical algorithms by which machines and computer programs operate): they invoke those rules to consolidate power, and perceive the constructive impulse of hackers as a threat.[48]

In contrast, hackers should mistrust authorities and promote decentralization. And hackers should judge each other "by their hacking, not bogus criteria such as degrees, age, race, or position."[49] The central doctrine of hacker ethics is to gain access to a system itself and not to settle for using ready-made end-user interfaces. Most likely Wernéry and Holland were not aware of Levy's book at the time of the hack but explicitly agreed later on.

For sure, Wernéry's and Holland's motivation was not as consumer protective as they pretended in *Datenschleuder* and in interviews. They felt it had also been a great opportunity to have their nemesis DBP meet its Waterloo. It matched the image of hackers as a technically enthusiastic, yet critical vanguard, demanding free access. This ambivalence of two impulses—a rage against the machine and a passion for some kind of utopia, in which not the contingent, anonymous institutions but the logical and rational algorithms would lead the way to democratic computer technology and a free information society—turned into a half-hearted demand for consumer protection, not the political agenda some leftist groups desired. However, it was this sugar-coated concept of hackers that had a significant impact on discourses criminalizing their activities.

---

[47] This behavior was investigated by group discussions which formed the main subject of secondary research literature at the time. A history of Btx technology comparing its design and appropriation is, in contrast, still to be written.

[48] Levy, *Hackers*, 41.

[49] Ibid., 43.

8.7 Legislation for White-Collar Crimes

In the combined issues 5+6 of *Datenschleuder* in 1984, the authors complained about a subtle criminalization of their hobby. For instance, they pointed out that a telecommunication journal had published a do-it-yourself guide for building an "illegal" modem a few years earlier, while the authors of that very journal accused the hackers of the same now.[50] They added: "Only those who are totally crack-brained would publish a journal like *Datenschleuder* and commit offenses at the same time." Nevertheless, discourses seeking to penalize hacking had already started, while consumer protection activism was also leaving its mark.

Before the 1980s, computer crimes were unknown to the German public. Companies had suffered from practices they considered to be crimes against their computer infrastructure. In most cases, they could only get compensation but not the satisfaction of having those acts prosecuted. At hearings and conferences outside the public domain, experts discussed ways to penalize what they considered computer crimes. The first hearing on computer crimes in Germany was held on May 13, 1974, while an influential monograph analyzing computer crimes was published in 1977.[51] In many studies and monographs of the 1970s, computer abuses were discussed, while in the 1980s, experts lamented the lack of legislation and rulings that resulted in courts finding defendants not guilty.

Computer crimes whether penalized or not were usually considered by the media as well as politicians to be white-collar crimes, committed by experts or business employees, not by petty criminals or young vandals. Although hackers and young computer enthusiasts were mistrusted, they were usually only looked down on or ignored. In 1983, the *Bundestag* Committee on Legal Affairs began to debate a draft bill to fight "white-collar crimes." The legislative process was restarted after being interrupted by early elections.[52] In the Ministry's draft law of 1978, the former Social Democrat and Liberal government had suggested penalizing computer fraud through a law against white-collar crimes. While the draft had indeed stated that the new technology offered ways to prevent crimes, for example, through safer computer systems, at the same time new crimes evolved that did not fit under the existing *Strafgesetzbuch* (StGB, Criminal Code).[53] The newly elected conservative government agreed and restarted negotiations addressing frauds in tender procedures

---

[50] *Datenschleuder* 5+6 (1984), 1.

[51] Ulrich Sieber. 1977. *Computerkriminalität und Strafrecht*. Köln: Heymann.

[52] Hans Achenbach. 1986. Das Zweite Gesetz zur Bekämpfung der Wirtschaftskriminalität. *Neue Juristische Wochenschrift* 30: 1835–1898. While the new coalition of conservatives and liberals coincided with changes in other European countries, one has to bear in mind that the former coalition was indeed fought by leftist movements. Especially after NATO's Double-Track Decision, the German peace movement alienated the government while the Green party was evolving as a collective movement out of many left-wing groups. Hence, while the change of government indeed meant a shift in economic policy, in Germany anyway it had little impact on the extra-parliamentary movement of the left.

[53] Ministry draft law for an anti-white-collar crime act of December 19, 1978, 41.

and computer crimes in one draft.[54] Since the part on computer crimes was undisputed, the introduction of computer crime statutory law seemed to be a more or less obvious development of the StGB. Aspects of an emerging computer culture, especially hackers, were seen as marginal, if seen at all. The explanation in the draft statute filed by the *Bundesjustizministerium* (BMJ, Federal Ministry of Justice) only spoke of criminal attacks as an American phenomenon:

> Due to the widespread use of computers by commercial and administrative entities in the past two decades, criminal attacks on computers – which first occurred in the U.S.A. but are increasingly being detected in the Federal Republic of Germany and other Western industrialized nations as well – pose a major threat. The draft statute proposes a new *corpus delicti* for computer fraud and a *corpus delicti* for falsification of recorded data as well as several amendments to statutes concerning the protection of deeds.[55]

The bill contained one paragraph penalizing computer fraud and another penalizing the counterfeiting of electronic deeds. The existing law against fraud was deemed inapplicable since it was considered impossible for computers to err.[56] The government suggested introducing §263a StGB which defined computer fraud. Under this new provision, a person was acting illegally if he or she entered wrong information, manipulated the work flow of a computer program, or changed or blocked accurate data from being processed. Furthermore, the law was restricted to cases in which the victim suffered financial loss.

A hearing on the draft was held on June 6, 1984. The invited experts supported the urgent need for new legislation: offenders in cases like computer sabotage or time theft were not just motivated by pleasure and profit but by political reasons as well. This is the first time the term "hacker" was mentioned in the debate. According to the expert Sieber, hackers just like computer crimes were an American phenomenon that had just started to spread to Germany.[57]

Other types of offenses should be recognized by the committee, Sieber continued: for instance, manipulation of a running program, hiding malicious code in programs, blocking calculations such as wage accounting, program theft, time theft, counterfeiting identification codes, and finally destroying hardware or data.[58] Because in time theft no private data is obtained, changed, or destroyed and no running programs are affected in their internal logic, the intended legislation did not cover them. Nevertheless, a "thief" benefited from foreign processing capabilities without causing a measurable loss. Written testimonies from stakeholders in the business community and German government stressed this point.

---

[54] Bundestagssitzungs-Protokoll (German Federal Parliament Protocol) 10/25 (September 29, 1983): 1665.

[55] Ibid., 1668. In the German legal system, the term "deeds" ("Urkunden") includes documents that can serve as evidence in court.

[56] Fritjof Haft. 1987. Das Zweite Gesetze zur Bekämpfung der Wirtschaftskriminalität (2. WiKG). *Neue Zeitschrift für Strafrecht* 1: 6–9.

[57] Protocol of the Committee for Legal Affairs, Parliamentary Archives (PA-DBT 3109 A 10/6), Prot. 26, 173.

[58] Ibid., 26, 174–184.

For instance, Nixdorf, the biggest computer firm in Germany at that time, demanded the penalization of underlying offenses such as unauthorized access which is needed to commit other offenses like time theft.[59] Unauthorized access without any manipulation of programs or data was already penalized under the *Bundesdatenschutzgesetz* (BDSG, Federal Data Protection Act), but only if personal data were involved. According to Nixdorf, unauthorized access was not just a legal policy issue. It was an issue of system integrity, since an offender could damage systems through negligence, causing high costs to regain system integrity. It turned out the bill was insufficient in meeting industry demand for penalizing computer crimes, while academics disputed its legal concept.[60] Committee members had previously agreed on the computer crime part of the draft but had to acknowledge the need to revise it.[61]

On September 26, 1984, Berlin's Commissioner for Data Protection filed a copy of the "Counterfeit Access Device and Computer Fraud and Abuse Act of 1984," adopted by the US Senate in the summer of 1984. In this bill, the Senate penalized fraud by counterfeit access devices like counterfeit or stolen credit cards, furthermore, unauthorized access to computer systems and using computer systems with authorized access. The latter regulation constrained the penalty to cases in which "anything of value (other than the use of the computer) aggregating $5,000 or more during any one year period" is obtained.[62] Thus, "time theft," the mere use of a foreign computer, was not to be punished.[63]

In the Senate report accompanying the draft, experts emphasized the need to penalize "hacking," which was nothing but "intellectual pranksterism."[64] As a consequence, the Senate Committee complained of a too indulgent attitude towards hackers. Their image contradicted that of computer revolution heroes or consumer protection advocates and was more in keeping with rascals playing intellectual, still boyish pranks. Here, the term "hacker" had been introduced by experts to denote pranksterism, while in Germany the experts had addressed hacking as an underestimated crime. In both ways, criminalization was at work: one either already agreed on the felonious character of hacking or one was still ignoring it as a supposedly harmless intellectual hobby that cost "the economy millions now and potentially billions in the future," according to the report.

About a year after the hearing, the BMJ announced it would extend the scope of the committee's draft legislation.[65] The BMJ explained this extension was motivated

[59] *Nixdorf's* statement for the public hearing concerning the 2. WiKG (June 4, 1984), 7.

[60] For example, Fritjof Haft of the University Tübingen cautioned when changing existing laws and even rejected the necessity to change anything at all. See: Committee Protocol – Prot. 26, 169. Haft, Das Zweite Gesetz zur Bekämpfung der Wirtschaftskriminalität (2. WiKG), 6.

[61] Ibid., 26, 195.

[62] H.R. 5616. Counterfeit Access Device and Computer Fraud and Abuse Act of 1984. In 98th Congress, 2nd Session, 5f.

[63] Report to accompany H.R. 5616, 20.

[64] Ibid., 11.

[65] Letter from the BMJ to the Committee, June 11, 1985.

not only by the hearing but also by a visit of German parliamentarians to the USA and the results of the Organisation for Economic Co-operation and Development (OECD) working group for Information, Computer and Communication Policy (ICCP). In the extended draft, the Ministry suggested introducing laws against spying out data and changing or deleting it without authorization. Just as requested by Nixdorf, the draft planned to penalize unauthorized access, with imprisonment of up to 1 year. The draft's explanatory statement included:

> A person fulfills the elements of the offense if he or she overcomes access guards, for example by repeatedly typing combinations of letters and numbers on the keyboard of a home computer ("hacking") and, as such, gains access to data not designated to be accessed by this person. Criminalizing such cases is justified by the legal wrong-doing in jeopardizing operator and user integrity caused by a successful unauthorized access of databases, by the possibility of causing too high system load, as well as by the creation of opportunities to engage in other computer-related offenses.[66]

The Ministry presented an explanation of "hacking," defining hackers as offenders who merely try passwords again and again till they gain access. Significantly, its definition ignored any form of technological skills described previously as intellectual pranksterism. Many articles in *Datenschleuder* dealt with technical problems by describing the functionality of phone networks or mainframe operating systems, showing hackers had at least some technical knowledge. Instead, the draft's opinion matched seamlessly that of DBP in the Committee on Posts and Telecommunications, denying hackers had any technical expertise or discovered any flaws in Btx at all. Nevertheless, this opinion dissented with the US Senate's report, which called hacking an "intellectual pranksterism." It is plausible that hackers were despised since they were not experts in a traditional sense. Most acts ascribed to hackers in the USA were committed by those operating within universities. While university students give the impression of future experts, the young Club members do not. Expertise is ascribed to professionals, not to hobbyists, whether or not the latter have a profound knowledge. Likewise, the statement completely ignored any notion of consumer protection, not to mention any political agenda. In contrast, it emphasized the notion of a punishable crime for mere unauthorized access.

On October 23, 1985, the Committee on Legal Affairs agreed to the BMJ's latest suggestions, while the Greens preferred to fight safety problems with technical measures instead of new criminal laws. Except for this point, the need for the bill was undisputed.[67] Still, some committee members considered exempting "good hackers" and "young computer enthusiasts" from punishment for their "beneficial work." They were impressed by hacks in which "hobbyists" proved large companies and organizations' security measures to be insufficient. The committee also mentioned a case in which two members of a computer club managed to transfer a large amount of money from a bank to their own account using Btx, thus proving that DBP's security guarantee was false. Even the conservatives agreed: they

[66] Attachment to the Letter from the BMJ to the Committee, June 11, 1985.

[67] Committee Protocol, Prot. 63, 38.

sympathized with hackers and were impressed by their "intellectual discipline." Nevertheless, it was necessary to limit their "hobby" to a "justifiable extent." The draft of §202a StGB was seen as an inevitable part of the new legislation. Nonetheless, the committee agreed to exempt hacking that revealed data protection issues from punishment.[68] Trying to avoid a legal definition of what "politically correct hacking" meant, the committee reshaped §202a in such a way that obtaining data without authorization was penalized, while unauthorized connecting to computer systems without causing loss or damage and without obtaining secret data was not. Only the Greens doubted if the wording was sufficient to exempt "good hackers" from punishment.[69]

We can see an interesting shift in this debate: while earlier hackers were seen as activists engaging in data and consumer protection against nontransparent technology, they were now discussed as young enthusiasts with an exciting *hobby* that nevertheless required strict boundaries to maintain acceptable social behavior. The implications of the shift in hacking's image are obvious. Shifting names for phenomena is a basic strategy in shaping political discourses where the actual context or meaning of the particular phenomenon is irrelevant. What does matter is the implication of a logic of representation in which hackers are either subsumed under the concepts of consumer protection or hobbyism, superficially distinguished from "intellectual pranksterism." Through this discursive shift, the committee adapted the image of hacking in the Senate's report step by step.

The Btx hack did have an impact on the legislative process. The intervention played a role in the debate on the role of hackers. However, this image of hacking as a kind of consumer protection has been superimposed by treating it as a mere hobby. Hacking shifted from a political to a personal affair and was thus marginalized in the political discourse: its alleged connection to public interests could now be ignored. Still, the sympathy towards hackers did not vanish completely but enabled exemption from punishment, not for political activists but for young enthusiasts whose hobby interfered with serious matters of state and the economy.

8.8 The Legal Implications for Hacktivism

From the hackers' point of view, the Greens' critique turned out to be correct. While hacking into a foreign computer system was now penalized only if foreign data were obtained, hackers thought it was impossible to hack into any system without obtaining any data.[70] While even hackers admitted the need for computer crime

[68] Ibid., 63, 47.

[69] Ibid., 71, 6.

[70] Stephan Ackermann. 1988. Die aktuellen Tarife fürs Hacken. In *Das Chaos Computer Buch. Hacking made in Germany*, ed. Wieckmann, 183–192. Reinbek bei Hamburg: Wunderlich, here 185, considers even passwords to be protected data. This interpretation is, however, to be argued from a juridical point of view, Günter Freiherr von Gravenreuth. 1989. Computerviren, hacker,

legislation to protect citizens and the economy from computer fraud, they considered the law as an "anti-hacker law" that included a "tariff list for hacking."[71] Other hackers were even more pessimistic. One lamented that the new statutes penalized hacking without exception for "honest hackers" who were doing nothing wrong.[72] However, most hackers also admitted the need for the new statutes: not to contest "juvenile hackers" but the "gigantic dimensions" of computer crimes. Nevertheless, without a doubt, the lawmaker had indeed intended to fight hackerism through an "Anti-hacker Act," as the media put it.[73] So, even if ambiguities in the law might have allowed hacking, it had certainly become more risky. Especially since using foreign identification codes had become computer fraud, a new Btx hack would have been illegal and consequently, its impact in the media impossible. While they could still look for ways to hack within the law, hackers had without doubt become the criminals of the computer revolution.[74] The Club drew a surprising conclusion from the shift: what had started as a "chaotic" regulars' table became a legally registered association in 1986. Protected by the basic right of freedom of association, the Club attempted to avoid further criminalization as a terrorist or criminal organization.[75] While authors in legal journals tried to maintain the impunity of hobbyist hacking, their attempts to tell "hackers" from "crashers" soon became silent.[76]

8.9 Conclusion

The ambivalent image of hackers as heroes and criminals that I examined in legal discourses also found their way into the media, into politics, and even with hackers themselves. The ambivalence in the various debates shaped hacktivism in Western Germany in the 1980s. Both the legal discourses and hackers' self-concept had strong roots in American images, yet appropriated in specific ways. Hacktivism in Germany together with post-1968 discourses led to a political hacktivism, inspiring actions that impressed journalists and politicians alike. Encouraged by the openmindedness of the public and politicians for data protection activism, the hackers began contesting their criminalization and marginalization. In their opinion,

---

datenspione, crasher und cracker. Überblick und rechtliche Einordnung. *Neue Zeitschrift für Strafrecht*, 201–206, here 204.

[71] Ackermann, Die aktuellen Tarife fürs Hacken.

[72] Thilo Eckoldt. 1988. Hacker-mit einem Bein im Knast. In *Das Chaos Computer Buch. Hacking made in Germany*, ed. Jürgen Wieckmann, 154–167. Reinbek bei Hamburg: Wunderlich.

[73] Ackermann, Die aktuellen Tarife fürs Hacken, 183.

[74] Ibid., 192.

[75] *Datenschleuder* 60 (1997), 25f.

[76] Haft, Das Zweite Gesetze zur Bekämpfung der Wirtschaftskriminalität (2. WiKG), 9; Von Gravenreuth, Computerviren, hacker, datenspione, crasher und cracker. Überblick und rechtliche Einordnung, 204; and Stefan Ernst. 2007. Das neue Computerstrafrecht. *Neue Juristische Wochenschrift* 37: 2661–2666, here 2661.

humankind could not yet relinquish them as a techno-political vanguard, especially since penalizing hacking indicated how little hacktivism was understood. Hence, there was alternating attraction and rejection between hackers and the state and between hackers and the media. Just as the hackers' merits were acknowledged in most political discussions, politicians and commentators underlined the need to control hacking. Thus, discourses tended to marginalize hackers by denying them any political legitimacy and declaring them to be mere hobbyists. The Club was in jeopardy of losing its unique selling point: a group interested in both technology and politics.

The gestures of differentiation against the left, the alternative movement and also the allegedly obstinate and overstrained politicians, created and shaped the atmosphere in which institutionalized hacktivism could evolve. The transforming appropriation of leftist techno-critique but also the recognition in the media and partly in the political arena created an environment which encouraged Club members. They had to endure frustrating hostilities and opposition. Nonetheless, successes and failures alternated in a primarily discouraging, but still motivating way. With the computer crime legislation, the conditions of hacktivism changed: despite trying to keep "good hacking" outside the law, the new law prepared the ground for harsh reactions of law enforcement and for an image shift in news coverage. When the 1986/1987 hacking attacks on networks of international institutions like CERN and NASA were discovered, few discussions took place about striking security flaws in critical digital infrastructures of authorities and companies in the western world.[77] Although hackers revealed again that these systems were not protected against industrial and governmental espionage, the thin-skinned authorities initiated investigations into the Club. They raided the Club's rooms and its members' apartments, providing the media with stories about computer criminals. Wernéry's arrest in France was just the icing on the cake.

Bibliography

Achenbach, Hans. 1986. Das Zweite Gesetz zur Bekämpfung der Wirtschaftskriminalität. *Neue Juristische Wochenschrift* 30: 1835–1898.

Ackermann, Stephan. 1988. Die aktuellen Tarife fürs Hacken. In *Das Chaos Computer Buch. Hacking made in Germany*, ed. Jürgen Wieckmann, 183–192. Reinbek bei Hamburg: Wunderlich.

Adorno, Theodor W., and Max Horkheimer. 1972. *Dialectic of enlightenment*. New York: Seabury Press.

Ammann, Thomas. 1988. Nach uns die Zukunft. Aus der Geschichte des Chaos Computer Clubs. In *Das Chaos Computer Buch. Hacking made in Germany*, ed. Jürgen Wieckmann, 9–31. Reinbek bei Hamburg: Wunderlich.

Bach, Hans-Peter. 1985. *Verfassungsrechtliche Grundfragen von Bildschirmtext*. PhD thesis, University of Mainz.

Brunner, John. 1975. *Shockwave rider*. New York: Harper & Row.

[77] Andy Müller-Maguhn, and Reinhard Schrutzki. 1988. Welcome to the NASA-headquarter. In *Das Chaos Computer Buch. Hacking made in Germany*, ed. Jürgen Wieckmann, 32–53. Reinbek bei Hamburg: Wunderlich.

Coleman, Gabriella. 2010. The hacker conference. *Anthropological Quarterly* 83(1, Winter): 47–72.
Dietrich, Ralf. 2009. *Das Erfordernis der besonderen Sicherung im StGB am Beispiel des Ausspähens von Daten, [Para] 202a StGB: Kritik und spezialpräventiver Ansatz*. PhD thesis, Universitat Tübingen.
Eckoldt, Thilo. 1988. Hacker-mit einem Bein im Knast. In *Das Chaos Computer Buch. Hacking made in Germany*, ed. Jürgen Wieckmann, 154–167. Reinbek bei Hamburg: Wunderlich.
Enzensberger, Hans Magnus. 1970. Baukasten zu einer Theorie der Medien. *Kursbuch* 20(1970): 159–186.
Ernst, Stefan. 2007. Das neue Computerstrafrecht. *Neue Juristische Wochenschrift* 37: 2661–2666.
Friesinger, Manfred. 1989. *Bildschirmtext in Frankreich*. München: Fischer.
Gibson, William. 1984. *Neuromancer*. New York: Ace Books.
Haft, Fritjof. 1987. Das Zweite Gesetze zur Bekämpfung der Wirtschaftskriminalität (2. WiKG). *Neue Zeitschrift für Strafrecht* 1: 6–9.
Holland, Wau, et al. (eds.). 1985. *Die Hackerbibel*. Löhrbach: Pieper Werner Medienexp.
Horkheimer, Max. 1974. *Critique of instrumental reason*. New York: Seabury Press.
Jakić, Bruno. 2014. Galaxy and the new wave: Yugoslav computer culture in 1980s. In *Hacking Europe. From computer cultures to demoscenes*, ed. Gerard Alberts and Ruth Oldenziel, 107–128. New York: Springer.
Kaps, Rolf Ulrich. 1983. *Die Wirkung von Bildschirmtext auf das Informationsverhalten der Konsumenten*, Schriftenreihe der Studiengruppe Bildschirmtext. Gröbenzell: Fischer.
Kromrey, Helmut, et al. 1984. *Bochumer Untersuchung im Rahmen der wissenschaftlichen Begleitung des Feldversuchs Bildschirmtext Düsseldorf/Neuss*. Bochum: Ruhr-Universität.
Kuhlmann, Wolf-Dieter. 1985. *Rechtsfragen des Bildschirmtext-Staatsvertrages vom 18. März 1983*. PhD thesis, Universität Bochum.
Kulla, Daniel. 2003. *Der Phrasenprüfer. Szenen aus dem Leben von Wau Holland*. Löhrbach: Pieper and the Grüne Kraft.
Levy, Steven. 1984. *Hackers: Heroes of the computer revolution*. Garden City, NY: Anchor Press/ Doubleday.
Marcuse, Herbert. 1964. *One-dimensional man*. Boston: Beacon Press.
Müller-Maguhn, Andy, and Reinhard Schrutzki. 1988. Welcome to the NASA-headquarter. In *Das Chaos Computer Buch. Hacking made in Germany*, ed. Jürgen Wieckmann, 32–53. Reinbek bei Hamburg: Wunderlich.
Nevejan, Caroline, and Alexander Badenoch. 2014. How Amsterdam invented the Internet: European networks of significance, 1980–1995. In *Hacking Europe. From computer cultures to demoscenes*, ed. Gerard Alberts and Ruth Oldenziel, 189–217. New York: Springer.
Pospischil, Rudolf. 1987. *Bildschirmtext in Frankreich und Deutschland: Grundlagen u. Konzeptionen*. Nürnberg: Verlag der Kommunikationswissenschaftlichen Forschungsvereinigung.
Sieber, Ulrich. 1977. *Computerkriminalität und Strafrecht*. Köln: Heymann.
Stolte, Dirk. 1983. *Personalsuche und Personalvermittlung mit Bildschirmtext*, Schriftenreihe der Studiengruppe Bildschirmtext. Gröbenzell bei München: Fischer.
Traut, Bernd M. 1987. *Rechtsfragen zu Bildschirmtext*. München: R. Fischer.
von Gravenreuth, Günter Freiherr. 1989. Computerviren, hacker, datenspione, crasher und cracker. Überblick und rechtliche Einordnung. *Neue Zeitschrift für Strafrecht*, 201–206.
von Randow, Thomas. 1984. Ein Schlag gegen das System. Ein Computerclub deckt Sicherheitslücken im Btx-Programm der Post auf. *Die Zeit* 49, November 30.
Warnecke, Christoph. 1983. *Bildschirmtext und dessen Einsatz bei Kreditinstituten*, Schriftenreihe der Studiengruppe Bildschirmtext. Gröbenzell: Fischer.
Wasiak, Patryk. 2014. Playing and copying: Social practices of home computer users in Poland during the 1980s. In *Hacking Europe. From computer cultures to demoscenes*, ed. Gerard Alberts and Ruth Oldenziel, 129–150. New York: Springer.
Wieckmann, Jürgen (ed.). 1988. *Das Chaos Computer Buch. Hacking made in Germany*. Reinbek bei Hamburg: Wunderlich.
Wiesenbauer, Ludwig. 1983. *Verhaltenswissenschaftliche Grundlagen der Bildschirmtextbenutzung*, Schriftenreihe der Studiengruppe Bildschirmtext. Gröbenzell: Fischer.

Chapter 9
How Amsterdam Invented the Internet: European Networks of Significance, 1980–1995

Caroline Nevejan and Alexander Badenoch

9.1 Nets and the City[1]

In his discussions on the use of the Internet in civil society, the internationally renowned sociologist Manuel Castells singled out Amsterdam as the key site of historical innovation in Europe. Looking at developments there in the early 1990s, he identified the city's digital network as "a new form of public sphere combining local institutions, grassroots organizations, and computer networks in the development of cultural expression and civic participation."[2] Many have traced the start of the new public sphere to January 15, 1994, when access to the Internet became available to the general public in the Netherlands via a new dial-in service and virtual access area called *De Digitale Stad* (Digital City, called DDS). Access to Digital City was open to all: anyone with a modem simply needed to dial an Amsterdam telephone number or use one of the public terminals installed in the city. Subsequently, the

[1] This paper describes how the digital culture evolved in Amsterdam. Although the authors appreciate that the Amsterdam's digital culture emerged in a global context, they focus on understanding the global context from the Amsterdam perspective. This chapter is the result of an extended dialogue between Nevejan, a social scientist who was one actor in many of the events described here, and Badenoch, a media historian, in consultation with print archives and other witnesses. The authors are grateful to Geert Lovink, David Garcia, Patrice Riemens, Marleen Stikker, Tjebbe van Tijen, and Frances Brazier for their comments and Ruth Oldenziel and Gerard Alberts for their valuable editorial work. See also Nevejan Caroline. 2007. *Presence and the design of trust.* PhD Thesis, University of Amsterdam, in which some of these events are described from a social science perspective.

[2] Manuel Castells. 2001. *The Internet galaxy: Reflections on the Internet, business, and society*, 146. Oxford: Oxford University Press.

C. Nevejan
Delft University of Technology, Delft, The Netherlands
e-mail: nevejan@xs4all.nl

A. Badenoch (✉)
Université Paris IV Sorbonne, Paris, France
e-mail: alecbadenoch@gmail.com

G. Alberts and R. Oldenziel (eds.), *Hacking Europe. From Computer Cultures to Demoscenes*, History of Computing, DOI 10.1007/978-1-4471-5493-8_9,

adoption of Internet services grew rapidly from about 300 private citizens with Internet access before the opening to 4,000 daily users a year later, rising to 50,000 in 1997. The short user manual was a nonfiction bestseller at bookstores in the city.[3] Once in, users found themselves in a text-based environment—a graphic interface would come a few months later—built around the metaphor of the city. Users could visit the "post office" (send emails), exchange gossip in cafés, visit a number of themed city "squares," and debate public issues.[4] Other parts of Digital City had their referents in the more material aspects of Amsterdam. One could visit the library and consult its catalogue, visit the town hall for municipal information, and even read pornographic stories in the sex shops. A number of online experiments and events also took place, not least in connection with the upcoming municipal elections. The "rooted" location of Digital City as portal to the global world, with reference to a specific lived-in city, was the key to its participatory appeal. For the first time in the Netherlands, a computer environment came into existence where Dutch was spoken and where the agenda was set by Dutch social morals and codes. Thus far, the Internet had been a specialized environment dominated by the United States, dominated by the English language, American industry, and international nongovernmental organizations (NGOs)—a focus also echoed in the historical literature.[5] With the opening of Amsterdam Digital City, part of the Internet turned Dutch as it was publicly connected to events in Dutch society and in a Dutch style.[6] The locally organized, broadly participatory design and use attracted a wide range of international attention. Amsterdam Digital City was held up as an example of how the Internet could potentially transform social life. Moreover, Amsterdam had long been a central node in the technical infrastructure of the Internet.

As Don Slater has cautioned, based on his ethnographic exploration of Internet use in Trinidad, we must not treat the Internet and World Wide Web as global monoliths, used the same way the world over, but as phenomena locally appropriated for very different purposes.[7] We take his point one step further to show how technologies

---

[3] Ibid., 147; Joost Flint. 2004. *DDS – 10 jaar anders*. http://www.dds.nl/downloads/achtergrondartikel.pdf. Accessed 16 July 2011.

[4] For a demonstration of Amsterdam Digital City (DDS) Version 3.0 from the late 1990s, see http://www.dds.nl/downloads/DDS-3.0-presentatie.swf; a new online archive of Digital City (in Dutch) is at http://re-dds.nl/. Accessed 21 Mar 2013.

[5] In most histories of computing, "the Internet" refers to the work done by the US-based military, research, and large-scale business actors. Similarly, the "heroes" of Internet history are described as the lone technological innovators. See Janet Abbate. 1999. *Inventing the Internet*. Cambridge, MA: MIT Press; Paul E. Ceruzzi. 2003 [1998]. *A history of modern computing*. Cambridge, MA/London: MIT Press; Stephen Segaller. 1998. *Nerds 2.0.1: A brief history of the Internet*. New York: TV Books; Tim Berners-Lee. 2000. *Weaving the Web: The original design and ultimate destiny of the World Wide Web*. New York: HarperBusiness; and Stephen Levy. 1984. *Hackers: Heroes of the computer revolution*. Garden City, NY: Anchor Press/Doubleday.

[6] Caroline Nevejan. 1995. Holiday in the Digital City of Amsterdam. Lecture to the Dutch Ministry of Economic Affairs, February 11, unpublished manuscript in Nevejan Archives.

[7] Don Slater. 2003. Modernity under construction: Building the Internet in Trinidad. In *Modernity and technology*, ed. Philip Brey, Thomas J. Misa, and Andrew Feenberg, 139–160. Cambridge, MA: MIT Press.

are appropriated to individual end users and how local cultures have a profound effect on the design of networks and interfaces, including their social embedding. In the United States, Senator and later Vice-President Al Gore of Tennessee played a key role in facilitating broad public access to computer networks for educational purposes. When touting those achievements as a presidential candidate, Gore was accused mockingly by his political adversaries of claiming to have "invented the Internet."[8] While Al Gore never actually made this claim, we argue here that such public displays of envisioning and advocating a new technology play a significant role in emphasizing the value of creating new technologies. In taking this line of argument, we see a stark contrast between the way the Internet was invented in Europe and in the United States. It was not political figures like Al Gore who played the key facilitating roles in Amsterdam but actors from a range of independent media labs and cultural centers who worked to enable this new digital public culture.

We trace this history by showing how various actors came to converge around digital developments over the course of the late 1980s. Firstly, we trace two parallel developments: the growth of Amsterdam as a central node and gateway of the Internet in Europe on the one hand and the rise of independent media and cultural centers in the 1980s on the other. Members of these centers would become important catalysts in shaping digital developments in the city.[9] Secondly, we show how these sectors came together in the late 1980s with the involvement of a third set of actors, the hacking community, to shape what would become Digital City and Amsterdam's booming digital culture.[10]

9.2 The Internet Comes to the Netherlands

Already a decade before the launch of Digital City, Amsterdam was a central node and gateway for the Internet in Europe. Since the 1950s, Dutch nuclear physicists had collaborated internationally with scientists from the United States and the USSR even at the height of the Cold War. For physicists, the Internet's predecessor

[8] See Seth Finkelstein's "Al Gore Invented the Internet Archive," at http://sethf.com/gore/. On Al Gore's role in the US digital development, see Janet Abbate. 2010. Privatizing the Internet: Competing visions and chaotic events, 1987–1995. *IEEE Annals of the History of Computing* 31 (1): 10–22, and for praise of his role in promoting the Internet by key architects, see http://www.politechbot.com/p-01394.html. Last accessed 15 July 2011.

[9] This chapter draws on Nevejan's archive, deposited at the International Institute for Social History (*Internationale Instituut voor Sociale Geschiedenis*) Amsterdam, hereafter Nevejan Archive). As these materials have not been catalogued at the time of writing, they will be referred to according to the way they are currently filed. Every attempt has been made to describe them such that they can be relocated as necessary.

[10] The events described here involved a large number of artists, theorists, and activists, all of whom were important actors in shaping Amsterdam's independent media cultures. For future reference, we've mentioned them in the footnotes.

was vital for exchanging large amounts of data in their international collaborations at CERN in Geneva, Switzerland.[11] The Dutch National Institute for Nuclear Physics (NIKHEF) and national research center for Mathematics and Computer Science (CWI) were next-door neighbors. In the early 1980s, Amsterdam's computer scientists jumped on the bandwagon by literally drilling a hole through the wall to connect a cable to the physicists' adjacent building. The connecting cable not only marked the start of the European backbone of the Internet; the connection symbolized CWI's role in pioneering a number of Internet developments.

In the early 1980s, it was not just academic researchers who were interested in the new possibilities for communication and collaboration that the emerging digital communication infrastructure offered. Smaller and larger businesses and NGOs also expressed interest in these services. Similar to University of California, Berkeley, CWI offered accounts on their server. Using modems in which one would put the telephone receiver in a rubber cradle, people would "phone in" through telephone lines on the server. Many individuals began to participate in Usenet newsgroups, which started up in 1980. One account could facilitate a group of people to get otherwise inaccessible news and information. In 1987, civil networks like PeaceNet and GreenNet designed bulletin board services to connect grassroots organizations for the first time.[12] Unlike today, when all involved would participate on the net, these networks consisted of connections between nodes, around which groups of people would organize themselves. Political organizations and solidarity movements like the antinuclear waste movement, unions, and women's groups sought to connect through the network in order to get around censorship regimes and share information directly with other organizations. Various grassroots movements in Amsterdam were linked into such networks in the 1980s.

The local interest in CWI's connection was paralleled by its importance internationally. The indication ".NL" became the first root domain outside the United States, and on November 17, 1988, CWI's Piet Beertema received Europe's first email, sent via the first nonmilitary Internet connection between Europe and the United States. In 1990, Dutch universities started to connect electronically and established SURF foundation, which has since become a key European academic player.[13] When CWI's Internet service became increasingly popular over the course of the 1980s, the organization decided to focus exclusively on research and in early 1989 allocated its services to a separate foundation, Stichting NLnet, the first independent provider in the Netherlands.[14] It was the first Internet backbone in the

---

[11] See Abbate, *Inventing*. Professor Kees Braams, director of the Nuclear Physics Institute in Rijnhuizen, was working on a regular basis with Soviet colleagues, using the ARPAnet.

[12] Bulletin board services for grassroots organizations, administered by the Institute for Global Communication: http://www.igc.org/html/aboutigc.html. Last accessed 16 July 2011.

[13] Annelies Vlap. 2011. Internet van en voor Nederland. Het verhaal van 25 jaar .nl, in *25 jaar .nl*. In Bex*communicatie. *Anniversary Publication SIDN*, 30–40. Arnhem: Stichting Internet Domeinregistratie Nederland.

[14] Founders of Stichting NLnet were Ted Lindgren, Marten van Gelderen, Piet Beertema, Frances Brazier, Wytze van der Raay, and Jos Alsters. For a brief overview of the organization's history, see: http://nlnet.nl/foundation/history/199804-usenix.html. Last accessed July 2011.

Netherlands, offering local dial-in and ISDN infrastructure covering the entire country. It designed and implemented a low-cost connectivity structure without anticipating individual service, focusing instead on institutional provision. Major NLnet customers were corporate clients like Philips but also independents such as SURFnet, InterDoc's Antenna, Hack-Tic Network, and later the Internet service provider XS4ALL, who all, as we will see, played an important role in our story.

While institutional clients caught the attention of Amsterdam's increasingly important network connection, public interest took another turn. Amateur computing was booming. The Dutch Hobby Computer Club, which was started in 1977, exploded to a membership of 46,000 a decade later, making the organization one of the largest in Europe.[15] Independent of the national telecom agencies offering coax-cable infrastructures, individual users like the computer hobbyists developed their own practices and formats. Amsterdam City Council was also in a position to play an important role in supporting the emerging digital developments. As owner of the local cable infrastructure until 1995, the Council facilitated a rich local television and radio scene with a variety of broadcasters catering to a city of only 700,000 inhabitants.[16] Public events brought these disparate communities together for the first time.

9.3 Reconstructing the City: Squatting and Free Cultural Spaces

The social actors who would go on to shape Amsterdam's Internet infrastructural node in Europe and make it publicly available came from the city's counterculture and squatter movement. Creating new media spaces was part and parcel of the movement—and the struggles—to create new forms of urban space. Many neighborhoods that had been home to the city's Jewish community, including the half-open ghetto formed in 1941, became the center of these struggles. Empty from the deportation of the city's Jewish residents, many buildings had all of the wood in them plundered for firewood in the difficult hunger winter of 1944/1945 and were nevertheless nearly fully occupied after 1945, though the question of who actually owned them remained unsettled. A law from 1947 passed to deal with the uncertain ownership of the buildings gave the occupants of a house right to remain there unless someone else could prove ownership. Such was the state of many old neighborhoods, like the old Jewish working-class Nieuwmarkt neighborhood, east of

---

[15] Frank Veraart. 2008c. *Vormgevers van Persoonlijk Computergebruik: De ontwikkeling van computers voor kleingebruikers in Nederland 1970–1990*. PhD thesis, TU Eindhoven.

[16] James Stappers, Frank Olderaan, and Pieter de Wit. 1991. The Netherlands: Emergence of a new medium. In *The people's voice: Local radio and television in Europe*, ed. Nick Jankowski, Ole Prehn, and James Stappers, 90–103. London: John Libbey; Nick Jankowski. 1988. *Community television in Amsterdam access to participation in and use of the "Lokale Omroep Bijlmermeer"*. Amsterdam: Amsterdam University Press.

Dam Square and the Red Light District, and a short walk from Amsterdam University. The port had long been home to immigrants (and remains so) as well as being the center of the city's once-thriving Jewish community. In the 1960s, it was one of a number of neighborhoods that came into focus for city planners and social activists alike. In technocratic plans for city (re)construction (some of which dated from before the war), these parts would be razed and rebuilt to accommodate more car and metro traffic through the city, as well as more non-mixed commercial zoning, and wide, open boulevards. For social activists, by contrast, the old building, in need of reconstruction and repair, represented a chance to build new forms of urban community. Old houses that had been condemned were squatted, and a new inner city communal life started to emerge in which new ways of living together with larger groups of people, including schools, shops, businesses, and workshops, were invented. Starting in 1964, squatting as it is currently understood, as both practical and utopian social action, began to gain increasing attention. The anarchist group Provo, which became famous for its "white plans" (including, most famously, free white bicycles for use in a car-free inner city), embraced the practice and announced a "white housing plan" in 1966, in which empty houses would have their doors painted white to announce they were available for living in.[17] Typically, for social-democratic Amsterdam, the neighborhood newspaper *Geïllustreerd Bethaniënnieuws*, among the first publications to advocate and advertise squatting, briefly received a (small) subsidy from the City Council.[18] From the late 1960s, activists had occupied and renovated the dilapidated, often historic buildings, resulting in violent confrontations with the authorities on several occasions. The action of squatting became known as *kraken* in Dutch, street slang for breaking in, after the start of the *Woningburo de Kraker* [housing agency for squatters], which helped to organize the movement in Amsterdam starting in 1969.[19] The Nieuwmarkt neighborhood became an important center for the 1960s and 1970s movement, whose leading figures came to play such an important role in shaping hacking culture and independent media production later on in the 1980s.

One such leading figure was Tjebbe van Tijen, a visual artist and cultural coordinator in Amsterdam, who both embodied and documented the squatter movement within the culture of the city. A founding member of the *Woningburo de Kraker*, he later also became a curator at the Amsterdam University Library where he established a collection on modern social movements. In an article published in 1992, he recalled an event called "Free Cultural Spaces" at a soon-to-be razed property in the

[17] Tjebbe van Tijen. 1966. 1966: Provo's Witte Huizenplan/White House Plan of Provo movement. *Witplan*. http://witplan.wordpress.com/1966/04/25/provos-witte-huizenplanwhite-house-plan-of-provo-movement/. Accessed 31 Mar 2013.

[18] Eric Duivenvoorden. 2000. *Een voet tussen de deur. Geschiedenis van de kraakbeweging 1964–1999*. Amsterdam: De Arbeiderspers.

[19] Tjebbe van Tijen notes that the use of the word *kraken* stems from a decision taken in naming the Woningburo de Kraker, in a meeting he attended that took place in the building of Hans't Mannetje, publisher of the *Geïllustreerd Bethaniennieuws*. Van Tijen, email communication with the authors, April 1, 2013. See also Duivenvoorden, *Een voet,* ch. 1.

Nieuwmarkt neighborhood in 1984.[20] Responding to the changing climate, the event sought to document and take stock of the movements in Amsterdam and abroad. In particular, the event highlighted the squatter movement's role in creating both places to live and "free cultural spaces," defined by their ability to create new possibilities for cultural expression and to form new communities. A manifesto poster produced for May 16, 1984, highlighted the importance of Amsterdam as a center: "In Amsterdam there are now around a hundred, in the rest of the Netherlands, many dozens." Van Tijen listed a wide range of spaces in the city such as music venues, theaters, galleries, and Paradiso, an old church occupied peacefully in the late 1960s that was transformed into one of the country's most important and internationally renowned pop venues.[21] He also mentioned virtual spaces in the "ether" in the form of independent radio stations.

Van Tijen stressed it was not always a matter of creating something permanent, but, especially and explicitly building on the situationist movement, the creation of new "situations" that demonstrate (now we would say perform) new forms of behavior.[22] In his words,

> The short and intense existence of a cultural 'free space' gives others the idea to follow the example in one form or another. Such brief existence of cultural 'free spaces' nevertheless leaves behind the image of a radiant young idea without any sign of less decay toward the loathed ruling cultural values, although it has proved unviable in the long run.

At the same time, and this would prove vital for the movement, "the creation of free cultural spaces was not always a simple choice between 'clean' uncompromising, radical action or execrable co-operation of traitors with the ruling order."[23] Indeed in many cases, including Paradiso, agreements regarding the use of empty buildings had been reached very quickly.

Towards the mid-1980s, when conservative parties came to power in many countries, articulating an ideology of law and order, the squatter movement changed both in Amsterdam and in other cities such as Berlin. When the police began to remove squatters forcibly from their houses, the new law-and-order politics polarized the political climate. In a political compromise, large quantities of squats were legalized, while other parts of the movement were criminalized. The compromise legitimized the squatters' claim that it was immoral for speculating house owners to leave spaces empty despite the housing shortages, while it acknowledged owners' property rights. A new law passed in 1981 required house owners to give up buildings for use if these were empty. The effect of the law on existing squatters, and the

---

[20] Tjebbe van Tijen. 1992. Vrije culturele ruimtes. In *Gebroken wit: politiek van de kleine verhalen*, ed. Mascarpone, Irene Janze, et al. Amsterdam: Ravijn. [Available online as Tjebbe van Tijen. 2004. Vrije Culturele Ruimtes. http://imaginarymuseum.org/VKULT. Last accessed 16 July 2011].

[21] Its status as music venue in Europe is on a par with that of the Warfield Theater in San Francisco, which was founded slightly earlier.

[22] Guy Debord. 1977. *Society of the spectacle*. Detroit: Black & Red. On the Situationist movement, see Greil Marcus. 2001 [1989]. *Lipstick traces: A secret history of the twentieth century*. London: Faber & Faber.

[23] Van Tijen, *Vrije Culturele Ruimtes*.

movement, was negligible, although it did allow house owners to create a new business in letting properties cheaply, especially to students, to avoid squatting without creating any legal rights for these renters so they can be forced to leave at any time.[24] Although the character of the squatter movement changed, the culture evolving in the many squats with their endless empty spaces, once the breeding ground for a vibrant youth culture, did not disappear. Many prominent members of the squatter movement began to reorganize themselves around cultural and media centers in the ensuing years.[25]

Such new cultural centers became centers for experiment. In the 1960s, artists discovered new media technologies as their primary medium of expression. Because making digital music and visual images were prohibitively expensive and required special production processes, individual artists had to organize themselves collectively around "production houses." In the 1960s, young modern composers created the musical laboratory STEIM, which pioneered and inspired internationally—and continues to inspire—many young composers and musicians seeking to engage in technical innovations and new musical ideas.[26] A decade later, artists established the foundations for visual electronic arts like Montevideo and Time Based Arts. One artist, David Garcia, would later become a key player in designing networking events for the Next 5 Minutes conference.[27] Music venues like Paradiso acquired capital-intensive PA systems beyond the means of music bands and made them available to young performers. The media centers collectively bought tools and technologies that were unaffordable for individuals—thus participating in a long tradition of communal (media) consumption, such as workers' radio clubs in the 1920s.

Such venues facilitated a culture of independent media production, including an active print, radio, and poster scene in which many of Amsterdam's digital culture pioneers participated.[28] The squatter movement's weekly magazine *Bluf!* was edited by (among others) Caroline Nevejan, Geert Lovink, and Peter van der Pouw Kraan, who played key roles in setting up later digital network events. A number of local and "pirate" radio stations operated from within the squatters' scene in the city center.[29] Marleen Stikker, who would go on to become the first "mayor" of Digital

---

[24] A.M. Kloosterman, H.J. Rossel, and J.P. van Stempvoort. 2008. *Hoofdlijnen in het huurrecht: met vragen en antwoorden*. Deventer: Kluwer.

[25] The Foundation for the Advancement of Illegal Knowledge (Dutch: Bilwet) started by Geert Lovink also stressed the connection between the squatter movement and its intricate and often ambivalent position with regard to "the media." See Adilkno [The Foundation for the Advancement of Illegal Knowledge]. 1994. *Cracking the Movement: Squatting Beyond the Media*. Trans. Laura Martz. New York: Autonomedia. http://thing.desk.nl/bilwet/Cracking/general.html. Last accessed 27 Sept 2011. See especially chapter 8.

[26] http://www.steim.nl

[27] http://www.montevideo.nl. Last accessed 16 July 2011. Time Based Arts and Montevideo merged in the early 1990s.

[28] For a large poster collection of the Nieuwmarkt neighborhood, see the International Institute for Social History in Amsterdam's website: http://zoeken.iisg.nl/search/search?action=transform&col=marc_images&lang=nl&xsl=marc_images-detail.xsl&docid=11014181_MARC

[29] Geert Lovink. 1992. The theory of mixing: An inventory of free radio techniques in Amsterdam. *Mediamatic Magazine* 6(4). http://www.mediamatic.net/page/5750/en?lang=en. Accessed 21

City, participated in two such radio stations and established the theater magazine *Alligator*, using available desktop publishing software, as well as *Live Magazine* that used new media to experiment with novel forms of political debate.[30] She further organized the Wetware conference with Geert Lovink in 1991, designed to explore the role of the human as body in the age of "virtual reality."[31] The *Zomerfestijn* (summer festivals) which Stikker organized in 1990 and 1991 included artists who were exploring technological frontiers such as Test Department, Survival Research Laboratories, and *Einstürzende Neubauten*.

From the start, the independent media communities were cosmopolitan and international, connected with networks beyond Amsterdam including Eastern Europe, where a vibrant, independent underground culture was flourishing. In 1987, the Amsterdam squatters' bookshop Sjakoo launched *Europe Against the Current,* offering venues to show alternative, independent, and radical views to confront what they saw as "mainstream" Europe where uniformity ruled.[32] Inspired by the 1985 "Alternative Cultural Forum" in Budapest and media fairs in London and Frankfurt, the organizers accumulated over 4,000 addresses, mobilizing an international network of alternative bookshops, publishers, and collectors by combing through catalogues, reviews, folders, and specialized guides. They supplied the addresses for the event's invitations but also became a permanent resource for further contacts. The catalogue listed 1,000 addresses. The *Europe Against the Current* event in September 1989 attracted 350 groups from 21 countries. At the event, Samizdat authors and publishers from Eastern Europe met with so-called pirate printers and often left-wing radicals from the West. In a retrospective published in 1990, Tjebbe van Tijen noted that

> [t]he multiformity, the multiplicity of opinions sought by the organizers was achieved but not all the participants and visitors were happy with it. The culturally-oriented found the event too political, the politicals blamed its far too cultural character. The participants from Eastern Europe, mostly for the first time in the West, were often surprised to see the Western European radical left groups present. Their passionate stand was exactly what they sought to free themselves of or what they tried at least to flee.[33]

Budding computer communication began to play an increasingly important role in connecting many local, independent media with networks beyond Amsterdam. Through PeaceNet and GreenNet, which, for example, reported the April 26, 1986, Chernobyl Nuclear plant disaster two whole days before the news appeared in

May 2011; Geert Lovink. 1995. *'Listen or Die': A history of the punk hard core pirate station 'Radio Death', Amsterdam 1985–1987*. Bilwet. http://thing.desk.nl/bilwet/TXT/DOOD.ENG.txt. Last accessed 27 Sept 2011.

[30] Interview with Stikker, September 26, 2011.

[31] See Adilkno, Foundation for the Advancement of Illegal Knowledge, "Hardware, Software, Wetware," posted June 17, 1996, by Geert Lovink on nettime: http://www.nettime.org/Lists-Archives/nettime-l-9606/msg00026.html; Geert Lovink, Rik Delhaas, and Laura Martz (eds.). 1991. *Wetware*. Amsterdam: De Balie.

[32] Tjebbe van Tijen. 1990. Europa tegen de stroom. *De Gids* 153(6): 466–471. [English translation available online Going against the grain, Europe against the current, http://www.imaginarymuseum.org/ETS/ETSeng.html. Accessed 30 Jan 2014]

[33] Ibid.

regular newspapers, the squatters' magazine *Bluf!* effectively scooped major newspapers. It featured news reports that were unavailable such as the revolution in Nicaragua and the anti-apartheid struggle in South Africa. *Bluf!* editor Geert Lovink left the magazine in 1983 and spent more and more time in West Berlin, where he built a network of squatters and media theorists. Like in Amsterdam, the squatter movement in Berlin maintained strong ties with the established intellectual and left political scenes but was more politically passionate and intense.[34] Building on contacts made at the Amsterdam *Europe Against the Current* event, Lovink established connections with like-minded people in Eastern Europe from his Berlin base, particularly after the wall came down, when he was able to travel throughout Eastern Europe. His contacts enabled Amsterdam's cultural centers to invite Central and Eastern Europeans to their conferences and to establish long-term relationships with some.

The Amsterdam cultural and media centers also collaborated with centers being set up at the same time elsewhere in the Netherlands. In the southern city of Den Bosch, V2, the center of Unstable Media, explored electronic arts in a squat in 1981. In the northern city of Groningen, long dominated by socialist politics, the Mediamatic Foundation began in 1986, first with *Mediamatic* magazine, before transforming around 1990 into a creative multimedia lab, organizing underground shows and performances as well as doing commercial consultancy.[35] In 1986, activist Michael Polman started up the Antenna network in the Catholic capital Nijmegen, hotbed of the emerging liberation theology movement, which connected grassroots organizations from all over the world on a daily basis. Through regular meetings, the organizations exchanged vital information and collectively decided how to mobilize politics for issues they shared.[36] Despite operating in the periphery of Amsterdam's evolving networks, Antenna's worldwide connections had a significant impact on Dutch digital culture. It opened up its worldwide network at various conferences, thus providing the counter movement with a global reach. While these groups were independently involved in a number of networks worldwide, they did not collaborate until a new network event, the Galactic Hacker Party (GHP), brought them together in 1989 to focus on digital issues.

[34] Freia Anders. 2010. Wohnraum, Freiraum, Widerstand. Die Formierung der Autonomen in den Konflikten um Hausbesetzungen Anfang der achtziger Jahre. In *Das alternative Milieu. Antibürgerlicher Lebensstil und linke Politik in der Bundesrepublik Deutschland und Europa 1968–1983*, ed. Sven Reichard and Detlef Siegfried, 473–498. Göttingen: Wallstein Verlag. See also the newly started online project: http://de.wikipedia.org/wiki/Wikipedia:WikiProjekt_Autonome_und_Hausbesetzer-Bewegung#Medien

[35] V2 was founded by Alex Adriaansens and Joke Brouwer; Mediamatic was an initiative of Willem Velthoven and Jans Possel.

[36] Antenna, founded to support NGOs, local government, and educational institutions by introducing and facilitating ICT, became the ICT partner for around 500 organizations worldwide. Since 1993, Antenna has supported almost all development, emancipation, and environment organizations in the Netherlands. An archive of the Association for Progressive Communication Newsgroups is online at Occasio Digital Social History Archive: http://socialhistory.org/en/collections/occasio. See also the introduction to the archive at http://socialhistory.org/sites/default/files/docs/archiving-electronic_messages.pdf. Both last accessed 1 Apr 2013.

9.4 Network Events in a Rapidly Changing World: Computer Squatting

As the squatter movement increasingly channeled its energy into media and cultural centers in the late 1980s, a new form of independent media engagement came to the fore: computer hacking. Much hacking culture had arisen as a countercultural movement, not only in the United States, aimed at what was seen as an increasingly technocratic society symbolized by computers. By understanding rather than fearing the tools of computers, hackers could subvert the process by appropriating them for their own goals.[37] In Dutch, many words to describe hacking came from English usage; the words "hacking" and "phone phreaking" filled the pages of the Dutch hacker zine *Hack-Tic*. Alongside these, however, came a Dutch translation: *computerkraken,* best translated as "computer squatting." The term had a similarly energizing effect on the way the practice was considered by proponents and skeptics alike.

In the summer of 1988, after the German Chaos Computer Club surprised the world with a spectacular hacking act, Nevejan, then programmer of Amsterdam's music temple Paradiso, sought to demonstrate the great potential of the Internet on its stage. With the help of *Bluf!* colleague Pouw Kraan and computer science professor I.S. Herschberg of the Delft University of Technology, who collaborated with 20-year-old hacker Rop Gonggrijp, she contacted Chaos Computer Club in the German social-democratic city of Hamburg.[38] Founded in 1981 by Wau Holland and others in the offices of the leftist newspaper *Die Tageszeitung*, the Chaos Computer Club hacked Deutsche Bank in the summer of 1988, wiring a hundred thousand German Marks into their own account within one night. At the press conference the next morning, they publicly wired the money back, stating that their act showed Deutsche Bank could not be trusted.[39] The breathtaking stunt inspired Paradiso to organize the Chaos Info Show on November 13, 1988.[40] Steffen Wernery, Wau Holland, and Bernd Fix presented Chaos Computer Club's work and ideas on Paradiso's stage. Among the audience were Dutch journalists, Hobby Computer Club members, and individuals interested in the emerging phenomenon of digital technology and hacking. The drama was not lost on the audience as fundamental issues were played out on stage. While publicly maintaining a "Robin Hood" image, Chaos Computer Club asked fundamental questions about democracy, privacy, and security. Wernery had just been released after serving 2 months in a French prison when Dutch electronic multinational Philips had sued him for hacking their work.

---

[37] Veraart, *Vormgevers*, 62.

[38] Gonggrijp, an established and prominent hacker at that time, has remained a public figure in the Netherlands. He initiated successful protests against the use of non-privacy-protected voting computers in the Netherlands; more recently, he made headlines as the "coproducer" of the video *Collateral Murder* released by Wikileaks in April 2010. See his website http://rop.gonggri.jp/

[39] See Kai Denker. 2014. Heroes yet criminals of the German computer revolution. In *Hacking Europe. From computer cultures to demoscenes*, ed. Gerard Alberts and Ruth Oldenziel, 167–188. New York: Springer.

[40] Program and production notes Nevejan Archive, Folder "Chaos Info Show."

From the beginning, the political debate focused on how to engage young hackers with their responsibility as "tech-savvy" citizens, who could use the new technology either to create or to destroy. All Chaos Computer Club's hacks and publicity in the late 1980s sought to challenge social democracy and promote grassroots democracy. As Kai Denker shows in his contribution, during the same period, however, hacking was also increasingly criminalized in Germany and internationally.[41]

After the event at Paradiso, Nevejan, Gonggrijp, and Patrice Riemens drove to Hamburg to meet Chaos Computer Club members in their home city for the annual conference in December 1988.[42] On the way home, Gonggrijp articulated his initial ideas for establishing the computer journal *Hack-Tic*. Together, the three formed plans to host an event in Amsterdam devoted to hacking.[43] The subsequent event, *Galactic Hacker Party* or *International Conference on Alternative use of Technology Amsterdam* (ICATA 89), brought together for the first-time hackers from all over the world in a public event, linked both physically and via Internet connection. Through communication expert professor Cees Hamelink at the University of Amsterdam, who was instrumental in developing UNESCO's policy on balanced flow of information (as opposed to free flow), the organizers made contact with UNESCO and participants in Brazil and Nairobi.[44] While the press focused on hacking and hackers, the organizers successfully assembled a broad coalition of stakeholders, including all the earlier mentioned initiatives, labs, and collectives. Only after the event did Amsterdam Council begin to realize the city's special status as a center of innovation and so supported the organizers' bid to have the conference's final manifesto published under the auspices of UNESCO. In its letter to UNESCO, the City Council pointed out that "the organization of this conference is possible because the Netherlands, unlike many other countries, do not as yet have legislation that makes 'hacking' without criminal motives an offense."[45] Indeed, the law in the Netherlands was not changed until March 1, 1993, and Dutch hacking law still counts as more limited than elsewhere.[46]

The Center for Cooperative Technology, led by professor Gerard de Zeeuw, supported GHP from the beginning, helping out with the physical network as well as inviting their network of cyberneticians. That is why Gordon Pask, the communications specialist, came to lecture on entropy. At the Paradiso event, several Chaos Computer Club (CCC) members as well as members of the New York-based hacker's club 2,600 were present. Nodes in Brazil, New Zealand, and Kenya reported their perspective on digital networks, suggesting that hacking be seen "not as a middle-class northern issue, but more as universal. Maybe the real hackers are

---

[41] Denker, op.cit. fn 39.

[42] Ralf Rudolf. 1988. Erste Eindrücke zum CCC Congress '88. *Die Datenschleuder* 28–29(1988) at http://www.offiziere.ch/trust-us/ds/28/010_Erste_Eindruecke.html. Last accessed July 2011.

[43] Nevejan, Holiday.

[44] Patrice Riemens to Cees Hamelink, July 2, 1989, Nevejan Archive, Galactic Hacker Party, Folder "Organisatie."

[45] A.W. Jansen to Claude Ondobo, director of UNESCO International Programme for the Development of Communication, October 25, 1989, Nevejan Archive, Galactic Hacker Party.

[46] A recent ruling (March 9, 2011) held that hacking into a Wi-Fi network was not a crime under Dutch Law (Article 138a) that strictly covers breaching the security of a physical computer.

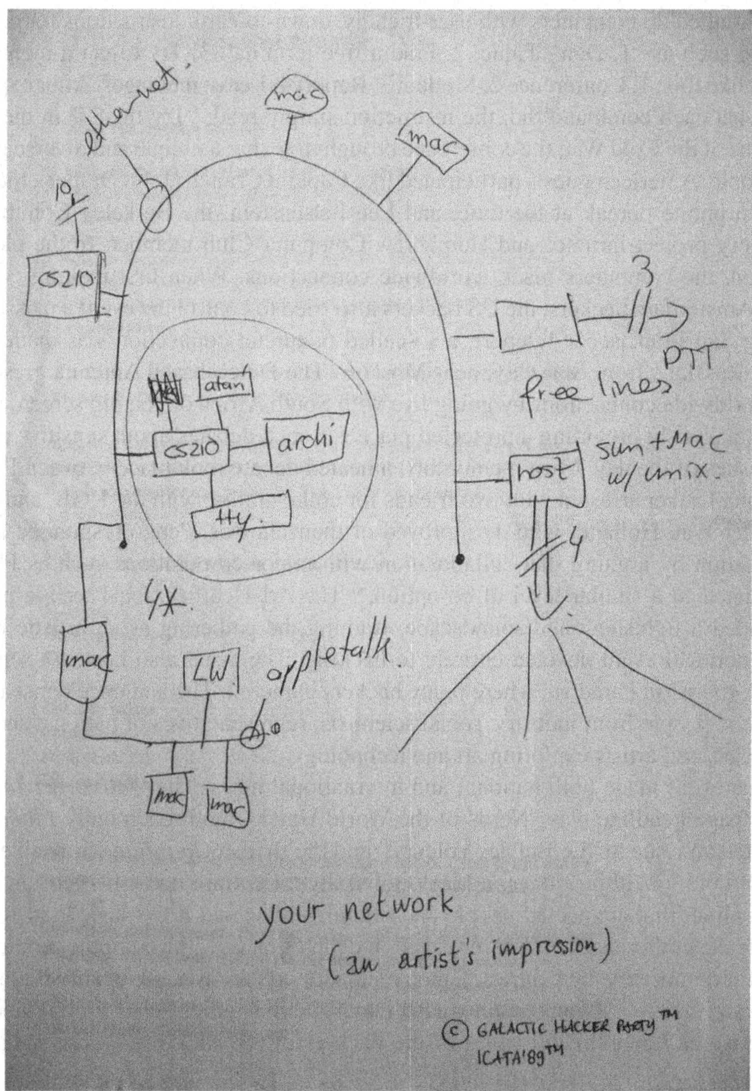

Fig. 9.1 "Your Network: An Artist's Impression." This sketch was created in preparation for the Galactic Hacker Party at the Paradiso in Amsterdam in 1989. A schematic diagram showing both the machines located at the event and the connections abroad, its simple, accessible form reflects the goals of the organizers: to demystify the Internet by turning it into a participatory technology. Source: International Institute for Social History in Amsterdam

found in the South instead of the North, because there they are no longer trying to see it as a universal possibility for communication."[47] For the event, the organizers created a computer infrastructure (Fig. 9.1) connecting Paradiso with other regions

[47] "Link with Nairobi," ICATA 1989 draft proceedings, Nevejan Archive, Galactic Hacker Party.

and installed 20 computers with user-friendly, down-to-earth instructions for conferencing such as "1. Don't Panic, 2. Find a free terminal, 3: Try to get a menu that looks like this: 1. Conference 2. Modem 3. Report 4. Leave message." After explaining what each command did, the instruction simply read: "Try this!"[48] In the final months of the Cold War, the conference brought together a unique and diverse group of people. American guests participated like Captain Crunch (John Draper), the best known phone phreak at the time, and Lee Felsenstein, the Berkeley Community Memory project initiator and Homebrew Computer Club member. In the plenary session, the computers made worldwide connections. When first making contact with Amsterdam hackers, the US hackers also tried to control the event's message.[49] Using San Francisco's Teleport, a so-called picturetel connection was made with three Russians from Star City, near Moscow. The Dutch-based Antenna presented its worldwide connections by going live with South Africa on the big screen, while simultaneously providing a protected place for open debates about sensitive political issues of the day. Most memorably, a heated debate took place between Pengo, a young hacker arrested with two friends for collaborating with the KGB, and CCC founder Wau Holland, who disapproved of their choices. Pengo responded to the accusation by arguing that collaboration with major corporations such as Philips amounted to a similar level of co-option.[50] The Art Heafties, local techno-punks, provided a lightshow and soundscape, framing the gathering as an artistic rather than political event devoted entirely to hacking. The event also hosted a separate "hack room" in Paradiso, where many hackers gathered. The audience consisted of hackers, people from industry, social scientists, representatives of national security agencies, and artists exploring art and technology.

The event made both national and international news. The *Wall Street Journal* front page headline was "Nerds of the World Unite," the French daily *Libération* devoted an issue to "Le Bal des Voleurs," and the British *Guardian* wrote an extensive article.[51] Within 3 days, a local/global digital culture had emerged, on stage and online, that connected people and organizations, and it has lasted since then. While the conference sessions engaged in debates on how the computer could be a tool for democracy, by contrast, Dutch media reports focused on legality issues and *computerkraken*.[52] Many mainstream Dutch media outlets also highlighted the secretive and anarchistic nature of the hackers in the hack room. The magazine

---

[48] "Conferencing," Unnumbered document, Nevejan Archive, Galactic Hacker Party.

[49] The US hacker Craig Larsen wrote to the organizers: "I feel this is an historical event of tremendous importance. This is the first time in history that the cyberheroes of the East Coast, West Coast and Europe will all be aligned together" and described the event as a "Euro-American techno summit," email Craig Larsen to Hack-Tic, July 20, 1989, Nevejan Archive, Galactic Hacker Party, Folder "Organisatie."

[50] ICATA 1989 draft proceedings, Nevejan Archive, Galactic Hacker Party.

[51] Mark M. Nelson. 1989. Nerds of the world unite – And defend their right to hack. *Wall Street Journal Europe*, August 7; Informatique: Le Bal des Voleurs. *Liberation* no. 2551 (August 5, 1989).

[52] Talks included "the computer as a tool for democracy" (Lee Felsenstein), "Citizen networks," and "Social Consequences of AI." Program, Galactic Hacker Party, Nevejan Archive, Galactic Hacker Party.

Hack-Tic rejoiced that the event "brought more hackers together than 10 laws could ban!"[53] Another independent magazine did express some reservations, though. "Those stealthily working the keys in the hack room did not answer questions or explain what they were up to. The visitor was shut out. "You know, I feel like an illiterate' said a curious but non-hacking visitor."[54] While the mainstream Dutch press either focused on hackers' activities as a problematic domain of the technically literate elite or sensationalized them, the alternative press forced the issue politically, demanding greater access to the tools that would unlock the new domain.

The second installment of the event occurred under radically changed circumstances. In Amsterdam, like in many other cities with a reputation for tolerance towards gays, the unfolding AIDS epidemic changed the cultural and political landscape fundamentally. With no cure in sight, a strong social prejudice reignited against gays. When blood transfusion and infected needles were identified as the cause and women also started to have AIDS, many young people were confronted with illness or friends dying. The sense of innocence and the joy of sexual liberation facilitated by contraception came to an end overnight. When in June of 1990 the US government prohibited people with AIDS or HIV from travelling to the states to attend the World AIDS conference in San Francisco, Paradiso decided to host a shadow conference and welcome people with HIV and AIDS. The Galactic Hacker Party organization, along with David Garcia, Heleen Riper, Matthew Lewis, and Rolf Pixley, decided to create the International Conference on Alternative Technology for AIDS (ICATA90) nicknamed the Seropositive Ball (Fig. 9.2). The Amsterdam branch of ACT UP, HIV Union, National Health Service, AIDS fund, parents of children with HIV organizations, the Buddy project, and others established a broad coalition with financial support from the Dutch Ministry of Health. The Center for Cooperative Technology at the University of Amsterdam, headed by Gerard de Zeeuw, assisted Pixley in creating a network that anticipated many of the features of the current World Wide Web graphical interface. The development notes stressed: "In the attempt to bypass the usual terminal interface and complicated command structures of E-news and E-mail, we are developing hypercard communication programs that will require only the address and message to be typed. All other actions will be executed by clicking on buttons with a mouse."[55] Using hypercard stacks distributed by mail and the university's digital infrastructure, the network succeeded in including the AIDS wards in Amsterdam's Academic Hospital, Cornell University in New York State, and San Francisco's General Hospital.[56] These stacks featured an online art gallery and "the AIDS stack" a large database of information developed by Michael Tidmus.[57] The

---

[53] *Hack-Tic* 5–6(1989): 3.

[54] ICATA '89 or Galactic Hacker Party?. *NN: Blad tegen de toekomst* 37 (August 10, 1989): 9.

[55] Notes from Rolf Pixley, May 12, 1990, Nevejan Archive, Seropositive Ball, Folder "0+0 Network."

[56] On hypercard, see "Hypercard gone but not forgotten," *Wired* (August 14, 2002) http://www.wired.com/gadgets/mac/commentary/cultofmac/2002/08/54365

[57] Artists who contributed to the first ever online art gallery were Max Kisman, Peter Mertens, and Jan Dietvorst among others. Unfortunately, due to digital erosion, the art gallery no longer exists.

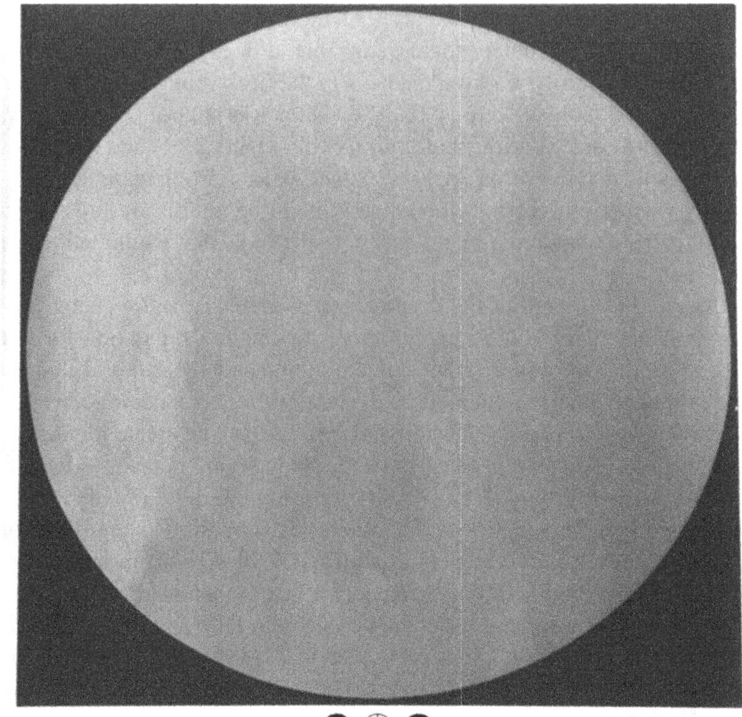

Fig. 9.2 Poster for the Seropositive Ball, ICATA 1990. Created by Jan Dietvorst, this simple, yet visually powerful design of a gold circle in an 'Yves Klein' blue square captures both the "zero" implied in the title, as well as the global nature of the crisis. The colors sought to evoke both the feelings of celebration and mourning represented by the event. Although hung mostly in the Netherlands, its text in English projected the underlining international community the poster was addressing within and beyond the city of Amsterdam

organization established public access points with Act Up in San Francisco, Simon Watson's Project Space in New York, several Amsterdam bookshops, and Paradiso. Some AIDS patients at home were connected as well. Computer company Apple

Samples of the AIDS stack can be found in Nevejan Archive, Seropositive Ball, Folder "0+0 Network."

had a policy of joining in the fight against AIDS at the time and provided dozens of computers both within Paradiso and other public spots, as well as in AIDS wards and for patients at home.[58] Under public pressure, even the US State Department felt a need to issue an official statement to explain the Reagan administration's AIDS policy at the opening of the conference by the Dutch Minister of Health with the HIV Union chairman. Over 150 artists contributed: musicians, theater performers, visual artists, filmmakers, and more. For those involved in the Seropositive Ball, the event was memorable. From a technology perspective, the Seropositive Ball network showed the significant impact of a good graphic interface for the uninitiated and for new network users. Network users needed no learning curve. One email from a small AIDS ward in the city shows how quickly caregivers and patients took to the interface:

> Currently we are looking after four patients. Unfortunately they are too ill to be able to participate in the Sero+net activities. The staff is too busy with their daily activities and therefore also unable to take part in the ongoing conversations, but they are very interested in the Ball. They admire the wonderful art gallery and value the information in the stack and the news. And they would like to hear from you in Paradiso about the events. Tonight the night shift will certainly have time to take note of your messages and will pass them on to patients and staff here.[59]

The newcomers used the new technologies with such intensity, driven by the desire to find treatments or to be in touch with people in the same situation. Often, tears were shed when the computers were collected again after the event. The idea of vital information as driver for technological innovation became the key lesson of the Amsterdam event.

Both events, at which hackers from all over the world met and engaged in debates with social activists, artists, politicians, administrators, large medical organizations, and security services, benefitted from the production sites and cultural centres that had emerged in the city since the 1960s. They also became the birthplace for foundations building a new media landscape. The events provided a platform for Dutch digital culture to present itself and helped identify key players who are still important today.

9.5 New Networks and Centers: 1993 as the Year of Change

The possibilities of the new digital age raised by the two ICATAs began to spin out and take root in strengthening Amsterdam as a network node locally and in forming new global networks. Internationally, the electronic border-crossings performed at the ICATA events became even more significant due to the dramatic political changes occurring in Europe. Cultural centers became important civil society sites

---

[58] The documentation folder for the event contains the booklet, "Where does Apple stand on AIDS," produced by Apple in Cupertino, April 1990. Caroline Nevejan to Helen Goossens, Apple Europe July 5, 1990, Nevejan Archive, Seropositive Ball, Folder "June 1990."

[59] Proceedings, Seropositive Ball, 1990, Nevejan Archive, Seropositive Ball.

in the process of democratization, most evident in Eastern Europe. After the Berlin Wall fell in 1989, the Soros Foundation deliberately funded society organizations such as media centers, conferences, and networks to facilitate democratic processes after the breakdown of the communist states, building on network connections already forged before the wall came down. Centers in this network such as the Fine Arts Documentation Center in Budapest—founded in 1985 already and one of the important centers in connection with Amsterdam—became major connection points.[60] The members of this network of independent media centers eventually formed the International Contemporary Art Network (iCAN) based in Amsterdam.

Building on these connections, Paradiso launched the *Next 5 Minutes* conference (January 8–10, 1993) to explore the role of independent media in these changing societies and global networks.[61] They felt the dichotomies between underground/dominant, right/left or independent/mainstream no longer matched the media landscape. To pinpoint the more flexible nature of new media configurations and identify cracks in the existing media landscapes, they chose the term "tactical television," drawing on the cultural theory of Michel de Certeau.[62] At first, they mostly ignored the Internet (although Hack-Tic did run a session at the conference) and focused on the new possibilities of independent television enabled by portable camcorders for spreading information and making connections outside formal communication channels.[63] The organizers were driven by the idea that such new affordable technologies could create an alternative media sphere to the rigid domination of the Reagan and Thatcher years. Through the Antenna network, media makers in the southern hemisphere from Brazil to Burma, from the Aboriginals' satellite in Australia to New York's Paper Tiger, were well represented. Lovink, with Soros Foundation funding, involved over 25 media makers from Eastern Europe, including those who had started the Romanian Revolution in Timisoara Television

[60] Soros Centers for Contemporary Arts, http://www.c3.hu/scca/index.html. Last accessed 6 Oct 2011.

[61] David Garcia (Time Based Arts), Geert Lovink (Bilwet), Geke van Dijk and Bas Raijmakers (Amsterdam Cultural Studies), Menno Grootveld (Robotnik TV), Raul Maroquin (Hoeksteen TV), and Caroline Nevejan (Paradiso) all sought new perspectives on the emerging media landscape, gathering best practices and new theory, which resulted in the publication of the Zapbook and the first Next Five Minutes (N5M) program. In the next installment, the second N5M, their media critique was directed mostly at the Internet. The nettime mailing list, moderated in several languages and including editors Patrice Riemens and Geert Lovink (Amsterdam), Pit Schulz (Berlin), and Ted Byfield (New York), was instrumental in this development. Since then, N5M has evolved into a larger network that organizes conferences and education around the globe. In 2013, Erik Kluytenberg, programmer at De Balie, is the catalyst in this network.

[62] Jeroen van Bergeijk, Geke van Dijk, Karel Koch, and Bas Raimakers (eds.). 1992. *N5M Zapbook: Working papers*. Amsterdam: Paradiso. http://www.tacticalmediafiles.net/TMF_documents/N5Mzapbook.pdf, esp. 25. Last accessed 6 Oct 2011; Michel de Certeau. 1984. *The practice of everyday life*. Berkeley: University of California Press.

[63] Karel Koch. 1992. Introduction: The camcorder revolution, in Bergeijk et al. eds., *N5M Zapbook*, 29. Program, "Next Five Minutes," January 8–10, 1993, Nevejan Archive, Folder "Press Now tot/met zomer 1995." The next installment of N5M expanded the idea to "tactical media" and brought the Internet into focus.

Studios.[64] The rich local television outlets in Amsterdam and other Dutch cities participated as well. In the wake of this and subsequent meetings, the nettime mailing lists forged an ongoing English-language discussion group for Internet critique.[65]

The war that broke out in Yugoslavia in 1991 threw the international situation into sharper relief. Young refugees from former Yugoslavia came to Amsterdam. Paradiso, De Balie, and Index on Censorship initiated Press Now and organized support for independent media in former Yugoslavia. Working through both diplomatic and underground channels, Amsterdam activists developed programs dealing with the war in collaboration with Belgrade's independent radio station B92, the beacon for many teenagers who had fled. The radio station cum music hall became an Internet center early on. B92 director Veran Matic and Dragan Pantic, director of their Internet group, regularly visited Amsterdam to participate in debates and share their experiences. Since the Balkan Wars fed on media propaganda, B92's counter information was vital as it created a network of independent radio stations, representing a youth culture determined to counteract the older generation's war propaganda. On July 1,1993, during the long siege of Sarajevo, B92 radio, Amsterdam Paradiso, and Belgrade B92's Internet group supported by the Dutch public broadcaster VPRO joined in the program "Music, War and Radio" for one night of broadcasting in the hope of accessing the network of independent radio stations using the Internet as well.[66] B92's organizers came to Amsterdam, while VPRO journalist Erwin Blom visited the radio studio in Belgrade. Well-known Dutch rock bands played the songs of Yugoslavian rock bands. Krist Novoselic, Nirvana's bass player, originally from Zagreb, gave a talk via telephone. Well-respected British journalist Misha Glenny for *The Guardian* and BBC, writer of *The Fall of Yugoslavia* (1992), addressed the crowd in a somber mood.[67] And when B92 was under siege and threatened with having all its broadcasts stopped, XS4ALL pioneered the new possibilities of Internet radio and granted the station a worldwide audience. Soon after, the BBC Internet department took over the connection, guaranteeing that B92 never stopped playing.

Besides these global connections, between 1990 and 1992, the Hack-Tic Network and its magazine were important catalysts in shaping public development of digital connections locally. The Dutch node in the international hacker communities' network, along with 2,600 in New York and Chaos Computer Club in Germany, created a steadily growing community. Even though boys with a specific sense of humor that excluded others dominated the network, *Hack-Tic* played a

---

[64] On the videos, see Tjebbe van Tijen. 1993. A context for collecting the new media. In *Next 5 Minutes Video Catalogue, catalogue of videotapes shown during the festival on tactical television held in Paradiso Amsterdam, 8–10 January 1993*, ed. Bas Raijmakers and Tjebbe van Tijen. Amsterdam: International Institute of Social History. Online at http://socialhistory.org/sites/default/files/docs/collecting-new-media.pdf. Accessed 1 Apr 2013.

[65] See http://www.nettime.org/

[66] Program, "Press, War and Radio," Nevejan Archive, Folder "Press Now tot/met zomer 1995."

[67] Ibid.

significant role in the ongoing political debates and practices. Its visual appearance and written tone reflected the subcultural Do-It-Yourself publishing aesthetics. As an indication of its importance, security services, policy makers, and large companies subscribed to *Hack-Tic* magazine. Equipped with a disclaimer ("information here is for educational purposes. Use of this information could be punishable/dangerous to the state/naughty") and a reassurance to readers that they could subscribe anonymously—the magazine was sent in a plain brown wrapper: "If you have a position in society, you just need to put money and your address in an envelope and send that to our PO Box. We know what to do."[68]

Hackers' ability to be "public" to the extent they were in the Netherlands changed almost literally overnight on March 1, 1993, when a new law on "computer criminality" went into effect that for the first time made it explicitly illegal to gain unauthorized access to a secured place on a computer.[69] In so doing, this act enshrined in Dutch legal code the cultural link between squatting and hacking that had been established in the years before. Section 138 of the code is on breaking and entering, called "huisvredebreuk" (literally "disturbing the peace of a home"); section 138a, which prohibits hacking, defines its crime as "computervredebreuk": disturbing the peace of a computer. In response to the new law, the Hack-Tic group shifted its focus beyond the hackers' community to explore more popular uses of the Internet.[70] As *Hack-Tic* told its readers: "It is important that the Internet community becomes a more balanced reflection of the 'normal' world. Right now people with money and power are over-represented."[71] In May 1993, the group started XS4ALL, a public access Unix system, open 24 h a day. Subscriptions were available to anyone for 75 Dutch guilders for 3 months to help cover the system's operating costs and lease of lines. Going public also carried a paradox, the activists realized. Creating broad access meant asking users *not* to hack via their system out of fear that the authorities would shut them down. The new owners cited the "free flow of information" upheld in the Galactic Hacker Party manifesto as the higher goal. "When you look at it, we become lackeys of the paranoid system administrators in the world. That would have been difficult to live with if we had not believed, that thanks to our combined presence on the Internet, we might also change the atmosphere on the net."[72] The declaration signaled the start of a new era seeking to create public engagement with the Internet. When XS4ALL began, it could hardly handle the number of new

---

[68] Colophon. *Hack-Tic* 1(1989): 2.

[69] Officially Wet van, December 23, 1992, Stb. 1993, 33. History and full text of the law in Kornelis I.J. Mollema, et al. 1993. *Computercriminaliteit: De wetgeving, de gevolgen voor bedrijven en de accountant.* Deventer: Kluwer. See also P. Kleve, R.V. Mulder, and C. van Noortwijk. 2010. ICT Criminaliteit. In *Criminaliteit en criminaliteitsbestrijding in Nederland*, ed. Erwin Roelof Muller, et al., 259–288. Deventer: Kluwer; Hanneke. 1993. Wet computercriminaliteit. *Hack-Tic* 20–21(1993): 4–11.

[70] See articles in *Hack-Tic* 20–21(1993); Reinder Rustema. 2001. *The rise and fall of DDS*. MA thesis, University of Amsterdam.

[71] *.hactic.nl. *Hack-Tic* 20–21(1993): 18.

[72] Ibid., 20. They did, however, offer one month's free access to anyone who could hack *their* system with instructions.

subscribers. Initially aiming for 500 subscribers in its first month, it got them within its first day.

A second generation of digital activists then took the lead. Marleen Stikker, a programmer at the center for political debate De Balie (adjacent to Paradiso), involved the center in the subsequent digital developments. De Balie was founded in 1982 by Felix Rottenberg, former chair of the young socialists and later of its parent organization the Dutch Labor Party PvdA, in order to engage young people politically and culturally in renewing the party with grassroots politics. By 1989 already, De Balie had organized a series of lectures and exhibitions on technological culture.[73] Stikker herself became particularly inspired by working with Press Now to explore the medium as a means of revitalizing public culture.[74] From De Balie, Stikker brought together a group of thinkers; developers and digital activists explore the possibilities to develop civic access to the Internet. The so-called city plan group was searching for a narrative that would facilitate "ordinary people" to engage in online civic initiatives. As a result, they invented the concept of the Digital City.[75] Later in the summer of 1993, Hack-Tic Network organized *Hacking at the End of the Universe* (HEU), a follow-up to the Galactic Hacker Party, at a campsite where 3,000 participants hooked up their computers in tents for the first time.[76] Besides collaborative hacking, debates centered on the information society, privacy, and security.

Right from the start, and thanks to their deep ties to the political establishment, Stikker and De Balie succeeded in mobilizing political and financial support as well as a commitment from Amsterdam City Council. Reineke van Meerten, then the Council's project manager for telecommunication and informatics policy, played a crucial role in steering the project through the Council. The city agreed to finance Digital City as a 10-week pilot project in the lead-up to the municipal elections. The Ministry of Economic Affairs also contributed. The start-up capital for Digital City totaled 300,000 guilders. In the fall of 1993, Digital City became a foundation. Together with XS4ALL (and Mediamatic), they moved into an old building at Prins Hendrikkade, sharing lines, modem and data centers, systems maintenance, and the helpdesk. NLnet sponsored the new initiatives.[77]

Digital City was an instant success. Within months it had over 10,000 inhabitants, receiving European and worldwide attention. The first interface to Digital City was a classic black screen with white letters.[78] Its success increased even more when the organizers launched Digital City's first graphical interface to the net. With the help of designers Michael van Eeden, Marjolein Ruig, Mieke Gerritsen, and Rob

---

[73] The organizers were Michiel Schwarz and Rein Jansma.

[74] Authors' interview with Marleen Stikker, September 26, 2011.

[75] Members of the City Plan Group included Geert Lovink, Menno Grootveld, Geke van Dijk, Bas Raijmakers, Joost Flint, Felipe Rodrigues, Paul Jongsma, Walter van der Cruijse, and Bert Mulder.

[76] Hacking at the End of the Universe. *Hack-Tic* 22–23(1993): 3.

[77] Interview with Stikker.

[78] Digital City 1.0 was designed by Marleen Stikker and Felipe Rodriguez. Digital City 3.0 was designed by Michael van Eeden, Marjolein Ruyg, Rob van der Haar, and Marleen Stikker.

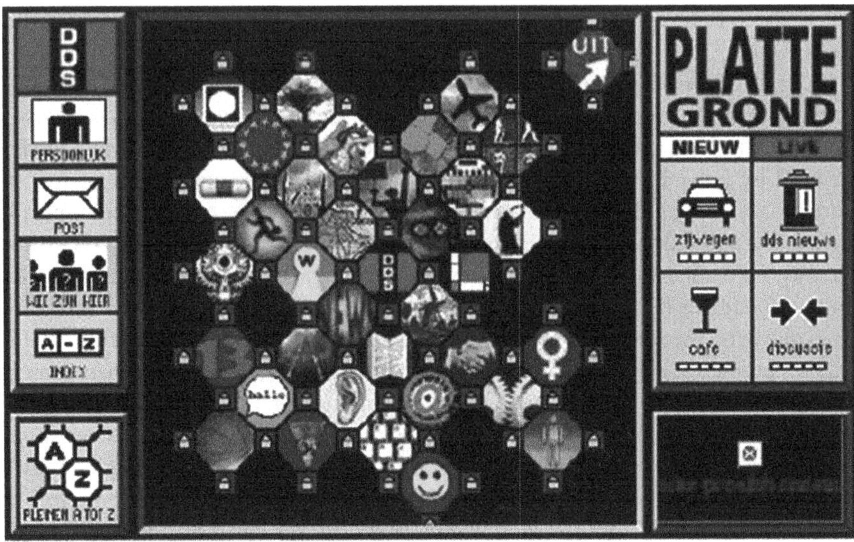

Fig. 9.3 Envisioning the Internet: It was 1994: the emerging Internet was still clunky, still steeped in the culture of the military and engineering, from which it came. Enter the Dutch "Digital City" project, an alliance of activists, squatters, and members of local government. These pioneering users broke with engineering-based interfaces of letters and code. Building on this ground breaking start, the design continued to develop rapidly, resulting in this third, updated interface introduced in 1995. This image—and Digital City's approach—imagines the Internet as a city unto itself. Each octagon on the screen represents different activist groups in the city, from Gay Square to news-junkie politicos, side-by-side in the city everyday institutions and places, such as city hall and the city library. Source: published online at re: DDS http://re-dds.nl/vondsten/FolderDDS3-telnr.pdf under creative commons licence CC BY-NC-SA 3.0 NL

van der Haar, Digital City boasted one of the most advanced appearances of an Internet City worldwide (Fig. 9.3). By inventing "interaction design" in the process, software developers and graphic designers were jointly engaging in a method to understand and create interaction. All their efforts were directed at facilitating the thousands of digital citizens who demanded services no one had thought of before. Not only interaction design but also participatory design and community management had to be invented on the fly. It was a constant conversation between developers, designers, and citizens exploring suggestions immediately and generating an exponential growth of ideas and manifestations of online life. Hackers, artists, and activists were crucial in the evolving dynamic.[79]

Citizens of Digital City were invited to create their own profile so others could see who was online. One could become a visitor or an inhabitant of Digital City,

[79] Interview with Stikker. See also Lovink, Geert Opkomst, Ondergang en Herrijzenis van de Digitale Stad. Interview met Marleen Stikker. Online at http://amsterdam.nettime.org/Lists-Archives/nettime-nl-0103/msg00038.html. Accessed 29 Mar 2013.

which offered various interaction possibilities. Squares were thematically structured and neighborhoods acquired character. Organizations including businesses, NGOs, and, for example, the library and some newspapers could experiment with how to profile themselves and invent services they could offer. Amsterdam City Council collaborated by offering their public and management information systems to be included in Amsterdam Digital City. The overall city plan provided a map which was redesigned several times, on which users could just click and go. Users built houses, cafés, gardens, shops, and even the first online cemetery called "Momento Mori."[80] In what was called The Metro, a text-based MOO (Multi-User Domain, Object Oriented), hundreds of users built this creative universe.[81] Beurs TV, a local broadcaster and organizer of the online elections in Digital City, managed for the first time to incorporate chat sessions on live television.[82]

Amsterdam Digital City provided a platform in a user-friendly, visually attractive, and Dutch-based environment to explore the potential of online communication. The graphical interfaces and interaction software that were developed triggered the imagination of many users. Besides online interaction, Digital City organized citizen meetings to discuss the implications and effects of Digital City and the new netiquette. It also incorporated a wide range of public events including parties, debates, and artistic experiments, to unlock the potential of the connective platform. Digital City was a great experiment of fundamental research into the future of the public domain. Being locked into the real city of Amsterdam, it took the human scale as its conceptual ground, integrating online life with real events in the city of Amsterdam. Whereas The WELL in the United States was a virtual community established online which then began to meet in person, DDS originated in communities that already existed outside the Internet and who experienced the online interaction as a welcome contribution.[83]

For the emerging scene of digital artisans, Digital City served as a playground full of inspiration, while the Dutch government founded the Netherlands Design Institute, whose director John Thackara launched the Doors of Perception conference.[84] Inspired by the TED conference and Siggraph, the leaders of the new designer generation gathered in Europe, including prominent IT companies, consultancies, scholars, and designers to present the latest software inventions. The Dutch digital scene went on display, while the conference offered a platform to explore fundamental differences between the United States and Europe.

---

[80] Created by Marjolein Ruyg.

[81] Created by Michael van Eeden.

[82] Beurs TV was initiated and directed by Nina Meilof.

[83] This is in many ways comparable to the internet use in Trinidad highlighted by Slater, Modernity under construction.

[84] Thackara launched the Doors of Perception Conference together with Willem Velthoven of Mediamatic. This conference was moved to India after the Netherlands Design Institute closed. See www.doorsofperception.com

With the introduction of graphical interface, the Internet had suddenly become commercial. It changed the political dynamics. Much discussion surrounding Digital City and what rapidly became known as the Amsterdam Public Digital Culture has been a tale of one moment of euphoria followed by decline before the project was pulled into the commercial domain.[85] Such narratives questioned the sustainability of open infrastructures while examining the willingness and ability of Digital City's organizers and administrators to maintain such structures in light of corporate competition and sought to explain Digital City's transformation in the second half of the 1990s. Confronted with an increasingly commercial environment, the organizers felt Digital City either had to reinvent itself or close shop. By the late 1990s, the government no longer supported the creative industries. The Netherlands Design Institute had to close its doors, causing the Netherlands to lose its position as front-runner in the digital revolution and test country for many industries involved. When Digital City decided to stop the site in 1999, many users felt the organization had no right to do so; it was their city. The organizers felt they had no choice but to close the gates.[86]

Since 1993 and through 1994, Internet use had spread at a dazzling speed, and its transformation into a commercial realm was becoming increasingly apparent. Some of the original initiators saw the space for public research in which networked events and public initiatives like Digital City offered scope for participatory development in the public domain, shrinking fast. To protect this space where such public research could be funded and designed, Paradiso and De Balie joined forces. Independent consultant Bert Mulder wrote an analysis of the possibilities of starting an independent media lab. In December of 1994, Stikker (De Balie) and Nevejan (Paradiso) founded the Society for Old and New Media, an independent media lab for culture and the public domain.[87] De Waag, a former city gate built in the fifteenth century where Rembrandt painted his anatomy lesson in its Theatrum Anatomicum, and located directly on the Nieuwmarkt, had been empty for over a decade. The city was seeking bids for its redevelopment, and the Society for Old and New Media entered the competition. It was funded and supported by two partners from culture (De Balie, Paradiso), two from education (Rietveld Academy's Sandberg Institute, the Utrecht School of Fine Arts), and two from business (the cooperative Rabobank, media company Weekbladpers), putting up a bid to create an institution to support public research into old and new media. The city awarded the contract to the new foundation, rejecting several proposals from commercial developers.

Although modeled on MIT's Medialab in Boston, the Amsterdam initiative did not share its US counterpart's focus on commercial competitiveness. In the oldest medieval building in town, the savviest technologies were gathered with an agenda defined by a civic perspective. Because they were pushing technology as well as finding new creative uses, their agendas were distinctly different. Whereas MIT

---

[85] This is definitely the narrative in Castells, *Internet*, 146–155; see also Rustema, *Rise and fall*; Flint, *DDS*.

[86] Interview with Stikker.

[87] http://www.waag.org

Medialab made an application for individual children in a smart room full of sensors, the Waag built a visual MOO for inner-city elementary schools, allowing children to learn to both reading and writing plus art history at the same time. Debates between these different approaches were heated. Since then, Waag Society has been a place of innovation, joining the ranks of established media labs (and several MIT Medialab students came as apprentices to the Waag). In the second half of the 1990s, Waag Society played a significant role in creating a European network of independent media labs and became a founding partner of Sarai, a New Delhi-based media lab.

Other media labs also joined the established ranks of digital arts and culture, while new labs emerged as well: Submarine, Worm, Fabchannel, and more. As of 1996, the media labs started to establish what is called the Virtual Platform, to better organize their lobbying activities and benefit from each other's experiences. They have taken joint political action while developing their own individual work and identity. Mediamatic continues to create award-winning exhibitions and performances that intervene in key cultural debates and has also developed the widely used Anymeta community management system. V2 is an established digital art platform and lab as well. STEIM invites many young artists to come and play and collaborates closely with mostly international conservatories. Since 2001, the Dutch government has supported digital culture, acknowledging e-culture as a discipline in its own right. In 2012, the government decided to abolish these funds once again, arguing that creative industries do not need public support.[88]

9.6 Conclusion

As we have shown here, the digital public culture of Amsterdam that Castells highlighted can best be understood as an outgrowth of the public media culture pioneered in a range of independent media centers. Their commitment to broad and popular access to media and active, creative networking shaped the digital culture that emerged in the 1990s. Digital City is indeed itself best viewed as such a media center, which focused all its experiments on the new virtual environment in an attempt to revitalize the city's culture. These media centers came into existence within larger cultural movements in which youth culture, intellectual underground, and political activism played an important role, in turn shaping their particular approach to the emerging digital media. Media centers functioned locally and translocally, making bridges between Eastern and Western Europe and beyond.

Because media centers were part of larger social movements, it is not surprising to see that crucial roles in the development of Europe's digital culture included nontechnical experts. Paradiso's network events and Amsterdam Digital City set an agenda in which technology's impact on society was at the forefront in a

[88] The current political debates can be followed at the Netherlands Council for Culture and the Arts: http://www.cultuur.nl/

collaborative effort by technical and nontechnical people alike. These actors' emphasis on the questions "What is this stuff for?" and "How will it enhance our lives?" had a deep impact on how the digital culture emerged in those first years. The digital culture that emerged in the United States, where a community like The WELL was built on the Whole Earth Catalogue, has also been defined by such non-industrial and mostly cultural developments.[89] It has sharpened and deepened the imagination of the first adaptors. Or, for example, Apple's Educational Object Index in the mid-1990s, building on a large movement of learning innovation, has influenced ideas about online learning that have only now become commercially available.

Janet Abbate has stressed that the title of her study *Inventing the Internet* points to a technology that has been repeatedly *reinvented* by the actors and shaped the Internet's path.[90] We have followed a similar line of argument here, but expanding our focus beyond the developments within the military (e.g., ARPAnet), scientific (e.g., CERN), and commercial communities that are the standard reference points of most Internet histories. Instead, we highlight the local mediators who adapted the Internet along different lines, pushing for universal free access, political engagement with the city and the world, and for a civil society with broad participation including state and countercultural actors. As one contemporary observer remarked, Digital City was the result of a "golden formula: gather professional activity-organizers around a table with hackers who understand all about network technology."[91] Such a "golden formula" emerged from a social and technological networking style that characterized the city. Alternative networks negotiated and cooperated with public institutions and industry in a political arena, where state, market, and civil society worked in close harmony to manage conflict and coordinate change. Radical behavior, as long as it conforms to certain social rules, will be engaged with rather than criminalized or excluded. Social-democratic city councils fostered such politics of consensus, turning Amsterdam into a relatively safe playground to explore new media and new forms of community. Digital City, in short, represented a broad social coalition and unique civic participation.

Fixing historical focus on the relationship between digital development and specific urban cultures in Amsterdam has highlighted three aspects of the story. Firstly, the historical focus shows the importance of a local youth and alternative culture in Amsterdam. The digital culture emerging in the early 1990s was rooted in the independent printing and broadcasting cultures that blossomed in 1980s Amsterdam. These were all connected with local activist communities involved in European and global networks, such as squatter movements, antinuclear movements, and other

---

[89] See WELL's website at www.well.com; Katie Hafner. 1997. The epic saga of the well. *Wired Magazine* 5(5, May). http://www.wired.com/wired/archive/5.05/ff_well_pr.html. Accessed 27 Sept 2014.

[90] Abbate, *Inventing*, 6.

[91] Marianne van den Boomen. 1995. "Digitale Steden en virtuele Gemeenschappen," excerpt from Marianne van den Boomen. In *Internet-ABC voor vrouwen*. Amsterdam: Institut voor Politiek en Publiek. http://www.xs4all.nl~boom/hs8.html. Accessed 15 June 2011.

social justice movements. Secondly, we highlight how actors whose core expertise lay not in the traditional sense of technological realms but with strong visions for the future of digital technologies, which played an important role in shaping the Internet's material, institutional, and cultural infrastructure in the Netherlands and Europe. While noting the roles of major institutions and actors connected to them, as well as that of technological amateurs—the ever-present boys with toys—this story also shows how community, governmental, and industry actors played a vital part in creating a media infrastructure.[92] Thirdly, we point to the important role of public events in constructing and designing communication infrastructures. Networked events are moments whereby design—as described here—or by accident, a communication structure is created, whereby actors are made meaningfully aware of their connections.[93] At such moments of linking, both human actors and technologies *perform,* confirming and/or transforming the meaning of the connections for those who witness the event. At events such as the Galactic Hacker Party and the Seropositive Ball, and the hacker camping events (which continue to this day), computer networks were placed literally center stage to allow participants to experience the potential of the new technologies for addressing issues (social, political, and personal) they were already involved in.[94] The shared, witnessed, and collaborative first-time experience of new ways of communicating or creating and accessing vital information had a major impact on the participants' sense of their own capacity to intervene. This is very different to the hacker culture of garages and back rooms stressed in many histories of computer innovation, in that it focuses on a shared, public experience. Likewise, the history of The WELL is defined by its local roots in the San Francisco Bay area and is known through its monthly parties. Amsterdam Digital City hosted very dynamic meetings with its citizens. People sharing first-time digital network experiences resulted not only in an exponential growth of their imagination as well as a sense of realism of the new opportunities.

---

[92] For the Dutch case, see Veraart, *Vormgevers,* 83. For a longer-term communication perspective, especially the key role of radio amateurs in both constructing and subverting the development of state infrastructures, see Susan J. Douglas. 2004 [1999]. *Listening in: Radio and the American imagination*. Minneapolis: University of Minnesota Press; Onno de Wit. 1998. *Telefonie in Nederland, 1877–1940. Opkomst en ontwikkeling van eengrootschalig system.* Amsterdam: Otto Cramwinckel, Adrian Johns. 2010. *Death of a pirate: British radio and the making of the information age*. New York: W. W. Norton & Company.

[93] See Nevejan, *Presence*, 102–104, 128; Alexander Badenoch and Andreas Fickers. 2010. Introduction: Europe materializing? Toward a transnational history of infrastructures. In *Materializing Europe: Transnational infrastructures and the Project of Europe*, ed. Alexander Badenoch and Andreas Fickers, 1–26. Basingstoke: Palgrave; Andreas Fickers, and Susan Lommers. 2010. Eventing Europe: Broadcasting and the mediated performances of Europe, respectively. In *Materializing Europe: Transnational infrastructures and the Project of Europe*, ed. Alexander Badenoch and Andreas Fickers, 225–251. Basingstoke: Palgrave.

[94] Hacker camps now occur every 4 years in the Netherlands and have included "Hacking in Progress" (1997), "Hackers at Large" (2001), "What the Hack"(2005), "Hacking at Random" (2009), and "Observe, Hack, Make" (2013).

Bibliography

Abbate, Janet. 1999. *Inventing the Internet*. Cambridge, MA: MIT Press.

Abbate, Janet. 2010. Privatizing the Internet: Competing visions and chaotic events, 1987–1995. *IEEE Annals of the History of Computing* 31(1): 10–22.

Adilkno [The Foundation for the Advancement of Illegal Knowledge]. 1994. *Cracking the Movement: Squatting Beyond the Media*. Trans. Laura Martz. New York: Autonomedia. http://thing.desk.nl/bilwet/Cracking/general.html. Last accessed 27 Sept 2011.

Anders, Freia. 2010. Wohnraum, Freiraum, Widerstand. Die Formierung der Autonomen in den Konflikten um Hausbesetzungen Anfang der achtziger Jahre. In *Das alternative Milieu. Antibürgerlicher Lebensstil und linke Politik in der Bundesrepublik Deutschland und Europa 1968–1983*, ed. Sven Reichard and Detlef Siegfried, 473–498. Göttingen: Wallstein Verlag.

Badenoch, Alexander, and Andreas Fickers. 2010. Introduction: Europe materializing? Toward a transnational history of infrastructures. In *Materializing Europe: Transnational infrastructures and the Project of Europe*, ed. Alexander Badenoch and Andreas Fickers, 1–26. Basingstoke: Palgrave.

Berners-Lee, Tim. 2000. *Weaving the Web: The original design and ultimate destiny of the World Wide Web*. New York: HarperBusiness.

Castells, Manuel. 2001. *The Internet galaxy: Reflections on the Internet, business, and society*, 146. Oxford: Oxford University Press.

Ceruzzi, Paul E. 2003 [1998]. *A history of modern computing*. Cambridge, MA/London: MIT Press.

de Certeau, Michel. 1984. *The practice of everyday life*. Berkeley: University of California Press.

de Wit, Onno. 1998. *Telefonie in Nederland, 1877–1940. Opkomst en ontwikkeling van eengrootschalig system*. Amsterdam: Otto Cramwinckel.

Debord, Guy. 1977. *Society of the spectacle*. Detroit: Black & Red.

Denker, Kai. 2014. Heroes yet criminals of the German computer revolution. In *Hacking Europe. From computer cultures to demoscenes*, ed. Gerard Alberts and Ruth Oldenziel, 167–188. New York: Springer.

Douglas, Susan J. 2004 [1999]. *Listening in: Radio and the American imagination*. Minneapolis: University of Minnesota Press.

Duivenvoorden, Eric. 2000. *Een voet tussen de deur. Geschiedenis van de kraakbeweging 1964–1999*. Amsterdam: De Arbeiderspers.

Fickers, Andreas, and Susan Lommers. 2010. Eventing Europe: Broadcasting and the mediated performances of Europe. In *Materializing Europe: Transnational infrastructures and the Project of Europe*, ed. Alexander Badenoch and Andreas Fickers, 225–251. Basingstoke: Palgrave.

Flint, Joost. 2004. *DDS – 10 jaar anders*. http://www.dds.nl/downloads/achtergrondartikel.pdf. Accessed 16 July 2011.

Hafner, Katie. 1997. The epic saga of the well. *Wired Magazine* 5(5, May). http://www.wired.com/wired/archive/5.05/ff_well_pr.html. Accessed 27 Sept 2014.

Hanneke. 1993. Wet computercriminaliteit. *Hack-Tic* 20–21(1993): 4–11.

Jankowski, Nick. 1988. *Community television in Amsterdam access to participation in and use of the "Lokale Omroep Bijlmermeer"*. Amsterdam: Amsterdam University Press.

Johns, Adrian. 2010. *Death of a pirate: British radio and the making of the information age*. New York: W. W. Norton & Company.

Kleve, P., R.V. Mulder, and C. van Noortwijk. 2010. ICT Criminaliteit. In *Criminaliteit en criminaliteitsbestrijding in Nederland*, ed. Erwin Roelof Muller et al., 259–288. Deventer: Kluwer.

Kloosterman, A.M., H.J. Rossel, and J.P. van Stempvoort. 2008. *Hoofdlijnen in het huurrecht: met vragen en antwoorden*. Deventer: Kluwer.

Koch, Karel. 1992. Introduction: The camcorder revolution. In *N5M Zapbook: Working papers*, ed. Jeroen van Bergeijk, Geke van Dijk, Karel Koch, and Bas Raimakers, 29. Amsterdam: Paradiso.

Levy, Stephen. 1984. *Hackers: Heroes of the computer revolution*. Garden City, NY: Anchor Press/Doubleday.

Lovink, Geert. 1992. The theory of mixing: An inventory of free radio techniques in Amsterdam. *Mediamatic Magazine* 6(4). http://www.mediamatic.net/page/5750/en?lang=en. Accessed 21 May 2011.

Lovink, Geert. 1995. *'Listen or Die': A history of the punk hard core pirate station 'Radio Death', Amsterdam 1985–1987*. Bilwet. http://thing.desk.nl/bilwet/TXT/DOOD.ENG.txt. Last accessed 27 Sept 2011.

Lovink, Geert, Rik Delhaas, and Laura Martz (eds.). 1991. *Wetware*. Amsterdam: De Balie.

Marcus, Greil. 2001 [1989]. *Lipstick traces: A secret history of the twentieth century*. London: Faber & Faber.

Mollema, Kornelis I.J., et al. 1993. *Computercriminaliteit: De wetgeving, de gevolgen voor bedrijven en de accountant*. Deventer: Kluwer.

Nelson, Mark M. 1989. Nerds of the world unite – And defend their right to hack. *Wall Street Journal Europe*, August 7.

Nevejan, Caroline. 2007. *Presence and the design of trust*. PhD Thesis, University of Amsterdam.

Rudolf, Ralf. 1988. Erste Eindrücke zum CCC Congress '88. *Die Datenschleuder* 28–29(1988) at http://www.offiziere.ch/trust-us/ds/28/010_Erste_Eindruecke.html. Last accessed July 2011.

Rustema, Reinder. 2001. *The rise and fall of DDS*. MA thesis, University of Amsterdam.

Segaller, Stephen. 1998. *Nerds 2.0.1: A brief history of the Internet*. New York: TV Books.

Slater, Don. 2003. Modernity under construction: Building the Internet in Trinidad. In *Modernity and technology*, ed. Philip Brey, Thomas J. Misa, and Andrew Feenberg, 139–160. Cambridge, MA: MIT Press.

Stappers, James, Frank Olderaan, and Pieter de Wit. 1991. The Netherlands: Emergence of a new medium. In *The people's voice: Local radio and television in Europe*, ed. Nick Jankowski, Ole Prehn, and James Stappers, 90–103. London: John Libbey.

van Bergeijk, Jeroen, Geke van Dijk, Karel Koch, and Bas Raimakers (eds.). 1992. *N5M Zapbook: Working papers*. Amsterdam: Paradiso. http://www.tacticalmediafiles.net/TMF_documents/N5Mzapbook.pdf, esp. 25. Last accessed 6 Oct 2011.

van den Boomen, Marianne. 1995. "Digitale Steden en virtuele Gemeenschappen," excerpt from Marianne van den Boomen. In *Internet-ABC voor vrouwen*. Amsterdam: Institut voor Politiek en Publiek. http://www.xs4all.nl~boom/hs8.html. Accessed 15 June 2011.

van Tijen, Tjebbe. 1966. 1966: Provo's Witte Huizenplan/White House Plan of Provo movement. *Witplan*. http://witplan.wordpress.com/1966/04/25/provos-witte-huizenplanwhite-house-plan-ofprovo-movement/. Accessed 31 Mar 2013.

van Tijen, Tjebbe. 1990. Europa tegen de stroom. *De Gids* 153(6): 466–471 [English translation available online Going against the grain, Europe against the current. http://www.imaginarymuseum.org/ETS/ETSeng.html. Accessed 30 Jan 2014]

van Tijen, Tjebbe. 1993. A context for collecting the new media. In *Next 5 Minutes Video Catalogue, catalogue of videotapes shown during the festival on tactical television held in Paradiso Amsterdam, 8–10 January 1993*, ed. Bas Raijmakers and Tjebbe van Tijen. Amsterdam: International Institute of Social History. Online at http://socialhistory.org/sites/default/files/docs/collecting-new-media.pdf. Accessed 1 Apr 2013.

van Tijen, Tjebbe. 1992. Vrije culturele ruimtes. In *Gebroken wit: politiek van de kleine verhalen*, ed. Mascarpone, Irene Janze, et al. Amsterdam: Ravijn. [Available online as Tjebbe van Tijen. 2004. Vrije Culturele Ruimtes. http://imaginarymuseum.org/VKULT. Last accessed 16 July 2011]

Veraart, Frank. 2008c. *Vormgevers van Persoonlijk Computergebruik: De ontwikkeling van computers voor kleingebruikers in Nederland 1970–1990*. PhD thesis, TU Eindhoven.

Vlap, Annelies. 2011. Internet van en voor Nederland. Het verhaal van 25 jaar .nl, in *25 jaar .nl*. In Bex*communicatie. *Anniversary Publication SIDN*, 30–40. Arnhem: Stichting Internet Domeinregistratie Nederland.

Chapter 10
Users in the Dark: The Development of a User-Controlled Technology in the Czech Wireless Network Community

Johan Söderberg

10.1 Introduction

About 10 years ago, if you happened to be standing on a rooftop in a Czech town looking out into the night sky, your attention might well have been drawn to some red lights glowing on the horizon. Perhaps an association to cyberpunk would have crossed your mind. Such aesthetic sensibilities were indeed cultivated by the members of the wireless network community who built the light-transmitting devices. Where the onlooker saw red light beams, there were in fact streams of data crossing back and forth over the rooftops. Many of the wireless network activists were students living in rented flats in large tower blocks. Some of them had elderly neighbors who did not share their appreciation for cyberpunk aesthetic. Furthermore, those neighbors tended to be the movers and shakers of local housing committees. They had the authority, in other words, to tell the young residents to take down the devices from the buildings. This happened frequently enough to motivate the wireless network community to start looking for a technical solution to the dispute. They came up with a modified version of the device where the data transmission took place in the infrared as opposed to the red region of the electromagnetic spectrum. The technical performance with regard to range, accuracy, and interference from rain and fog was roughly the same for both kinds of light. The problem of interference from neighbors, however, was much reduced with infrared light. The stream of data could now flow, cunningly, behind the backs of unwitting neighbors.

The light-transmitting device was called "Ronja," an abbreviation for Reasonable Optical Near Joint Access. Invented in 2001 by Karel Kulhavy, the technology was widely used in the Czech Republic for about 5 years. Ronja offered the cheapest,

J. Söderberg (✉)
Göteborgs Universitet, Göteborg, Sweden

Laboratoire Techniques, Territoires et Sociétés/Institut Francilien Innovation et Société, Université Paris-Est, Paris, France
e-mail: johan.soderberg@sts.gu.se

G. Alberts and R. Oldenziel (eds.), *Hacking Europe. From Computer Cultures to Demoscenes*, History of Computing, DOI 10.1007/978-1-4471-5493-8_10,

fastest, and most reliable method to connect computers at the time. The project was guided by the idea that anyone without previous knowledge in electronics should be able to build a Ronja device. To make that vision come true, the mechanics and electronics were designed from generally available, off-the-shelf components. Improvements to the technology were discussed in a community of developers and users, and designs and schematics were published under a free software license. These principles were thematized under the label "user-controlled technology." Interest in the Ronja project fizzled out at about the same time as the phenomena of "open-source hardware," and hackerspaces begun to proliferate elsewhere in the world, often with the pretext of democratizing manufacturing. Hence, the experimentation with a user-controlled technology in the Czech wireless network community can be seen as a forerunner to recent trends.[1]

In this chapter, I begin with giving a brief technical description of how Ronja worked, in order to give the reader an idea of the extraordinary amount of effort and ingenuity that went into building the device. Thereafter I move on to describe the Ronja project and the wireless network community in the Czech Republic.[2] The case study is strategically placed for advancing the theoretical argument that I have in mind. On the face of it, the Ronja project was driven by users standing outside well-defined institutions. Still, even when an innovation stems from users (as opposed to employees inside universities and firms), it is the product of institutions or, differently put, of history. I make this point in support of those writers who, before me, have complained that the historical perspective is largely absent from discussions about users of technology.[3] The topic has chiefly been investigated in the field of Innovation Studies and the constructivist wing of Science and Technology Studies. But, for various reasons that I will come back to in the second half of the chapter, both of these traditions have a poor understanding of historical processes. Similar shortcomings are therefore likely to be reproduced once more when the same discussions are applied to hackers developing open-source hardware.[4] I advance my theoretical claim by broadening the context of Ronja to

[1] Denisa Kera. 2012. Hackerspaces and DIY-bio in Asia: Connecting science and community with open data, kits and protocols. *Journal of Peer Production* 1(2), 1–8. Available http://peerproduction.net/issues/issue-2/peer-reviewed-papers/diybio-in-asia/. Accessed 5 May 2013.

[2] My research is based on 21 in-depth interviews with people who used, built, or in other ways contributed to the Czech Ronja project in five countries: Sweden, the Netherlands, Switzerland, Czech Republic, and Slovakia. Most of the study was done during a 6-month field trip to the Czech Republic in autumn 2008. A secondary source of information has been websites related to the Ronja project. The most important document is the mailing list of the official Ronja site (http://ronja.twibright.com/) and the discussion forum run by the Czech wireless network community (http://czfree.net). All interviews were held in English, but most of the written documents were in Czech or Slovakian.

[3] Ruth Oldenziel, Adri Albert de la Bruhèze, and Onno de Wit. 2005. Europe's mediation junction: Technology and consumer society in the twentieth century. *History and Technology* 21(1): 107–139; Lorraine Daston. 2009. Science studies and the history of science. *Critical Inquiry* 35(4): 798–813; Dominique Pestre. 2013. *À contre-science – Politique et savoirs des sociétés contemporaines*. Paris: Seuil.

[4] Scholars abiding to Innovation Studies were the first ones to jump on this latest trend, see Kerstin Balka, Christina Raasch, and Cornelius Herstatt. 2009. Open source enters the world of atoms:

include the historical setting from which the project emerged. In this way I hope to demonstrate that the ebb and flow of the Ronja project were tied up with social relations which in part took place "behind the backs" of the practitioners in the Czech wireless community.

10.2 How a Ronja Link Worked

A Ronja link consisted of two devices mounted in line of sight of each other. The main part of the device, the so-called head, was made out of two chimney pipes. One pipe was equipped with a transmitter, a so-called Tx, and the other pipe contained a receiver, a "Rx." Between the head and the computer sat a box called a "Twister," which processed the signal from the head to be read by the network card in the computer. The key component in the transmitter was a light-emitting diode (LED). Originally the diode was designed to be used in traffic lights. The diode operated in the red or, in a modified version of Ronja called "Inferno," in the infrared end of the electromagnetic spectrum. The light would pass through a 130 mm lens that gave focus to the beam. At the opposite side of the link was another Ronja device. The incoming light was registered by a photodiode placed in the receiver of the other device. The photodiode translated the pulses of light into electronic charges, which then passed through an amplifier that reinforced the signal and reduced noise. In this way, the "blinks" of light were translated into the "1" and "0" of a digital communication network.

Ronja was able to send 10 Mb per second of data. It was much faster than what could be achieved with Wi-Fi transmissions on the 2.4 GHz wavelength used at the time. The original design had a maximum range of 1.4 km. The main drawback with free-space optics was that both red and infrared lights are sensitive to fog. To ensure that the link worked irrespectively of weather conditions, it had to be backed up with a normal Wi-Fi antenna. But apart from bad weather and mechanical interference which blocked the line of sight, Ronja was a remarkably stable technology. It did not have the same problems of packet losses and collisions commonly experienced in Wi-Fi networks. Since a Wi-Fi signal is broadcast over an area, it will always come up against the problem of crowding. This became more of a problem to the Czech wireless network activists as their success in spreading the technology increased. Another disadvantage with Wi-Fi is that data can travel in only one direction at a time. In other words, computer transmissions going back and forth have to share the same lane. The twin pipes of the Ronja head, on the other hand, sent and received data separately and simultaneously. In technical terms, this was known as "full duplex." There was no upper limit to the number of Ronja links that could operate in the same area since the optical device was truly point-to-point. Such

---

A statistical analysis of open design. *First Monday* 14(11). Accessed 5 May 2013; Sonali Shah. 2006. Open beyond software. In *Open sources 2.0 – The continuing evolution*, ed. Chris DiBona, Danese Cooper, and Mark Stone, 339–360. Beijing: O'Reilly.

technical considerations meant that Ronja had a major advantage over the Wi-Fi equipment then sold in the Czech Republic at the time.

The main drawback of the Ronja project was that the task of building an optical link, aiming it, and then doing maintenance work was extremely time-consuming and labor intensive. Just assembling all the parts was a challenge. The users had to make do with general-purpose components. Furthermore, as the customers who purchased the parts were usually firms rather than hobbyists, parts were sold in much larger quantities than the users had need for. Once the parts had been found, the work of assembling them into a working unit began. An experienced builder had to spend a couple of days just to solder the electronics, which was done manually with a soldering iron. To make the mechanical construction could take weeks. The original version was built from metal parts which had to be cut, drilled, and welded into the right shape. No less time-consuming was the task of sealing the holes afterwards with silicon. This was necessary as the Ronja link typically was mounted on rooftops and exposed to harsh weather conditions. If the chassis had not been properly sealed, humidity in the air would damage the electronics inside. Furthermore, the mechanics had to be built in such a way that it could withstand howling winds and storms without the link being knocked out of position.

Aiming the device was critical for getting the transmission of data to flow effortlessly over the rooftops. As the power of the LED was fairly weak, this had to be compensated for by using a lens to focus the beam. The light cone was consequently very narrow. This, in turn, made aiming much harder, especially since the Ronja link on the opposite side could be up to a kilometer away. Usually it took a couple of hours to aim a link, a task that was preferably done at night. By holding up a car reflector at the opposite end, it was possible to see when the transmitter was pointing in roughly the right direction. The receiver then had to be placed in line with the incoming light. A voltmeter was connected to the head to indicate the strength of the incoming signal. Thereafter the whole procedure was repeated to position the second transmitter and receiver on the opposite side. This operation could be rather challenging if it was done in the dark, on a sloped roof. Even after the Ronja link had been aimed, it might need adjustments. Since the metal was compressed after it had been mounted, the first attempt at aiming the link was only temporary. During the next few weeks it had to be fine-tuned. In addition, it might be necessary to repeat the process every couple of years, due to changes in temperature and winds.

10.3 The History of Ronja and the Czech Wireless Network Scene

The inventor of Ronja, Karel Kulhavy, was known among his peers as "Clock." He got the idea to build Ronja from a TV remote control, which made him realize that light waves could be used to communicate at a distance. The direct incentive for building such a device arose from the wish to communicate with a friend who lived across the street.[5] They first experimented in 1998, but it took another 2 years before Clock started to pursue his ideas more systematically. Initially his plan was nothing more ambitious than sending Morse code, but while working on it he realized that the principle of free-space optics allowed him to do a lot more. Crucially, he discovered that light waves could be used to transmit data. The first public version of Ronja was released on December 21, 2001, under the name Metropolis.[6]

Although Clock was at the center of the innovation story, it should be stressed that the idea of using free-space optics to connect computers was in the air. A similar experiment was taking place at about the same time independently, without knowledge of the Ronja project's existence. In a village in Podkrkonoší to the north of Prague, Petr Seliger had felt the same urge to be connected with his friends. He too came to think of the possibility of using light as a means of data transmission. Seliger used an ordinary laser pointer as the light source for his device. He called his machine "Cheapo." In 2003, the machine was reliable enough to build a local computer network. When asked where the idea and the motivation came from, Seliger stressed the topology of the place where he lived. The village is located at the bottom of a valley in such a way that Wi-Fi signals tend to be blocked out. The Cheapo enabled Seliger to connect to a friend who happened to live on a hilltop and from where they could mount a Wi-Fi antenna. Cheapo had many limitations, especially with regard to Internet access. When Seliger learned about Clock's project, he switched to Ronja. For an idea of the difference in scale and ambition, the number of electronic parts in the two designs can be compared. Whereas the different versions of Ronja had between 2000 and 3000 electronic parts, i.e., capacitors, coils, and resistors, Cheapo had been built with less than 50 components. Cheapo was a hack meant to solve a local problem encountered by a single inventor, who had the misfortune of living in a valley.[7] During my stay in the Czech Republic, I also heard of another construction similar to Cheapo, which suggests that there may have been many more experiments at the time that Ronja was launched.

What made the Ronja project stand out was that the creator wanted more than a device that fulfilled his own needs. Clock's aspiration to spread the use of Ronja required a different approach from the outset. The design had to be made with consideration for a second, unknown user. In other words, it had to be generalizable. Ideally, an inexperienced user should be able to build a machine by following the instructions. The availability and cost of parts was another hurdle which had to be taken into account in the design. This can best be exemplified with the lens. While commercial free-space optical devices use specially crafted optical lenses which can cost thousands of Euros, the Ronja machine did the same job with an ordinary magnifying glass, the diameter of which happened to fit the chimney pipe. The magnifying glass was imported from China and sold at a flea market in Prague for a few Euros. Likewise, the electronics used in the original version of Ronja were

[5] Jan Hudec, 2008-12-08.

[6] Karel Kulhavy, 2008-11-16.

[7] Petr Seliger, 2008-10-21.

based on components that were more than 30 years old. They had to be soldered by hand by the user to make an electronic part which was aptly called "the bird's nest." Sometimes it took months of extra design work to get cheap, general-purpose components to do what could otherwise have been achieved instantly with a special purpose but expensive electronic component or one that would have been difficult to obtain.[8] Besides these additional hurdles in the design of the machine, a lot of time had to be spent on documenting the machine. The challenge here was that the addressee was not a trained engineer who shared a body of tacit knowledge and common practices with the inventor. Rather, the intended audience consisted of teenagers and students who had no engineering training to rely on. When asked about his motives for all his efforts, Clock replied that the only way for him to justify to himself the time he had spent on Ronja was that it enabled more people to benefit from the technology:

> At the beginning it was the beauty of the technological elegance. I can do things which I thought were impossible. And then, then you get some recognition from people. And comments like someone builds Ronja and writes that it was the most exciting moment in my life when it started to work. That makes me feel special, like I have some relevance.[9]

The subsequent rapid spread of Ronja should be seen against the backdrop of a strong movement around wireless community networks in the Czech Republic. These communities sprang up in many places around the world in the early 2000s. Wireless networks utilized a small patch of the electromagnetic spectrum which until then had been left unregulated by governments because it was deemed unsuitable for commercial and military purposes. When the first equipment was marketed, government regulators and the computer industry designated the unlicensed part of the spectrum for indoor purposes. The ideal customer was a company connecting computers in an office building or at a trade fair. As prices fell and Wi-Fi antennas became more accessible, community activists started to build local networks in their neighborhoods.[10] To put the equipment to such a different purpose required a lot of tweaking by the activists, some of which could qualify as innovation in its own right. For instance, in the early days the activists built their own antennas using pineapple cans. The signal was thus given direction and could travel a longer distance.

Nothing, however, compares to the ambitions and complexity of the innovations which emerged from the Czech wireless community, out of which the Ronja machine was a showcase example. Part of the explanation for the unusual circumstances was that the Czech activists, in comparison to their counterparts in the USA and Western Europe, had difficulties affording Wi-Fi equipment. Another reason was that the Internet infrastructure and the commercial alternatives in the Czech Republic lagged behind neighboring countries in Western and Central Europe.

---

[8] Karel Kulhavy, 2008-11-16.

[9] Karel Kulhavy, 2008-11-16.

[10] Ellen Oost, Stephan Verhaegh, and Nelly Oudshoorn. 2009. From innovation community to community innovation: User-initiated innovation in wireless Leiden. *Science, Technology, & Human Values* 34(184): 182–205; Christina Dunbar-Hester. 2009. 'Free the spectrum!' Activist encounters with old and new media technology. *New Media & Society* 11(1–2): 221–240.

These circumstances created a strong impetus to build an alternative communication infrastructure. According to one estimate, at one point there may have been as many as 250 independent wireless networks in Prague alone.[11] Some were made up of just a handful of friends; others gathered hundreds or even thousands of members. The largest single, nonprofit wireless community network in the Czech Republic was established in the city of Plzen with more than 8,000 members. It is still in existence, and activists in the region have been relatively successful in coordinating their efforts with neighboring towns and villages. By connecting separate wireless networks through high-speed links, they have set up a local intranet, which at one point included an estimated 20,000 users.[12] It comes as no surprise, then, that the Czech Republic is the country in Europe which has the largest proportion of users connected to the Internet through Wi-Fi technology.[13]

In the same year as the Ronja project was launched, CZFree.net was inaugurated and became the hub of discussions and information exchanges among wireless network activists in the Czech Republic. Free-space optics was quickly recognized as an attractive alternative to the standard Wi-Fi technology. When the first community networks were established, the price for one Wi-Fi point was over 20,000 Czech korunas. In comparison, the parts for building a complete Ronja link cost between 1,000 and 3,000 koruna. In terms of functionality, free-space optics had many advantages over Wi-Fi, one of which appealed particularly strongly to activists with anarchist leanings. Ronja links could be connected in a long chain so that the signal jumped from one node to the next without the transmission being slowed down or losing much in quality. In theory, at least, a local computer network could be extended in this way to cover a metropolitan area. A communication infrastructure could thus be built where all the hardware was owned entirely by the users. Although it was technically feasible to do the same thing with Wi-Fi technology, the speed and quality of the data transmission would be seriously compromised. Hence, in practice, larger wireless network communities relied on a centralized backbone, such as fiber optical cables. Often access to the cable was rented from a corporation. The idea of running the backbone through Ronja links promised to fulfill one of the original dreams of the wireless network community. One founder of the CZFree.net explained their vision as follows:

> The idea in the beginning was not only to create a network which connects people to the Internet but to create a network which is resistant to political pressures. This is free as freedom, not as cheap connection, but really as freedom of speech. And the freedom of this network should have been made by keeping it in private, actually it is a network-of-networks which peer together to form a big network. And going after private citizens is much, much more problematic than against business subjects. These people who were for the idea of freedom were trying to keep it distributed on many parties who were participating in this bigger idea.[14]

---

[11] Petr Simandl, 2008-10-27.

[12] Michael Polak, 2009-01-16.

[13] COM. 2009. *Progress report on the single European electronic communications market 2007, 14th report*. 24 March 2009. Brussels: EC.

[14] Lada Myslik, 2008-01-09.

Two major sources of inspiration lay behind the sentiments expressed in the above quote. First, since free software was often used to run the servers, there was an inflow of people and ideas from the computer scene. With that came the cultural figure of the hacker with its 1960s countercultural connotations.[15] Second, the wireless network community was preceded by an earlier generation of community radio stations. In the large cities in Western Europe, many radio stations had been set up in squatted buildings by anarchists. They saw radio technology as a means of creating a grassroots alternative to the state and bourgeois media.[16] However, on the community radio scene, just as in the hacker "underground," the line between radical politics and free-wheeling commerce was blurred. Another major impetus came from pirate radio stations which began sending commercial radio from boats on international waters. Those stations were chiefly preoccupied with circumventing national regulations on commerce and taxation laws.[17] In the Eastern Bloc, and as the 1980s drew to a close, community radio became important for organizing dissent.[18] This legacy implanted a touch of radicalism in the wireless community in the Czech Republic, typically with a bent towards antistatism. As the above quote hints, political zeal was however mixed with less idealistic motives, especially the wish to have a cheap connection. The quote also suggests that the latter prevailed over the former. Given that the level of idealism was not a constant over time and differed markedly from one local wireless network community to another, my decision to use the word "activist" to denote all the people who were involved in building wireless networks is open to debate. Perhaps it would have seemed less loaded if I had chosen the generic word "user" instead. I will return to defend my choice of terminology towards the end of the chapter.

A mixture of political motives, low costs for acquiring the material, and superior technical functionality came together for a time and created a soaring interest in the Ronja project. One indicator of how widespread the machine became can be found on the official website. People were encouraged to post photos on their Ronja links on the website, which boasted 153 installed and working Ronja links. The actual number of machines built was probably much higher. Another sign is the number of people who distributed key components for Ronja. For example, the light-emitting diode came in quantities of 120 diodes per package. One member of the wireless community who ordered packages and distributed the diodes to individuals claimed that he had distributed over 800 diodes to users who just wanted to build a few links

[15] Fred Turner. 2006. *From counter culture to cyberculture: Stewart Brand, the Whole Earth Network, and the rise of digital utopianism*. Chicago: Chicago University Press. See also Nevejan, Caroline, and Alexander Badenoch. 2014. How Amsterdam invented the Internet: European networks of significance, 1980–1995. In *Hacking Europe. From computer cultures to demoscenes*, ed. Gerard Alberts and Ruth Oldenziel, 189–217. New York: Springer.

[16] Maxigas. 2012. Hacklabs and hackerspaces: Tracing two genealogies. *Journal of Peer Production* 1(2), 1–10. Available: http://peerproduction.net/issues/issue-2/peer-reviewed-papers/hacklabs-and-hackerspaces/. Accessed 5 May 2013.

[17] Adrian Johns. 2009. Piracy as a business force. *Culture Machine* 10, 44–63. Accessed 5 May 2013.

[18] Richard Barbrook. 1987. A new way of talking: Community radio in 1980s Britain. *Science as Culture* 1(1): 81–129.

for private use.[19] He furthermore related that he had known some larger wireless network communities which built many Ronja links and ordered their packages directly from the USA. Another indicator of the Ronja's popularity is the spread of electronic parts. In a modified version of the Ronja device which became very popular, the "bird's nest" electronics were replaced with electronics based on printed circuit boards (PCB). Although it is possible to home brew simpler PCBs, it is also much easier to have them made by a firm. The drawback of ordering from a firm is that it demands an economy of scale, due to the high costs of getting the manufacturing process up and running. Once in place and producing large quantities, however, the cost per unit becomes negligible. A few people in the wireless network community have begun to order batches of PCBs and sell them to fellow hobbyists. One, who started a website called Ronja shop, estimates that he shipped 1,000 PCBs to people who wanted to build Ronja links.[20] The number of diodes and PCBs may tell us little about how many Ronja machines were built in the end, yet the interviewees involved in the wireless network communities in the Czech Republic and Slovakia suggest that the machine was widespread. Outside of these two countries, however, few people have heard of the Ronja project. An exception is the Netherlands, another country with a strong tradition in wireless networks. Awareness about the Czech project has spread thanks to the workshops for building Ronja links organized by the Wireless Community Camp, a summer camp loosely tied to Wireless Leiden.[21]

The same conditions that enabled the Ronja project to grow in the Czech Republic impeded its diffusion to other countries. One possible explanation may be the geographical confinement of language. In the beginning, the documentation was in Czech, as were the discussions on CZFree.net. This changed gradually as the Ronja website was set up: instructions were translated into English and German, allowing people from other countries to become involved in the forum discussions. Yet most knowledge sharing, especially with regard to modifications of Ronja, took place by word of mouth, creating a barrier even to the wireless network community in Slovakia. The Ronja project spread more slowly in the neighboring country, where components were more difficult to find and more expensive. For instance, Slovakian activists collected money to allow a member to go to Prague and buy magnifying glasses of the right size. But a more important explanation is underscored by a wireless network activist in Bratislava: "In Prague, you had quite a lot of people who could actually help you with building Ronja."[22] Hence, newcomers could ask for help in their extended friendship circles. In some cities, activists more systematically organized the diffusion of learning practices. For instance, members of the CZFree.net set up a physical space in Prague where beginners could get help with troubleshooting their almost-working equipment.[23]

---

[19] Ondrej Tesar, 2008-10-05.

[20] Jakub Horky, 2009-01-17.

[21] WifiSoft.org Foundation. 2007. *Annual report 2007*. http://wifisoft.org/trac/. Accessed 20 Jan 2012.

[22] Marcel Hecko, 2008-12-17.

[23] Lada Myslik, 2008-01-09; Petr Seliger, 2008-10-21.

The focus on spreading learning practices expressed one of the goals of the Ronja activists. They had to come up with a design which did not require users to have an engineering degree, or else the project would not go very far. Users were nevertheless expected to climb a rather steep learning curve, as basic understanding of how electronics works, familiarity with programming, and some soldering skills were indispensable. At least to some of the activists, this was perceived as a feature of the Ronja project, rather than as a bug. Accordingly, the many modifications which were made to simplify the building process were not welcomed by everyone. It was not sufficient for users to acquire a network device and join a decentralized communication network; the social and political transformations wished for by some of the activists required them to develop an informed and active relation to the technology in question. This goal can be said to have been achieved, in so far as many of the Ronja links were built by teenagers who lacked any formal technical training. However, it also hindered the spread of the technology. To learn those skills required a very keen interest in technology and a lot of spare time. At the end of the day, many users only really wanted to connect their computers to a local computer network and had little interest in learning about the technology.

The involvement of this type of new user group generated a demand for preassembled Ronja devices. Most people who had been involved in the project for a couple of years made one or two links on request, helping to spread the knowledge and use of Ronja. Even independent Internet service providers began to order Ronja links from activists. In response, some activists started businesses selling modified Ronja links or parts. A case in point is a local businessman in the small town of Chrudim, who noticed the growing demand for the product when his firm was asked to make metal casings for Ronja devices. This prompted him to attempt a more ambitious approach. He involved a member from the local wireless network community in Chrudim with some experience with the technology. When an Internet service provider commissioned them to build their first link, they experimented with the design and the best way to go about producing the device. Five employees were engaged from time to time to speed up this process. In spite of their efforts and investments, they failed to get the equipment to work in time. After a number of delays and disappointments, the technically experienced partner withdrew from the project. Reflecting upon the failure, the partner suggested to me that the impossibility of making Ronja links for sale was integral to the project. This he explained in terms of the huge amount of motivation and energy it required to build, install, and operate a Ronja link (Fig. 10.1):

> I told that he [the businessman] has employees, but they are doing other projects and I think that they felt that they could not be bothered with Ronja. Because he told somebody who was doing something completely different from Ronja, I would say, building a house or doing metal boxes, he told this person to go with me on the roof of the building and try to do something. The employee had no motivation to have success on this project. I guess he had motivation to fail the project and not be bothered with it anymore.[24]

[24] David Kolovratnik, 2008-12-14.

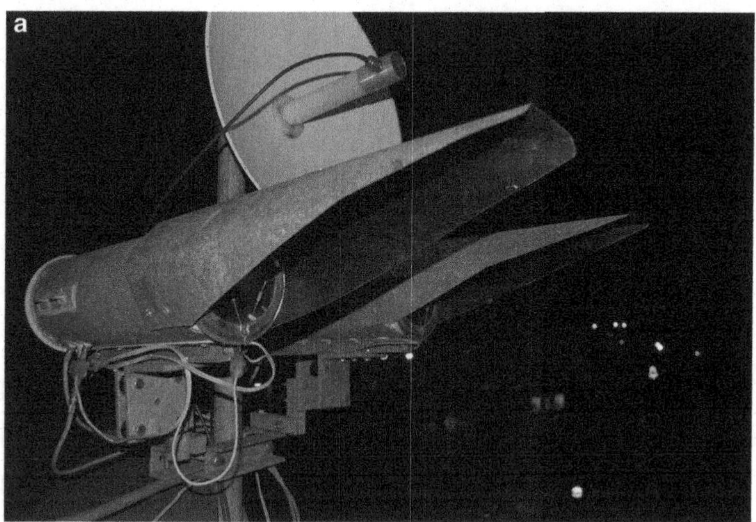

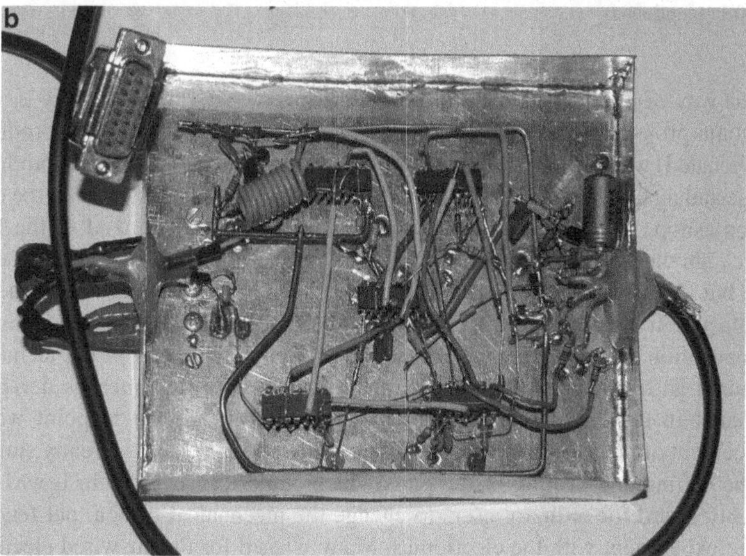

Fig. 10.1 Archeology of an Open-Source Wifi System. (a–c) In the small town of Chrudim in the center of the Czech Republic, one still finds Ronja devices mounted on top of roofs and walls. In one of the metal pipes sits a light emitting diode (*LED*), in the second pipe a photodiode that registers incoming light. The light carries data from one Ronja device to a second device mounted on the opposite side. In this way, Czech wireless activists built computer networks on a frequency entirely unregulated by the state, that is to say: visible, red light. Because the designs for the device were published under a free license, the construction of the machine too was in the control of its users. Source: Photographer Johan Söderberg

Fig. 10.1 (continued)

One way of interpreting the above quote is to say that, due to the way in which the Ronja project had been conceived, the technology was ill-suited to production by (alienated) wage labor. In other words, the design was biased towards production for use and against production for sale. The same thing was attested to by the owner of Ronjashop, who, having operated a small-scale business linked to the Ronja project, should know: "Generally, Ronja is a project which is simple to do on the knee, but is very hard if you want to send documentation to China so that they can manufacture it in bulk."[25] Many saw this as an obstacle when the market demand for the innovation surged. Their wish to see the commercialization of the technology prompted an overhaul of the design of the Ronja device. Numerous derivatives circulated in the Czech wireless network community. A case in point was the replacement of metal pipes with plastic pipes in the Ronja chassis, greatly simplifying the cutting and drilling of the parts which could take over 20 h. It was fairly straightforward for ordinary users to change the mechanical design, but few were able to experiment with the electronics. Many wished for the air-wired electronics to be replaced with surface-mounted PCB electronics. Clock was reluctant to heed the call which he thought departed from the ideal of self-reliance and user-control. As a result of his reluctance, Jan Skontorp released the first PCB design for Ronja in 2004. It turned out that PCB also had some advantages from the standpoint of user-control. With the original electronics it was hard to translate the three-dimensional space of crisscrossing wires and components into a two-dimensional drawing in a way that was intelligible to inexperienced users. The air-wired electronics intimidated newcomers, resulting in many failures. Moreover, the push

[25] Jakub Horky, 2009-01-17.

for a leaner production process of Ronja parts was not driven by sales alone. The redesign was part and parcel of the definition of a network device, as a single unit is useless. Conversely, having more of them increased the utility of every unit. People in the wireless network communities needed many links and wanted to reduce the time and effort to produce a series of units. Still, underlining the observation above on alienation and the need for motivation, one member of the wireless network community in Chrudim testified that he had more fun soldering air-wired electronics than working with a batch of PCBs.[26]

The idea of making money from selling Ronja links was not controversial in itself. Indeed, when someone asked on the Ronja mailing list for permission to build one of the components of Ronja and make a profit from it, he was encouraged to do so. He was even told that he did not need to ask for permission. All that was required of him was to respect the free license under which the technology had been published. The license specified that changes to the original design had to be made publicly available to the community.[27] The various design changes made to speed up the production of Ronja links did actually stir up some controversy. According to Clock, some modifications compromised the performance of the optical link. At other times, he felt that such changes contradicted the original vision of having a user-controlled technology. Clock's strict adherence to the vision of user-controlled technology turned many people away from the project. They ran off to do their own thing with free-space optics, resulting in the lack of a unified community of developers and activists with a shared sense of moral obligation towards the license agreement. This became evident when core members of the CZFree.net started a business based on the invention without publishing their modifications. Clock accused them of having violated the free license.[28]

With hardware design, however, as opposed to software code, it is less self-evident what counts as a derivative. Complicating the matter still further, it is debatable whether the free license grants any legal protection to hardware development at all. The free license depends on a copyright agreement and is therefore limited to literary works. Hence, the only way to enforce a license in this case would have been through the norms of the community. When I talked to the people who had been involved in the Ronja project and asked them about the incident, they were divided as to what had happened and who was wronged. By then it was clear that no community existed any longer in which a shared development project could unfold. The community fell apart as people became increasingly reluctant to cooperate around an open development project.[29] In 2008, there were several attempts to improve and develop a second generation of free-space optics, using lasers instead of light diodes. Those projects, however, were run as traditional start-up firms, keeping information about the development process secret.

---

[26] Ondrej Zajicek, 2008-12-14.

[27] Karel Obadal, Ronja mailing list, 2004-11-01.

[28] Karel Kulhavy, Ronja mailing list, 2003-07-20.

[29] Michal Elias, 2008-09-27.

The conflict over commercialization in the Ronja project was mirrored in similar divisions in the Czech wireless network community. Over the years, tensions grew between those who wanted to professionalize the service and those who wanted it to remain a hobby. Suspicion was fuelled by occasional attempts to high-jack nonprofit wireless network communities. A high-jacking occurred when a group of people were elected to the governing committee of a community network with the intent of turning it into a for-profit service. Some community networks connected hundreds of users, which became a potentially valuable asset to an Internet service provider.[30] Aside from such hostile takeovers, commodification was working in less dramatic ways. In the beginning, the wireless networks were built by enthusiasts who derived as much satisfaction from tinkering with the technology as from having a fast and cheap Internet connection. This changed when members with more of a consumer attitude started to benefit from the service. Hence, fewer were willing and able to volunteer to do the maintenance work. Today it is common for nonprofit, wireless network communities to hire someone to get the job done.[31] Some administrators have preferred their wireless network communities to stay small and convivial and have turned down the opportunity to make a living out of their hobby.[32]

10.4 Situating the Success and Decline of the Ronja Project

As indicated in the introduction, I present the Ronja project with the intent of engaging in a larger, theoretical debate about the notion "user." Amateur innovators often imagine themselves to be "outsiders" vis-à-vis institutions and professions. This implies a vacuous space outside institutions, populated by atomistic, free-floating – albeit networked – users. Indeed, the very term "user" suggests an agent detached from collective identities, institutional confinements, and historical processes. The only thing determining him/her as a "user" is the technology he/she is using. One can easily see why this notion has become so popular in Innovation Studies, being a subdiscipline of economics. The user is a stand-in for the individual market agent.[33] But the idea of the user is also acclaimed in the poststructuralist wing of Science and Technology Studies (STS). The user here personifies the belated hopes of putting the notion of "structure" to rest – and history along with it.[34] From this theoretical perspective, the user is but an emergent effect of the

[30] Jakub Horky, 2009-01-17; Lada Myslik, 2008-01-09.

[31] Jakub Sykora, 2008-11-27; Jiri Bohac, 2008-09-14.

[32] Petr Simandl, 2008-10-27; Ondrej Zajicek 2008-12-14.

[33] Carliss Baldwin, Eric von Hippel, and Christoph Hienerth. 2006. How user innovations become commercial products: A theoretical investigation and case study. *Research Policy* 35: 1291–1313; Eric von Hippel. 2005. Open source projects as user innovation networks. In *Perspectives on free and open source software*, ed. Joseph Feller, et al., 267–278. Cambridge, MA: MIT Press.

[34] For a critique along these lines, see Dominique Pestre. 2004. Thirty years of science studies: Knowledge, society and the political. *History and Technology* 20(4): 351–369.

network, capable of subverting any given constraint, whether technical or otherwise, ad infinitum. The same goes for the user himself or herself, who is treated as an empty placeholder for an endless play of identities.[35] What such argument boils down to, as many critics of constructivist STS have pointed out before, is an unqualified endorsement of agency.[36] Constructivist STS research has thus grown insensitive to the historical momentum of institutions and economic relations and fails to historically situate its analysis of the user and the technology being used. For sure, there are other traditions within the heterogeneous field of STS with a developed sense of historical processes. Here, tellingly, the notion of "user" has often been played down, and pride of place is given to other analytical categories, such as the formation of a collective identity and/or an idea about the life-world within which technological change unfolds.[37]

The Ronja case study is strategically placed for developing my critique of the atomistic notion of the "user." This is because, at first glance, the project conforms so well with aforementioned theoretical approaches.[38] The Ronja device was, indeed, developed and built outside of any recognizable institution. Furthermore, the people involved spoke and thought of themselves as users. After all, Ronja was branded as a *user*-controlled technology. As an offshoot of the wireless network community, the project had inherited a stroke of similarly anarchistic ideas and values. This influence owed much to the fact that in many cities on the European continent, the first nodes in the wireless network had been set up in squats. Creating a local computer network for the neighborhood was seen as an extension of other alternative media outlets, such as publishing fanzines, sending community radio, and broadcasting street TV. Ultimately, the aim was to build an independent communication infrastructure replacing the cables and satellites owned by states and multinational companies.[39] The Ronja project corresponded well with this broader outlook. Crucially, it showed that with modest means and technical ingenuity, it was possible to offset state powers (i.e., over Wi-Fi frequencies). Hence, the case study offers an ideal example of free-floating "change agents" which take a given (infra)

---

[35] Steve Woolgar. 1991. Configuring the user: The case of usability trials. In *A sociology of monsters: Essays on power, technology and domination*, ed. John Law, 57–102. London/New York: Routledge; Vololona Rabeharisoa, and Michel Callon. 2003. Research 'in the wild' and the shaping of new social identities. *Technology in Society* 25(2): 193–204.

[36] Olga Amsterdamska. 1990. Surely you are joking, Monsieur Latour. *Science, Technology & Human Values* 15(4): 495–504; Johan Söderberg, and Adam Netzén. 2010. When all that is theory melts into (hot) air: Contrasts and parallels between actor network theory, autonomist Marxism, and open Marxism. *Ephemera: Theory & Politics in Organization* 10(2): 95–118.

[37] This taxonomy of approaches in STS is proposed by Andrew Jamison, and Mikael Hård. 2003. The storylines of technological change: Innovation, construction and appropriation. *Technology Analysis & Strategic Management* 15(1): 81–91.

[38] Hence I have selected and delimited my case study in accordance with Bent Flyvbjerg's qualified defense of this approach within the social sciences. Bent Flyvbjerg. 2006. Five misunderstandings about case-study research. *Qualitative Inquiry* 12(2): 219–245.

[39] Christian Sandvig. 2004. An initial assessment of cooperative action in Wi-Fi networking. *Telecommunications Policy* 28(7–8): 579–602.

structure and bend it to serve other purposes than those originally intended. Closer inspection will reveal, however, that the life cycle of the Ronja project depended on legal and economic relations about which the activists were at best dimly aware. The activists influenced (or coproduced, as it were) these relations in turn but only to a limited extent. The extent to which a group, such as the Czech wireless network community, can influence "back" depends on how well the group has rendered visible and become conscious of the social relations that it is – at one and the same time – part of and up against. The emphasis I place on historical processes in studies of users of technology is grounded in this praxis-oriented outlook.

A key historical fact about the Ronja project is that it took place in a country which only 10 years earlier had officially declared itself to be a communist state. This set the stage for the Ronja project in more than one way. To begin with, many young people had technical qualifications yet were economically disadvantaged in comparison with their counterparts in Western Europe. They were thus compelled to find cheaper alternatives to commercial Wi-Fi equipment in order to be able to do the same things as activists in London and Berlin did. It was pointed out to me on several occasions that the Ronja project was not an isolated phenomenon, but conformed to a long-established tradition of tinkering in the Czech Republic. In the Czech countryside, it is not uncommon to find homemade band saws and tractors along with many other weird and wonderful things.[40] Making things at home has been incorporated into the national identity and is spoken of as the *"zlaté ruce"* or "golden hands" of Czech people. Allegedly, this reputation was earned in the second half of the nineteenth century when a large Czech minority lived and worked in Vienna as craftsmen and industrial laborers. According to a census made at the turn of the last century, more than 100,000 of the city's residents stemmed from the Czech hinterlands.[41] When those lands were later annexed to the Soviet empire, due to chronic shortages, the habit of repairing and tweaking became a necessity of life.[42] It can be argued that this history created a fertile ground for the Ronja project in at least two respects. First, there was technical know-how among an older generation that could be passed down to the young. Second, many homes in the Czech Republic were equipped with simple workshops. The tools needed for building Ronja machines were therefore relatively easy to come by.

Another leftover from the communist days was the Czech phone company, Ceskoslovenské Spoje. In more than one way, the phone company had inspired the activists to experiment with free-space optics. The straightforward method for creating a point-to-point optical link was to hang an optical cable across the street, from window to window. The idea was borrowed from the Czech telephone company, since this had been the cheapest way to connect people to the phone service. The practice was however stopped in the large cities, sometimes by intervention from local authorities. As the Czech Republic was incorporated in the

---

[40] Pavel Klvač, et al. (ed.). 2007. *Na tom našem dvoře*. Prague: KSB.

[41] Monika Glettler. 1982. The organization of the Czech Clubs in Vienna circa 1900: A national minority in an imperial capital. *East Central Europe* 9(1): 124–136.

[42] Petr Seliger, 2008-10-21.

global tourist economy, keeping the streets tidy had become a new imperative.[43] More importantly, perhaps, was the fact that the phone company's services were rather poor. For many years, the company refused to lease its cables to competing Internet service providers. In 2005, it was finally forced by the EU to change its monopolistic policy. But until then the company had not been in a hurry to provide its customers with high-speed ADSL connections. When the technology was introduced in neighboring countries, many customers in the Czech Republic were still using dial-up modems. Not only were phone modems slow, but users were charged per minute – a cost structure that was particularly frustrating to young males who wanted to download large files (in violation of international copyright laws, no doubt) and play games over the computer network. The wireless network movement channeled those frustrations into a political force of a sort:

> I think the Wi-Fi community showed up to the regulatory domain, the Czech telecommunication bureau, which is the regulating domain for all telecommunications in our republic, showed that people are unhappy about the state, and they started to regulate more the monopoly of Czech telecom. Because I think that if we didn't build Wi-Fi networks we would have dial-up until today.[44]

This quote lends weight to the claim that the users exercised agency through their use of technology. Indeed, they did so to the point of influencing state policies and that without having to engage in lobbying or electing their own representatives. That assessment needs to be qualified, however. Given the resentment against Ceskoslovenské Spoje and state regulators, it might sound paradoxical to propose that the restrictions imposed by the state were what created the preconditions for home-brewed, free-space optics to exist in the first place. Nonetheless, as much is suggested by what happened after the Czech regulators decided to allow more frequencies for private uses:

> The central regulatory committee in Czech [Republic] told that 5.5 GHz band is not illegal, so we have started to use it, and that was a killing for Ronja.[45]

To be precise, it took another year, until 2006, before the activity in the Ronja project peaked. In Slovakia, where the new rules had been implemented earlier than in the Czech Republic, there was a similar time lag. Ronja continued to be used because initially it was difficult to build wireless networks based on the latest 5.5 GHz technology. One problem was that the activists needed drivers for their servers running GNU/Linux. Adoption of European standards came slowly because most Linux kernel programmers lived in the USA. Furthermore, it took time for manufacturers to perfect the production process and bring down the price to the point where it became affordable to the activists.[46] At the time of writing, the cost for Wi-Fi equipment is only slightly higher than the cost for the parts needed to assemble a Ronja link. Wi-Fi still has many technical flaws compared to free-space

---

[43] Karel Snajdrvint, 2008-12-14.

[44] Jakub Sykora, 2008-11-27.

[45] Petr Simandl, 2008-10-27.

[46] Marcel Hecko, 2008-12-17.

optics. Those drawbacks are more than compensated for, though, by the convenience of acquiring Wi-Fi equipment compared to building a Ronja link. There were also some strictly local conditions which favored or disfavored the continued use of Ronja links. I was told by an activist in Prague that in his neighborhood the Ronja links had quickly been dismantled once there was an affordable alternative. The reason for this was that he lived close to the river where fog was very common, causing the optical link to dysfunction.[47] To stay attractive, the Ronja project would have to keep pace with the industry, above all it would have to develop a faster, 100 Mb/s optical link. The topic was discussed on the Ronja mailing list from time to time and a couple of attempts were made. But even a 100 Mb/s link would soon be outdated. Clock reckoned that a head-to-head race against the industry in terms of functionality and price would be futile. Instead, he hoped Ronja would stay relevant because the system catered to needs which the companies failed to address:

> I think in fact here I am doing something which people want and which the commercial companies do not want to provide. Transparency. And… direct communication. I think people will always appreciate if there are no hidden interest from them, and will always appreciate if they can communicate with the author. Without him saying: 'Ah, we can't tell you this because it is secret, we are going to lose our revenues.'[48]

One such "hidden interest" concerns privacy. Internet service providers are now mandated by the EU and Czech laws to monitor their customers' Internet traffic for law enforcement purposes. Among other things, the aim is to combat file sharing of copyrighted material. In a near future, customers could well have their Internet access closed down if they are suspected of violating copyright law. If the enforcement of intellectual property law on the Internet becomes truly effective one day, then perhaps legislators will have given a new lease of life to home-brewed, free-space optics.

10.5 Conclusion

The Ronja project flourished in a space which had been created by the legal prohibition on the use of certain Wi-Fi frequencies. Hence, even in its absence, the state was present. When the restriction on frequencies was lifted, the Ronja project came up against an even mightier foe: global commodity production. Admittedly, the project would not have existed in the first place had it not been for cheap electronic parts such as resistors and capacitors, that is, components which had previously been made available by the world market. Much the same can be said about the activists themselves. As noted above, a strong impetus to build Ronja came from the desire to consume entertainment in the form of music, films, and games – desires which bore the mark of the culture industry and commodity production in a different sense. The political aspirations of the Ronja project acquired wider relevance because it successfully piggybacked on such desires. But this success bore the mark of its own downfall.

[47] Ondrej Tesar, 2008-10-05.

[48] Karel Kulhavy, 2008-11-16.

The technology was used only for as long as it was better than competing, industrial standards at "delivering the goods." The benchmarks for "better," i.e., low cost and high functionality, had been taken over by the wireless network community from the society at large. There was also a more utopian fringe who rejected those benchmarks, instead giving priority to political, ethical, and pedagogical values. This outlook was soon marginalized in the project. What I want to stress with this recapitulation is that at both ends of its life cycle, the Ronja project was shot through with social relations. In part, those social relations transcended the horizon and self-understanding of the practitioners. For instance, most of the participants in the project saw themselves as users and spoke of themselves as such. And yet the innovation did not have, and could not have been, the accomplishment of atomistic user-consumers. This can easily be seen when the Ronja project is contrasted with similar experiments which took place at the same time in the Czech Republic. An unknown number of individuals cobbled with free-space optical devices in order to have a computer network for themselves and their closest friends. Those projects ended when the consumer need had been satisfied, and they have since been forgotten about. The Ronja project was developed to a point where it could cater to preestablished consumer expectations and beat technical benchmarks, because the activists did so while striving for something more: to conquer the world with user-controlled technology. This suggests that the term "activist" is more accurate than "user," even though, paradoxically, the political vision of the Ronja project was framed in a language about users. That choice of terminology is hardly surprising, given that talk about the "user" is so prevalent in technical and design settings. The political vision of the Ronja project built on an inconsistent but overlapping body of ideas and values within the Czech wireless network community. It combined engineering tropes and anarchist influences with a local specificity, the dissident legacy. The outcome hereof was a strong belief in the technical ingenuity of (networked) individuals, empowering them to circumvent bodies of political representation and collective decision making, be that the local housing committee or state regulators. For a while, it seemed as if this dream would come through thanks to community-owned wireless networks and free-space optics. The move from Wi-Fi signals to light waves was a move into an unregulated space or, differently put, into a bandwidth where the Czech state could no longer "see." By evoking seeing and blindness, I want to close my discussion with a point about epistemology. Where an unsuspecting onlooker on a rooftop could only see red lights in the horizon, someone in-the-know saw a transmission of data. Occasionally the light beam could not be detected at all with the naked eye. Hidden in the light were a private communication channel, a potential neighbor dispute, and probably a breach of intellectual property law. In short, a social conflict rendered unrepresentable by the epistemological gap between the technically ingenious and the technically disingenious. In spite of this, the pedagogical mission of user-controlled technology was to close the epistemological gap. This was to be done by raising the level of technical awareness among average, disingenious users. The observations just made about the relative transparency/opaqueness of electromagnetic waves applies with equal force to the social relations that shot through the Czech wireless network community. Three examples of social relations discussed in the text are a state that is present in its absence, norms and ideas about the "user" that have been internalized by the practitioners, and the commodity form. To render such social relations visible takes sociological concepts about a "social whole" and the *longue durée* found in the historical discipline. Granted, this implies another kind of epistemological gap and thus a risk for abuse. The egalitarian response is not, as adherers of constructivist STS believe, to do away with totalizing concepts, representations, and historical perspectives. On the contrary, it mandates a pedagogical responsibility from sociologists and historians, equal to the one felt by the Czech wireless network activists towards technically inept users. It is only thus we stand a chance, collectively, to make sense of this confusing world and impose an enlightened order on some small part of it.

Acknowledgements The case study in the Czech Republic was made possible, thanks to a grant which was awarded to me by .SE-stiftelsen. I also received financial support from Laboratoire Techniques, Territoires et Sociétés (LATTS) for finalizing the text. My gratitude is also extended to Marie Wenger and Liz Libbrecht who gave me important feedback. Finally, I want to express my appreciation for the people I met in the Czech wireless network scene.

Bibliography

Amsterdamska, Olga. 1990. Surely you are joking, Monsieur Latour. *Science, Technology & Human Values* 15(4): 495–504.

Baldwin, Carliss, Eric von Hippel, and Christoph Hienerth. 2006. How user innovations become commercial products: A theoretical investigation and case stud. *Research Policy* 35: 1291–1313.

Balka, Kerstin, Christina Raasch, and Cornelius Herstatt. 2009. Open source enters the world of atoms: A statistical analysis of open design. *First Monday* 14(11). Accessed 5 May 2013.

Barbrook, Richard. 1987. A new way of talking: Community radio in 1980s Britain. *Science as Culture* 1(1): 81–129.

COM. 2009. *Progress report on the single European electronic communications market 2007, 14th report*. 24 March 2009. Brussels: EC.

Daston, Lorraine. 2009. Science studies and the history of science. *Critical Inquiry* 35(4): 798–813.

Dunbar-Hester, Christina. 2009. 'Free the spectrum!' Activist encounters with old and new media technology. *New Media & Society* 11(1–2): 221–240.

Flyvbjerg, Bent. 2006. Five misunderstandings about case-study research. *Qualitative Inquiry* 12(2): 219–245.

Glettler, Monika. 1982. The organization of the Czech clubs in Vienna circa 1900: A national minority in an imperial capital. *East Central Europe* 9(1): 124–136.

Jamison, Andrew, and Mikael Hård. 2003. The storylines of technological change: Innovation, construction and appropriation. *Technology Analysis & Strategic Management* 15(1): 81–91.

Johns, Adrian. 2009. Piracy as a business force. *Culture Machine* 10, 44–63. Accessed 5 May 2013.

Kera, Denisa. 2012. Hackerspaces and DIY-bio in Asia: Connecting science and community with open data, kits and protocols. *Journal of Peer Production* 1(2), 1–8. http://peerproduction.net/issues/issue-2/peer-reviewed-papers/diybio-in-asia/. Accessed 5 May 2013.

Klvač, Pavel, et al. (ed.). 2007. *Na tom našem dvoře Kličova*. Prague: KSB.

Maxigas. 2012. Hacklabs and hackerspaces: Tracing two genealogies. *Journal of Peer Production* 1(2), 1–10. http://peerproduction.net/issues/issue-2/peer-reviewed-papers/hacklabs-and-hackerspaces/. Accessed 5 May 2013.

Nevejan, Caroline, and Alexander Badenoch. 2014. How Amsterdam invented the Internet: European networks of significance, 1980–1995. In *Hacking Europe. From computer cultures to demoscenes*, ed. Gerard Alberts and Ruth Oldenziel, 189–217. New York: Springer.

Oldenziel, Ruth, Adri Albert de la Bruhèze, and Onno de Wit. 2005. Europe's mediation junction: Technology and consumer society in the twentieth century. *History and Technology* 21(1): 107–139.

Oost, Ellen, Stephan Verhaegh, and Nelly Oudshoorn. 2009. From innovation community to community innovation: User-initiated innovation in wireless Leiden. *Science, Technology & Human Values* 34(184): 182–205.

Pestre, Dominique. 2004. Thirty years of science studies: Knowledge, society and the political. *History and Technology: An International Journal* 20(4): 351–369.

Pestre, Dominique. 2013. *À contre-science – Politique et savoirs des sociétés contemporaines*. Paris: Seuil.

Rabeharisoa, Vololona, and Michel Callon. 2003. Research 'in the wild' and the shaping of new social identities. *Technology in Society* 25(2): 193–204.

Sandvig, Christian. 2004. An initial assessment of cooperative action in Wi-Fi networking. *Telecommunications Policy* 28(7–8): 579–602.

Shah, Sonali. 2006. Open beyond software. In *Open sources 2.0 – The continuing evolution*, ed. Chris DiBona, Danese Cooper, and Mark Stone, 339–360. Beijing: O'Reilly.

Söderberg, Johan, and Adam Netzén. 2010. When all that is theory melts into (hot) air: Contrasts and parallels between actor network theory, autonomist Marxism, and open Marxism. *Ephemera: Theory & Politics in Organization* 10(2): 95–118.

Turner, Fred. 2006. *From counterculture to cyberculture: Stewart Brand, the Whole Earth Network, and the rise of digital utopianism*. Chicago: Chicago University Press.

von Hippel, Eric. 2005. Open source projects as user innovation networks. In *Perspectives on free and open source software*, ed. Joseph Feller, et al., 267–278. Cambridge, MA: MIT Press.

WifiSoft.org Foundation. 2007. *Annual report 2007*. http://wifisoft.org/trac/.

Woolgar, Steve. 1991. Configuring the user: The case of usability trials. In *A sociology of monsters: Essays on power, technology and domination*, ed. John Law, 57–102. London/New York: Routledge.

Interviews

Bohac, Jiri, contributed mechanical inventions for Ronja, user of Ronja (Prague, September 14, 2008)

de Stigter, Johan, running a company selling wireless equipment, sponsor of Ronja (telephone interview, September 30, 2008)

Elias, Michal, experimented with Ronja design, vendor and user of Ronja (Prague, September 27, 2008)

Gullik, Webjorn, experimented with Ronja design (phone interview, August 10, 2008)

Hecko, Marcel, developed PCB for Ronja, administrator of a nonprofit, wireless network, user of Ronja (Bratislava, December 17, 2008)

Horky, Jakub, vendor of Ronja (Prague, January 17, 2009)

Hudec, Jan, tested the first versions of Ronja (Prague, December 8, 2008)

Kamenicky, Tomas, developer of a second generation of free space optics (Prague, December 4, 2008)

Krishnan, Arun, developer and user of Ronja in India (telephone interview, October 17, 2008)

Kolovratnik, David, user of Ronja (Prague, December 14, 2008)

Kulhavy, Karel, main developer of Ronja (Zurich, November 16, 2008)

Michnik, Jakub, vendor of Ronja (Brno, December 17, 2008)

Myslik, Lada, main developer of Crusader (Prague, January 9, 2008)

Nemec, David, vendor of Ronja (Chrudim, December 14, 2008)

Polak, Michael, running an Internet Service Provider, user of Ronja and Crusader (Prague, January 16, 2009)

Seliger, Petr, developed PCB for Ronja, user of Ronja (Prague, October 21, 2008)

Simandl, Petr, administrator of non-profit wireless network and independent developer of open hardware designs (October 27, 2008)

Snajdrvint, Karel administrator of a non-profit wireless network, user of Ronja (Chrudim, December 14, 2008)

Sykora, Jakub, user of Ronja (Prague, November 27, 2008)

Tesar, Ondrej, developed PCB for Ronja, distributed light diodes, user of Ronja (Prague, October 5, 2008)

Zajicek, Ondrej, administrator of nonprofit, wireless network, user of Ronja (Chrudim, December 14, 2008)

Bibliography

Aarseth, Espen. 1997. *Cybertext: Perspectives on ergodic literature*. Baltimore: Johns Hopkins University Press.

Abbate, Janet. 1999. *Inventing the Internet*. Cambridge, MA: MIT Press.

Abbate, Janet. 2010. Privatizing the Internet: Competing visions and chaotic events, 1987–1995. *IEEE Annals of the History of Computing* 32(1): 10–22.

Abramovitch, D. 2005. Analog computing in the Soviet Union. An interview with Boris Kogan. *IEEE Control Systems* 25(3): 52–62.

Achenbach, Hans. 1986. Das Zweite Gesetz zur Bekämpfung der Wirtschaftskriminalität. *Neue Juristische Wochenschrift* 30: 1835–1898.

Ackermann, Stephan. 1988. Die aktuellen Tarife fürs Hacken. In *Das Chaos Computer Buch. Hacking made in Germany*, ed. Jürgen Wieckmann, 183–192. Reinbek bei Hamburg: Wunderlich.

Adamson, Ian, and Richard Kennedy. 1986. *Sinclair and the sunrise technology: The deconstruction of a myth*. Harmondsworth: Penguin.

Adilkno [The Foundation for the Advancement of Illegal Knowledge]. 1994. *Cracking the Movement: Squatting Beyond the Media*. Trans. Laura Martz. New York: Autonomedia. http://thing.desk.nl/bilwet/Cracking/general.html. Last accessed 27 Sept 2011

Adilkno [The Foundation for the Advancement of Illegal Knowledge]. 2013. *Hardware, software, wetware*. http://www.nettime.org/Lists-Archives/nettime-l-9606/msg00026.html. Accessed 15 May 2013.

Adorno, Theodor W., and Max Horkheimer. 1972. *Dialectic of enlightenment*. New York: Seabury Press.

Advisory Council for Applied Research and Development. 1978. *The applications of semiconductor technology*. London: HMSO.

Akera, Atusushi. 2001. Voluntarism and the fruits of collaboration: The IBM user group, SHARE. *Technology and Culture* 42(4): 710–736.

Akrich, Madeleine. 1992. The de-scription of technical objects. In *Shaping technology/building society: Studies in sociotechnical change*, ed. Wiebe E. Bijker and John Law, 205–224. Cambridge, MA: MIT Press.

Akrich, Madeleine, and Bruno Latour. 1992. A summary of convenient vocabulary for the semiotics of human and nonhuman assemblies. In *Shaping technology/building society: Studies in sociotechnical change*, ed. Wiebe E. Bijker and John Law, 259–264. Cambridge, MA: MIT Press.

Albert de la Bruhèze, Adri, and Ruth Oldenziel. 2009. *Manufacturing technology, manufacturing consumers. The making of Dutch consumer society*. Amsterdam: Aksant.

Ammann, Thomas. 1988. Nach uns die Zukunft. Aus der Geschichte des Chaos Computer Clubs. In *Das Chaos Computer Buch. Hacking made in Germany*, ed. Jürgen Wieckmann, 9–31. Reinbek bei Hamburg: Wunderlich.

G. Alberts and R. Oldenziel (eds.), *Hacking Europe. From Computer Cultures to Demoscenes*, History of Computing, DOI 10.1007/978-1-4471-5493-8,

Amsterdamska, Olga. 1990. Surely you are joking, Monsieur Latour. *Science, Technology & Human Values* 15(4): 495–504.

Anders, Freia. 2010. Wohnraum, Freiraum, Widerstand. Die Formierung der Autonomen in den Konflikten um Hausbesetzungen Anfang der achtziger Jahre. In *Das alternative Milieu. Antibürgerlicher Lebensstil und linke Politik in der Bundesrepublik Deutschland und Europa 1968–1983*, ed. Sven Reichard and Detlef Siegfried, 473–498. Göttingen: Wallstein Verlag.

Antonić, Voja. 1983. *Galaksija*. http://www.paralax.rs/pr83.htm. Accessed 17 June 2010.

Aspray, William. 1997. The Intel 4004 microprocessor: What constituted invention. *IEEE Annals of the History of Computing* 19(3): 4–15.

Atkinson, Paul. 2005. Man in a briefcase: The social construction of the laptop computer and the emergence of a type form. *Journal of Design History* 18: 191–205.

Bach, Hans-Peter. 1985. *Verfassungsrechtliche Grundfragen von Bildschirmtext*. PhD thesis, University of Mainz.

Badenoch, Alexander, and Fickers Andreas. 2010. Introduction: Europe materializing? Toward a transnational history of infrastructures. In *Materializing Europe: Transnational infrastructures and the Project of Europe*, ed. Alexander Badenoch and Andreas Fickers, 1–26. Basingstoke: Palgrave.

Bagnall, Brian. 2006. *On the edge: The spectacular rise and fall of Commodore*. Winnipeg: Variant Press.

Baldwin, Carliss, Eric von Hippel, and Christoph Hienerth. 2006. How user innovations become commercial products: A theoretical investigation and case study. *Research Policy* 35: 1291–1313.

Balka, Kerstin, Christina Raasch, and Cornelius Herstatt. 2009. Open source enters the world of atoms: A statistical analysis of open design. *First Monday* 14(11). Accessed 5 May 2013.

Bancroft, Ralph. 1984. What the retailers said when they looked at the spectrum. *The Times*, December 4.

Barbrook, Richard. 1987. A new way of talking: Community radio in 1980s Britain. *Science as Culture* 1(1): 81–129.

Bardini, Thierry. 2000. *Bootstrapping: Douglas Engelbart, coevolution, and the origins of personal computing*. Stanford: Stanford University Press.

Bardini, Thierry, and A.T. Horvath. 1995. The social construction of the personal computer user. *Journal of Communication* 45(3): 40–66.

Barker, Flo. 1984. Programs lighten the load of a methodist minister. *Sinclair User*, January, 102–103.

Barryman, J. 1988. The Soviet Union and Yugoslavia's defence and foreign policy. In *Yugoslavia's security dilemmas – Armed forces, national defence and foreign policy*, ed. M. Milivojevic, J.B. Allcock, and P. Maurer, 192–260. Oxford: Oxford University Press.

Bassett, Ross Knox. 2002. *To the digital age: Research labs, start-up companies, and the rise of MOS technology*. Baltimore: Johns Hopkins University Press.

Batanović, Vladan, and Jovan Kon. (ed.). 2006. *IMP Riznica znanja*. Belgrade: M. Pupin Institute and PKS.

Berners-Lee, Tim. 2000. *Weaving the Web: The original design and ultimate destiny of the World Wide Web*. New York: HarperBusiness.

Bertsch, Gary K. (ed.). 1988. *Controlling East–West trade and technology transfer: Power, politics, and policies*. Durham: Duke University Press.

Bertsch, Gary K., and Thomas W. Ganschow. 1976. *Comparative communism: The Soviet, Chinese, and Yugoslav models*. San Francisco: W.H. Freeman.

Bex*communicatie, *25 jaar .nl*. Arnhem: Stichting Internet Domeinregistratie Nederland, 2011.

Bijker, Wiebe E., Thomas P. Hughes, and Trevor J. Pinch (eds.). 1987. *The social construction of technological systems. New directions in the sociology and history of technology*. Cambridge, MA: MIT Press.

BloomBecker, Buck. 1990. *Spectacular computer crimes: What they are and how they cost American business half a billion dollars a year!* Homewood: Dow Jones-Irwin.

Blundell, Gregory S. 1983. Personal computers in the eighties. *BYTE*, January, 166–182.

Bošković, Ratko. 1984. Kako je rodjena Galaksija. *Magazine Start*, February, 25–26.

Botz, Daniel. 2011. *Kunst, Code und Maschine – Die Ästhetik der Computer-Demoszene* [Art, code and machine – The aesthetic of the computer demoscene]. Bielefeld: Transcript Verlag.

Bourne, Chris. 1984. Digging up the past. *Sinclair User*, August, 110–111.

Bourne, Chris. 1985. Fool's gold from the funny farm? *Sinclair User*, January, 138.

Brian, Bagnall. 2005. *On the edge: The spectacular rise and fall of Commodore*. Winnepeg: Variant Press.

Bronckers, R.P.N. 1986. Microcomputer buiten werktijd. *De Automatisering Gids*, November 5, 30–32.

Brunner, John. 1975. *Shockwave rider*. New York: Harper & Row.

Bubenko, Janis, John Impagliazzo, and Arne Sølvberg (eds.). 2005. *History of Nordic computing: IFIP WG9.7 first working conference on the history of Nordic computing (HiNC1), June 16–18, 2003, Trondheim, Norway*. New York: Springer.

Cain, Frank. 2005. Computers and the Cold War: United States restrictions on the export of computers to the Soviet Union and Communist China. *Journal of Contemporary History* 40(1): 131–147.

Calic, Marie-Janine. 2011. The beginning of the end: The 1970s as a historical turning point in Yugoslavia. In *The crisis of socialist modernity. The Soviet Union and Yugoslavia in the 1970s*, ed. Marie-Janine Calic, Dietmar Neutatz, and Julia Obertreis, 66–86. Göttingen: Vandenhoeck & Ruprecht.

Campbell-Kelly, Martin. 2003. *From airline reservations to sonic the Hedgehog: A history of the software industry*. Cambridge, MA/London: MIT Press.

Campbell-Kelly, Martin, William Aspray, Nathan Ensmenger, and Jeffrey R. Yost. 2014 [1996]. *Computer: A history of the information machine*. Boulder: Westview Press.

Carleer, Gerrit J., and H.D. Valkenburg. 1985. *Burgerinformatica, meer dan computers alleen, resultaat van het Landelijk Onderzoek Burgerinformatica en Evaluatie-onderzoek 100-scholenproject*. Den Haag: Ministerie van Onderwijs en Wetenschappen.

Carlsson, Anders. 2009. *The forgotten pioneers of creative hacking and social networking – Introducing the demoscene*. Paper presented at the Re:live: Media Art Histories. Conference proceedings, Melbourne.

Carr, Diane, David Buckingham, Andrew Burn, and Gareth Schott. 2006. *Computer games: Text, narrative and play*. Cambridge: Polity Press.

Castells, Manuel. 2001. *The Internet galaxy: Reflections on the Internet, business, and society*. Oxford: Oxford University Press.

Central Intelligence Agency. 1990. *World factbook*. Washington, DC: Central Intelligence Agency.

Ceruzzi, Paul E. 1996. From scientific instrument to everyday appliance: The emergence of personal computers, 1970–77. *History and Technology* 13(1): 1–31.

Ceruzzi, Paul E. 1999. Inventing personal computing. In *The social shaping of technology*, 2nd ed, ed. Donald MacKenzie and Judy Wajcman, 66–68. Buckingham: Open University Press.

Ceruzzi, Paul E. 2003 [1998]. *A history of modern computing*. Cambridge, MA/London: MIT Press.

Chandler Jr., Alfred D. 2007. *Inventing the electronic century: The epic story of the consumer electronics and computer industries*. New York: The Free Press.

Chirillo, John. 2001. *Hack attacks encyclopedia: A complete history of hacks, cracks, phreaks, and spies over time*. New York: Wiley.

Chposky, James, and Ted Leonsis. 1988. *Blue magic: The people, power and politics behind the IBM PC*. New York: Facts on File.

Cieraad, Irene. 2009. The radiant American kitchen: Domesticating Dutch nuclear energy. In *Cold War kitchen. Americanization, technology, and European users*, ed. Ruth Oldenziel and Karin Zachmann, 113–136. Cambridge, MA: MIT Press.

Cohen, Scott. 1984. *Zap! The rise and fall of Atari*. New York: McGraw-Hill.

Coleman, Gabrielle. 2010. The hacker conference. *Anthropological Quarterly* 83(1, Winter): 47–72.

COM. 2009. *Progress report on the single European electronic communications market 2007, 14th report*. 24 March 2009. Brussels: EC.

Cooke, Claudia. 1983a. User of the month: Retiring to the sea, the ship and his Sinclairs. *Sinclair User*, April, 48.

Cooke, Claudia. 1983b. User of the month: Taking the strain out of calculating wages. *Sinclair User*, August, 78–79.

Cooke, Claudia. 1983c. User of the month: Leading athletes quest for gold is boosted by ZX-81. *Sinclair User*, September, 84–85.

Cookson, Clive. 1982. The times guide to information technology. *The Times*, January 14.

Cortada, James W. 2004. *The digital hand: How computers changed the work of American manufacturing, transportation, and retail industries*. Oxford: Oxford University Press.

Cowan, Ruth Schwartz. 1987. The consumption junction: A proposal for research strategies in the sociology of technology. In *The social construction of technological systems*, ed. Wiebe E. Bijker, Thomas P. Hughes, and Trevor J. Pinch, 261–280. Cambridge, MA: MIT Press.

Cox, John K. 2005. *Slovenia: Evolving loyalties*. London: Routledge.

Cringely, Robert X. 1992. *Accidental empires: How the boys of Silicon Valley make their millions, battle foreign competition, and still can't get a date*. Reading: Addison-Wesley.

Crowley, David, and Susan E. Reid (eds.). 2002. *Socialist spaces: Sites of everyday life in the Eastern bloc*. Oxford: Berg Publishers.

Curtis, Glenn E. 1990. *Yugoslavia: A country study*. Washington, DC: Library of Congress, Federal Research Division.

Dale, Rodney. 1985. *The Sinclair story*. London: Duckworth.

Daston, Lorraine. 2009. Science studies and the history of science. *Critical Inquiry* 35(4): 798–813.

de Certeau, Michel. 1984. *The practice of everyday life*. Berkeley: University of California Press.

de Grazia, Victoria. 2005. *Irresistible empire. America's advance through twentieth-century Europe*. Cambridge, MA: Belknap Press.

de Wit, Onno. 1998. *Telefonie in Nederland 1877–1940: Opkomst en ontwikkeling van een grootschalig technisch systeem*. Amsterdam: Otto Cramwinckel.

Debord, Guy. 1977. *Society of the spectacle*. Detroit: Black & Red.

Denker, Kai. 2014. Heroes yet criminals of the German computer revolution. In *Hacking Europe. From computer cultures to demoscenes*, ed. Gerard Alberts and Ruth Oldenziel, 167–188. New York: Springer.

Department of Education and Science. 1981. *Microelectronics education program: The strategy*. London, Department of Education and Science.

Dietrich, Ralf. 2009. *Das Erfordernis der besonderen Sicherung im StGB am Beispiel des Ausspähens von Daten, [Para] 202a StGB: Kritik und spezialpräventiver Ansatz*. PhD thesis, Universitat Tübingen.

Donig, Simon. 2010. Appropriating American technology in the 1960s: Cold War politics and the GDR computer industry. *IEEE Annals of the History of Computing* 32(2): 32–45.

Douglas, Susan J. 2004 [1999]. *Listening in: Radio and the American imagination*. Minneapolis: University of Minnesota Press.

Dulić, Tornislav, and Roland Kostić. 2010. Yugoslavs in arms: Guerrilla tradition, total defence and the ethnic security dilemma. *Europe-Asia Studies* 62(7): 1051–1072.

Dunbar-Hester, Christina. 2009. 'Free the spectrum!' Activist encounters with old and new media technology. *New Media & Society* 11(1–2): 221–240.

Durnová, Helena. 2010. Sovietization of Czechoslovakian computing: The rise and fall of the SAPO project. *IEEE Annals of the History of Computing* 32(2): 21–31.

Duivenvoorden, Eric. 2000. *Een voet tussen de deur. Geschiedenis van de kraakbeweging 1964–1999*. Amsterdam: De Arbeiderspers.

Dybowski, Klaudiusz, and Michał Silski. 1986. Maniak. *Bajtek*, May–June, 30.

Eckoldt, Thilo. 1988. Hacker-mit einem Bein im Knast. In *Das Chaos Computer Buch. Hacking made in Germany*, ed. Jürgen Wieckmann, 154–167. Reinbek bei Hamburg: Wunderlich.

Economist. 1984. Yugoslavia. In *The world in figures*, 240–242. London: MacMillan.

Edgerton, David. 2006. *The shock of the old: Technology and global history since 1900*. London: Profile Books.

Edwards, Paul N. 1996. *The closed world: Computers and the politics of discourse in Cold War America*. Cambridge, MA: MIT Press.

Elfimov, Konstantin. 2008. Brief history of Russian Speccy demoscene and the story of Inward. *Mustekala Kulttuurilehti* [online journal]. http://www.mustekala.info/node/35580. Accessed 30 Jan 2014.

Enzensberger, Hans Magnus. 1970. Baukasten zu einer Theorie der Medien. In *Kursbuch*, 20(1970): 159–186.

Ernst, Stefan. 2007. Das neue Computerstrafrecht. *Neue Juristische Wochenschrift* 37: 2661–2666.

Evans, Christopher. 1979. *The mighty micro: The impact of the computer revolution*. London: Victor Gollancz.

Fickers, Andreas, and Suzanne Lommers. 2010. Eventing Europe: Broadcasting and the mediated performances of Europe. In *Materializing Europe: Transnational infrastructures and the Project of Europe*, ed. Alexander Badenoch and Andreas Fickers, 225–251. Basingstoke: Palgrave.

Flint, Joost. 2004. *DDS – 10 jaar anders*. http://www.dds.nl/downloads/achtergrondartikel.pdf. Accessed 16 July 2011.

Flyvbjerg, Bent. 2006. Five misunderstandings about case-study research. *Qualitative Inquiry* 12(2): 219–245.

Frasca, Gonzalo. 2003. Simulation vs. narrative: Introduction to ludology. In *The video game theory reader*, ed. J.P. Mark Wolf and Bernard Perron, 221–236. London: Routledge.

Frasca, Gonzalo. 2007. *Play the message: Play, game and videogame rhetoric*. PhD thesis, University of Copenhagen.

Freiberger, Paul, and Michael Swaine. 1999. *Fire in the valley: The making of the personal computer*. Berkeley: Osborne/McGraw-Hill.

Frey, Franco. 1984. Dk'tronics revisited. *Crash*, October, 52–53.

Friesinger, Manfred. 1989. *Bildschirmtext in Frankreich*. Munich: Fischer.

Gates, Bill. 1976. Open letter to hobbyists. *Homebrew Computer Club Newsletter* (Letter dated February 3, 1976). http://en.wikipedia.org/wiki/Open_Letter_to_Hobbyists. Accessed 31 Dec 2011.

Gates, Bill. 1995. *De weg die voor ons ligt*. Amsterdam: Meulenhoff.

Gates III, William H. 1995. *The road ahead*. New York: Penguin.

Gibson, William. 1984. *Neuromancer*. New York: Ace Books.

Gillies, Constantin. 2003. *Wie wir waren: die wilden Jahre der Web-Generation*. Weinheim: Wiley-VCH.

Glennie, Paul. 1995. Consumption within historical studies. In *Acknowledging consumption: A review of new studies*, ed. Daniel Miller, 164–203. London/New York: Routledge.

Glettler, Monika. 1982. The organization of the Czech clubs in Vienna circa 1900: A national minority in an imperial capital. *East Central Europe* 9(1): 124–136.

Gowling Marketing Services. 1984. *The attitudes of parents and children to home computers and software*. Liverpool: Gowling Marketing Services.

Guerreiro-Wilson, Robbie, Lars Heide, Matthias Kipping, Cecilia Pahlberg, Adrienne van den Bogaard, and Aristotle Tympas. 2004. Information systems and technology in organizations and society (ISTOS): Review essay. In *Tensions of Europe. Network first plenary conference proceedings*, ed. Johan Schot, et al., Budapest, Hungary (CD-ROM). [Also accessible as: Tensions of Europe Working Paper http://www.tensionsofeurope.eu/www/en/files/get/Review_IT_Guerreiro.pdf. Accessed 30 Jan 2014]

Haddon, Leslie G. 1988a. The home computer: The making of a consumer electronic. *Science as Culture* 2: 7–51.

Haddon, Leslie G. 1988b. *The roots and early history of the British home computer market: Origins of the masculine micro*. PhD thesis, University of London.

Haddon, Leslie. 1990. Researching gender and home computers. In *Technology and everyday life: Trajectories and transformations*, ed. Knut Sørensen and Anne-Jorn Berg, 89–108. Trondheim: University of Trondheim.

Haddon, Leslie. 1992. Explaining ICT consumption: The case of the home computer. In *Consuming technologies: Media and information in domestic spaces*, ed. R. Silverstone and E. Hirsch, 82–96. London: Routledge.

Haddon, Leslie, Enid Mante-Meijer, Bartolomeo Sapio, Kari-Hans Kommonen, Leopoldina Fortunati, and Annevi Kant (eds.). 2005. *Everyday innovators: Researching the role of users in shaping ICTs*. Dordrecht: Springer.

Hafner, Katie. 1997. The epic saga of the well. *Wired Magazine* 5(5, May). http://www.wired.com/wired/archive/5.05/ff_well_pr.html. Accessed 27 Sept 2014.

Hafner, Katie, and John Markoff. 1991. *Cyberpunk: Outlaws and hackers on the computer frontier*. London: Touchstone.

Haft, Fritjof. 1987. Das Zweite Gesetze zur Bekämpfung der Wirtschaftskriminalität. *Neue Juristische Wochenschrift* 1: 6–9.

Hammond, Thomas Taylor. 1954. *Yugoslavia between East and West*. Washington, DC: Foreign Policy Association.

Hanneke. 1993. Wet computercriminaliteit. *Hack-Tic* 20–21(1993): 4–11.

Hapnes, Tove. 1996. Not in their machines: How hackers transform computers into subcultural artefacts. In *Making technology our own? Domesticating technology into everyday life*, ed. Lie Merete and Knut H. Sørensen, 121–150. Oslo/Stockholm/Copenhagen/Oxford/Boston: Scandinavian University Press.

Haring, Kristen. 2007. *Ham radio's technical culture*. Cambridge, MA: MIT Press.

Heritage, John. 1984. Sinclair business user: A systematic start. *Sinclair User*, July, 120.

Himanen, Pekka. 2001. *The hacker ethic: A radical approach to the philosophy of business*. New York: Random House.

Hodges, Lucy. 1985. Average school has nine micros. *The Times*, January 25.

Holland, Wau, et al. (eds.). 1985. *Die Hackerbibel*. Löhrbach: Pieper Werner Medienexp.

Horkheimer, Max. 1974. *Critique of instrumental reason*. New York: Seabury Press.

Huizinga, Johan. 1949 [1938]. *Homo ludens: A study of the play-element in culture*. London: Routledge & Kegan Paul.

Hyysalo, Sampsa. 2009. Figuring technologies, users and designers – Steps towards an adequate vocabulary for design–use relation. In *Use of science and technology in business: Exploring the impact of using activity for systems, organizations, and people*, ed. Frans Prenkert, Enrico Baraldi, Håkan Håkansson, and Alexandra Waluszewski, 291–313. Bingley: Emerald Publishing Group.

Impagliazzo, John, Timo Jrvi, and Petri Paju (eds.). 2009. *History of Nordic computing 2: Second IFIP WG 9.7 conference, HiNC 2, Turku, Finland, August 21–23, 2007, revised selected papers*. New York: Springer.

Irek, Małgorzata. 1998. *Schmugglerzug Warschau-Berlin-WarschMaterialien einer Feldforschung*. Berlin: Das Arabische Buch.

Irwin, John. 1977. *Scenes*, 23. London: Sage.

Jacobs, Marc A. 1993. *Software kopen of kopiëren? Een sociaal- wetenschappelijk onderzoek onder pc-gebruikers*. Den Haag: [s.n.].

Jakić, Bruno. 2014. Galaxy and the new wave: Yugoslav computer culture in 1980s. In *Hacking Europe. From computer cultures to demoscenes*, ed. Gerard Alberts and Ruth Oldenziel, 107–128. New York: Springer.

Jamison, Andrew, and Mikael Hård. 2003. The storylines of technological change: Innovation, construction and appropriation. *Technology Analysis & Strategic Management* 15(1): 81–91.

Janjatović, Petar. 1998. *Ilustrovana Enciklopedija Yu Rocka 1960–1997*. Belgrade: Geopoetika.

Jankowski, Nick. 1988. *Community television in Amsterdam access to participation in and use of the "Lokale Omroep Bijlmermeer"*. Amsterdam: Amsterdam University Press.

Janssen, Hans G. 1982. In *Basicode*, ed. N.O.S. Hobbyscoop. Hilversum: Nederlandse Omroep Stichting.

Janssen, Hans G. 1984. In *Basicode-2*, ed. N.O.S. Hobbyscoop. Hilversum: Nederlandse Omroep Stichting.

Jędrzejewski, Marek. 1987. Gdykomputer jest bożkiem [When a computer becomes an idol]. *Argumenty*, September 27, 12.

Jenkinson, Paul. 2007. *Spectrum hardware page*. http://www.worldofspectrum.org/hardware/. Accessed 15 Oct 2007.

Johns, Adrian. 2009. Piracy as a business force. *Culture Machine* 10, 44–63. Accessed 5 May 2013.

Johns, Adrian. 2010. *Death of a pirate: British radio and the making of the information age*. New York: W. W. Norton & Company.

Johnson, J. 1983. Letters: Illustrations waste space. *Sinclair User*, June, 17.

Johnstone, Bill. 1984. More small firms buy computers. *The Times*, June 14.

Jordan, Tim, and Paul A. Taylor. 2004. *Hacktivism and cyberwars. Rebels with a cause?* London: Routledge.

Kaiserfeld, Thomas. 1996. Computerizing the Swedish welfare state: The middle way of technological success and failure. *Technology and Culture* 37(2): 249–279.

Kaps, Rolf Ulrich. 1983. *Die Wirkung von Bildschirmtext auf das Informationsverhalten der Konsumenten*, Schriftenreihe der Studiengruppe Bildschirmtext. Gröbenzell: Fischer.

Kent, Steven L. 2001. *The ultimate history of video games: From Pong to Pokémon and beyond: The story behind the craze that touched our lives and changed the world.* New York: Three Rivers Press.

Kera, Denisa. 2012. Hackerspaces and DIY-bio in Asia: Connecting science and community with open data, kits and protocols. *Journal of Peer Production* 1(2), 1–8. http://peerproduction.net/issues/issue-2/peer-reviewed-papers/diybio-in-asia/. Accessed 5 May 2013.

Kidder, Tracy. 1981. *The soul of a new machine*. Boston: Little Brown.

King, Brad, and John Borland. 2003. *Dungeons and dreamers. The rise of computer game culture from geek to chic*. New York: McGraw-Hill.

Kipping, Mattias, and Ove Bjarnar (eds.). 1998. *The Americanisation of European business. The Marshall plan and the transfer of US management models*. London: Routledge.

Klaver, Marie-José. 1998. De Digitale Vluchtweg. *NRC Handelsblad*, October 29.

Klaver, Marie-José. 1999. Boem, boem uit de chatroom. *NRC Handelsblad*, May 17.

Kleve, P., R.V. Mulder, and C. van Noortwijk. 2010. ICT Criminaliteit. In *Criminaliteit en criminaliteitsbestrijding in Nederland*, ed. Erwin Roelof Muller, et al., 259–288. Deventer: Kluwer.

Kling, Rob, and C. Suzanne Iacono. 1995. Computerization movements and the mobilization of support for computerization. In *Ecologies of knowledge. Work and politics in science and technology*, ed. Susan Leigh Star, 119–153. Albany: State University of New York Press.

Kloosterman, A.M., H.J. Rossel, and J.P. van Stempvoort. 2008. *Hoofdlijnen in het huurrecht: met vragen en antwoorden*. Deventer: Kluwer.

Klvač, Pavel, et al. (ed.). 2007. *Na tom našem dvoře Kličova*. Prague: KSB.

Koch, Karel. 1992. Introduction: The camcorder revolution. In *N5M Zapbook: Working papers*, ed. Jeroen van Bergeijk, Geke van Dijk, Karel Koch, and Bas Raimakers, 29. Amsterdam: Paradiso.

Kornfeld, Lewis. 1992 [1983]. *To catch a mouse: Make a noise like a cheese*, Revs. and 3rd ed. Fort Worth: The Summit Publishing Group.

Kornfeld, Lewis. 1997. *To catch a mouse make a noise like a cheese*. Irving: The Summit Publishing Group.

Krige, John. 2006. *American hegemony and the postwar reconstruction of science in Europe*. Cambridge, MA: MIT Press.

Krige, John. 2008. The peaceful atom as political weapon: Euratom and American foreign policy in the late 1950s. *Historical Studies in the Natural Sciences* 38(1): 5–44.

Kriwaczek, Paul. 1997. *Documentary for the small screen*. Oxford: Focal Press.

Kromrey, Helmut, et al. 1984. *Bochumer Untersuchung im Rahmen der wissenschaftlichen Begleitung des Feldversuchs Bildschirmtext Düsseldorf/Neuss*. Bochum: Ruhr-Universität.

Kuhlmann, Wolf-Dieter. 1985. *Rechtsfragen des Bildschirmtext-Staatsvertrages vom 18. März 1983*. PhD thesis, Universität Bochum.

Kuisel, Richard F. 1993. *Seducing the French: The dilemma of Americanization*. Berkeley: University of California Press.

Kulla, Daniel. 2003. *Der Phrasenprüfer. Szenen aus dem Leben von Wau Holland*. Löhrbach: Pieper and the Grüne Kraft.

Kushner, David. 2003. *Masters of doom. How two guys created an empire and transformed pop culture*. New York: Random House.

Large, Peter. 1984. Indian summer of cheaper micro. *The Guardian*, December 20.

Latour, Bruno. 1992. Where are the hidden masses. Sociology of a few mundane artifacts. In *Shaping technology/building society: Studies in sociotechnical change*, ed. Wiebe E. Bijker and John Law, 225–258. Cambridge, MA: MIT Press.

Latour, Bruno. 2005. *Reassembling the social: An introduction to actor-network-theory*. Oxford: Oxford University Press.

Law, John. 1991. *A sociology of monsters: Essays on power, technology and domination*. New York: Routledge.

Lean, Thomas. 2004. *'What would I do with a computer?' The shaping of the Sinclair computer 1980–1986*. MA thesis, University of Kent.

Lean, Thomas. 2008a. From mechanical brains to microcomputers: Representations of the computer in Britain 1948–1984. In *Science and its publics*, ed. A. Bell, S. Davies, and F. Mellor, 179–200. Newcastle: Cambridge Scholars Publishing.

Lean, Thomas. 2008b. *'The making of the micro': Producers, mediators, users and the development of popular microcomputing in Britain (1980–1989)*. PhD thesis, University of Manchester.

Lean, Thomas. 2012. Mediating the microcomputer: The educational character of the 1980s British popular computing room. *Public Understanding of Science*, first published online on 30 October 2012 as doi:10.1177/0963662512457904.

Lean, Thomas. 2014. 'Inside a day you'll be talking to it like an old friend': The making and remaking of Sinclair personal computing in 1980s Britain. In *Hacking Europe. From computer cultures to demoscenes*, ed. Gerard Alberts and Ruth Oldenziel, 49–71. New York: Springer.

Lécuyer, Christophe. 2005. *Making Silicon Valley: Innovation and the growth of high tech, 1930–1970*. Cambridge, MA: MIT Press.

Lehtonen, Turo-Kimmo. 2003. The domestication of new technologies as a set of trials. *Journal of Consumer Culture* 3(3): 363–385.

Lekkas, Theodore. 2014. Legal Pirates Ltd: Greek home computing cultures in early 1980s Greece. In *Hacking Europe: From computer cultures to demoscenes*, ed. Gerard Alberts and Ruth Oldenziel, 73–103. New York: Springer.

Levy, Steven. 1984. *Hackers: Heroes of the computer revolution*. Garden City, NY: Anchor Press/Doubleday.

Levy, Steven. 2010. *Hackers: Heroes of the computer revolution – 25th anniversary edition*. Sebastopol: O'Reilly Media.

Lindsay, Christina. 2003. From the shadows: Users as designers, producers, marketers, distributors, and technical support. In *How users matter: The co-construction of users and technology*, ed. Nelly Oudshoorn and Trevor J. Pinch, 29–50. Cambridge, MA: MIT Press.

Lipartito, Kenneth. 2003. Picturephone and the information age: The social meaning of failure. *Technology and Culture* 44(1): 50–81.

Lönnblad, H. 1997. Kahden tietokonedemon vertaileva analyysi [A comparative study of two computer demos]. *Musiikin Suunta* 19(2): 28–34. http://www.kameli.net/demoresearch2/.

Lovink, Geert. 1992. The theory of mixing: An inventory of free radio techniques in Amsterdam. *Mediamatic Magazine* 6(4). http://www.mediamatic.net/page/5750/en?lang=en. Accessed 21 May 2011.

Lovink, Geert. 1995. *'Listen Or Die': A history of the punk hard core pirate station 'Radio Death', Amsterdam 1985–1987*. Bilwet. http://thing.desk.nl/bilwet/TXT/DOOD.ENG.txt. Last accessed 27 Sept 2011.

Lovink, Geert, Rik Delhaas, and Laura Martz. 1991. *Wetware*. Amsterdam: De Balie.

Lubar, Steven. 1992. 'Do not fold, spindle or mutilate': A cultural history of the punched card. *Journal of American Culture* 15(4): 43–55.

Lubar, Steven. 1993. *Infoculture. The Smithsonian book of information age inventions*. Boston/ New York: Houghton Mifflin Company.
Lydall, Harold. 1989. *Yugoslavia in crisis*. Oxford: Clarendon.
Mackay, Hughie, and Gareth Gillespie. 1992. Extending the social shaping of technology approach: Ideology and appropriation. *Social Studies of Science* 22(4): 685–716.
MacKenzie, Donald A., and Judy Wajcman. 1985. *The social shaping of technology: How the refrigerator got its hum*. Milton Keynes: Open University Press.
Maines, Rachel P. 2009. *Hedonzing technologies. Paths to pleasure in hobbies and leisure*. Baltimore: Johns Hopkins University Press.
Marcus, Greil. 1990. *Lipstick traces: A secret history of the twentieth century*. Cambridge, MA: Harvard University Press.
Marcus, Greil. 2001 [1989]. *Lipstick traces: A secret history of the twentieth century*. London: Faber & Faber.
Marcuse, Herbert. 1964. *One-dimensional man*. Boston: Beacon Press.
Markoff, John W. 2005. *What the dormouse said: How the 60s counterculture shaped the personal computer*. New York: Viking.
Markovic, Nikola. 2009. E-Potencijali Srbije nr1. *CEPiT E-volucija*, 3–11. Belgrade: Studeni.
Marković, Predrag. 2011. 'Where have all the flowers gone?' – Yugoslav culture in the 1970s. In *The crisis of socialist modernity. The Soviet Union and Yugoslavia in the 1970s*, ed. Marie-Janine Calic, Dietmar Neutatz, and Julia Obertreis, 118–133. Göttingen: Vandenhoeck & Ruprecht.
Martin, C.D. 1993. The myth of the awesome thinking machine. *Communications of the ACM* 36(4): 120–133.
Mastanduno, Michael. 1992. *Economic containment: CoCom and the politics of East–West trade*. Ithaca: Cornell University Press.
Maxigas. 2012. Hacklabs and hackerspaces: Tracing two genealogies. *Journal of Peer Production* 1(2), 1–10. http://peerproduction.net/issues/issue-2/peer-reviewed-papers/hacklabs-and-hackerspaces/. Accessed 5 May 2013.
Mäyrä, F. 2002. Introduction: All your [base are] belong to us. In *Computer games and digital cultures conference proceedings studies in information sciences*, 5–8. Tampere: Tampere University Press.
McDonald, Christopher. 2010. Technology in the political landscape. *IEEE Annals of the History of Computing* 32(2): 87–88.
McNeil, Maureen. 1991. The old and new world of information technology in Britain. In *Enterprise and heritage: Crosscurrents of national culture*, ed. John Corner and Sylvia Harvey, 120–124. London: Routledge.
Mesarić, Milan. 1971. *Suvremena znanstveno tehnička revolucija*. Zagreb: Ekonomski Institut.
Miller, Daniel. 1995. *Acknowledging consumption: A review of new studies*. London: Routledge.
Misa, Thomas J. (ed.). 2010. *Gender codes: Why women are leaving computing*. Hoboken: Wiley.
Misa, Thomas J., and Johan Schot. 2005. Inventing Europe: Technology and the hidden integration of Europe. *History and Technology* 21: 1–19.
Misina, Dalibor. 2008. *'Who's that singing over there?' Yugoslav rock-music and the poetics of social critique*. PhD thesis, University of Alberta, Alberta.
Modli, Zoran. 2011. *Ventilator 202 recollections*. http://www.modli.rs/radio/ventilator/ventilator.html. Accessed 20 Feb 2011.
Mollema, Kornelis I.J., et al. 1993. *Computercriminaliteit: De wetgeving, de gevolgen voor bedrijven en de accountant*. Deventer: Kluwer.
Moody, Fred. 1999. *The visionary position. The inside story of the digital dreamers who are making virtual reality a reality*. New York: Times Business.
Moritz, Michael. 1984. *The little kingdom: The private story of Apple computer*. New York: W. Morrow.
Morton, David L. 2000. *Off the record: The technology and culture of sound recording in America*. New Brunswick: Rutgers University Press.
Müller-Maguhn, Andy, and Reinhard Schrutzki. 1988. Welcome to the NASA-headquarter. In *Das Chaos Computer Buch. Hacking made in Germany*, ed. Jürgen Wieckmann, 32–53. Reinbek bei Hamburg: Wunderlich.

Nelson, Mark M. 1989. Nerds of the world unite – And defend their right to hack. *Wall Street Journal Europe*, August 7.

Nevejan, Caroline. 2007. *Presence and the design of trust*. PhD thesis, University of Amsterdam.

Nevejan, Caroline, and Alexander Badenoch. 2014. How Amsterdam invented the Internet: European networks of significance, 1980–1995. In *Hacking Europe. From computer cultures to demoscenes*, ed. Gerard Alberts and Ruth Oldenziel, 189–217. New York: Springer.

New Scientist Technology Review. 1971. Yugoslavia Grows Ripe for computer boom. *New Scientist and Science Journal* 51(768): 576.

Nissen, Jörgen. 1993. *Pojkarna vid datorn: Unga entusiaster i datateknikens värld* [Boys in front of computers. Young enthusiasts in the world of computer technology]. PhD thesis, Lynköping Universitet.

Nora, Simon, and Alain Minc. 1978. *L'informatisation de la société: rapport à M. le Président de la République*. Paris: La Documentation française.

Norberg, Arthur L. 2005. *Computers and commerce: A study of technology and management at Eckert-Mauchly Computer Company, Engineering Research Associates, and Remington Rand, 1946–1957*. Cambridge, MA: MIT Press.

Nordli, Hege. 2003. *The net is not enough: Searching for the female hacker*. Trondheim: Norwegian University of Science and Technology.

Oldenziel, Ruth. 2001. Woman the consumer: The consumption junction revisited. In *Feminism in twentieth-century science, technology and medicine*, ed. Angela N.H. Creager, Elizabeth Lunbeck, and Londa Schiebinger, 128–148. Chicago: Chicago University Press.

Oldenziel, Ruth, and Adri Albert de la Bruhèze. 2009. Theorizing the mediation junction for technology and consumption. In *Manufacturing technology, manufacturing consumers. The making of Dutch consumer society*, ed. Adri Albert de la Bruhèze and Ruth Oldenziel, 9–40. Amsterdam: Aksant.

Oldenziel, Ruth, and Mikael Hård. 2013. *Users, tinkerers, rebels. The people who shaped Europe*. London: Palgrave.

Oldenziel, Ruth, and Karin Zachmann (eds.). 2009. *Cold War kitchen. Americanization, technology, and European users*. Cambridge, MA: MIT Press.

Oldenziel, Ruth, Adri Albert de la Bruhèze, and Onno de Wit. 2005. Europe's mediation junction: Technology and consumer society in the twentieth century. *History and Technology* 21(1): 107–139.

Oost, Ellen, Stephan Verhaegh, and Nelly Oudshoorn. 2009. From innovation community to community innovation: User-initiated innovation in wireless Leiden. *Science, Technology & Human Values* 34(184): 182–205.

Ortiz-Arroyo, D., F. Rodriguez-Henriquez, and C.A. Coello. 2010. The turing-850 project: Developing a personal computer in the early 1980s in Mexico. *IEEE Annals of the History of Computing* 32(4): 60–71.

Oudshoorn, Nelly. 1996. Genderscripts in technologie: Noodlot of uitdaging? *Tijdschrift voor Vrouwenstudies* 17(4): 350–368.

Oudshoorn, Nelly, and Trevor J. Pinch (eds.). 2003a. *How users matter. The co-construction of users and technology*. Cambridge, MA: MIT Press.

Oudshoorn, Nelly, and Trevor J. Pinch. 2003b. How users and non-users matter. In *How users matter: The co-construction of users and technology*, ed. Nelly Oudshoorn and Trevor J. Pinch, 1–28. Cambridge, MA: MIT Press.

Owen, Kenneth. 1978. Microelectronics: This could be man's greatest leap forward. *The Times*, October 10.

Owen, Chris. 2010. *Planet Sinclair: Clones and variants*. http://www.nvg.ntnu.no/sinclair/computers/clones/clones.htm. Accessed 10 Jan 2010.

Paju, Petri, and Helena Durnová. 2009. Computing close to the iron curtain: Inter/national computing practices in Czechoslovakia and Finland. *Comparative Technology Transfer and Society* 7(3): 303–322.

Parr, Joy. 1997. What makes washday less blue? Gender, nation, and technology choice in postwar Canada. *Technology and Culture* 38(1): 153–186.

Patterson, Patrick H. 2003. *Consumer culture, the new 'New Class,' and the making of the Yugoslav dream, 1950–1965*. Paper presented at states and social transformation in Eastern Europe 1945–1965. London: The Open University Conference Center.

Patterson, Patrick H. 2006. Dangerous liaisons: Soviet-bloc tourists and the Yugoslav good life in the 1960s and 1970s. In *The business of tourism: Place, faith and history*, ed. Philip Scranton and Janet F. Davidson, 186–212. Philadelphia: University of Pennsylvania Press.

Patterson, Patrick H. 2009. Making markets Marxist? The East European grocery store from rationing to rationality to rationalizations. In *Food chains: From farmyard to shopping cart*, ed. Warren Belasco and Roger Horowitz, 196–216. Philadelphia: University of Pennsylvania Press.

Pearson, Jamie Parke. 1992. *Digital at work: Snapshots from the first thirty-five years*. Burlington: Digital Press.

Pells, Richard. 1997. *Not like us: How Europeans have loved, hated, and transformed American culture since World War II*. New York: Basic Books.

Perry, Marvin, Myrna Chase, Margaret C. Jacob, et al. 2007. *Western civilization: Ideas, politics, and society*. Boston: Wadsworth.

Pestre, Dominique. 2004. Thirty years of science studies: Knowledge, society and the political. *History and Technology: An International Journal* 20(4): 351–369.

Pestre, Dominique. 2013. *À contre-science – Politique et savoirs des sociétés contemporaines*. Paris: Seuil.

Péteri, György (ed.). 2006. *Nylon curtain. Transnational and transsystematic tendencies in the cultural life of state-socialist Russia and East-Central Europe*, vol. 18. Trondheim: TSEECS.

Péteri, György (ed.). 2010. *Imagining the West in Eastern Europe and the Soviet Union*. Pittsburgh: University of Pittsburgh Press.

Pfadenhauer, Michaela. 2005. Ethnography of scenes: Towards a sociological life-world analysis of (post-traditional) community-building. *Forum: Qualitative Sozialforschung/Forum: Qualitative Social Research* 6(3): 1–15.

Pinch, Trevor J., and Wiebe E. Bijker. 1984. The social construction of facts and artefacts: Or how the sociology of science and the sociology of technology might benefit each other. *Social Studies of Science* 14(August): 399–441.

Polgár, Tamás. 2005. *Freax. The brief history of the demoscene*, vol. 1. Winnenden: CSW Verlag.

Polgár, Tamás. 2008. *The brief history of the computer demoscene*. Berlin: CSW Verlag.

Poppe, Ine, and Sandra Rottenberg. 2000. *De KRAAKgeneratie*. Amsterdam: De Balie.

Portes, Alejandro, Manuel Castells, and Lauren A. Benton (eds.). 1995. *The informal economy: Studies in advanced and less developed countries*. Baltimore: John Hopkins University Press.

Pospischil, Rudolf. 1987. *Bildschirmtext in Frankreich und Deutschland: Grundlagen u. Konzeptionen*. Nürnberg: Verlag der Kommunikationswissenschaftlichen Forschungsvereinigung.

Potter, William C., Djuro Miljanić, and Ivo Slaus. 2000. Tito's nuclear legacy. *Bulletin of the Atomic Scientists* 56(2): 63–70.

Poznański, Roman. 1985. Informatyka na Perskim [Informatics on the Persian Bazaar]. *Bajtek*, October, 24–25.

Proctor, Alan. 1984. Sinclair business user: ZX-81 in the antique shop. *Sinclair User*, November, 163–164.

Projectgroep Burgerinformatica. 1985. *Burgerinformatica of informatiekunde*. Enschede: Stichting voor de Leerplanontwikkeling.

Protić, Jelica, and Dejan Ristanović. 2011. Building computers in Serbia: The first half of the digital century. *Computer Science and Information Systems* 8(3): 549–571.

Pugh, Emerson W. 1995. *Building IBM: Shaping an industry and its technology*. Cambridge, MA: MIT Press.

Rabeharisoa, Vololona, and Michel Callon. 2003. Research 'in the Wild' and the shaping of new social identities. *Technology in Society* 25(2): 193–204.

Radcliffe, John, and Robert Salkeld. 1983. *Towards computer literacy: The BBC computer literacy project*. London: BBC Education.

Ramet, Sabrina P. 2006. *The three Yugoslavias: State-building and legitimation, 1918–2005*. Bloomington: University of Indiana Press.

Rehn, Alf. 2001. *Electronic potlatch – A study on new technologies and primitive economic behaviors*. Stockholm: Royal Institute of Technology.

Rehn, Alf. 2004. The politics of contraband – The honor economies of the warez scene. *Journal of Socio-Economics* 33(3): 359–374.

Reid, Susan E., and David Crowley (eds.). 2000. *Style and socialism. Modernity and material culture in post-war eastern Europe*. Oxford/New York: Berg Publishers.

Reunanen, Markku. 2010. *Computer demos – What makes them tick?*. Licentiate thesis, Aalto University School of Science and Technology, Helsinki.

Reunanen, Markku, and Antti Silvast. 2009. Demoscene platforms: A case study on the adoption of home computers. In *History of Nordic computing 2*, IFIP advances in information and communication technology, ed. John Impagliazzo, Timo Järvi, and Petri Paju, 289–301. Berlin: Springer.

Rimmer, Bryan. 1978. Tomorrow's world. In the eye of a needle. *Daily Mirror*, September 21.

Rodney, Dale. 1985. *The Sinclair story*. London: Duckworth.

Rogers, Everett M. 2003. *Diffusion of innovations*, 5th ed. New York: Free Press.

Rommes, Els. 2002. *Gender scripts and the Internet: The design and use of Amsterdam's digital city*. PhD thesis, University Twente.

Rooker, G.A. 1983. Letters: Technical uses need promoting. *Sinclair User*, October, 19.

Rosen, Margit. 2011. *A little-known story about a movement, a magazine, and the computer's arrival in art; New tendencies and bit international, 1961–1973*. Cambridge, MA: MIT Press.

Rothstein, Robert L. 1968. *Alliances and small powers*. New York: Columbia University Press.

Rudolf, Ralf. 1988. Erste Eindrücke zum CCC Congress '88. *Die Datenschleuder* 28–29(1988) at http://www.offiziere.ch/trust-us/ds/28/010_Erste_Eindruecke.html. Last accessed July 2011.

Rustema, Reinder. 2001. *The rise and fall of DDS*. MA thesis, University of Amsterdam.

Saarikoski, Petri. 2004. *Koneen lumo. Mikrotietokoneharrastus Suomessa 1970-luvulta 1990-luvun puoliväliin* [The Lure of the machine. The personal computer interest in Finland from the 1970s to the mid-1990s]. Nykykulttuurin tutkimuskeskuksen julkaisuja 83. Jyväskylä: Jyväskylän yliopisto.

Saarikoski, Petri. 2005. Club activity in the early phases of microcomputing in Finland. In *History of Nordic computing*, ed. Janis Bubenko, John Impagliazzo, and Arne Sølvberg, 277–287. Berlin: Springer.

Saarikoski, Petri, and Jaakko Suominen. 2009. Computer hobbyists and the gaming industry in Finland. *IEEE Annals of the History of Computing* 31(3): 20–33.

Sandvig, Christian. 2004. An initial assessment of cooperative action in Wi-Fi networking. *Telecommunications Policy* 28(7–8): 579–602.

Schot, Johan, and Adri Albert de la Bruhèze. 2003. The mediated design of products, consumption and consumers in the twentieth century. In *How users matter: The co-construction of users and technology*, ed. Nelly Oudshoorn and Trevor J. Pinch, 229–246. Cambridge, MA/London: MIT Press.

Segaller, Stephen. 1998. *Nerds 2.0.1: A brief history of the Internet*. New York: TV Books.

Selwyn, Neil. 2002. Learning to love the micro: The discursive construction of educational computing in the UK, 1979–89. *British Journal of Sociology of Education* 23: 427–443.

Serge, Nicola. 1984. User of the month: Paddle your own canoe with the ZX81. *Sinclair User*, February, 58–59.

Shah, Sonali. 2006. Open beyond software. In *Open sources 2.0 – The continuing evolution*, ed. Chris DiBona, Danese Cooper, and Mark Stone, 339–360. Beijing: O'Reilly.

Shurkin, Joel N. 2006. *Broken genius: The rise and fall of William Shockley, creator of the electronic age*. London/New York: Palgrave Macmillan.

Sieber, Ulrich. 1977. *Computerkriminalität und Strafrecht*. Köln: Heymann.

Silvast, Antti, and Markku Reunanen. 2010. The demoscene – An overview. Editorial for the *Rhizome* special issue on the demoscene, 17 May 2010.

Silvast, Antti, and Markku Reunanen. 2014. Multiple users, diverse users: Demoscene and the appropriation of the personal computer. In *Hacking Europe. From computer cultures to demoscenes*, ed. Gerard Alberts and Ruth Oldenziel, 151–163. New York: Springer.

Silverstone, Roger, and Eric Hirsch. 1992. *Consuming technologies: Media and information in domestic spaces*. London: Routledge.

Siwiński, Waldemar. 1989. Poza priorytetem [Outside the priority]. *Bajtek*, March, 2.

Skinner, David Ian. 1992. *Technology, consumption and the future: The experience of home computing*. PhD thesis, Brunel University.

Slater, Don. 2003. Modernity under construction: Building the Internet in Trinidad. In *Modernity and technology*, ed. Philip Brey, Thomas J. Misa, and Andrew Feenberg, 139–160. Cambridge, MA: MIT Press.

Smith, Merritt Roe, and Leo Marx. 1994. *Does technology drive history? The dilemma of technological determinism*. Cambridge, MA: MIT Press.

Söderberg, Johan. 2014. Users in the dark: The Development of user-controlled technology in the Czech Wireless Network Community. In *Hacking Europe. From computer cultures to demoscenes*, ed. Gerard Alberts and Ruth Oldenziel, 219–239. New York: Springer.

Söderberg, Johan, and Adam Netzén. 2010. When all that is theory melts into (hot) air: Contrasts and parallels between actor network theory, autonomist Marxism, and open Marxism. *Ephemera: Theory & Politics in Organization* 10(2): 95–118.

Sołtysiński, Paweł. 1992. Na dobry początek… [To make a good start…]. *Kebab*, January, 2.

Sotamaa, O. 2005. Creative user-centred design practices: Lessons from game cultures. In *Everyday innovators: Researching the role of users in shaping ICTs,* ed. Leslie Haddon et al., 104–116. Dordrecht: Springer.

Spufford, Francis. 2004. *Backroom boys*. London: Faber and Faber.

Stappers, James, Frank Olderaan, and Pieter de Wit. 1991. The Netherlands: Emergence of a new medium. In *The people's voice: Local radio and television in Europe*, ed. Nick Jankowski, Ole Prehn, and James Stappers, 90–103. London: John Libbey.

Stolte, Dirk. 1983. *Personalsuche und Personalvermittlung mit Bildschirmtext*, Schriftenreihe der Studiengruppe Bildschirmtext. Gröbenzell bei München: Fischer.

Sumner, J. 2003. *The mighty microcosm: Home computers and user identity in Britain, 1980–90.* Paper presented to the annual meeting of the Society for the History of Technology, Atlanta, GA, Oct 2003.

Sumner, James. 2005. Retrieving micro histories: The strange case of the domestic microcomputer. Paper presented to University College London seminar series, London.

Sumner, James. 2007. What makes a PC? Thoughts on computing platforms, standards, and compatibility. *IEEE Annals of the History of Computing* 29(2): 87–88.

Sumner, James. 2008. Standards and compatibility: The rise of the PC platform. *History and Technology* 28 [=Sumner and Gooday. 2008]: 101–127.

Sumner, James, and J.N. Graeme Gooday (eds.). 2008. *By whose standards? Standardization, stability and uniformity in the history of information and electrical technologies* [Special issue *History and Technology* 28]. London: Continuum International Pub. Group.

Sundhaussen, Holm. 2012. *Jugoslawien und seine Nachfolgestaaten 1943–2011. Eine ungewöhnliche Geschichte des Gewöhnlichen*. Wien: Böhlau.

Sysło, Maciej M., and Anna B. Kwiatkowska. 2008. The challenging face of informatics education in Poland. In *Informatics education – Supporting computational thinking*, ed. Roland T. Mittermeir and Maciej M. Syslo, 1–18. Berlin/Heidelberg: Springer.

Szlemiński, Maciek. 1993. Polska scena C-64 teraz i kiedyś [Polish C-64 scene: Past and present]. *Commodore & Amiga*, July, 36.

Szperkowicz, Jerzy. 1987. Skąd się biorą komputery? [Where computers came from?] *Horyzonty Techniki*, special issue *64 strony o komputerach* (*64 pages on computers*), 34.

Tasajärvi, L., B. Stamnes, and M. Schustin (eds.). 2004. *Demoscene: The art of real-time.* Even Lake Studios & katastro.fi.

Tatarchenko, Ksenia. 2010. Not lost in translation: How did English become the common language of information processing (1960–1974)? Paper presented at the Software for Europe workshop. Lorentz Center, Leiden, The Netherlands, September 2010.

Tedlow, Richard S. 2006. *Andy Grove: The life and times of an American business icon*. New York: Portfolio.

Thatcher, Margaret. 1982. *Speech opening conference on information technology*, London.

The C-64 scene database. http://csdb.dk/. Accessed 12 Nov 2013.

Thomas, David. 1991. *Alan Sugar: The Amstrad story*. London: Pan Books.

Thomas, Douglas. 2002. *Hacker culture*. Minneapolis: University of Minnesota Press.

Tinn, Honghong. 2011. From DIY computers to illegal copies: The controversy over tinkering in Taiwan, 1980–1984. *IEEE Annals of the History of Computing* 33(2): 75–88.

Tomczyk, Michael S. 1984. *The home computer wars: An insider's account of Commodore and Jack Tramiel*. Greensboro: Compute! Publications.

Tomović, R., A. Mandžić, and T. Aleksić, et al. 1960. Cifarski Elektronski Računar CER10 IBK Vinča. *ETAN-1960* 1: 305–330.

Traut, Bernd M. 1987. *Rechtsfragen zu Bildschirmtext*, 1987th ed. München: R. Fischer.

Turkle, Sherry. 1984. *The second self: Computers and the human spirit*. New York: Simon & Schuster.

Turner, Fred. 2006. *From counterculture to cyberculture: Stewart Brand, the Whole Earth Network, and the rise of digital utopianism*. Chicago: University of Chicago Press.

Tympas, Aristotle. 2006. Electronic era technologies, the European experience: Historiographical omissions and ambitions. In *Tensions of Europe network second plenary conference proceedings*, ed. Johan Schot, et al., Lappeenranta, Finland (CD-ROM).

Tympas, Aristotle, Fotini Tsaglioti, and Theodore Lekkas. 2008. *Universal machines vs. national languages: Computerization as production of new localities*. Paper presented at the international conference 'Technologies of Globalization', Darmstadt.

Usselman, Steve. 1993. IBM and its imitators: Organizational capabilities and the emergence of the international computer industry. *Business and Economic History* 22(1): 1–35.

van Baalen, Carla, Anne Bos, Jan Willem Brouwers, Peter van Griendsven, Ron de Jong, and Jan Ramakers. 2005. *Koningin Beatrix aan het woord, 25 jaar troonredes, officiële redevoeringen en kersttoespraken*. Den Haag: Sdu.

van Bergeijk, Jeroen, Geke Van Dijk, Karel Koch, and Bas Raimakers. 1992. *N5M Zapbook: Working papers*. Amsterdam: Paradiso. http://www.tacticalmediafiles.net/TMF_documents/N5Mzapbook.pdf, esp. 25. Last accessed 6 Oct 2011.

van den Boomen, Marianne. 1995. "Digitale Steden en virtuele Gemeenschappen," excerpt from Marianne van den Boomen. In *Internet-ABC voor vrouwen*. Amsterdam: Institut voor Politiek en Publiek. http://www.xs4all.nl~boom/hs8.html. Accessed 15 June 2011.

Van den Boomen, Marianne, and Harm Ramkema. 1995. *Internet-ABC voor vrouwen: een inleiding voor datadames en modemmeiden*. Amsterdam: Instituut voor Publiek en Politiek.

Van der Heide, Martijn, et al. 2010. *World of spectrum*. www.worldofspectrum.org. Accessed 10 Jan 2010.

Van der Vleuten, Erik. 2008. Toward a transnational history of technology: Meanings, promises, pitfalls. *Technology and Culture* 49(4): 974–994.

Van Eeden, Ed. 2002. *Allemaal enen en nullen*. Utrecht: A.W. Bruna.

Van Elteren, Mel. 1994. *Imagining America, Dutch youth and its sense of place*. Tilburg: Tilburg University Press.

Van Elteren, Mel. 2006. *Americanism and Americanization. A critical history of domestic and global influence*. Jefferson/London: McFarland.

Van Muylwijk, Bert, and Jef Moonen. 1985. Computerapparatuur op school. *Computers op School* 6: 15–19.

Van Rooij, Arjan, Eric Berkers, Mila Davids, and Frank Veraart. 2008. National innovation systems and international knowledge flows. An exploratory investigation with cases of the Netherlands. *Technology Analysis and Strategic Management* 20(2): 149–168.

van Tijen, Tjebbe. 1966. 1966: Provo's Witte Huizenplan/White House Plan of Provo movement. *Witplan*. http://witplan.wordpress.com/1966/04/25/provos-witte-huizenplanwhite-house-plan-ofprovo-movement/. Accessed 31 Mar 2013.

van Tijen, Tjebbe (ed.). 1989. *Europe against the current: Catalogue on alternative, independent and radical information carriers*. Amsterdam: IISG.

van Tijen, Tjebbe. 1990. Europa tegen de stroom. *De Gids* 153(6): 466–471. [English translation available online Going against the grain, Europe against the current. http://www.imaginarymuseum.org/ETS/ETSeng.html. Accessed 30 Jan 2014]

van Tijen, Tjebbe. 1993. A context for collecting the new media. In *Next 5 Minutes Video Catalogue, catalogue of videotapes shown during the festival on tactical television held in Paradiso Amsterdam, 8–10 January 1993*, ed. Bas Raijmakers and Tjebbe van Tijen. Amsterdam: International Institute of Social History. Online at http://socialhistory.org/sites/default/files/docs/collecting-new-media.pdf. Accessed 1 Apr 2013.

van Tijen, Tjebbe. 1992. Vrije culturele ruimtes. In *Gebroken wit: politiek van de kleine verhalen*, ed. Mascarpone, Irene Janze, et al. Amsterdam: Ravijn. [Available online as Tjebbe van Tijen. 2004. Vrije Culturele Ruimtes. http://imaginarymuseum.org/VKULT. Last accessed 16 July 2011]

Veit, Stan. 1993. *Stan Veit's history of the personal computer: From Altair to IBM, a history of the PC revolution*. Asheville: WordComm.

Veladžić, Edin, Goran Miloradović, et al. 2010. *Yugoslavia between East and West; Ordinary people in unordinary country*. Online project EUROCLIO – HIP http://www.cliohip.com. Accessed 24 Nov 2011.

Veraart, Frank. 2008a. Basicode: Co-producing a microcomputer Esperanto. *History and Technology* 28: 129–147. [= Special issue *By whose standards? Standardization, stability and uniformity in the history of information and electrical technologies*, ed. J. Sumner and J.N. Graeme Gooday, 129–147]

Veraart, Frank. 2008b. De domesticatie van de computer in Nederland 1975–1990. *Studium* 2(1): 145–164.

Veraart, Frank. 2008c. *Vormgevers van Persoonlijk Computergebruik: De ontwikkeling van computers voor kleingebruikers in Nederland 1970–1990*. PhD thesis, TU Eindhoven.

Veraart, Frank. 2011. Losing meanings: Computer games in Dutch domestic use, 1975–2000. *IEEE Annals of the History of Computing* 33(1): 52–65.

Veraart, Frank. 2014. Transnational (dis)connection in localizing personal computing in the Netherlands, 1975–1990. In *Hacking Europe. From computer cultures to demoscenes*, ed. Gerard Alberts and Ruth Oldenziel, 25–48. New York: Springer.

Vlap, Annelies. 2011. Internet van en voor Nederland. Het verhaal van 25 jaar .nl, in 25 *jaar .nl*. In Bex*communicatie. *Anniversary Publication SIDN*, 30–40. Arnhem: Stichting Internet Domeinregistratie Nederland.

von Gravenreuth, Günter Freiherr. 1989. Computerviren, hacker, datenspione, crasher und cracker. Überblick und rechtliche Einordnung. *Neue Juristische Wochenschrift*, 201–206.

von Hippel, Eric. 2005. Open source projects as user innovation networks. In *Perspectives on free and open source software*, ed. Joseph Feller, 267–278. Cambridge, MA: MIT Press.

von Randow, Thomas. 1984. Ein Schlag gegen das System. Ein Computerclub deckt Sicherheitslücken im Btx-Programm der Post auf. *Die Zeit* 49, November 30.

Vuorinen, Jukka. 2007. Ethical codes in the digital world: Comparisons of the proprietary, the open/free and the cracker system. *Ethics and Information Technology* 9(1): 27–38.

Walen, Robert J., Stevan Dedijer, and Pavle Savić of IBK Vinča. 1953. *O dva bitna uslova za razvitak atomske energije kod nas*. Belgrade, Yugoslavia.

Wark, Mackenzie. 2004. *A hacker manifesto*. Cambridge, MA: Harvard University Press.

Warnecke, Christoph. 1983. *Bildschirmtext und dessen Einsatz bei Kreditinstituten*, Schriftenreihe der Studiengruppe Bildschirmtext. Gröbenzell: Fischer.

Wasiak, Patryk. 2010. Computing behind the iron curtain: Social impact of home computers in Polish People's Republic. In *Tensions of Europe and Inventing Europe Working Paper series*, working paper No. 2010/08. Accessible online at http://tensionsofeurope.eu/www/en/publications/working-papers.

Wasiak, Patryk. 2014. Playing and copying: Social practices of home computer users in Poland during the 1980s. In *Hacking Europe. From computer cultures to demoscenes*, ed. Gerard Alberts and Ruth Oldenziel, 129–150. New York: Springer.

Weber, Ursula. 2002. *Der Polenmarkt in Berlin: zur Rekonstruktion eines kulturellen Kontakts im Prozeß der politischen Transformation Mittel- und Osteuropas*. Neuried: Ars Una.

Wedel, Janine (ed.). 1992. *The unplanned society, Poland during and after communism*. New York: Columbia University Press.

Weizenbaum, Joseph. 1976. *Computer power and human reason: From judgment to calculation*. San Francisco: W. H. Freeman.

Wevers, Henk. 1980. Softtalk. *HCC Newsletter* 18, June/July, 23.

Wieckmann, Jürgen (ed.). 1988. *Das Chaos Computer Buch. Hacking made in Germany*. Reinbek bei Hamburg: Wunderlich.

Wiesenbauer, Ludwig. 1983. *Verhaltenswissenschaftliche Grundlagen der Bildschirmtextbenutzung*, Schriftenreihe der Studiengruppe Bildschirmtext. Gröbenzell: Fischer.

WifiSoft.org Foundation. 2007. *Annual report 2007*. http://wifisoft.org/trac/.

Willison, Robert, and Mikko Siponen. 2008. *Software piracy: Original insights from a criminological perspective*. Paper presented at the proceedings of the annual Hawaii international conference on system sciences, Maui.

Winner, Langdon. 1993. Upon opening the black box and finding it empty: Social constructivism and the philosophy of technology. *Science, Technology & Human Values* 18(3): 362–378.

Woolgar, Steve. 1991. Configuring the user: The case of usability trials. In *A sociology of monsters: Essays on power, technology and domination*, ed. John Law, 57–102. London/New York: Routledge.

Wozniak, Steve. 2006. *iWoz, computer geek to computer icon*. New York: W.W. Norton and Company.

Yost, Jeffrey R. 2005. *The computer industry, Emerging industries in the United States*. Westport: Greenwood Press.

Young, Jefferey S., and William L. Simon. 2005. *iCon Steve Jobs, the greatest second act in the history of business*. Hoboken: Wiley.

Zeitlin, Jonathan, and Gary Herrigel (eds.). 2000. *Americanization and its limits. Reworking US technology and management in post-war Europe and Japan*. Oxford: Oxford University Press.

Zemanek, Heinz. 2002. Computers in small countries. In *Computing technology past & future*, ed. J. Folta, 157–170. Prague: National Technical Museum in Prague.

Zhuk, Sergei. 2010. *Rock and roll in the Rocket City: The West, identity and ideology in Soviet Dnepropetrovsk*. Washington, DC: Woodrow Wilson Center Press.

Zimmerman, William. 1972. Hierarchical regional systems and the politics of system boundaries. *International Organization* 26(1): 18–36.

Zimmerman, William. 1987. *Open borders, non-alignment and the political evolution of Yugoslavia*. Princeton: Princeton University Press.

Γεωργιάδης, Φ. 1986a. Εισαγωγή στο Hacking [Introduction to hacking]. *Pixel* 23: 103.

Γεωργιάδης, Φ. 1986b. Η πρώτη αντιγραφή [First copy]. *Pixel* 25: 128–133.

Ηλίας Γεωργάκης. 2010. Μείωση εισφορών έως 25 %. *TA NEA*, December 21. http://www.tanea.gr/default.asp?pid=2&ct=3&artid=4609892. Accessed 2010.

Καραιωσηφόγλου, Γ. 1984. Τα νέα του *Pixel* [Pixel's news]. *Pixel* 2: 5.

Καράλης, Κ. 1990. Στα άδυτατης ελληνικότητας. *RAM*, April, 69.

Κυριακός, Χ. 1986a. Οι Hackers αποκαλύπτουν [Hackers reveal]. *Pixel* 27: 76–81.

Κυριακός, Χ. 1986b. Οι πειρατές του software [Software pirates]. *Pixel* 21: 55.

Κυριακός, Χ. 1986c. Ο πόλεμος των computer shops [The war of computer shops]. *Pixel* 19: 71.

Μανδρινός, Μ. 1983. Προγράμματα για τον ZX-81 [Programs for ZX –81]. *Pixel* 1: 12.

Μανούσος, Ν. 1983. Γράμμα από τον Εκδότη [Letter from the Editor]. *Pixel* 1: 3.

Νικολάου, Μ. 1985. Νίκος Λουκίδης: Ο Έλληνας 'Mr. Chips' [Nikos Loukidis: The Greek "Mr. Chips"!]. *Pixel* 15: 158.

Τσουάνας, Ν. 1984. Σπάστε το Manic Miner [Break Manic Miner]. *Pixel* 3: 16.

Τσουάνας, Ν. 1985. Επεμβάσεις: Ξεκλειδώστε το Pole Position [Interferences: Unlock pole position]. *Pixel* 15: 134.

About the Authors

Gerard Alberts teaches History of Computing and Mathematics at the University of Amsterdam. He has been project leader in history of software in the context of European Cold War history and Dutch history. The *Software for Europe* was part of the ESF Eurocores Inventing Europe.

Alexander Badenoch is postdoc at the University of Paris IV-Sorbonne on the LABEX "Écrire une nouvelle histoire de l'Europe" (EHNE) and Lecturer in Media Studies at Utrecht University, where he is a lead researcher on the project "Transnational Radio Encounters." He is the author of *Voices in Ruins: West German Broadcasting Across the 1945 Divide*, and most recently editor, with Christian Henrich-Franke and Andreas Fickers, of *Airy Curtains in the European Ether: Broadcasting and the Cold War*, as well as the chief content editor of the online exhibition "Inventing Europe" (www.inventingeurope.eu).

Kai Denker studied computer science, philosophy, and history in Darmstadt (TU), Germany. In 2009, he graduated in philosophy with a work on Gottlob Frege and Ludwig Wittgenstein and in computer science with a work on global cellular automata. Currently, he holds a PhD scholarship at Darmstadt (TU). His PhD project connects a reconstruction of Gilles Deleuze and Félix Guattari as rigorous readers of Bernhard Riemann to historical and current phenomena of digital activism.

Bruno Jakić is a Yugoslav-born, Amsterdam-based engineer, consultant, and entrepreneur in the field of artificial intelligence. He has a fascination with history, in general, and the history of computational machinery, in specific. He collaborated with Gerard Alberts.

Thomas Lean holds a PhD in the History of Science, Technology, and Medicine from the University of Manchester, carried out in collaboration with the Museum of Science and Industry in Manchester as an ESRC-funded CASE studentship. His thesis examined the development of popular home computing in 1980s Britain. Prior to this he wrote his Master's thesis on the development of Sinclair computing, at the University of Kent. He currently works for National Life Stories at the British Library as an oral historian of science and technology on *An Oral History of British Science*.

G. Alberts and R. Oldenziel (eds.), *Hacking Europe. From Computer Cultures to Demoscenes*, History of Computing, DOI 10.1007/978-1-4471-5493-8,

Theodoros Lekkas teaches History and Philosophy of Science in Secondary Education. He studied History and Philosophy of Science at the University of Athens and he holds Master's degrees in History and Philosophy of Science and Technology from the University of Athens and from the International Master Program in European Studies of Society, Science and Technology (ESST). He has broad professional experience in project management and business analysis with major IT companies. He is writing his PhD thesis on aspects of the history of home computing in 1980s Greece. His research interests include the adaptation of computer technology at the local level (localization), computer subcultures in use, the intervention between social and technical in the personal and home computing, and the mediation process of computer use.

Caroline Nevejan has been involved with the developing digital culture since the 1980s. She orchestrated many networked events in Paradiso Amsterdam, was cofounder/director of Waag Society, and director Educational Research and Development of the Hogeschool van Amsterdam. After her PhD "Presence and the Design of Trust" at the University of Amsterdam in 2007, she became researcher at Delft Technical University, where she, together with Frances Brazier, focuses on participatory systems designs. Working in interdisciplinary fashion, including with ronments. In 2012, she published "Witnessing You, on Trust and Truth in a Network World." Nevejan is crown member of the Dutch Council for Culture and the Arts.

Ruth Oldenziel is professor at Eindhoven University of Technology and is a Fellow at the Rachel Carson Center for Environment and Society, Munich, in the fall of 2013 and 2014. She received her PhD from Yale University in American History in 1992 after graduate training in American Studies at Smith College, the University of Massachusetts at Amherst, and the University of Amsterdam. Her publications include books and articles in the area of American, gender, and technology studies. Her most recent publication coauthored with Mikael Hård is *Consumers, Tinkerers, Rebels: The People Who Shaped Europe* (London: Palgrave, 2013).

Markku Reunanen, Lic.Sc., M.A., is the lecturer of interactive visualization at the Aalto University School of Arts, Design and Architecture. He started as a researcher in the field of virtual reality and has gradually shifted toward digital cultural heritage and cultural studies during the last ten years. Currently, he is working on a doctoral thesis on the demoscene, a creative hobbyist subculture born in the mid-1980s.

Antti Silvast, M.Soc.Sc., in sociology, has a PhD (2013) from the University of Helsinki, Department of Social Research, Discipline of Sociology in 2013. He specializes in large technical systems and infrastructures, everyday practices of infrastrucure use, the sociology of risk, and qualitative research methods of sociology.

Johan Söderberg is a postdoc researcher at Laboratoire Techniques, Territoires et Sociétés/Institut Francilien Innovation et Société, Université Paris-Est. Theoretically, he works in the intersection between STS, critical theory, and labor process theory. For more information, please visit www.johansoderberg.net

Frank C.A. Veraart is a researcher at the Foundation of the History of Technology (SHT), Eindhoven, the Netherlands. In 2008, he completed his dissertation *Designers of Personal Computing in the Netherlands, 1970–1990,* which analyzes the introduction of home and personal computers in the Netherlands with a special focus on computers in educational programs, small industries, and private households. His publications include studies about computer games and a microcomputer "esperanto" called Basicode. Currently, he is involved in the historical analysis of technological transitions, in particular in the project *Historical Roots of the Dutch Sustainability Challenge: The Impact of the Utilization of Material Resources on the Modernization of Dutch Society, 1850–2010*, in which he focuses on the material flows and utilization of minerals and metals as well as on the transnational and transgenerational issues of sustainability.

Patryk Wasiak is affiliated with the Institute for Cultural Studies, University of Wrocław, Poland. After completing his M.A. degrees in sociology and art history at the Warsaw University, Wasiak wrote his dissertation on the transnational informal contacts between visual artists in Soviet Bloc. He held postdoctoral fellowships at the Center for Contemporary History Potsdam and the Netherlands Institute for Advanced Study. His research interests include cultural history of the Cold War, history of computing, and consumer electronics. Currently, he works on a second book on consumer electronics, home appliances and social identities in Poland during system transition of 1989.

Index

A

Access, 1, 4, 6, 10, 17, 34, 40, 61, 83, 89, 93, 119, 123, 125, 132–134, 139, 142, 159, 160, 167–169, 171, 173–175, 179–181, 183, 193, 194, 198, 199, 203, 204, 207, 211, 213, 224
"A computer on a chip," 7
ACORN, 8, 43, 50, 56, 57, 61, 62, 64, 79
Activism, 10, 76, 160, 170, 171, 177, 203
Activist, 3, 12, 129, 132, 138, 160, 161, 176, 181, 184, 188, 195, 197–200, 204, 207, 209, 212–217, 219, 222–226
Actors, 4, 6, 15, 16, 26, 36, 40, 46, 72, 77, 78, 82, 88, 96, 97, 123, 125, 134, 147, 148, 179–181, 183, 203–205, 221
Adoption, 4, 14, 26, 37, 72, 75, 77, 80, 139, 144, 146, 152, 153, 179, 223
Advertisements, 41, 49, 55, 56, 83, 86, 94, 96, 113, 128, 129, 132, 135
AIDS, 193–195
Alberts, Gerard, 1–18, 25, 123, 179
Alienation, 10, 32–39, 219
Allen, P., 10, 29
Altair, 27, 29, 35, 73, 79, 97
Amateur, 27, 29, 30, 62, 71, 73–75, 79, 80, 82, 83, 85, 86, 88–90, 92, 116, 137, 183, 204, 220
Amateur Computer Club (ACC), 28
Amateur radio, 11, 27, 28, 31, 59
American corporate culture, 4
The American dream, 25
Americanization, 4, 16, 25, 26, 47
American model of commercialization of the Internet, 5
American story, 3
Amiga, 13, 38, 124, 126, 129, 131–133, 137, 138, 140, 145, 149–152
Amsterdam, 1–3, 5–7, 10, 15, 17, 25, 26, 112, 113, 119, 170, 179–205
Anarchist, 184, 213, 214, 225
Antenna network, 188, 196
Anti-piracy, 128, 145
Anti-statism, 214
Apple, 12, 13, 16, 31, 33, 38, 43–45, 53, 54, 62, 74, 194, 195, 204
Appropriated, 1, 6, 14–16, 18, 120, 126, 141, 167, 177, 180, 181
Appropriation, 4, 5, 11, 12, 15, 16, 18, 26, 46–47, 78, 101, 123, 139, 140, 143–154, 162, 170, 178, 221
Art movement in computing, 108, 109
Association of Polish Socialist Youth, 8, 129
Aster CT-80, 41, 43
Atari, 38, 44, 67, 74, 80, 124, 128, 129, 131, 134, 135, 137, 140, 142
Athens, 1, 71, 82, 86, 88, 94, 95
Atomistic notion of the "user," 201
Audio tapes; cassettes, 81
Australia, 32, 137, 196
Austria, 41
Automatisering Gids, 28, 36
Autonomy, 9, 10, 17

B

Bajtek, 124, 127, 129–134, 136–138, 140
Baltona, 124, 128–129
Barnhoorn, Dik, 28
Basicode, 29–32, 41, 46, 74

G. Alberts and R. Oldenziel (eds.), *Hacking Europe. From Computer Cultures to Demoscenes*, History of Computing, DOI 10.1007/978-1-4471-5493-8,

BASIC programming language, 35, 41, 53, 55, 56, 60, 65, 67, 81, 84, 85, 91, 94, 130, 131, 133, 136, 137, 140
BBC, 8, 9, 30, 32, 50, 51, 56, 57, 61, 80, 119, 177
Belgium, 32, 71, 145
Belgrade, 17, 102, 104, 105, 108, 111, 113, 119, 197
Berlin, 8, 14, 77, 126, 130, 138–141, 144, 163, 174, 185, 188, 196, 222
Big system, 2
Bildschirmtext (Btx), 159–170, 175–177
Birds nest electronics, 192, 195
Black market, 112, 126
Bosnia and Herzegovina, 101, 102
Botz, Daniel, 144
Bourgeois media, 214
B92 radio, 119, 197
Bratislava, 215
British, 8, 9, 16, 27–31, 33, 34, 40, 41, 49–54, 56–58, 61, 62, 64, 68, 69, 80, 90, 192, 197, 205
British Association of Microcomputer Users in Secondary Education (MUSE), 30, 31
Broadcasting of computer software, 30
Building kits, 12
Bundesdatenschutzgesetz (BDSG, Federal Data Protection Act), 173
Byte, 35, 52, 74, 88, 130, 131

C

Capitalist, 124, 126
Captain Crunch (John Draper), 192
CCC. *See* Chaos Computer Club (CCC)
Ceefax, 41
Censorship, 111, 117, 182, 197
Central Europe, 124, 212, 222
Centralization, 7, 27
Chaos, 1, 3, 14, 17, 161–163, 165–167
Chaos Computer Club (CCC), 1, 3, 14, 17, 160–165, 189, 190, 197
Cheapo, 211
Chip, 7, 8, 51–53, 56, 73, 80, 131
Chip Shop, 32
Chopping games, 1
Chrudim, 216, 217, 219
Clock, 59, 210–212, 218, 219, 224
Clones, 12, 31, 38, 44, 68, 69, 108, 124
Club, 1, 3, 8, 14–18, 27–29, 33–37, 39, 58, 60, 65, 90, 92, 93, 96, 132–134, 136–138, 160–171, 175, 177, 178, 186, 189, 190
Co-construct, 5, 6, 13, 26, 51, 75, 96, 124, 144, 148
Coder, 140, 141, 152
Cold War, 4, 13–16, 101, 102, 119, 125, 181, 192
Commercialization, 5, 10, 18, 218, 220
Commodification, 10, 220
Commodore, 12, 13, 16, 31, 33, 38, 42, 43, 53, 69, 74, 81, 92, 124, 128, 129, 131–133, 137–140, 142, 145, 148, 149
Commodore, 64, 80, 113, 124, 126, 127, 132, 134, 145, 148, 149
Communism, 103, 127
Communist regime, 123, 125, 133
Communities, 1–3, 5–7, 10, 13–18, 26, 37, 68, 75, 77, 80, 144, 146–148, 151, 183, 185, 187, 197, 201, 204, 212, 213, 215, 219, 220
Community innovation, 212
Compis, 8, 9
Compudata, 8, 43
Compulsive programmer, 2
Compute!, 74, 130, 140
Compute!'s Gazette, 140
Computer(s)
  adaptation of, 54, 72, 87, 117
  bazaars, 123, 124, 127–129, 134–136, 138–140, 142
  clubs, 8, 14–18, 28, 29, 34, 36, 39, 58, 60, 65, 90, 92, 93, 96, 132–134, 136
  crime, 123
  cultural dimensions of, 76
  education, 8, 57, 58, 60, 117, 130
  Esperanto, 29–32
  games, 3, 8, 17, 37, 39, 64, 75, 125, 128, 131–137, 150
  hobbyists, 14, 29, 31, 32, 36, 37, 59, 75, 97, 124, 148, 183
  imports, 53, 101, 112, 113
  industry, 7, 13, 49, 52, 73, 74, 89, 101, 103, 107, 117, 120, 212
  kits, 28, 53
  literacy,7–9, 16, 41, 42, 50, 56, 59, 63, 66, 68
  literate, 8
  localization of, 92
  magazine(s), 16, 17, 52, 61, 63, 66, 71, 83, 88, 92, 94, 96, 102, 123, 124, 127–133, 135, 137, 138, 140, 142
  professionals, 29, 36
  stores, 15, 18, 53, 80, 86–88, 90, 92–97
  use, 6, 10, 16, 59, 60, 68, 96, 97, 123, 129, 131, 133, 134, 153

Computerization movement, 123, 127, 129–132, 141
Computer-oriented subcultures, 138
"Computer studios," 127, 128, 132, 135, 138
Compute!'s Gazette, 140
Computing, 1, 25–47, 49–69, 71–97, 102, 134, 144, 162, 180, 209
  Hobbyist and amateur, 28, 75
  in schools, 8, 42, 45, 46, 57
  in Yugoslavia, 102, 105, 115, 119
Configuring the user, 6, 75, 124, 147, 221
Constructivist STS, 221, 226
Consumentenbond, 34
Consumer culture, 107, 108, 123, 126, 144
Consumption junction, 6, 7, 96
Control, 3, 7, 9, 10, 12, 26, 27, 38, 62, 101, 104, 105, 108, 117, 118, 152, 162, 163, 177, 192, 217, 218
Coordinating Committee for Multilateral Export Controls (COCOM), 125
Copying, 8, 15–17, 35–37, 39, 81–83, 85–87, 93, 95, 97, 123–142, 164
Copyright(s), 35, 46, 77, 89, 93, 123, 128, 132, 136, 162, 219, 223, 224
Counter-cultural, 14, 17, 50, 51, 63, 76, 163, 189, 204, 214
Countercultural communities, 10, 16
Counterculture, 1–3, 7, 10, 17, 27, 74, 76, 102, 113, 160, 163, 167, 183
Cracking, 16, 17, 32–39, 77, 81, 83, 86, 87, 138, 140, 141, 149, 186
  culture, 16, 37
  scene, 138, 149
Crack intros, 139–141
Criminalization, 160, 161, 171, 174, 177
Cultural distinction, 142
Cultural practice, 6
Cultural script, 6, 13, 18
Cultural studies, 144, 196
Cyber culture, 17
Cyberpunk, 3, 14, 207
Czech Republic, 15, 207, 208, 210–215, 217, 222, 223, 225

D

Data transmission, 207, 211, 213
De Balie, 2, 187, 196, 197, 199, 202
De Digitale Stad (digital city), 6, 10, 15, 17, 119, 159–161, 166, 179–185
Demo, 3, 68, 116, 143–145, 149, 150, 152
Democratization; ideology of, 76
Demo-makers, 150
Demoscene, 3, 6, 15, 17, 77, 123, 136–141, 143–154, 164
Demoscene Research, 144
Denmark, 32
Deutsche Bundespost (DBP) Germany's Federal Mail, 159
Dial-up modems, 223
Diffusion of innovations, 144, 146
Digital city (DDS), 10, 15, 17, 179–181, 186, 199–205
Digital public domains, 15
Disk magazines, 144, 150, 154
Diskmags, 139–141, 144, 145, 149, 154
Dissidents, 123, 126, 225
DIY computing, 14
Domesticate(d), 5, 7, 14, 15, 18, 123
Domestication, 14, 53, 80, 126, 130, 134, 142
Domestication of technology, 80, 142, 144, 146
Dybowski, Klaudiusz, 132, 133

E

Early adopters, 152
Eastern Europe, 8, 11, 16, 68, 107, 110, 125, 126, 128, 140, 187, 188, 196
Economic pathology, 126
Education, 8, 11, 25, 27, 30, 33, 36, 41–45, 47, 49, 50, 54, 56–61, 65–67, 97, 111, 117, 130, 133, 196, 202
Educational machines, 7
Electronic magazines, 144
Electronics TOP International (ETI), 28
Elektuur, 28
Elwro Junior, 124
End-user, 144, 150, 170, 171
Entrepreneurs, 32, 57, 123, 126, 127
Epistemological gap, 225, 226
64'er, 140
ESPRIT, 14
ETI. *See Electronics TOP International (ETI)*
Europe, 1, 4–8, 10, 11, 13–18, 27, 30, 37, 40, 46, 68, 73, 75–77, 97, 103, 112, 123, 125, 139, 140, 142, 143, 149, 159, 160, 169, 179, 181–183, 185, 187, 188, 195, 201, 204, 205, 212, 213
European, 1–18, 25, 30, 33, 35, 38, 40, 41, 45, 46, 75, 96, 108, 110, 125, 126, 138, 141, 159, 163, 172, 179–205, 213, 221, 223
European Community, 14
Exidy Sorcerer, 31, 43

F
Felsenstein, Lee, 192
Finland, 8, 11, 13–15, 33, 75, 90, 97, 145
France, 11, 46, 71, 104, 120, 160, 178, 179, 182, 207
Free-floating "change agents," 221
Free software, 32, 85, 137, 208, 214
Free space optics, 209, 211, 213, 219, 222–225
Fun, 15, 140, 149, 151, 219

G
Galactic Hacker Party (GHP), 188, 190–193, 198, 199, 205
Galaksija computer, 113–116
Games, 2, 3, 8, 13, 14, 17, 36, 37, 39, 51, 62, 64–68, 75, 77, 81, 83, 84, 86, 88, 90, 96, 102, 115, 117, 118, 125, 128–140, 142, 145, 149, 150, 160, 162, 170, 223, 224
Gaming, 1, 9, 14, 36, 37, 39, 51, 59, 64–67, 72, 97, 132, 134–136, 143, 153
Gaming scripts, 134
Garcia, David, 179, 186, 193, 196
Gates, Bill, 25, 29, 35, 44
GDR, 13, 107, 126, 128
Gendered encoding, 6
Gender specificity, 6
Gender studies, 144
Germany, 11, 14, 16, 17, 46, 71, 76, 77, 113, 159–164, 170, 172–174, 177, 190, 197
GHP. *See* Galactic Hacker Party (GHP)
Global commodity, 224
GNU/Linux, 223
Golden hands, 222
Gonggrijp, Rop, 169
Graphical interfaces, 38, 44, 193, 199–201
Grassroots alternative, 214
Grzybowska Street, 127, 136

H
Hacker culture, 1–6, 10, 13, 15, 17, 29, 77, 82, 97, 138, 144, 151, 160, 185
Hackers, 1–5, 10–15, 17, 18, 29, 50, 58, 73, 76–78, 81–83, 86–88, 90, 96, 138, 142–154, 159–162, 164–178, 189, 191–193, 195, 197, 198, 200, 204, 205, 208, 214
Hackers-as-outsiders, 2
Hacker's ethos, 2
Hackers' identity, 87
Hackerspaces, 208, 214
Hacking, 1–5, 8–10, 12, 14–16, 63, 65, 83, 86, 87, 97, 131–133, 143, 154, 160–162, 164–168, 171, 174–178, 181, 184, 189–192, 198, 199, 205
Hack-Tic, 183, 189, 190, 192, 193, 196–199
Hacktivism, 10, 160, 161, 165, 176–178
Hacktivist, 10, 165
Hamburg, 1, 3, 15, 126, 159, 163, 165, 168, 169, 189, 190
Hamburg bank, 3
Hamburger *Sparkasse*, 3
Hamelink, Cees, 190
Harvard, 29, 39, 77
HCC. *See* Hobby Computer Club (HCC)
Hobby, 11, 12, 18, 27, 28, 33–35, 53, 59, 60, 62, 120, 129, 136, 138, 143, 154, 160, 171, 174–176, 183, 189, 220
  computers, 12, 17
Hobby Computer Club (HCC), 18, 28, 33–36, 39, 41, 136–138, 183, 189
Hobbyism, 176
Hobbyists, 9, 14, 17, 28–39, 44, 46, 47, 49, 50, 52–54, 58, 59, 74, 75, 79, 89, 97, 124, 132, 138, 148, 160, 175, 177, 183, 210, 215
  culture, 148
Hobbyscoop, 30–32
Holland, Wau, 3, 159, 161, 189, 192
Holy Grail, 2
Home
  computer, 115, 117–119, 123–144, 152, 163, 164, 174
  computing, 16, 17, 49, 50, 56, 59, 65, 68, 71–97, 102, 114–116, 119, 134, 141, 162, 163
Home-brew, 203, 204
Homebrew Computer Club, 101
Home microcomputers, 72, 74, 80, 82, 84, 87–89, 94, 95
  home micros, 81
The Housebreakers, 140
Hugi, 145, 150, 151
Hungary, 76, 103, 105, 106, 125, 128, 140, 141

I
IBM, 3, 6, 9, 12–14, 37, 38, 43–45, 47, 71–75, 78–82, 89, 91, 96, 97, 107, 108, 119, 124, 145, 149, 150
IBM-clones, 12, 108
IBM-compatible, 12–14, 38, 43–45, 91
Ideology, 76, 78, 92, 111, 185

IFIP. *See* International Federation of Information Processing (IFIP)
Imphobia, 145, 150, 152
Indigenous computer development, 120
Informal economy, 123, 126, 127, 141
Informatics, 8, 11, 27, 41, 43, 71, 79, 82, 97, 127, 129–131, 133, 199
Information society, 40, 41, 167, 171, 199
Innovation, 7, 12, 15, 16, 26, 50, 63, 73, 144, 146, 151, 179, 186, 190, 195, 202, 204, 205, 208, 211, 212, 218, 220, 221, 225
Innovation studies, 208, 220
INPUT64, 140
Inside-outside opposition, 3
Institutions, 6, 15, 26, 38, 90, 96, 104, 105, 109, 110, 117, 118, 124, 137, 160, 171, 178, 183, 188, 202, 204, 208, 220, 221
Intel, 7, 29
"Interfering"(Επεμβάσεις), 3
Intermediaries, 26, 39, 96, 129, 134
Intermediary actors, 26, 96 *See also*: Mediators
Internal export, 128
International Federation of Information Processing (IFIP), 11, 33, 90, 139
Intershop, 128
Iron Curtain, 4, 13, 109, 124, 125
Iskradata, 112
Italy, 16, 45, 46
Ivo Lola Ribar Institute, 105, 117

J
Japan, 57, 144
Jaruzelski, W., 125
Jordan, T., 10
Journal, 7, 12, 16, 28, 29, 35, 36, 50, 54, 86, 117, 125, 144, 148, 160–163, 165, 170, 171, 177, 190, 192, 208, 214, 220

K
Kansas City code, 30, 32
Keyboard, 11, 55, 56, 60, 61, 63, 64, 67, 118, 126, 127, 140, 174
Kidder, T., 2
Komputer, 124, 126, 128–132, 134, 137
Kraken, 2, 184
Kulhavy, K., 207, 210–212, 219, 224

L
Learning about computers, 51, 58, 59, 62
Lévi-Strauss, 143
L'informatisation de la société, 8
Lingua franca, 11
Linux kernel, 223
Listing, 60, 61, 64, 66, 80, 83–86, 89–91, 96, 131, 136, 142
Local communities, 1, 13
Local networks, 212
LOGO, 130, 133, 134
Lola-8, 117, 118
London, 3, 6, 10, 18, 25–27, 29, 33, 34, 49–52, 57, 61, 66–68, 74, 75, 77, 78, 90, 97, 107, 112, 124, 125, 127, 138, 142, 147, 148, 183, 185, 187, 221, 222
Longue durée, 226
Lovink, Geert, 179, 186–188, 196, 199, 200
Ludological element, 2, 15

M
Magazine, 15–17, 27, 28, 32, 45, 52, 53, 55, 59–61, 63–66, 68, 71, 72, 76, 79, 80, 82–90, 92–97, 102, 108, 109, 112–115, 117, 123, 124, 127–135, 137–140, 142, 144, 145, 149, 150, 154, 160, 164, 169, 170, 186–188, 193, 197, 198, 203
Magic disk, 140
Mastery, 2, 4, 68, 152, 153
MCN. *See* Micro Computer Club Netherlands (MCN)
MCP. *See* Music-print Computer Products (MCP)
Media art, 143, 144
Mediation junction, 6, 7, 96, 124, 134, 208
Mediators; roles of, 88–95 *See also*: Intermediary actors
Meritum, 9, 124
Metropolis, 211
Microcomputer, 1, 5, 7–9, 14, 29–34, 36–38, 40–43, 45, 49, 50, 52, 56–58, 61, 62, 67, 72, 74, 79, 82, 84, 87, 89, 91–95, 112, 127, 131, 138, 143, 147, 152, 162, 164
Micro Computer Club Netherlands (MCN), 33
Microcomputer Esperanto, 32, 74, 137
Microcomputer revolution, 8
Micro processor revolution, 7
Microsoft, 13, 25, 29, 33, 40–47
Middle class, 6, 8, 56, 144, 191
Midnight programmer, 2
Military, 7, 10, 15, 16, 27, 73, 76, 103–106, 109, 117, 118, 180, 182, 204, 212
Minitel, 41, 159, 161
Modernity, 26, 110, 111, 126, 180, 201

Motorola, 29
Mouse control, 38
MS-DOS, 13, 43, 124
MSX computers, 38
Music-print Computer Products (MCP), 41, 42

N
Narratives, 3, 26, 72, 120, 199, 201
Negotiation, 74, 147, 172
Netherlands, 8, 11, 14–17, 25–47, 71, 96, 113, 119, 123, 139, 179–183, 185, 188–190, 192, 198, 201–205, 208, 215
Network, 3, 5, 9, 17, 26, 39, 90, 92, 97, 123, 128, 129, 134–136, 139, 160, 162, 164, 167, 175, 179–205, 207–226
Nevejan, Caroline, 17, 170, 179–205, 214
New wave music, 163
Next Five Minutes Conference (N5M), 186, 196
Niche markets, 28, 49
1980s, 7–10, 12, 14–16, 18, 25, 29–31, 33–40, 42, 44, 49–69, 71–97, 101–120, 123–143, 151, 159, 160, 162–165, 167, 168, 170, 172, 177, 179–205, 214
NLnet, 182, 183, 199
N5M. *See* Next Five Minutes Conference (N5M)
Non-aligned movement, 106, 108, 110
Non-users, 144, 153
Nora and Minc-report, 8
Nordli, H., 144
Norway, 8
Now the Chips are down, 8, 51, 52, 56

O
Oldenziel, Ruth, 1–18, 25, 26, 96, 123, 124, 208
Olivetti, 12, 45
Open culture, 76, 92, 94, 96, 97
Openness, 10, 102, 139
Open source hardware, 208
Operating system, 13, 16, 29, 41, 45, 46, 79, 152, 175
Optical link, 190, 199, 202, 204
Osborne, 13, 73
Otaku culture, 144
Outsider role, 2
Outsiders, 2–4, 39, 200
Ownership, 1, 10, 13, 49, 113, 163

P
Padua, 141
Papermags, 139
PC. *See* Personal computer (PC)
The People's Voice, 130, 183
Pengo, 192
The Persian bazaar, 127
Personal computer (PC), 3, 4, 7, 10–18, 25–28, 38, 39, 43–45, 47, 49–51, 62, 69, 71, 73–83, 88–90, 97, 114, 124, 143–154
Pewex, 124, 128–129, 135, 137
Pfadenhauer, Michaela, 146
Philips, 8, 12, 31, 41–45, 183, 189, 192
Phreaking, 7, 9, 189
Pirate radio stations, 186, 187, 214
Pirates, 5, 82, 83, 86, 87, 123, 128, 187
  software, 65, 78, 82, 88, 95, 127, 128, 134, 136, 140, 141, 187
Pixley, Rolf, 193
Players, 34, 39, 68, 135, 139, 182, 186, 195, 197
Playfulness, 1, 2, 10
Plzen, 213
Podkrkonoší, 211
Poland, 8, 11, 13–15, 17, 103, 123–142
Policy, 4, 9, 14, 16, 40, 41, 44, 45, 56, 57, 77, 103–105, 110, 111, 117, 125, 128, 172–174, 185, 190, 194, 195, 198, 199, 220, 223
  educational, 8
Polish Association of Informatics, 8, 129
Politicization, 10
Polonus, 136, 139, 141
Popular computing, 49, 56, 68, 69
Popular Electronics, 27, 79
Post-structuralist, 220
Prague, 11, 15, 105, 211, 213, 215, 224
Pranksterism, 174–176
Press Now, 196, 197, 199
Prestel, 41
Privacy, 10, 165, 168–170, 189, 199, 224
Professions, 7, 11, 28, 29, 35, 36, 45, 66, 74, 75, 86–89, 116, 120, 131, 132, 146, 147, 204, 220
Programming, 2, 27, 29–32, 34, 36, 51, 54–56, 58–60, 63–68, 81, 83–85, 87–89, 97, 111, 113, 118, 125, 130–133, 136, 139, 140, 143, 150, 164, 216
Programming language, 29, 31, 53, 60, 128
PTT (Dutch Postal, Telegram, Telephone Company), 41
Public Understanding of Science, 49, 56
Public understanding of technology, 129

Q
Quartet, 141
Quartet Inc., 140
Queen Beatrix, 40

R
Radio, 11, 17, 18, 28–32, 59, 79, 101, 115–117, 119, 126, 138, 161, 183, 185–187, 197, 204, 214, 221
Radio Rotor, 28
Rathenau, G.W., 8, 40, 47
R.A.W., 145
Reasonable optical near joint access, 207
Riemens, Patrice, 179, 190, 196
Risan, 113
Rites of passage, 2, 6
Robers, Klaas, 31
Roberts, Ed, 27
Rock music, 111
Rogers, E.M., 144, 146, 152
Ronja, 17, 18, 207–220, 222–225
Russia, 124, 141

S
Saarikoski, Petri, 14, 33, 75, 90, 97, 143, 144, 152
Sarajevo, 102, 111, 112, 197
Scenario, 5, 6, 13, 35
The Scene, 148–150
Scenes, 1–18, 32, 51, 77, 101–115, 117, 119, 120, 138–141, 143–154, 183, 186, 188, 201, 210–220
School, 8, 36, 41, 43, 57, 65, 87, 117, 128, 135, 144, 163
Science 451, 141
Science and Technology Studies (STS), 147, 188, 200, 201, 206
Script, 5–8, 10–13, 16, 18, 123, 124, 129, 132–134, 136, 141, 142, 144, 147, 148, 150–154
Security, 3, 10, 162, 163, 165, 166, 168, 169, 175, 178, 189, 190, 192, 195, 198, 199
Self-stylization, 146
Seliger, P., 211, 215, 222
Serbia, 101, 102, 105, 107, 108, 113, 114, 117–119
Seropositive Ball, 193–195, 205
Sex'n'Crime, 145
Siemens, 12
Silicon Valley, 73, 86, 131
Silvast, Antti, 3, 17, 77, 123, 139, 143–145
Sinclair
  ZX80, 49, 50, 53, 55, 58, 74, 79
  ZX81, 50, 55, 58, 59, 61, 69, 74, 79
  ZX Spectrum, 16, 50, 58, 64, 74, 137
Skill, 31, 36, 53, 81, 92, 93, 97, 118–120, 130, 131, 133, 144, 147–154, 164, 175, 216
Skontorp, Jan, 218
Slot, Gerard, 28
Slovakia, 208, 215, 223
Sneakernets, 134–136
Social class, 144
Socialism, 3
Socialist, 8, 9, 16, 103, 110, 111, 123–127, 130, 133, 137, 138, 141, 143, 188, 199
Social movement, 76, 184, 203
Social Shaping of Technology, 62, 78
Social systems, 146
Social whole, 226
Society for Old and New Media (Waag Society), 202
Söderberg, Johan, 17, 207, 217, 221
Software
  copy of, 83
  crack, 32, 86, 139
  modification, 87, 97
Software packages, 39, 86, 94
Software piracy, 77, 93, 132, 136
Software sharing, 76, 92
Soldering, 12, 63, 132, 210, 216, 219
Solidarity movement, 125, 182
Sołtysiński, Pawel, 134
Soros Foundation, 196
Southwest Technical Systems Co., 28
Soviet Bloc, 106, 125, 141
Squatter movement, 1, 183–186, 188, 189, 204
Squatting, 2, 183–195, 198
Stalin, Joseph, 103, 105
Standards, 4, 5, 8, 9, 11–17, 38, 42, 44, 49, 63, 74, 78, 79, 86, 107, 109–111, 118, 124, 127, 159, 204, 213, 223, 225
State control of information, 10
Stikker, Marleen, 179, 186, 187, 199, 200, 202
Strafgesetzbuch (StGB) Criminal Code, 162, 171, 173, 175
STS. *See* Science and Technology Studies (STS)
Style, 50, 53, 55, 111, 145, 147, 150, 180, 204
Sub-cultural spaces, 16

Subculture, 3, 15–17, 27, 60, 68, 77, 101–103, 118, 138, 139
Sweden, 8, 14, 40, 46, 126, 141, 208
System, 2–4, 7, 9, 13, 16, 25, 27, 29–31, 38, 40, 41, 43–46, 51, 57, 62–64, 79, 105, 107, 108, 113, 114, 118, 125, 127–129, 136, 146, 152, 159, 162, 163, 165–178, 186, 198–200, 205, 224
Szczecin, 140, 141

T

Taiwanese parts, 12
Tandy, 31, 43
Taylor. P., 10
Technical University Delft, 28, 189
Technological change, 221
Technological script, 147, 148, 150, 153
Technology diffusion, 97, 144
Technophile, 6, 27, 32, 163, 164
TELEAC. *See* Television Academy (TELEAC)
Teletext, 41, 159
Television Academy (TELEAC), 30
Television (TV), 8, 28, 30, 31, 34, 41, 50, 54–57, 60, 73, 74, 123–127, 159, 166, 170, 183, 196, 197, 200, 210, 221
Tinkering, 1, 7, 12, 15, 28, 95, 96, 129, 143, 149, 153, 200, 202
Tito, 103, 104, 110
Tjebbe van Tijená, 112, 179, 184, 185, 187, 197
Top Secret, 132, 135, 136
Trade fair, 32, 212
Transnational, 4, 8, 9, 13, 14, 16, 17, 25–47, 124
Trust, 10, 189
Tulip, 8, 9, 43–45
Turkle, S., 2, 29, 75, 142, 143, 152
Turku, 1
Twentieth century, 1, 16, 25

U

Underground, 104, 113, 119, 125, 167, 168, 176, 177, 183, 194
Unemployment, 8, 40, 51, 52
UNESCO, 170
United States (USA), 4, 7, 8, 10, 11, 16, 18, 25–27, 40, 45, 46, 52, 53, 69, 71, 73–75, 77, 103, 106–111, 120, 124–126, 137, 144, 146, 159, 160, 174, 175, 180–182, 189, 200–203, 210, 212, 215, 223
Universality, 3, 4, 7, 18
Use of computers, 1, 32, 34, 51, 59, 63, 66, 76, 83, 88, 90, 91, 101, 107, 109, 112, 120, 134, 172, 174
Use of technology, 1, 68, 203
User-controlled technology, 18, 187–206
User groups, 6, 7, 27, 44, 136–139, 146, 196
Users, 1–18, 26, 27, 29, 30, 32, 34–37, 39, 44, 46, 49–51, 53–55, 58, 60–69, 71, 72, 74–90, 92–97, 114–116, 123–142, 164, 168, 170, 171, 175
User's conscience, 35
Users Matter, 5

V

van Duffelen, Jaap, 28
van Spaandonk, Rob, 28
Ventilator 202, 115–117
Veraart, F., 8, 14, 16, 25–47, 74, 88, 96, 136, 137, 183, 189, 204, 17139–141
Viditel, 41
Vienna, 41, 222
View-data, 40, 41
Vroom en Dreesmann (V&D), 33

W

Warsaw, 1, 126–128, 135, 139, 140
Warsaw Pact, 14, 101, 106, 108
Wasiak, Patryk, 5, 6, 8, 13, 14, 17, 123–142, 164
Web, 3, 5, 6, 13, 161
Weizenbaum, Joseph, 2, 9
Wernery, S., 189
West Berlin, 126, 188
Western, 17, 101, 108, 110–112, 118–120, 124, 125, 128, 129, 131, 137, 141, 142, 144, 172, 177, 178
Western Europe, 17, 18, 72, 74, 82, 91, 92, 110, 123, 125, 128, 137, 139, 140, 167, 183, 192, 194, 202
Windows, 13, 25, 44–47, 152, 222
Wireless Community Camp, 215
Wireless Leiden, 212, 215
Wireless networks, 207, 208, 213–216, 219–221, 223, 225
Woolgar, Steven, 124, 147, 221
World Cracking Federation, 140
World Wide Web (WWW), 13, 180, 193

X

XS4All, 119, 183, 197–199

Y
The Young Technician, 8, 129
Your computer, 130
Yugoslav, 3, 5, 8, 9, 17, 101–120, 163
Yugoslavia, 11, 14–17, 101–113, 115, 117–120, 128, 163, 197
Yugoslav Lola, 9

Z
Zagreb, 1, 15, 102, 105, 107, 108, 111, 114, 197
Zemanek, H., 11
Zilog, 29, 41, 74
Zine, 145
Zines, 139, 145, 149, 150, 189

Printed in the United States
By Bookmasters